They Also Serve

Methodist and United Methodist Bishops' Spouses, 1940–2018

Jane P. Ives

Abingdon Press
Nashville

THEY ALSO SERVE:
METHODIST AND UNITED METHODIST
BISHOPS' SPOUSES
1940–2018

Every effort was made to verify information prior to publication. As far as possible, all information was accurate as of December 31, 2018.

All links in this book were functional at the time of writing. However, some links may no longer be active at the time of publication.

Library of Congress Control Number: 2020933266

20 21 22 23 24 25 26 27 28 29 —10 9 8 7 6 5 4 3 2 1
MANUFACTURED in the UNITED STATES of AMERICA

DEDICATION

I dedicate this book to my sisters and brothers in the United Methodist Episcopal Family with profound respect, love, and gratitude for those who have traveled with me (both literally and figuratively), providing encouragement, support, wisdom, and friendship.

I pray that this book will prove helpful for those who in the future find their lives suddenly changed by the words, "We have an election."

—Jane P. Ives, January 7, 2020

CONTENTS

Part Three: Bishops' Spouses in The United Methodist Church 1968–2000

Part Four: United Methodist Bishops' Spouses in a New Century 2000–2018

Part Five: Profiles of Methodist and United Methodist Bishops' Spouses 1940–2018

ACKNOWLEDGMENTS

I could not have completed this book without the contributions and support of the following persons:

Robert Williams, former Executive Secretary of the United Methodist General Commission on Archives and History, who agreed that this story and these stories need to be told and encouraged me to undertake this project;

Alfred Day, current General Secretary of the United Methodist General Commission on Archives and History, whose excellent feedback, guidance, and advocacy for the commission's financial support helped bring this to publication;

The staff at the United Methodist archives building at Drew University, who provided access to the bishops' spouses' scrapbooks and records and who assisted with research (**Frances Lyons**, **Dale Patterson**, and student researchers, **Nazlin Shakir** and **Daniel Michalak,** in particular);

Mary Catherine Dean, who began the editing process before her untimely death in 2018, and other editors and staff at The United Methodist Publishing House who finished the task;

Prema Devadhar, my sister in Christ in the UM Episcopal Family, who made the first visit to the Archives to begin the research, and **all my other episcopal sisters and brothers** who have shared their stories and helped gather information;

My husband, **Bishop S. Clifton Ives**, with whom I have traveled this amazing journey and who has encouraged my writing by cheerfully assuming more than his share of the household tasks;

Our children and grandchildren, for their patience with my distraction and for the joy they bring to us in so many ways.

Finally, **thanks be to God** for all the gifts I have received through the years, for the experiences that have shaped me, for loving companions along the way, and for the church that has nurtured and informed my spiritual growth.

—Jane P. Ives, October 2018

ABBREVIATIONS TABLE

Throughout this text, the following abbreviations will be used for citations to frequently used sources and references:

Biographical Directory of United Methodist Bishops, Spouses, and Surviving Spouses	*Biographical Directory*, Years
The Council of Bishops in Historical Perspective: Celebrating 75 Years of the Life and Leadership of the Council of Bishops of the United Methodist Church by William B. Oden and Robert Williams (Nashville: Abingdon Press, 2014)	Oden & Williams, page #
The Encyclopedia of World Methodism, Volume I [or *Volume II*], edited by Nolan B. Harmon, (Nashville: The United Methodist Publishing House, 1974)	*Encyclopedia of World Methodism*, vol. #, page #
The Faith We Sing (Nashville: Abingdon Press, 2000)	*TFWS*, hymn #
History of the Council of Bishops of The United Methodist Church, 1939-1979, by Roy H. Short (Nashville: Abingdon, 1980)	Short, page #
Methodist Bishops' Spouses' Fellowship Scrapbooks, various years, housed in the UM Archives and History Center in Madison, New Jersey	Spouses' Scrapbooks, Years
Notes from Marj Tuell's diary	Tuell Diary
The United Methodist Book of Discipline (Nashville, The United Methodist Publishing House, 2016)	the *Discipline, BOD*
The United Methodist Hymnal (Nashville: The United Methodist Publishing House, 1989)	*UMH*, hymn #
United Methodist Women	UMW

INTRODUCTION: "THEY ALSO SERVE . . ."

"They also serve who only stand and wait." These words from "On His Blindness" by the English poet John Milton became a mantra of sorts for me when I found myself waiting after church for my preacher husband to finish conversations and be ready to go home. It was always important for me, however, to find my own ministry wherever we were—in each appointment, at each event, and during each encounter. Shaped by my experiences in Methodist Youth Fellowship, where "Christ Above All" was our motto, I taught church school and worked with youth groups, participated in United Methodist Women (UMW) groups and mission projects, and considered my teaching in public schools a ministry. Later, when I became the "Bishop's Wife" and followed Cliff around while he visited and preached at local churches and gatherings of all sorts and sizes, I still found meaning through my own projects and commitments, sometimes simply by getting to know at least one person in each place we visited, listening to his or her story, and offering empathetic listening, encouragement, and prayers.

When someone greeted me with, "I never shook hands with a Bishop's Wife before," I smiled warmly, even though I felt that those words had little to do with who I am as a person. I could freely give that experience to a stranger because I had other places and relationships where I felt known as myself. I especially enjoyed serving on the annual conference task force for "A Church for All God's Children," where I could participate freely in brainstorming and offer ideas, enjoying feedback from those who didn't agree with my suggestions and didn't feel they must defer to my role. Occasionally, in other settings, I was dismayed when my casual suggestion was translated into a mandate, "Because the Bishop's Wife says so." Fortunately that was not the case everywhere I went.

My husband's election to the episcopacy brought me into the United Methodist Bishops' Spouses' Association, a fascinating group of unique individuals. Friendship with others in this diverse group grows quickly out of the need to connect with persons dealing with similar circumstances, joys, and challenges. We don't need to explain to each other the overwhelming nature of moving to a different area and annual conference(s), sometimes miles from home and family, finding our mental databases almost useless as we try to learn new geography (names of rivers, counties, and neighboring states), politics (names of elected leaders and local and statewide issues), and history. Some episcopal assignments include multiple states and annual conferences, increasing the amount of new information to be absorbed. Not all bishops' spouses have to move long distances, and I know of a few who continued to work at their former jobs—but that is not the norm. Itinerancy is a fact of life for United Methodist pastors and their families, and even more so for those elected to the episcopacy. The spouses of newly elected bishops may wonder how they will use their gifts and graces in a new area, with its unknown distinctive characteristics, assets, and needs.

I have delighted in meeting and getting to know at a deeper level other bishops' spouses, both contemporaries with whom I have shared so many experiences and adventures and those who came before. At Memorial Services for the Council of Bishops, I have listened in awe to the stories and tributes shared about each deceased bishop and bishop's spouse. Most of those elected from our Northeastern Jurisdiction within my lifetime were already familiar to me. My new colleagues from other jurisdictions have shared stories of their mentors and friends, some of whom are truly legendary, revered for their hospitality, kindness, leadership, missionary zeal, talents, wisdom, and courage. Our fellowship includes teachers, writers, health-care providers, musicians, preachers, business managers, homemakers, organizers, artists, and more. We are also parents, grandparents, sons and daughters, brothers and sisters; sharing and celebrating family events such as births, deaths, illnesses, graduations, and the like. The more I have learned about individual episcopal spouses, the more I have felt called to share their stories and the history of our association, which has evolved remarkably through the years, reflecting cultural shifts in our society at large as well as changes in the church. We have been most noticeably reshaped by the changing roles of women and men, deeper understanding of racism/sexism, and globalization.

I began by interviewing individual spouses and encouraging each to write about his or her "Faith Journey." Because the Bishops' Spouses' Association's scrapbooks and meeting records are housed in the UM Archives and History Center on the campus of Drew University in Madison, New Jersey, I spent some time there learning about the history of our Association and about bishops' spouses from different times and places. Someone handed me copies of information about Ellen Simpson, whose husband was elected to the episcopacy of The Methodist Church in 1852. Although she did not live during the time period I have chosen as the focus of this book, the tributes expressed about her are perhaps typical of comments made about many bishops' spouses. "The church owes much to Mrs. Simpson for watching over the Bishop . . . ; for relieving him of family cares . . . ; for bearing cheerfully her share of the self-denial involved in his many and prolonged and distant absences; for sweetening, warming, and solidifying the social life of the churches in the communities where she lived; for zealously devoting her extraordinary energies to the welfare and progress of Methodism; and especially for her judicious, sympathetic, and eminently successful efforts on behalf of certain great and necessary charities of the Church" (Address by Rev. Dr. William V. Kelley, Services in Arch Street Methodist Episcopal Church, December 27, 1897, [Methodist BY1542, 56135, 5491s]).

My intent, however, in writing this book is to explore the real lives and personalities beyond such exalted impressions, to share the human struggles as well as the public achievements of persons who have shared in this unique experience. I think it is important to recognize that bishops and their spouses are people who deal with the whole range of human experience. From my point of view, this conveys a much more powerful message than putting them on pedestals and pretending that they never struggle with ordinary human challenges.

Research, reading, and interviewing has been walking on "holy ground" for me. I am eager to share with you the adventures and reflections of persons who, because their spouses served as bishops in the Methodist and United Methodist churches from 1940 through 2018, embarked on a life-changing journey, each bringing to it her or his own unique gifts and graces. The spouse profiles located in Part 5, especially those for whom we found ample information, reveal both personal differences and the influence of historical context. I pray that this book will deepen your understanding of United Methodist bishops' spouses and increase your appreciation of their common journey.

> Therefore, since we are surrounded by such a great cloud of witnesses, let us throw off everything that hinders and the sin that so easily entangles. And let us run with perseverance the race marked out for us.
>
> (Hebrews 12:1 NIV)

Structure of This Book

Part 1 consists of three chapters that set the stage, so to speak. The first describes the episcopal election process through the experiences of individual spouses, and the second provides an overview of adjustments faced after election, as described by several different spouses. The third chapter narrates the evolution of our association, describing how it has changed through the years in response to changes in church and society and to the interests and enthusiasms of the spouses themselves.

Parts 2, 3, and 4 contain separate chapters for each quadrennium. Each of these chronological chapters provides a list of spouses who joined the episcopal family that quadrennium, highlights of spouses' experiences during Council of Bishops' meetings or Council actions that impacted the spouses, and personal reflections and stories written by or about some of the spouses. "Windows on History" segments describe the impact of historical events on bishops' spouses during or before the time when they were part of the episcopal family.

Part 5 provides profiles of all the spouses from 1940 through 2018, including those from earlier elections still living in 1940, when several branches of our church reunited. The first paragraph of each profile tells how that person became part of the episcopal family, followed by the bishop's assignment(s), to provide an overview of where and when they served. The second paragraph of each profile focuses on the spouse and the uniqueness she or he brought or brings to the role of Bishop's Spouse. We worked diligently to gather as much information as possible, but in some cases, we could find only very limited information. Spouses still living (or their children, in some cases) were given the opportunity to edit their own profiles and to write about their experiences and feelings, but we were not able to get responses from everyone. To the best of our ability, we verified all facts through December 31, 2018, and we have not included events (meetings, births, deaths, marriages) that took place after that date.

I hope and pray that the material contained in this book will increase understanding of and appreciation for persons often introduced simply as the "Bishop's Spouse" and for the evolution of our fellowship through the years. I apologize for any omissions or errors caused by the large amount of information gathered and by conflicting information in some sources.

Part 1

LIVES TURNED UPSIDE DOWN

Chapter 1

"WE HAVE AN ELECTION"

Allen Johnson reported in a 2018 email that the morning after his wife was elected bishop in 2016, he overheard the spouse of another newly elected bishop say, "I went to bed at home and woke up on Mars." He acknowledged that it has felt that way for him too, sometimes.

Every four years, in the summer following General Conference, the Jurisdictional Conferences in the United States convene to listen to reports and debate resolutions. The Central Conferences in Africa, Europe, and the Philippines meet later in the year. Most participants at these gatherings focus primarily on the election of new bishops to replace those who have retired or died in office or to serve newly designated episcopal areas. Each time ballots are cast, business continues until a teller walks across the platform and hands an envelope to the presiding bishop. What used to be a relatively long wait, when written ballots were counted by hand, has now become a much shorter time, thanks to electronic voting. A hush falls over the gathered assembly, waiting to hear either "We have an election" or "We have no election," followed by resounding cheers or a collective groan of dismay, especially if the balloting has gone on for hours or days.

Somewhere in the crowd, family members wait with quickly beating hearts to hear their fate: Will the old familiar life continue, or will we move into an unknown future? Will we continue to live near family and friends, or will we move miles away from those most dear? In the United States, bishops are elected for life, with assignment to specific episcopal areas for four years at a time until they reach retirement age. In some of the Central Conferences (United Methodist churches outside the United States), bishops are elected for one quadrennium, after which they stand for re-election—in some areas repeatedly, in others achieving lifetime status after a second election. Retired bishops still participate in the Council of Bishops with voice but not vote.

Reflections

Jane Ives's Story

At the time of their ordination, United Methodist elders may be told that they have, in effect, volunteered for the episcopacy. I suspect that few actually expect to be elected. Cliff and I used to laugh when someone assured us that he would someday become a bishop. Through our early involvements in the Maine Annual Conference, now merged into the New England Conference, and our experiences at the General Church level, we came to know a number of bishops personally. When Cliff was elected as an alternate to General Conference in 1972, our local church secretary, who had once served as secretary to the Secretary of General Conference, insisted that the church fund his expenses to attend. In order for me to attend as well, we drove to Atlanta from Bangor, Maine, leaving our three young children with friends in Raleigh, North Carolina, and stayed in the cheapest hotel we could find. Cliff has participated in every General Conference since then, and I have attended at least part of most of them as well. In 1976, when General Conference met in Portland, Oregon, I served as a reserve delegate and spent long days seated in the balcony watching the debate and marveling at the carefully orchestrated dance of parliamentary process.

Almost 16 years later, in July 1992, I sat in another balcony during the Northeastern Jurisdictional Conference at Albright College in Reading, Pennsylvania, trying to stay calm and centered by piecing together a quilt square while the election process wore on. After one of the two episcopal vacancies was filled by the election of an ethnic person, we knew that a white male might be elected next. I sat in the balcony, thinking about my mother and Cliff's mother, both of them having recently moved into assisted-living facilities back in Maine; our three grown children, two of them married and one engaged, all living in New England; and our two young grandchildren, a third due in September, and who knew how many in the future. Our children, grandchildren, and Cliff's brother were still waiting back home, having borrowed a van for the nine-hour drive to Reading, should Cliff be elected. When I called them around 11:00 p.m. to report that the election outcome was still uncertain, they decided to drive as far as the home of our daughter in Massachusetts, hoping to find out by the time they got there whether or not to keep coming.

Although torn by thoughts of leaving New England, part of me wanted Cliff to "win." I also found myself savoring the "unknowing" of the past days, months, and years. Cliff had come close to election in 1988, withdrawing when he was one of three with the most votes, the others being a woman and a Korean. He did not want to be elected by default because some delegates might choose a white male over the others. We returned to Portland, Maine, where Cliff was serving as a district superintendent. I was teaching special education in an elementary school, a job that I loved, and our youngest son was finishing high school. During the next four years, I completed my masters in special education at a local university and flung myself into my work, quietly aware of the election to be held in 1992. Typically organized by nature, I labeled all plans for the years after that as "tentative." I walked to school each day, toting my paperwork, humming to myself, "Great is thy faithfulness, O God my Father," willing myself to trust that all would be well, whatever might happen.

Shortly after midnight, I heard the announcement, "We have an election," followed by my husband's name. Rejoicing erupted among the Maine delegation, as Cliff was the first person ever to be elected bishop while serving as a member of the Maine Annual Conference (Patricia J. Thompson, *Roots and Wings: 200 Years of Methodism in Maine, 1793-1993* [Winthrop, ME: Maine Annual Conference Commission on Archives and History, 1993], 37–38). Two bishops made their way through the clapping and hugging to escort Cliff to the platform, and two others made their way to the balcony to fetch me. Cliff and I embraced quickly when we arrived on the platform and then turned, stunned, to smile our thanks for the applause and affirmation. Cliff received an episcopal pin, and we both were given new name tags attached to purple ribbons. We were whisked off for a media interview and meeting with the General Commission on Finance and Administration to fill out forms related to compensation and health insurance.

I made a hasty phone call to our daughter's home to say, "Keep coming." Eventually we found ourselves back in our room with a few hours to sleep before we would learn our assignment. The Episcopacy Committee, unable to complete its work until the elections were finished, usually met through the night to decide where each bishop would be assigned. From his 16 years of experience on that committee, Cliff knew that the previous custom of calling bishops in the middle of the night to tell them where they were going had been replaced by a scheduled 6:00 a.m. visit by the representative from that conference. I told Cliff that he had an unfair advantage, because he knew the members of the committee and would therefore know as soon as he opened the door where we would spend the next four years and possibly more (bishops are assigned for the quadrennium, and those who have served for just four years in one place are often reassigned for another four, occasionally for a total of 12). We tried to catch some sleep, but my mind spun with uncertainty and with prayers for our children, traveling down the highway. We had set the alarm for 5:30 a.m. so that we could be up and dressed when the messenger of our future arrived. A knock on the door sounded, as I stood facing the mirror, adjusting my earrings. "Ah," Cliff exclaimed, "my friend from West Virginia." I took a deep breath and turned to greet him.

West Virginia is as far from Maine as you can go, both south and west, in the Northeastern Jurisdiction. Bishops are not usually assigned to the area out of which they have been elected, but because of where our family lived, we had partly hoped for an assignment near New England. In July of 1988, however, the Northeastern Jurisdictional Conference had met on the campus of West Virginia Wesleyan College, where we experienced the beauty of the West Virginia hills and the graciousness of its people. After Cliff withdrew from that election process, we quietly confessed to each other that we felt called to this beautiful place. We tucked that thought away and happily returned to our life in Maine.

And now I walked with Cliff and Richard Wright to a special breakfast, where we found the bishops and some spouses eating with members of the Episcopacy

Committee from their newly assigned areas. We glanced around, noting who would be going where. Not long after breakfast, our family arrived, somewhat rumpled and weary after driving all night. I had just a moment to tell them where we would be going before the conference convened for the official announcement of the assignments. Following a brief session, the delegates and guests went to assigned rooms where they greeted their new bishops. Our family, including our two toddler grandchildren, joined the receiving line. I had no idea of the wonderful adventures that lay ahead, the amazing opportunities to learn and serve, and the very special people with whom we would share in ministry and friendship.

Staying connected with our family and friends back in Maine involved a 15-hour drive or airplane tickets, with the additional help of email and telephone calls. Sometimes it felt as if we lived in two different worlds, shifting back and forth between them with surprising ease. I never did finish the quilt square I was working on during the election process.

* * *

Meanwhile, others were experiencing a similar life-changing event.

Mackie Norris's Story

"Over the weekend, Alfred and I had traveled from Atlanta, Georgia, to Fort Worth, Texas, for the South Central Jurisdictional Conference. He was serving as president of Gammon Theological Seminary, and I was in a faculty position at Emory University as an associate professor in the School of Nursing, a position that I enjoyed very much and with which I was very well contented (I was also three credit hours and a dissertation away from completing my PhD).

"On the morning of Monday, July 13, 1992, as we readied ourselves to go to the opening session, we paused for a time of reflection, prayer, clarification, and verbal confirmation. I looked at Alfred and said, 'Here we go! Are you ready for this?' His countenance was calm and peaceful. We discussed the 'What ifs,' and we agreed that we were committed to the process and would be responsive to the leading of the Holy Spirit. We talked about where and when we would meet for lunch after the morning session, shared a warm embrace, and then we were on our way to the gathering room for the beginning of the conference.

"The conference was called to order at 8:30 a.m. with the customary singing and greetings. Following opening reports and general "housekeeping" duties, the first ballot was taken. The episcopal address was given by the host bishop, and then it was time for the report from the Elections Committee. I was seated in the visitor's section and not in a place where I could make eye contact with Alfred, but I knew where he was. As is usually the case, all the data related to the balloting was given: number of ballots cast, number of invalid ballots, number of valid ballots, number needed to be elected. Then I heard the phrase 'We have an election.' I had heard the phrase before at other Jurisdictional Conferences, but this time it had a direct impact on my life.

"I would be hard pressed to recount much of anything else that happened at that time. I do remember seeing two bishops escorting Alfred from his seat to the front of the auditorium, and I felt arms around me lifting me from my seat and ushering me toward him. I do remember that we received a warm and rousing greeting from the conference attendees. The rest is a blur! Neither of us had time to speak with family members or to make any phone calls at that time because we were whisked away to meet with reporters, GCFA representatives, and others. We learned that his election was the first for the 1992 election cycle. It was not yet noon, and our plans for the rest of the day had to be rearranged.

"Alfred's election happened very quickly, but the waiting had just begun. The jurisdiction was electing six episcopal leaders, and that had to be accomplished before any discussion of episcopal assignments could take place. Finally, I learned that I would have to practice spelling Albuquerque! We were assigned to the Northwest Texas/New Mexico Area, with its residence in that city. It was a cultural and geographical dichotomy to Atlanta, where we had been living for the past seven years. Our 18-month old grandson could not understand why we were leaving *him*. I soon learned the flight schedule for the most convenient and cost-effective airline, could recite it verbatim, and used it frequently. New terrain, new rhythm of life, new church family, new . . . new . . . new. And in the midst of all the 'newness,' old concepts and beliefs emerged that lent familiarity to the experience: the warmth of colleagues, the acceptance and welcoming of people, the beauty of the region, the mission of the church." —written 2016

Zoe Wilson's Story

"In the spring of 1991, when Joe came home to tell me that the Texas Conference Delegation had elected him as its nominee for the episcopacy, my first thoughts were *What is ahead for us now? Will we remain happily serving in our appointment in our native East Texas, or will we find ourselves organizing for a move to the great beyond of episcopal assignments in the South Central Jurisdiction?* I had begun to feel at home in our local congregation. While singing 'Here I Am, Lord' at the Texas Annual Conference closing worship, however, I found myself moved to tears at the assuring words 'I will hold your people in my heart.' These words became my pledge to serve Christ's body however events unfolded, wherever they took me as a supportive spouse. During the South Central Jurisdictional Conference session in July, my attention was divided because we had become good friends with several of the other candidates and their spouses. Alfred and Mackie Norris had traveled with us on a long flight to Singapore for the World Methodist Conference in 1991, and Ann Sherer had served as a pastor in the district Joe served as a district superintendent. Since we had spent two weeks at the Lydia Patterson Institute in El Paso, Texas, in 1990 with Fritz and Etta Mae Mutti, we were very interested in his election process as well. It was an exciting time, and 'We have an election' became a cause for celebration as these friends were elected and we moved together into the ministry of the Council of Bishops."

—written 2016

Henriette Yemba's Story

"In 2005, the Congo Central Conference held its first election for many years as the three bishops serving there had been elected in 1972, 1980, and 1996 successively, then re-elected for life. My husband, David, had been serving as the Founding Dean and Professor of Theology at Africa University, where I worked closely with him, since expatriate spouses of Africa University employees were not allowed to work in Zimbabwe. We had kept close connection with our home conference, West Congo, attending as many of its annual conferences as possible. At the 2003 session, the West Congo Annual Conference elected David as a nominee for the episcopacy. In February 2005, he took three weeks off from Africa University, and we flew to the Congo Central Conference session in Kamina.

"After the opening worship, the representative from the Council of Bishops who had come to preside began the voting. There were a total of eleven candidates from all three of the annual conferences in the Central Congo Episcopal Area. On the third ballot, the presiding bishop announced that David had been elected. We were surprised because we did not expect things to happen so quickly. The shouts of joy, singing, crying, and celebrations began and continued throughout the whole Central Congo Episcopal Area, as well as at Africa University. Although bishops in Africa are often assigned to the area out of which they were elected, David was assigned to the Central Congo Episcopal Area, from which Bishop Onema was retiring after 32 years in office. David served three quadrennia there, working hard to start a fourth Episcopal Area, now the East Congo Episcopal Area, in our Central Conference, and retiring in 2017. Because we did not know pictures were being taken and videos recorded, we were wonderfully surprised the next day to receive a photo album and videotape of all the activities of the election day. David's election made me a member of the Bishops' Spouses' Association, that I love so much. I felt good about David's election, but also realized the big challenges ahead. The episcopacy moved us, taught us, used us, humbled us, and allowed us to be at the highest office of the church. We thank God for all He has done for us as a couple, as a family, through His service."

—written 2019

* * *

And sometimes an election bears the weight of historical significance.

Robin Ridenour's Story

"There is no doubt in my mind that God has had a plan for Karen's life and for mine and has been preparing us for this moment through the work of the Holy Spirit. For years, United Methodists on both the east and west coasts of the United States have been asking to submit Karen's name for bishop. This year, when friends asked us to consider again, we made plans to talk with them about it on the afternoon of June 11, 2016. That turned out to be the day of the massacre of queer people at a dance club in Orlando, Florida. As Karen and I talked about the episcopacy, we considered the fact that people are still being murdered because of their sexual orientation and gender identity and our belief that the church has been complicit in discrimination. I was terrified about retaliation in the aftermath of General Conference and the Orlando shooting, but God reassured us through 1 John 4:8: 'There is no fear in love. Perfect love casts out fear.' We knew it was time. The words of a hymn also came to mind:

'My heart shall sing of the day you bring.'
(Rory Cooney, 'Canticle of the Turning' [GIA Publications, Inc., 1990])

"When Karen was elected as the endorsed candidate from the California-Nevada Annual Conference, my immediate response was, 'Oh no, this is happening.' At the beginning of the Western Jurisdictional Conference, all of the episcopal candidates and their support persons were sequestered in a room with a spiritual guide, Rev. Mark Calhoun. Everyone was respectful, gracious, and funny. The process was explained to us, but we were not told how little sleep we would get over the next four days. We averaged about two or three hours a night. The most significant aspect of the episcopal election process, for me, was the truly loving kindness the candidates showed each other and the ways in which the Holy Spirit moved. The atmosphere at the conference was tangible and electric, breathing love and hope into each one of us. As the balloting progressed and candidates began to withdraw, each poignant withdrawal speech moved the election process toward the Western Jurisdiction's ethos of inclusion and justice.

'Let the fires of your justice burn.' (Cooney, 'Canticle')

"Rev. Siusifa Hingano, a delegate from the Pacific Islands, whose son is gay, boldly declared, 'I am willing to lay down my life and my body and my faith to hold the door open so some people can walk freely. I am willing to kick the door, and I pray that people will open their minds, so that my son and all gay and lesbian people will walk freely on the bridge . . . to a wide door where people with open arms and open hearts [will] welcome them all home.' The people of the Western Jurisdiction erupted in tears and hugs, showering each other with love. Likewise, Rev. Frank Wulf, Rev. Lida Pierce, and Rev. Walter 'Skip' Strickland each withdrew, emphasizing that it was time to be bold, to let the Spirit of God move us, to remember those who are forgotten, and to make sure all voices are heard and considered. Rev. Donna Pritchard went on to say, 'Thank you for recognizing that every child of every ethnicity, every sexual orientation, and every gender identity is not only a child of God but is a child of ours.'

"Finally, the election was between Rev. Dottie Escobedo-Frank and Karen, and then the unexpected and incredulous happened. Rev. Dottie Escobedo-Frank rose and went to the microphone. Breathless, I thought, '*What?! Why?!*' As she read her withdrawal speech, I sobbed, overwhelmed that something so profound, so self-sacrificing, so loving could happen.

'Wipe away all tears, for the dawn draws near . . .' (Cooney, 'Canticle')

"The last ballot, #17, with only Karen's name on it, was ready. Randall Miller, lay delegate from the California-Nevada Conference, came over to tell me what I should do after the election. Minnie Brown, wife of Bishop Warner Brown, followed and told me to come with her. She held my arm tightly and led me to the edge of the plenary floor. The last ballots were cast, and soon we heard, 'We have an election.' Minnie and I worked our way through the wave of people. Karen and I hugged and cried. I followed Karen up to the stage, with Minnie holding me tightly, then releasing me at the platform just behind Karen. As Karen spoke a few words, I looked over the body and wept for all of the love in that room, for the sacrifices made by all of the candidates, and for the way in which the Holy Spirit was moving in all of our lives and the life of our church. I thought, 'Wow, THIS is the church, a place where everyone is truly welcome. THIS is the church I love.'

'. . . and the world is about to turn!' (Cooney, 'Canticle')"

—written November 2016

Others Remember

During the balloting process leading up to Dale White's election in 1976, **Gwen White** recalled fingering the gold-plated cross she wore on a chain around her neck, praying, "Only if it is your will, dear Lord." By the time Dale's election was announced, the cross was worn down to a silvery finish. Four years later, watching the election process from the Bishops' Spouses' reserved seating area, she empathized with the spouses of the newly elected bishops, remembering the shock she had felt when she realized that her life had instantly changed and turned in a new direction.

Jean Stockton remembered arriving late for the Southeastern Jurisdictional Conference at Lake Junaluska in July 1988. "My husband, Tom, was a candidate for bishop, but so were a lot of other people, and we didn't really think it would happen. I spent all day playing tennis, and after I had returned to our home near the conference center, the phone rang. A voice I did not recognize suggested that I should arrive at the auditorium by early evening and wear a simple cotton dress. I took a hurried bath and put on my tennis dress, since it seemed to fit the description of what I should wear, although it was very short. When I arrived in the assembly hall, the first ballot was being processed. Soon a loud voice announced, 'We have an election.' Tom was elected on the first ballot. We were completely unprepared and surprised! Our oldest daughter, Lisa, who had just arrived at the time of the announcement, came running over to me with tears rushing down her cheeks. 'Is this a life sentence?' she asked. I replied, 'I think so!' And so it was!"

Marilyn Brown Oden, in her article "A Bishop's Wife on the Road Unchosen" (*Circuit Rider*, July/August 1992, 8–9), noted that, while the words "We have an election" opened doors for her husband, they "dropped like a guillotine on my life as I knew it. They severed me from the sense of purpose and personal identity I experienced from my job, from my beloved community of faith, from a quarter-of-a-century support group of clergy and spouses in our home conference; and they distanced our children by 1,000 miles." Later she told me, "I thought I was going to have to give up what I love to do, but that is not what happened."

Before her own husband's election, one woman watched a friend whose husband was elected bishop being led to the roped off area where the bishops' spouses sat. "*The corral*," she thought. Four years later that image came back to haunt her when her husband was also elected. Another spouse compared being whisked off after the election to going through a heavy curtain that completely cut her off from the life she knew. Still another told me that she felt as if a giant eraser had rubbed out all she had been and done to date. In spite of the traumatic change involved, many of us have found meaning and value in our new role as the spouse of a bishop. We are grateful for the new opportunities, even if we may not have felt that way at the time of our spouse's election.

Different Situations

Sometimes, the impact of the election is complicated by family concerns and crises. One spouse, whose mother died shortly after the election, expressed frustration at being torn between grieving and the demands of the episcopacy.

Lucrécia Domingos recalls her husband's election: "We felt so happy with his election in 2000 and his reelection four years later (according to their Central Conference practice, reelection made him a bishop for life). On the day of his reelection, however, I lost one of my brothers. My joy was mixed with sorrow, but the church consoled me, and God helped me live through that day. I was nervous about following a woman like Marilina DeCarvalho as the bishop's spouse of the area, but I prayed, and God helped me overcome my fear. I have been many places, had many opportunities, and learned many things. I thank God for everything that He has done for me and my family. May God continue to bless us."

—written Spring 2016

* * *

Not every bishop's spouse comes into this organization through the election process. **Susan Thomas** married Bishop Neil Irons some years after his first wife died.

Susan Thomas's Story

"Most of the other bishops' spouses had come 'up through the ranks' as wives of ordained ministers, and of course I had not. It was a huge learning curve for me, not only within the Harrisburg Pennsylvania Area where Neil was serving, but also in the Council of Bishops. Although the bishops and their spouses were very welcoming and warm to me, I felt like a fish out of water. Having been married to an attorney and having socialized with an entirely different group of people, and then having suffered through a miserable divorce and having to start a career from scratch at age 40, not to mention having lived on my own for

15 years, I was, at first, quite overwhelmed by the role of bishop's wife. Fortunately, my sweet understanding Neil never had any expectations of me in that role and has allowed me to continue to be myself. 'Being me' meant that I could continue to work as a successful residential realtor without having to worry about getting to all the Council meetings. Because Neil and I were raised in similar family and community environments, we share the same values and religious experiences. These have been the backbone of our incredible marriage. I especially appreciate that the other spouses accept my limited participation. They are a wonderful group of people, and I feel blessed to have been able to meet them and share in some of their activities." —written 2016

Wayne Simpson's Story

"In 2008, after I had been divorced for about four years, I decided that I wanted to meet someone, so I contacted a dating service through which I arranged about three dates, none of which I found particularly appealing. Around this same time, Ann Sherer, who had been single for about 16 years, also decided that she would like to meet someone interesting. Since she was still serving as an active bishop, she was somewhat apprehensive about dating within the structure of the church. She contacted the same dating service through which I had been working, and she also went on several dates, none of which were very appealing.

"We both felt discouraged and not very optimistic that future dates would be different. I drew Ann's name, however, and gave her a call. She agreed to meet during her break at a coffee house not far from where she worked. This coffee house just happened to be halfway between my home and a fitness center about six miles away where I worked out several days a week. Since it was a nice day, I decided to ride my bike to the fitness center, stopping along the way to meet Ann for coffee. I was dressed in shorts and a T-shirt, with white socks that had an orange band across the tops. I guess I was feeling that I had nothing to lose. After all, if there was any appeal there in either direction, the manner of dress should pose no stumbling block. Besides, I was not bursting with confidence that this date would be different from any of the others, in which case, I didn't care about how my manner of dress might be perceived. I rode up to the coffee shop on my very old, one-speed bicycle with its wide handlebars, my preferred bike for riding for exercise in the hills east of Lincoln, Nebraska.

"I had not told her I would be coming on a bicycle, dressed in workout clothes, but as I walked into the cafe, she seemed to sense who I was and introduced herself. We got coffee and sat at a table outside. When I asked her what she did for a living, she said, 'I work for the church.' I didn't pursue what that meant, and we continued to talk about ourselves and our interests. In hindsight, I'm a little surprised she put up with me, because she is pretty adamant about proper dress for most occasions. I went away feeling quite positive about her. Something about her piqued my interest, and I called her again, this time inviting her on a date to a Glenn Miller concert at the Lied Center for Performing Arts in Lincoln. This time I dressed in a suit.

"At some point during our second or third date, she told me that she was a bishop. I was a little surprised, but after having heard her talk about various things, it didn't surprise me that much that she would hold such a position. It seemed to fit her. We continued to date and grew more serious about each other, and we were married in August 2009.

"Meeting so many new people—pastors and laypeople, district superintendents, bishops, and bishops' spouses—has been an awesome experience. So many new names! Most of them already knew Ann and knew who I was, so I just kept introducing myself, hoping they would introduce themselves in return. Most did, and most have made a real effort to make me feel welcome and comfortable. So many good people. It's been quite a ride, and we're still on the move!"

—written January 2017

* * *

The following chapters of this book offer more of the personal stories told by the close to 500 spouses who joined the Methodist and United Methodist episcopal families between 1940 and 2018. We thank God for the unique experiences and privileges that have been given to us, and we thank God for the grace and the wonderful surprises we have known in this life that we probably would never have chosen.

Dear friends, now we are children of God, and what we will be has not yet been made known. But we know that when Christ appears, we shall be like him, for we shall see him as he is. (John 3:2 NIV)

I consider that our present sufferings are not worth comparing with the glory that will be revealed in us. For the creation waits in eager expectation for the children of God to be revealed. (Romans 8:18-19 NIV)

What, then, shall we say in response to these things? If God is for us, who can be against us? (Romans 8:31 NIV)

Chapter 2

MAKING AN ADJUSTMENT

A Volunteers-in-Mission coordinator, Tom Clark of West Virginia, with whom we traveled on several mission trips, predicted that team members would surprise themselves by "making an adjustment" to unexpected situations in which they would find themselves while on mission journeys. In the same way, bishops' spouses "make an adjustment" to situations and experiences they did not expect and often likely would not have chosen. **Marilyn Brown Oden**, in her article "A Bishop's Wife on the Road Unchosen" (*Circuit Rider*, July/August 1992, 8–9), describes three major losses facing newly elected bishops' spouses: deep relationships, dependable rhythm, and direct responsibility. As the role of women has shifted in our society and as more women are elected to the episcopacy, fewer bishops' spouses are as completely uprooted now as they used to be. However, many do still experience a major change and the challenge of figuring out who they are and what they will do in this new situation. When younger persons are elected bishop, their spouses may find themselves staying home with their children instead of traveling with their spouse. Some find ways to continue in their vocations. Some become leaders in their new annual conferences; some continue to speak up for justice and social change. In the following testimonials, you will see how different individuals have found ways to use their gifts to serve Christ in new situations. Challenges often turn out to be opportunities.

Greater Nhiwatiwa spoke for many of us when she said, "My spouse's election to the episcopacy expanded my world."

Greater Nhiwatiwa's Story

"One afternoon in 2004, I met Teclah Chambara, a layperson in our local church, in downtown Mutare. She bounced forward to hug me as she shouted congratulations. Surprised, I stopped to listen as she told me that my husband had been elected a bishop of the Zimbabwe Episcopal Area at the conference meeting in South Africa. The impact of the surprise doubled two days later when Bishop Nhiwatiwa returned home from South Africa. We had never thought this could happen to us. Friends and relatives came to congratulate us while we were still adjusting to the idea.

"My husband was lecturer of homiletics at Africa University full time, and we had lived in Mutare for over 20 years. I had worked in the government there for 17 years as an occupational health and safety inspector, taking early retirement in 2002. I then got another job as an evaluation officer with Family Aids Caring Trust, a nongovernmental organization. I had worked in this inspiring field for a year and a half, developing a passion for working with the children and orphans of AIDS victims. I did a lot of traveling to both rural and urban areas in order to monitor these vulnerable children, assuring them that they would survive even though their parents had died. I checked door to door to see which children needed school fees, clothes to wear, and food to eat. I enjoyed being there for these orphans, and I felt like a mother to them. From my training as a nurse, I knew I was not in danger of catching AIDS from them. A lot of people who did not know how AIDS is transmitted from one person to another were afraid to touch the children and even items in their houses.

"Now we had to move to the episcopal residence in Harare. All was well with Eben in his new office, but I missed caring for the orphans and vulnerable children. The organization I worked for had no branch in Harare to which I could transfer and continue my work. I felt frustrated, missing my job and the joy I felt working with the children. Staying at home was a big change for me and a dislocation to my life. I joined a church choir, but that was not satisfying. Members of the UMW realized what I was feeling and asked the church to provide an office for me to use as their leader. In Zimbabwe, the pastor's spouse automatically becomes the leader of the UMW's organization, which is called Rukwadzaro Rwe Wadzimai (RRW). Being the bishop's spouse, I became the leader of the women throughout the area.

"The conference had given two centres to the women. Now I had to strategize how the centres could be used to provide the most benefit for women. The centre in the East Conference had been made available as a residence for female employees in town who needed accommodation. Since I came into this office, I have helped the centres become income-generating places for the women while empowering them through skills training. Currently, Africa University is renting the space there to accommodate female students, and renovations are underway to meet university standards. The money we get from the rentals goes toward the building of early childhood development classrooms for the orphans at our United Methodist Mission at Old Mutare and for children in the surrounding communities.

"The centre in the West Conference was a farm and has also been converted into an income-generating place. I sat down with the women executives, and we now lease the place for those who want to hold workshops, meetings, and outdoor weddings. We offer sewing, beading, cooking, and baking skills training to empower the women, after which they go home to teach others. I chair four executive meetings a year, four conventions (revivals)—each attended by about 8,000 people, mostly women. These conventions all include a topic taught by a professional person; for example, this year our topic was 'Climate change and waste management.' All conventions end with Holy Communion. The women are beautiful in their uniforms, which they always wear for Holy Communion and other special occasions such as revivals and Holy Week. The uniforms show our unity and bridge economic differences between us. Through my work with women, I can make a real difference in their lives and in the community, including children.

"Although I thought my career was over when Eben was elected bishop, God has given me even more meaningful work to do. God provides!"

—written 2016

Jane Ives's Story

I chose to retire from teaching in order to travel with Cliff because I wanted to share in his new life. We budgeted money for my travel expenses so that I could go with him to meetings across the country and around the world, as well as visit churches around the episcopal area. I have had such amazing adventures that I never would have experienced had I not taken advantage of those opportunities. Although I missed teaching school, I taught in Schools of Christian Mission and was able to negotiate a contract for administering individualized tests to students being evaluated for referral to special education in the county where we lived. As a certified leader couple through Better Marriages (formerly Association for Couples in Marriage Enrichment), Cliff and I had been leading workshops and training events, and I expected we would no longer be able to do so. However, couples in West Virginia encouraged us to provide leadership there and helped us recruit and train couples who became active as a Marriage Enrichment Leadership Team. All these involvements came together with opportunities for me to write and publish books, a childhood dream come true. At the time of Cliff's election, I bought a laptop computer, on which I wrote in motel rooms wherever we were. His election opened doors for me beyond my wildest expectations!

I was surprised to discover, however, the assumptions some people made. When people suggested that I must know about private personnel matters dealt with by the bishop, I was glad I could honestly state that I didn't. After a simple suggestion I made was translated into "The bishop's wife said we should," I learned to keep some opinions to myself. Sometimes my ideas were assumed to be my husband's as well, and I learned to clarify that he disagreed with me or that I did not know his thoughts on the subject.

Margaret Watson's Story

"I was enjoying my work as a high school guidance counselor, mainly helping seniors apply for scholarships, find jobs, join the military, and make plans as they graduated from high school. That was my ministry. I had always been a supportive pastor's spouse and felt my ministry also was to take care of our two wonderful children and our home so that Mike's time was freed up for congregational needs. Since I was not a vocal soloist or pianist, I found myself serving best through hospitality. I love people, and it was easy being friendly to everyone. I also joined the choir, participated in UMW activities, and taught children and youth in Sunday school and Vacation Bible School.

"When Mike was elected a bishop in 2000, I knew God's plan was for me to continue to support him; however, my ministry of helping high school students came to an abrupt end. No other bishop's spouse in the Southeastern Jurisdiction continued to work after election, so I thought I should devote my life to helping Mike full time. On September 1, 2000, we moved to Macon, Georgia, and I plunged into my new role, driving him from event to event and serving as a sounding board. Of course, my mother role continued as well, with our married son, who had a two-month-old son, and with our daughter, who was a sophomore at The University of Alabama, our alma mater.

"Our longtime friend, Dr. Jim Ridgway, Founder of Educational Opportunities in Lakeland, Florida, thought I began to look like a lost puppy. Since 1977, Mike and I had traveled with his company to the Holy Land; to Methodist heritage sites in England, Scotland, and Wales; to Greece, Turkey, and Italy, tracing Paul's journeys; and to other countries as well. Jim offered me a way to use my love of travel and my ministry of hospitality by serving on his staff aboard cruise ships all over the world. I started in 2003 and have worked two or three cruises each year ever since! I feel so blessed to be able to do work I love part time and still get to be part of Mike's episcopal adventures in our conference and elsewhere." —written 2016

Mike Johnson's Story

"When Peggy became a bishop, I took a leave of absence, giving up my pastoral appointment to go with her to the Philadelphia Area. Within a few weeks of our arrival, I was asked to serve an interim appointment and after that two others. After serving several interim appointments for the first four years, I asked to be appointed to school for two years as I pursued a graduate certificate in Spiritual Direction at Moravian Theological Seminary. I am now on extension ministry as a spiritual director, which allows me to be in ministry while still attentive to the changing needs of my spouse. Many just think that I have retired.

"Through all these changes, I have experienced the conflict of multiple roles. My parishioners did not feel free to complain. I had a unique relationship with the district superintendents, as both a pastor under their supervision and the spouse of their bishop. All have been gracious, and for the short term it has often been helpful, although it's not healthy for them or me long term.

"Finding my place has been a struggle. As an elder in The United Methodist Church, I feel I have been placed in limbo. When other elders might vest for the worship of the conference, I do not, after being advised not to 'let my ordination get in my way.' I am often not treated as active clergy. My new place is with the other spouses. While I am honored to be in their company, I am mindful of no longer being treated as clergy and often not even addressed as such. Although titles have never been that important to me, I do feel a sense of loss after 38 years of ordained ministry.

"As the spouse of a bishop, I have often felt invisible. When meeting her delegation for the first time, I held out my hand to greet those coming into the room, but they passed me by—as if I were not there. Being the spouse of a female bishop has caused me to struggle with gender roles in new ways. In 2009, my wife was honored and lifted high, placed in a chair and carried into the village during her visit to Wembo Nyama in the Democratic Republic of Congo, while I just followed behind.

"The power dynamics between us shifted from that of clergy colleagues, which we had enjoyed throughout most of our marriage, to my being the spouse of a person of power and authority. I became her support staff more than ever and took over many of the household chores. I went from being an equal financial contributor to the family to being dependent upon the career of my spouse. Maybe I am now best known as the 'holder of the bishop's purse.' None of this was bad, but it was different, and it caused me to ask important questions about who I was and about my calling. I have always viewed my marriage as part of my call, part of my ministry, but as the spouse of a bishop it felt different.

"The bishop spouses' organization has been helpful in connecting me with some of the greatest people of the church. They have provided a respite from the loneliness that comes with my position. Their shared wisdom has given me great comfort, but I have not always reached out when times are tough.

"I have observed Peggy, as a woman in the Council of Bishops, feeling ignored and unsupported by the active bishops in the Northeastern Jurisdiction. I have heard her frustration when her suggestion is rejected until one of the male bishops makes her idea his own. During the 2015 trial of Frank Schaefer (former pastor of Iona United Methodist Church in the Eastern Pennsylvania Conference) for conducting a same-sex wedding, her colleagues were silent when she sought advice, then criticized her decisions after the fact. During this time, she received a call from only one fellow bishop. She was deluged with hate mail from the left and the right. As her husband, this was painful to live through. Like many episcopal families, sometimes all we have for support is each other. Life in the Council and in the College of Bishops can seem socially polite and distant, for the most part. Covenant groups have provided a place to tell our stories and to receive a little more compassion and support. When the full Council started meeting less often, however, it became difficult to see each other often enough to form meaningful relationships."

—written 2016

Elaine Hopkins's Story

"John was serving as pastor in a local church when he was elected bishop in 1996. We had two sons in college and a third ready to begin his senior year of high school. Clearly, his election—while a gift—was quite a surprise! Three years earlier, we were surprised by an appointment change just as I was about to be vested in my pension plan at work. As a result, I decided to start my own training and consulting group. Now, moving several states away meant I would need to adjust my career path again. Why did I ever think I could control what God had in mind for our ministry? I say 'our' ministry because I have always felt a partner in serving the church. What to do this time?

"Because I could not transition my training and consulting firm from Indiana to Minnesota in six weeks, and since our youngest son, Ben, wanted to stay where we were for his senior year, we decided to purchase the parsonage we were living in from the church and postpone my move until the following June. That winter was challenging. John and I found it hard to live 12 hours apart. We had been side by side since marrying at age 18 and completing college, John's

Divinity School, and my MA program. That was a big adjustment, in addition to his learning to work as an episcopal leader and my learning to manage a growing business start-up.

"But God was truly with us, and by June of 1997, Ben was off to Hyde Park, New York, to begin culinary school, and I relocated to the Twin Cities. Our older sons, who spent their college summer vacations there with us, began to call Minneapolis home. All five of us fell in love with Minnesota.

"Running my little company, however, required a whole lot of travel. Our staff helped executive leadership of bank holding companies, insurance companies, and a large retail tire chain create work environments focused on service and product quality. Consequently, I found myself flying out of the Minneapolis-St. Paul airport every Sunday night for destinations in Indiana, Michigan, Illinois, and Kentucky, where clients had operations. On Thursday nights, I flew back home, where I did laundry, caught up on paperwork, and went to churches across the state with my husband, only to fly out again Sunday evening.

"Our joint ministry there felt strong, meaningful, and fulfilling; I would do it again in a heartbeat. It was stimulating for me, gave John and me much to talk about from Friday to Sunday, and paid many of the tuition bills for our three college kids. I loved learning more at the General Church level as well, when invited to Nashville and Washington, DC, to train staff members for the General Council on Finance and Administration and the General Board of Church and Society. I so appreciate having my own career. I know I'm happier and more informed about what interests me personally for having persisted.

"John was assigned to the East Ohio Area in 2004. As we transitioned to the rolling hills, Lake Erie shoreline, and a conference with many more United Methodists than there were in Minnesota, I decided I had had enough of weekly air travel.

"Before I knew it, John was calling on me to assist district superintendents seeking solutions to complex church staff challenges. I also found a new freedom to say yes to invitations to speak on UMW Sundays. I now had time to lead workshops for district leadership training events and for lay leaders. My experience and expertise in the business sector was a tremendous resource that I could share as a volunteer. Our ministries had truly merged. What's more, reducing travel gave me time to help organize and resource clergy spouse retreats and to become part of a meaningful fellowship circle at my local church. How special those years became for me personally, prompting me to affirm from yet another perspective, 'All the time, God is good!'" —written Fall 2016

Laurinda Quipungo's Story

"I am a medical doctor and have been the wife of Bishop José Quipungo for 40 years. I am the mother of three boys and two girls and grandmother of seven boys and three girls. Before José was elected to the episcopacy in 2000, we lived in Luanda, the capital of the country. In 1992, he was elected as a member of the Angola National Assembly, where he served until 1998, when he was appointed as pastor to the Central Church in Luanda.

"After my husband's election to the episcopacy, he was assigned to the East Angola Area, and we moved to Malange, in the interior of the country. Our life changed for the better, both spiritually and materially, allowing us to contribute more to both church and society. As a pediatrician in Luanda, I worked at the largest pediatric hospital in the country; in Malange, I was able to open a small clinic for children and adults. We opened an orphanage, providing food, clothing, health care, and schooling for the children. With my husband, I visited churches, some very far from the episcopal office, offering spiritual support and health care resources. I always brought medicines, clothing, and food for the people there, even for those not members of the church. We opened a Women's Training Center where they can learn cooking, sewing, and knitting. As a health professional, I was director of the Provincial Health government agency in Malange for three years. I now am director of the Provincial Hospital for women and children in Malange, which has 120 beds for pediatrics and 130 beds for maternity care. I contributed financially to the construction of three new church buildings in the South Lunda, Moxico, and Quela Districts. I participate actively in my local church, and I am a deaconess. I am so happy with my work. God has blessed us and continues to bless us every day." —written 2016

Dania Soriano's Story

"Even before my husband became a bishop, I was active in church work and programs in both our local church and the Davao Episcopal Area (DEA) as a whole. Bishop Gamboa appointed us as Persons-in-Mission in Health Ministries. We focused on Community Based Primary Health Care, traveling around the whole Davao Area. Leo and I were still young, and our bodies were able. Since we didn't have our own vehicle, we traveled by boat, tricycle, motorcycle, horse, or simply by walking. While Leo finished medical school, I taught at local churches and started a kindergarten school. When Leo passed his board exam, we were overjoyed. Leo practiced his profession through a mobile medical clinic, which is community-based, and I assisted him. We enjoyed visiting the annual conferences to give medical services, teach, and implement health programs.

"When we heard that Leo's friends were pushing him to be a candidate for bishop, we did not really expect him to be elected. We did not campaign, but he was elected anyway. As the acting secretary of the Central Conference, he had traveled to many meetings and guest-preached in many churches. Many of his seminary classmates were now district superintendents. Because he was so well known, the election went smoothly.

"I had never really wanted this life but was content living in the barrios and serving through the mobile clinic. We rode on logging trucks and slept at the side of the streets wrapped in a malong, a cloth wrapped around our bodies. We ate banana leaves and sardines, and we were happy.

"Now we found ourselves in the public eye. I was uncomfortable, as I did not feel that I measured up. I wanted to hide when people would call on me during gatherings to ask my opinion about certain things. I just wanted to be on the sidelines, a spectator. I wanted a simple life, but when Leo became bishop, I could no longer wear T-shirts and shorts. When I came to Manila during meetings, I had to wear formal clothes and shoes. I no longer used a backpack but bought a shoulder bag instead. What is painful is that my friends, who I thought would push, encourage, enlighten, and inspire me, seemed to be the ones who kept on noticing my clothes, shoes, and even my curtains. They would say that I could afford to buy things now because I was a bishop's wife and that I had enough money to buy medicines and to consult with the doctor when I was sick. I just smiled and smiled, keeping my heartaches inside because I had no place to vent. I am grateful for one good friend of mine, who remained faithful and supportive.

"After Leo's first term as bishop, we were accused of favoring and pushing our children into leadership positions. We encouraged and supported them, but I do not think we kept others back. Leo took the criticisms in stride, but I was very hurt. I couldn't understand why people who had been our friends would treat us so. Not all experiences were bitter, however. I was happy with the women in the local church and the clergy spouses in the Davao Episcopal Area.

"My chronic kidney failure started in 2010. My creatinine was very high, and the doctor said it could not be healed without a kidney transplant. After the transplant, in 2014, I thought I would return to normal, go back to traveling and being active, but I soon realized that I must take extra good care of myself. I could no longer do the things that I used to do when I was younger, although I still traveled with Leo. During annual conferences, I organized the clergy spouses and the workers' children and had fellowship with them. We held gatherings every December with the district superintendents throughout all 12 years of Leo's term.

"Because he had so many meetings to attend and travels here and abroad, Leo missed many important family experiences, including my father's wake and the deaths of my brother and mother, and even of his mother and sister. I became accustomed to his absence, but had a hard time accepting it when he missed our son's wedding, arriving only in time for the photo session.

"Now that I am retired, I do some gardening, go for checkups, visit with friends, go to prayer meetings and Bible study, prepare Sunday school lessons, and, of course, worship on Sundays. I also get to spend time with our granddaughter when she comes home from school. Sometimes, when I am physically able, I attend conferences outside Davao City." —written 2016

Irene Innis's Story

"My experience of being a bishop's spouse is unique, because during most of my husband's episcopacy, I was absent from Liberia, the area he served. During the height of the Liberian Civil War, which began in 1989, the mission station where John was serving became a place of refuge for thousands of displaced persons. The campus was closed in 1993, after rebels raided it, severely beating and almost killing John. Our family moved to the United States for safety in September 1996.

"John served as executive secretary of the General Board of Global Ministries in New York and in Baldwin, Louisiana, respectively. Our family lived in Worcester, Massachusetts.

"In early 1999, John moved back to Liberia to work for UMCOR, and on December 16, 2000, he was elected a bishop. Upon his election, our family was separated, and I took responsibility to raise our four children in the United States while John was busy with the leadership of the church. The price that our family paid was a severe stress that almost took my life. John suffered his share of stress while working in Liberia for nearly 16 years without his family being with him.

"We count ourselves blessed because our children all finished their education and are independent and successful. For the past four years of my husband's ministry (2012–2016), I decided to go to Liberia more often to get to know the church people. It was a bit hard because I found myself living in two worlds, frequently saying good-bye to friends. This deprived me and them from sharing the love that we desired to share with each other.

"The last four years have gone by quickly, and John is now retired. I am grateful for the success of his ministry. Also, I am glad that God enabled me to go back to Liberia to get to know the church people and to experience their love and generosity. I truly cannot pay them back for all their prayers and support that sustained our family.

"We have all kinds of stories to tell, including the endless story of severe stress that I encountered while living in the United States and the story of not having any private time in our home in Liberia. However, the joy is to hail the name of Jesus Christ for giving us the chance to serve. We praise and thank God for leading us with love and helping us to overcome all obstacles with victory in Jesus Christ."

—written November 2016

Edith Jokomo's Story

"Growing up in a family of 11 children was quite an experience. My father was a bus driver and my mother a farmer and housewife, so you can imagine how poor we were. My parents instilled in us the importance of sharing, something we had to do with so many siblings. Dinner time was always very challenging. The food was dished onto two plates for us to share, one plate with the starch (Sadza), and the other with the relish (beans or vegetables, anchovies). Often, some of our neighbors would come for dinner. Because we couldn't afford much, my mother would do her best to plate the food we had cooked so as to serve everyone. I remember counting and dividing beans among us, to make sure we were being fair to one another. Little did I know that this was preparing me for a calling as a spouse of a clergyperson (Jeremiah 29:11: 'I know the plans I have for you')! I learned that you don't stop giving because you lack resources, but you give because there is need and more work to be done. I also learned that there are many more things to give apart from money and resources; you can give yourself in service to God and others.

"When I married Chris, my late husband, I discovered that marrying a pastor in Zimbabwe came with a package of responsibilities, most of which one is trained for while you are in service. You automatically became the mother of all, and everyone expects you to know everything and to be an adviser to all. I still remember one of the most shocking encounters I experienced during the honeymoon stage of my marriage. A member of United Methodist Women died, and I was called into the house by the elders. There I found a few relatives and United Methodist Woman (RRW) leaders in the hut where the body was lying in the opened coffin. They were holding the RRW uniform. With great respect, they said, 'Mama, we were waiting for you so that we can clean up the body and dress it up.' At first, I thought they were joking or that it was one of those terrible nightmares. I tried very strongly to refuse, but they insisted that, since I was their pastor's wife, it was the member's right to have this done by me. When I realized that they meant it and would not give up, I took the small dish with some water and using the soap and towel they had handed to me, I cleaned up the body with their guidance. We dressed the corpse in the RRW uniform. It was frightening, but I later discovered that it was the beginning of a permanent journey, as I was called on to do this several times, even when Chris was the bishop. I still remember when some would actually state, before dying, that they wanted Mai Bishop and her team to dress them up when they die.

"Having been raised by parents who had an open house approach to running a home, I didn't find hosting many people at home unusual or challenging. Many people just came without an appointment to spend some time at the episcopal residence. Being called to fix real meals for large groups of visitors who came unexpectedly required creativity and discernment. Moving around with Chris throughout his ministry, preaching the gospel, organizing women's programs, being there for him and the ministry in every possible way, and participating in this call has opened my eyes to what needs to be done. Blessed are those with eyes that see, ears that hear, and minds that notice that Jesus has called them into supportive ministry, for the Lord enlarges their territory. The episcopal residence was home for all, and I praise God for grooming me for a higher calling and blessing me with the opportunity to serve Jesus at that level of commitment." —written October 2016

Neil Irons Remembers Inez Rossey Irons

"Inez was diagnosed with stage 3 breast cancer in 1989, a time when that disease was not often mentioned in public settings. At the next session of the Southern New Jersey Annual Conference, however, Inez requested permission to speak at one of the sessions. She came to the microphone and shared that she had been diagnosed with breast cancer. She then invited any women struggling with this disease to call her. Several women responded to that invitation, creating a small supportive network that proved to be a great help. Subsequently other women joined Inez in establishing a network for women who needed to find caring and support for a number of other issues.

"Professionally, Inez was a social worker, trained in gerontology. During our time in New Jersey, she worked as director of a senior daycare center sponsored by the Quakers for the elderly, urban poor in Trenton, New Jersey. Under her guidance, the program grew quite large. Inez saw to it that every man and woman there received at least one hug every day. She maintained contact with their families, seeking to build bridges to them as well as providing a healthy and caring environment for the elderly. Upon her death, a garden was planted and dedicated in her name.

"A story that illustrates her caring and generous nature was shared at her memorial service. She had taken another staff member with her on a round of visitation in the poorer area of Trenton. In one of the homes, an elderly woman asked Inez if she would lend her $25 in order to purchase some materials for needlework projects, which she could then sell. Inez handed her the money with no strings attached. After they had left the apartment, the other staff member told Inez that she would never get the $25 back. Yet several months later, this same woman repaid Inez out of the profits she was making from her handiwork. Inez believed in people, regardless of their station in life." —written 2016

Supporting and Encouraging Clergy Spouses

Many bishops' spouses seek to support and encourage the clergy spouses in their new annual conferences. When **Phenola Carroll** came to the New England Area with her husband in 1972, her warm, open manner fostered friendship, and she encouraged clergy spouse gatherings in each of the three conferences.

Many bishops' spouses work with conference leadership to plan retreats and other activities, sometimes leading such events themselves. **Gwen White** led spiritual growth workshops and retreats for clergy spouses and laywomen. She also advocated for and helped form covenant groups for sharing and spiritual support.

After the spouses of the class of 1992 created a *Thrival Kit,* a notebook filled with tips and coping strategies contributed by many different members of the group, **Janene Pennel** took that idea back to the Virginia Conference and helped them create a similar notebook for their clergy families.

Elaine Hopkins worked with others in the East Ohio Conference to develop a ministry with surviving clergy spouses, helping them to connect with one another and offering a way for them to donate clerical items they no longer need. A local church houses these donations, and those coming into ministry are invited to select from the robes, chalices and platens, and books. The conference mission coordinator also ships some of these overseas or sends them with Volunteer-in-Mission teams. Elaine also helped plan and resource clergy spouse retreats for the East Ohio and Western Pennsylvania conferences, working with **Sally Bickerton**, whose husband was bishop of the Western Pennsylvania Area. These events, scheduled for Friday afternoon through Saturday afternoon and now in their seventh year, helped to build cross-conference relationships.

Martha Chamberlain's Story

"Having spent nearly 43 years as the spouse of a clergyperson and a lifetime as the daughter of clergy, I felt a strong connection with the spouses of clergy in our new assignment. However, 'the way we were' no longer exists. No longer are most spouses female; no longer are pastors' wives expected to work for the church (gratis); no longer do most spouses work primarily in the home; no longer are all pastors male; and, in fact, clergy couples have further changed the landscape. Here are some of the ways I chose to connect with the spouses of the cabinet, dubbing them the 'SPICE Cabinet.' (After all, if mouses are mice, why shouldn't spouses be SPICE?)

"Working with the spouses of cabinet members seemed to be the best way to connect with the spouses of clergy throughout this very large conference. I wrote welcome letters to new persons and farewell letters to those leaving the cabinet. Partnering as Covenant Friends, we each developed a close relationship with at least one other person in the SPICE Cabinet. We were loosely organized, with a president, treasurer, and a prayer partner.

"Each year, through a monthly newsletter I sent them, I invited them to join me in a mission outreach project, and they in turn connected with the spouses of clergy on their districts. Once I asked the SPICE to encourage folks to bring children's shoes for refugees that I would store in my garage and send to UMCOR for Afghanistan. They took my invitation to the churches on their districts, and we ended up with (if I recall correctly) 40,000 pairs. Other years, we covenanted to connect with children outside our families or to participate in disaster response, Volunteers-in Mission, Change for Children, Prison Ministry, and the like.

"Scheduling time for the SPICE Cabinet to meet became increasingly more difficult each year, but we tried, usually meeting at the same time as the Cabinet. Establishing relationships with spouses of pastors throughout the conference, however, was even more challenging. With more than 900 churches in our conference, I could not even hope to visit everyone during that tenure. However, by accompanying Ray when he preached, I connected with the pastor's spouse, opening the door to an ongoing relationship. Knowing how easily I would forget my promise to pray for someone, I carried a pocket prayer calendar with me to jot down names and needs. In addition to attending district events, participating in the annual conference spouses' retreat was a comfortable setting for fellowship.

"The Holston Conference organized 'Partners in Crisis' in 1995, just prior to our arrival, with the encouragement and leadership of Dot Lee, wife of Bishop Clay Lee. I worked on compiling, writing/rewriting guidelines for this program. This group acted as an 'emergency room' or 'safety net' for the spouses of clergy whose marriage or family life was in crisis, offering temporary housing, emergency funds (from donations), financial and legal advice, one-on-one emotional support, and professional counseling through the conference/episcopal offices (with strict confidentiality). This group addressed numerous emergency needs as well as initiating and supporting marriage enrichment events for clergy couples.

"Extraordinary possibilities for meaningful service multiplied exponentially as I transitioned from the roles of pastor's wife and district superintendent's wife to that of a bishop's spouse. My history, temperament and profession—in addition to my age/cohort—all shaped my choice to engage or not in the larger arena. Remembering that we are human beings, not human 'doings,' I prayed that God would lead the way, and I was rewarded!" —written 2004

Linda Edwards Foster's Story

"It was a great privilege to be the wife of a United Methodist bishop. I did not really feel that I was 'good' enough to serve in that role. I remember how hard it was even to go down the aisle of Stewart Auditorium to sit with the other bishops' spouses after hearing those life-changing words, 'There is an election!' and after Marion was escorted to the stage at Lake Junaluska, North Carolina, in July 1996. To be truthful, I really had prayed that he would not be elected so that we could go back to our comfortable home, church, and family in Columbus, Georgia. We had served all of our married life in the South Georgia Conference, raised and educated our children there, and served many wonderful congregations as well as Marion's term as district superintendent. It was home and it felt comfortable. Now we were to be assigned to a new annual conference in a new state! All those new people to get to know and learn to love! I felt overwhelmed!

"We were assigned to the North Carolina Conference and moved to Raleigh about six weeks later. We had not even unpacked when a hurricane hit our area. It was then that we knew that this was where God wanted us to serve. We learned a lot from that experience as we helped the churches and parsonage families recover from the damage. Marion helped organize the conference before another disaster might hit by establishing the Merci Center, where volunteers can assemble flood buckets and other supplies that can be stored until needed.

"We made many new friends while we were there and made many trips together to Council meetings and abroad for the church. These are good memories for me, but then it came time for us to decide about our next assignment. Marion had had a heart attack, and we decided to retire in 2004. We bought our first home, which we named 'Finally,' and moved back to Georgia, where we lived until Marion died in 2011. Then the hard part began for me. I lost my identity when he died. I had always been 'Marion's wife,' 'the preacher's wife,' or 'the bishop's wife,' and now I had to figure out who I was. For a long time, I felt that I was lost at sea without a life preserver. There was no one with whom I could discuss major decisions. My children tried to help; but in the long run, I had to learn to stand on my own two feet.

"I went through all the stages of grief, and I am not sure I will ever get through them completely. I thought about all of the 'what ifs,' wondering if I could have done something more for Marion. People treated me differently. I was alone. I struggled with depression and sleepless nights. I had to realize that my life as I had known it for all those 48 years of our marriage was over. Even going to church and to Council of Bishops meetings was different. Support from friends and family, participation in a grief support group at the local Hospice House, and Martha Whitmore's *Healing After Loss* devotional book helped me through.

"After several years as a widow, I realized that my life wasn't over just because I had lost my husband. While I was at Epworth-by-the-Sea for a Council of Bishops' meeting, a retired United Methodist minister from South Georgia came into my life. He had also lost his wife. I had known her, but really had not known Fred even though we had lived in the same town at one time years earlier. Fred and I married in July 2013, and I found myself back in the role of preacher's wife, as he was serving an interim appointment in retirement. Since he has now retired permanently, we can do more of the things we enjoy, traveling and fishing, in particular.

"I learned that there is no 'getting over' the loss of your spouse, but the challenge is to learn how to live with it and to live a new normal. I am lucky to have good health and hopefully many good years to come. I can't see what's ahead, but I'm enjoying each new day, still trying to find my new identity, but discovering joy in the journey. I am blessed!" —written 2016

One of the translators for the Council of Bishops' meetings was overheard commenting, "I hope in my next life I return as a bishop's spouse. I think it must be the best job in the world!

Chapter 3

OUR EVOLVING FELLOWSHIP

In December 1940, during a meeting of bishops of the newly formed Methodist Church, some of their wives met to establish a Methodist Bishops' Wives Fellowship. Similar organizations had been formed within two branches of the church—The Methodist Episcopal Church and the Methodist Episcopal Church, South—before union in 1939. The third branch, The Methodist Protestant Church, did not have bishops. The women primarily planned social activities, hoping to build bonds of friendship and support comparable to what they saw developing among their husbands, who now met regularly as the Council of Bishops to oversee the "spiritual and temporal life of The Methodist Church" (Oden & Williams, 42). Many of those bishops had also worked together for years to reunite the church that had split over the issues of slavery and authority in 1844 (Oden & Williams, 27–28).

A collection of scrapbooks and notebooks stored in the United Methodist Archives and History Center on the campus of Drew University records the many changes that have taken place in this organization and provides glimpses into the lives of its members through the next almost 80 years. The first Methodist Bishops Wives Fellowship scrapbook, which appears to have been created during or after the 1952 General Conference in San Francisco, contains a "Brief History" handwritten by **Frances Corson**, summarizing the actions and activities of the organization dating back to 1940, along with a few memorabilia items from 1948–1951. Starting with the 1952 General Conference, newspaper clippings, program booklets, printed invitations, and other original items document the spouses' activities during Council of Bishops' meetings and General Conferences (Spouses' Scrapbooks, 1940—1964).

The spouses relate to one another primarily within the context of the bishops' meetings, except, of course, for those who knew each other before election. Shortly after episcopal elections, new bishops and their spouses are invited to an orientation session, where they learn more about this new role and get to know one another, often developing strong bonds with other members of their "class." Spouses meet during the Council of Bishops' meetings, usually held twice a year, including before and during the quadrennial General Conference. During the Jurisdictional College of Bishops' meetings, held between meetings of the Council, smaller groups of spouses may gather informally. Spouses develop even deeper friendships when they travel with teams of bishops and spouses on Global Visitations and special assignments.

Early gatherings of the Bishops' Wives Fellowship focused on getting to know one another and sharing news of their families. Those present at meetings also corresponded with absent members, in order to include them in the circle of fellowship, sometimes establishing prayer partners for mutual spiritual support. Until 2014, members elected officers, developed bylaws, contributed voluntary dues, and planned activities to encourage fellowship and friendship. For years, a "big sister/big brother" program paired newcomers with "veteran" spouses who volunteered to welcome them by letter or telephone, share information, and answer questions. "Veteran" spouses intentionally invited newcomers to sit with them on bus rides in order to get to know them. For some years, jurisdictional representatives served as liaisons with spouses in their areas, sending personal notes and copies of the minutes to those not present.

Leaders of the spouses' organization plan at least one official gathering early in the Council meeting to greet and introduce spouses of newly elected bishops and other first-time attendees, to deal with necessary business, and to share information about activities and projects planned for this time together. Typical meetings through 2014 began with a welcome by the president and host area's bishop's spouse, followed by devotions and prayer. An attendance pad and a dues envelope were circulated, and the recording secretary and the treasurer shared their reports. The corresponding secretary shared news of spouses who were ill, bereaved, celebrating family milestones, or facing difficulties, and brought appropriate cards for the members to sign. For a number of years, the organization honored the host bishop's spouse by making a financial gift of $75 to a charity chosen by that person. The spouses often held a brief memorial service, honoring those who had died since the previous meeting. The Nominating Committee, which was named in the fall, if not earlier, presented its slate of officers in the spring, followed by election and installation of the new officers. After announcements, the group sometimes had a speaker, skit, program of music, or mixer games.

The Executive Committee (now the Leadership Team) coordinates and schedules activities such as book group, choir, Mission Support Network, covenant groups, and other interest groups that have come and gone through the years, depending on the enthusiasm and energy of our members and on time and space available. In a hotel or retreat center, it is not always easy to find a space available without charge for such gatherings. We sometimes use the bishops' plenary space when they are in small-group meetings elsewhere. Covenant and interest groups may meet in corners of a hotel lobby or even in a member's room.

Homes Away from Home

The Council meets frequently at two United Methodist conference and retreat centers, each in a uniquely beautiful setting. At Lake Junaluska in western North Carolina, the Terrace Hotel and Lambuth Inn, along with other facilities and private homes, overlook a man-made lake nestled in the hills. At Epworth by the Sea on St. Simon's Island in Georgia, hotels and meeting places stand near the Federica River, where marshgrass abounds, dolphins often frolic, and walkways wind between majestic live oaks with Spanish moss trailing from their branches. When the Council meets in cities around the country, the members live in a hotel, where ballrooms are converted into plenary and small-group meeting spaces. Living in retreat centers and hotels presents some small practical challenges: remembering our room numbers from one place to the next, finding out where our closest friends are (easier now with cell phones), keeping track of room keys, remembering to wear the name tags that admit us to meetings and "Family Dinners," standing in the laundry room line, and finding inexpensive places to eat.

Spouses must pay their own way for Council events and for other travel with the bishops, whose expenses are covered by the Council. Sometimes there is no extra charge for spouses to stay in a hotel room, but they are responsible for their meals (except those to which they are specifically invited), travel, and other incidentals. The high cost of hotel meals prompts spouses to seek out and share information about nearby restaurants and grocery stores so that they can eat less expensively. The Council sometimes helps with the costs for Central Conference spouses, especially for those serving as president of the spouses' organization. The spouses have occasionally used money from the treasury to help those who feel they cannot afford to sign up for outings for which they are asked to pay.

Hospitality

An area hosting committee, including the host bishop's spouse, often plans sightseeing trips in the area, informal luncheons, and other outings for the spouses. Some annual conferences or episcopal areas have spent generous amounts of money and energy staffing hospitality rooms and providing snacks and beverages. Some area committees cover transportation, entry fees, and meal costs for visits to places of historical or cultural interest. Outings now also include opportunities for spouses to visit and volunteer at local United Methodist mission sites: soup kitchens, thrift stores, and activity centers, for example. Some spouses, uncomfortable with having so much money spent on them, have offered to pay their own way for bus tours and the like. Other spouses have reminded us that in some cultures refusing hospitality is considered rude.

Over the years, spouses have been increasingly welcomed and included in activities of the full Council, except, of course, Executive Sessions, which are convened for dealing with confidential matters. In 1972, **Marji Tuell** recalls, the spouses were "only grudgingly allowed to attend worship with the bishops." A few years later, when no bishop-pianist was available, considerable discussion took place before a spouse was invited to play for worship. In the fall of 1978, **Marji**

Tuell was invited to lead singing during worship, which felt like a major breakthrough. More recently, the bishop who is preaching may invite a spouse to read the Scripture or other liturgy; and in the fall of 1998, the spouses were invited to plan and lead one of the Council worship services. Now it is no longer remarkable for spouses to participate in leading worship and serving Communion. Such inclusion helps spouses feel recognized and appreciated as part of the "team."

The Council meeting usually opens with a memorial service, honoring both bishops and spouses who have died since the last meeting, followed by a "family dinner" to which relatives may be invited, especially the families of those being memorialized in the service. In recent years, spouses have sometimes been invited to eulogize deceased spouses. Spouses have long been invited to special dinners and program presentations for the Council, at which speakers might tell about local mission projects or area church history, local choirs or musicians might perform, and individual bishops might tell about their faith journeys. Many spouses also sit faithfully through open plenary sessions to hear reports of interest to them and to better understand what the bishops are doing.

Early on, the wives wore formal gowns and hats and gloves for some of their gatherings. A former district superintendent's wife, who had volunteered to help transport the bishops' wives to a luncheon, recalls her surprise when she arrived at the hotel and found them wearing evening gowns. Pictures taken in 1960 reveal many hats, but fewer appear in subsequent years. **Gwen White** commented that she decided against wearing a hat and gloves because she felt that made the Central Conference spouses uncomfortable. Some members of the class of 1988 wore jogging suits to meetings and meals, in gentle rebellion against the fancy dress of others. Attendees at Council meetings now wear a wide variety of clothing, with gratitude for the availability of easy-care fabrics and styles. Some of the Central Conference spouses have shared that they feel pressure to dress well while traveling in their home areas, because their church people expect the bishop and his/her spouse to represent them well.

The spring meeting before and during General Conference involves at least a two-week stay. During General Conference sessions, the bishops' spouses are seated in a designated area and also have a designated hospitality room. Spouses often enjoy reunions with delegates from former annual conferences and with friends made around the world. Some spouses like to be present when their spouse is presiding over the General Conference sessions or preaching during worship and when legislation of particular interest is discussed. Bishops have no vote during General Conference proceedings and little influence, unless assigned to preach, and bishops' spouses even less. But spouses often find ways to stand with and support those who may be affected by legislation—and there is a lot of praying going on.

Challenges

The ability to maintain a well-organized association is limited by meeting only twice a year, geographic distances, difficulty finding meeting spaces, language differences, and the extremely busy lives spouses lead between meetings. Sometimes they have to make last-minute adjustments in plans because of changes made by the Council of Bishops. The spouses have frequently rewritten bylaws and job descriptions of officers, striving for consistency and trying—with moderate success—to keep things from slipping through the cracks. Nominating Committees have tried hard to include representatives from each Jurisdiction and from the Central Conferences, but there are not always enough active spouses in each area. There have been lively discussions in business meetings about possibly having the spouses of retired bishops serve as officers, but many of them do not attend regularly. More vocal members sometimes dominate discussions, and differences of opinion about how things should be done can sometimes lead to hurt feelings. One member recalls how structured the organization was and how each quadrennium's newly elected class has brought new ideas and attitudes to the group. Some of these new ideas have lasted, and others have been dropped after a while. Some surviving spouses of deceased bishops struggle to still feel a part and sometimes attend meetings, pairing up with another surviving spouse or bringing along a family member to share housing costs.

Changes Resulting from Changes in The Council

As an auxiliary organization, the spouses' group is affected by changes in how the Council of Bishops functions. The 1939 plan of union ended the practice of bishops being elected and assigned to an area by the General Conference, which emphasized their role as general superintendents of the whole church. Election and assignment of bishops is now the responsibility of the Jurisdictions in the United States and of the Central Conferences elsewhere, contributing, perhaps, to increasing regionalism. Some Jurisdictions have characteristic points of view, more conservative or progressive, for example. These differences may show up in the spouses' organization from time to time, but they are not often spoken of, at least publicly.

Since more and more Central Conferences in Africa, Europe, and the Philippines began electing indigenous bishops, our membership has become increasingly diverse, although the difficulty involved in traveling sometimes keeps Central Conference spouses from participating. When Central Conferences become autonomous churches, their bishops no longer participate in the Council, except for special cases, like Puerto Rico, whose bishops still do. After The Methodist Church in India became autonomous in 1980, for example, Indian women who had been active with the Bishops' Wives Association before then were sadly missed by those who had developed deep friendships with them.

Another major change impacting the spouses was the decision of the Council, in the spring of 2012, to experiment with its schedule and hold only one full meeting each year. The active bishops met once a year without the retirees. This action was reversed in the spring of 2016, and retirees are now included in both meetings, with voice but no vote, as before. The active bishops now usually meet for a day or two after the meeting of the full Council.

When my husband and I joined the episcopal family in 1992, he was expected to make a Global Visitation at least once each quadrennium. Teams of bishops were assigned to visit episcopal areas in other parts of the world, and spouses often traveled with them, at their own expense. The teams usually spent 10 days or more traveling in the assigned area, visiting churches and mission projects and learning about the ministry and mission there, as well as the needs. Such visits changed the perspectives and sometimes the lives of those who participated. Increasingly many bishops and spouses have participated in Volunteer-in-Mission projects, as well. Some bishops are assigned to travel to other areas of the world to preach, teach, or provide supervision or consultation. Official Global Visitations do not currently take place, but bishops and their spouses have many other opportunities to travel.

Changes Resulting from Cultural Shifts

The Role of Women

Early records of the spouses' organization do not include the first names of the spouses. By the 1960–1964 quadrennium, the first names of the spouses appear more frequently in reports, picture identification, and lists of participants, either along with or sometimes instead of the husband's names. Newspaper clippings still identified the women exclusively by the husband's name.

As **Shirley Skeete** discovered when she attended her first Council meeting after her husband's election in 1980, very few of the women worked outside the home then. As a tenured teacher employed in New York City, she was placed on leave, giving her the opportunity to return to work anytime. She taught six of the 16 years that Herb was an active bishop, commuting to New York City, first from Philadelphia and later from the Boston area. Having a home and family in New York City made it easier for her to travel back and forth from where they were living (interview with Shirley Skeete, May 2016).

Eleanor Lyght, moving from northern New Jersey to New York in 1996, was able to continue in her same teaching job. Through the years, fewer spouses have opted to become a "full-time bishop's spouse," resulting in fewer available to attend meetings regularly and to provide leadership for the organization.

Male Spouses

In 1980, the North Central Jurisdictional Conference elected its first female United Methodist bishop, Marjorie Swank Matthews. This was 24 years after the 1956 General Conference passed legislation adding the following words to the *Book of Discipline*: "Women are included in all provisions of the *Discipline* which refer to the ministry" (Oden & Williams, 132). Two more were elected in 1984, but it was not until 1988 that the election of a married woman bishop, Sharon Brown Christopher, introduced a male spouse into the Bishops' Wives Association (Oden & Williams, 132). **Charles Christopher** was promptly elected president. In 1991, the organization changed its name to the Bishops' Spouses' Association, recognizing the increasing number of female bishops being elected. The statement of purpose was also updated to be more inclusive: "The purpose of the Bishops' Spouses' Association shall be to promote fellowship and a feeling of

Christian family among the spouses and widows/widowers of United Methodist bishops, both active and retired."

The husbands of female bishops have varied in their level of participation with the spouses' organization, but many seem to have moved into easy partnership with others active in the group. Outings have changed to include such activities as golf or kayaking tours. Some male spouses have assumed various leadership roles, serving as officers, leading activities, and implementing new projects, such as the closed group **Lee Padgett** has established on Facebook, titled "Association of Bishop Spouses."

Changes Related to Integration and Inclusion

The 1939 plan of union created the Central Jurisdiction, a non-geographic grouping of all African American churches and pastors, reflecting the continuing racism that divided the church in 1844 and fueled resistance to full integration. Racism was on the Council agenda in the 1950s (Oden & Williams, 69–70), and some spouses were very active in the civil rights movement of the 1960s. Although the Central Jurisdiction was abolished in the 1968 merger with the Evangelical United Brethren, racism has continued, sometimes hidden, and sometimes quite obvious. From time to time, the Council of Bishops has named a task force to work on racism within their organization. During the spring 1999 meeting, after several spouses expressed concern about a lack of inclusivity in the group, the spouses' Executive Committee assigned a team to plan and lead a community-building workshop for our next meeting. During that workshop, a panel of four spouses shared experiences of feeling excluded by the group. Out of the discussions that followed, the group produced a list of actions that could be taken to help the group be more inclusive. Participants signed a covenant, agreeing that 10 such actions would be put into practice, and the covenant document was added to the Thrival Kit.

Some of our book group discussions (see Spring Council meeting 2007, p. 224, and Spring Council meeting 2010, p. 232) prompted uneasy heart-searching and poignant conversation as African-American spouses described similar injustices they had experienced and white spouses struggled with their responsibility for slavery and current institutional racism. In a private interview, an African American spouse, who wishes to remain anonymous, expressed gratitude for the opportunities provided her through the church and for the warm welcome she received when she joined this group. "Because my husband was elected to this office, I have become a part of this community," she commented, "and I want you to know how important you all have been to me." She recalled that her father and mother always told her to get a good education and prepare herself for the end of segregation and reduction of the white privilege that impacted and limited their possibilities. She has felt a sacred commitment to take advantage of the doors that have opened for her on behalf of her parents, who did not have such opportunities (interview, October 2010).

In the fall of 2002, **Kashala Katembo** offered suggestions to help the group be more "global." The Central Conference spouses appreciated **Raquel Martinez** serving as host for them during that meeting, making sure they had copies of the schedule, answering questions, and encouraging them to participate in activities. Occasionally, one of the Council translators has been available to come to the meetings or, more often, one of the multilingual spouses will assist with communication.

The ongoing controversy over our church's position on homosexuality has been very stressful for many bishops' spouses. Episcopal families who have acknowledged and accepted their gay family members and friends suffer while listening to negative statements about marriage and ordination of LGBTQ+ persons (see Etta Mae Mutti's story, p. 191). Other spouses fear what will happen if the church softens its stance. Conflict over full inclusion of homosexual persons has been brewing since 1972. Before then, the *Discipline* was silent on the subject. At the 1972 General Conference, a special commission assigned to rewrite the Social Principles proposed adding these words: "Homosexuals no less than heterosexuals are persons of sacred worth, who need the ministry and guidance of the church in their struggles for human fulfillment, as well as the spiritual and emotional care of a fellowship which enables reconciling relationships with God, with others, and with self. Further we insist that all persons are entitled to have their human and civil rights ensured." After intensive debate on the conference floor, an amendment was made and quickly passed, changing the period to a comma and adding, "although we do not condone the practice of homosexuality and consider this practice incompatible with Christian teaching" (See "Lucile Wheatley's Window on History: The Struggle for Inclusion," p. 151).

At each General Conference since then, some persons have worked to remove these words, while others have worked for legislation to maintain this stance and to tighten enforcement of the prohibitions against ordination of "self-avowed practicing homosexuals" and participation in same-gender weddings. At the 2016 General Conference, delegates voted to ask the bishops to lead the church in resolving this division, which they did by establishing a special "Commission on a Way Forward" to bring together persons of different opinions to dialogue and develop proposals to bring to a special General Conference in February 2019. The results of that gathering and the General Conference of 2020 are beyond the scope of this volume.

In the summer of 2016, the Western Jurisdiction elected Bishop Karen Oliveto, the first openly gay bishop in our church, bringing her spouse, **Robin Ridenour**, into the Bishops Spouses' Fellowship, where she has been warmly welcomed (see Robin's story, p. 20). Some have expressed outrage at such defiance of the rules they want enforced; others refuse to comply with what they consider to be against God's will. Bishops' spouses, although unable to vote or speak on the conference floor, may advocate and work for a desired outcome through their own channels of influence. Collectively they agonize over this division in their beloved church, the threat to its ministry and mission, and hurtful things that are said.

Changes Influenced by Individual Interests and Convictions

Other changes in our organization have come about because of personal interests. When **Eunice Mathews** was working with a committee to plan activities for the spouses for the spring meeting of 1961, scheduled for Boston, her husband, Jim, asked if the spouses ever studied anything. Later, in the spring of 1977, when she was president, Eunice and **Mary Ella Stuart** invited a speaker to address the group, surprising some of the older members. Since then some sort of educational or cultural experience has often been part of the Association's meetings.

Sharing Ideas

The opportunity to share ideas has long been an important aspect of our life together. Informally, over meals or riding on a bus or just waiting for a bishops' meeting to end, spouses have asked each other how they handle various challenges. A group of spouses in the class of 1992 worked together to produce a

Thrival Kit for the next incoming class. Focused on the premise that there is no one way to thrive as a bishop's spouse, the loose-leaf notebook contained articles written by many different spouses, describing a variety of strategies and tips that worked for them. Spouses continued to update and produce these notebooks for several quadrennia.

Sometime between 2008 and 2012, inquiries by spouses of newly elected bishops about ideas for Christmas gifts and for entertaining the Cabinet and leadership teams in their areas inspired **Elaine Hopkins** to begin holding "Sharing What Works" sessions where answers to such questions could be explored. A posted invitation read, "Come and share how YOU have successfully transitioned and learn from others who have achieved goals you're still working on." These sessions were scheduled for an open time when we could find a room booked by the Council but not in use. Elaine reports, "I tried to select a theme for each session and usually asked one or two spouses to be prepared to share ideas that had worked for them. The themes ranged from 'annual conference gatherings of clergy spouses' and 'retreats' to 'finding your own church or networking group when assigned to a new episcopal area.'"

Covenant Groups

At the spring 1994 meeting in Rochester, New York, a small group of spouses, having observed how meaningful the bishops' covenant groups seemed to be, formed such a group for themselves. Those who chose to participate found this a very enriching experience, a confidential setting for personal sharing that provided mutual support and deepened friendships. Other spouses expressed interest, and the movement grew. Someone agreed to reorganize the groups at the end of the quadrennium, in order to include spouses of newly elected bishops and allow relationships to develop with different people. This activity continued through recent years, with varying levels of participation. During the years when retired bishops attended only one of the two Council meetings each year, it became more difficult to sustain involvement and interest. The groups often had difficulty finding space and time to meet in the schedule. At the fall meeting in 2017, the Leadership Team used the meeting time for table sharing and prayer, a rich experience for those present. The Association seems to be moving toward covenantal sharing as a way of being for the entire group, rather than assigning small groups.

Episcopal Spouses' Directory and Communication

Members of the class of 1996 conceived the idea of a spouses' directory, easily tucked into a purse or pocket, providing contact and personal information about each spouse. They produced a very professional booklet, with the help of staff in **Elaine Hopkins**'s business, but the Association voted not to invest money in continuing this project. In 2000, **Valerie Whitfield** graciously offered to update the document herself. In 2004, **Carol Paup** and **Jane Ives** took on this responsibility, and in 2009 the Association voted to add a new officer, membership secretary, to the Executive Committee to manage the directory information and the email listserv.

By then most spouses were using email, which improved communication, and the Episcopal Office was sending out information about meetings that way. The membership secretary made sure that those without email access had "Snail Mail Buddies" to print and pass along messages to them and also checked regularly to make sure we had correct emails. This position and the production of the directory were discontinued when the spouses' group reorganized in 2014. It became the responsibility of the spouses or their bishops to see that the Episcopal Office has correct email addresses for them.

Mission Support Network

At the fall 1997 Council Meeting, **Phyllis May** shared with her covenant group her experience visiting camps for refugees from Rwanda in the Democratic Republic of Congo (see the full story in chapter 19). She made an appeal for shoes for the children, whose battered feet she described eloquently. The spouses initiated a church-wide drive, and the overwhelming response alerted UMCOR to the potential of the bishops' spouses to provide mission education and promotion. After touring camps for Kosovo refugees with her husband in June 1999, **Hannah Meadors** recruited a team of bishops' spouses to visit Kosovo that fall. Traveling with an UMCOR team, they visited four different schools, delivering school kits and sports equipment to children and teachers who had survived the war and meeting with various agencies and personnel working with the people there. At the fall Council meeting, a few weeks later, these spouses reported on their experience to the full Council, and the first meeting of what would become the Mission Support Network was held.

During the next several quadrennia, this group continued to meet and evolve, honoring Hannah after her death in 2003 by continuing the work for which she had such passion. The group crafted a mission statement and an informational flyer, updated each year to communicate ways to participate and actions taken.

Mission Statement

The Mission Support Network (MSN) supports the United Methodist Committee on Relief, focusing on the Mother/Child Survival Program (CBPHC) and other global mission priorities by:

- maintaining contact with UMCOR
- praying daily for persons in need and for those who serve them
- studying global needs
- sharing and interpreting information
- traveling to mission sites for learning and service
- practicing good stewardship
- soliciting practical donations (e.g., UMCOR kits for Health, School, and Healthy Family and emergency needs, such as blankets for refugees)
- promoting financial contributions (e.g., One Great Hour of Sharing, Advance Specials)

[See "Minutes of Mission Support Network," in the Bishops' Spouses' collection, UM Archives and History Center]

UMCOR personnel offered training and informational programs for the spouses during a number of Council meetings and encouraged them to promote the One Great Hour of Sharing offering for UMCOR's undesignated giving.

In the fall of 2000, **Martha Chamberlain** visited the JAMKHED project in India to study maternal/child health as it relates to comprehensive Community Based Primary Health Care (CBPHC) in urban Bombay (now Mumbai) and areas surrounding Jamkhed. CBPHC trains persons from local communities to teach others and work for better sanitation, nutrition, and health care. Martha wrote a report of that visit, "Ignore? or Act?," which she presented to the General Board of Global Ministries in 2001 (report available at The UM Archives and History Center). In 2001, **Jo Stith** visited CBPHC projects in Venezuela, Bolivia, and Brazil. She also wrote a moving summary of her experience. Jo said, "Hannah urged me to do some things that I would never have done. She called me and asked me to go to Latin America, an experience that changed my life, really grabbed my attention." **Melba Whitaker** took clergy spouses from the Florida Conference to visit CBPHC projects in Brazil, Guatemala, and Peru, providing life-changing experiences for those participating and increasing missional giving in their annual conference. Several of these spouses went on to lead mission trips to Peru and Guatemala and became very involved in local mission in their churches.

The Mission Support Network continued to meet during Council meetings until 2014, inviting individuals to share about their missional involvements both at home and abroad, planning promotion of the One Great Hour of Sharing offering and implementing other projects, such as sending a large container of medications to Angola. The Network also organized and presented Mission Awareness Sessions during General Conference in 2000 and 2004 and organized an alternative Christmas-card project, sending out a message inviting members to make a donation to UMCOR equal to the amount we would have spent on postage by sending each other individual greetings. The spouses' group created a bulletin board where bishops and spouses could post a card during the November meeting and sent out a group Christmas card by email listing those who donated, raising $8,721.56 for UMCOR in 2007, and more than $10,000 each of the following Christmas seasons until 2014.

Interest Groups

In the fall of 2004, five interest groups were proposed, with **Margaret Watson** serving as interest group coordinator. **Char Ough** began a book group, **Raquel Martinez** volunteered to lead a Spanish class, **Brad Kiesey** offered to lead a choir, and **Martha Chamberlain** proposed a journaling group. Because illness and family needs kept Raquel and Brad from coming to the next meetings, the Spanish and choir groups did not happen. The book group continues, led by **Mary Lou Reece**, then by **Jennifer Davis**, and currently by **Jolynn Lowry**. At each meeting, members share titles of books they recommend; the group chooses two books, usually one fiction and one nonfiction for the next meeting, when volunteers present a review and lead a discussion of the books chosen.

Greater Nhiwatiwa was especially pleased when the book group read *The Blessings and the Bling* by Sharon Patterson, a breast cancer survivor. She later wrote, "I have plans to meet with some of the ladies here in Zimbabwe and discuss after they read the book. It is going to be helpful to motivate my people to have tests done early. . . . When you see me coming to the Council of Bishops, this is one of the reasons—to learn and to be exposed to good ideas that will help my people back home. Thanks be to God."

Martha Chamberlain's journaling group continued until 2012, with **Joyce Gwinn** assuming leadership in 2008. Members gathered at least once during each Council meeting to share their individual experiences with journaling. Some of those who brought journals with them volunteered to read selected passages aloud. This time together encouraged many to practice journaling more consistently and deepened awareness of how this practice can nurture spiritual growth. Listening to what others chose to share felt like sacred time.

A New Way of Functioning

In 2014, a long-standing struggle to improve the spouses' organization culminated in a movement to do away with the bylaws and simplify how it functions. The organization is hampered by the length of time between meetings, geographic distance between members, the fact that plans must often be changed because of changes made by the Council, difficulty finding meeting space in some settings, and the increasing number of spouses who are employed and thus not available to provide leadership for the group. Business meetings often dragged on at length and sometimes became contentious. Some decisions that were made were never implemented. A small group of spouses drafted a proposal, which was unanimously approved by the members present, calling for a two-year trial period of functioning as a Bishops' Spouses' Fellowship (BSF).

The proposal called for a leadership team composed of one representative from each US Jurisdiction, plus one each from Africa and Europe/Philippines, equaling a total of seven on the team. The team may delegate tasks, such as keeping track of membership records, historical records, book club, journaling, covenant groups, or any other spouses' activity that requires leadership. During Council of Bishops meetings, spouse activities will focus on fellowship, hospitality, diversity, inclusiveness, nurture, and care for all members. The team will provide a posted sign near the Council of Bishops' "command center" listing all spouse activities, with places and times so that all spouses will be informed and know where to look for information. Ahead of the meeting, as much information as possible will be emailed to the full fellowship. The Fellowship will not collect dues. Instead, a love offering will be taken if a need arises. Instead of sending cards signed by members present at a meeting, all members of the BSF are encouraged to send cards and emails to those who are ill or have lost loved ones.

The group continues to discuss matters that still need to be fine-tuned, such as keeping records, maintaining and updating the spouses' email list, and communicating with those absent from meetings. Our hope is to have, as **Helen Springer** said of the spouses' organization after John's election in 1936, "as much of an organization as [we] need" to sustain our fellowship of common interests and mutual care.

Moving into the Future

As in the past, the bishops' spouses' organization will continue to be influenced by changes in our church, our culture, and our world, as well as by the personal decisions and actions of its members. God has led us through crises and conflicts in the past, and we pray for openness to God's continued guidance and will for our world.

Part 2

BISHOPS' SPOUSES IN THE METHODIST CHURCH

PRE-1940–1968

Chapter 4

PRE–1940

Spouses from Prior Elections Still Living in 1940

The women listed below by predecessor church and in order of the year of their husbands' elections were still living in 1940 and may or may not have been involved in the new organization. Chapter 12 lists spouses from the Evangelical United Brethren Church and its predecessor churches who were still living in 1968. See detailed profiles of the spouses and citation information in Part 5, beginning on page 251.

From The Methodist Episcopal Church, North

Spouse	Bishop	Year Elected	Elected From	First Episcopal Assignment
Helen Bartlett Graves Burt	William Burt	1904	Italy AC	Europe
Jennie Lulah Ketcham Anderson	William Franklin Anderson	1908	New York area	Chattanooga

Spouse	Bishop	Year Elected	Elected From	First Episcopal Assignment
Jeanette Gertrude Fuller Leete	Frederick Deland Leete	1912	Detroit AC	Atlanta
Eva Thomas McConnell	Francis McConnell	1912	New York AC	Denver
Elizabeth Fisher Robinson	John Wesley Robinson	1912	Des Moines AC	Southern Asia
Sarah Tilsley Johnson	Eben Samuel Johnson	1916	Northwest Iowa AC	Africa
Mary Luella Day Leonard	Adna Wright Leonard	1916	Cincinnati AC	San Francisco
Clara Aull Mitchell	Charles Bayard Mitchell	1916	USA	St. Paul
Evelyn Riley Nicholson	Thomas Nicholson	1916	USA	Chicago
Adelaide Frances McGee Welch	Herbert Welch	1916	West Ohio AC	Korea and Japan
Laura Close Birney	Lauress John Birney	1920	Massachusetts	Shanghai, China
Laura P. Carson Burns	Charles Wesley Burns	1920	USA	Helena
Eva F. Wilson Clair	Matthew Wesley Clair	1920	USA	Liberia
Harriet Elizabeth Brown Jones	Robert Elijah Jones	1920	USA	New Orleans
Mina Wood Locke	Charles Edward Locke	1920	USA	The Philippine Islands
Eleanor M. Smith Mead	Charles Larew Mead	1920	USA	Denver
Anna Elizabeth Isenberg Richardson	Ernest Gladstone Richardson	1920	Connecticut and New York City	Atlanta
Ida L. Martin Smith	Harry Lester Smith	1920	New York State	Bangalore, India
Flora Janet Irish Waldorf	Ernest Lynn Waldorf	1920	New York State	Kansas City

Spouse	Bishop	Year Elected	Elected From	First Episcopal Assignment
Mary Putnam Stearns Badley	Brenton Thoburn Badley	1924	India	Bombay, India
Gertrude Virgil Brown	Wallace Elias Brown	1924	New York State	Helena
Lucy Dickerson Grose	George Richmond Grose	1924	USA	China
Edith Eglantine Egloff Lowe	Titus Lowe	1924	USA	Singapore
Margaret Ross Miller	George Amos Miller	1924	California, Philippines, Costa Rica	Mexico
Welthy Honsinger Fisher	Frederick Bohn Fisher	1920	USA and India	Calcutta
Lena Sarah Benson Baker	James Chamberlain Baker	1928	Illinois AC	Japan, Korea, Manchuria
Edna Dorman Lee	Edwin Ferdinand Lee	1928	Iowa, Manila, Batavia, Java, Malaya, Singapore	Manila
Myrtle L. Mudge Wade	Raymond J. Wade	1928	North Indiana AC	Stockholm
Satyavati Chitambar	Joshwant Rao Chitamber	1930	North India AC	Area included North India, Lucknow, Central Provinces Conferences, and the Bhabua Mission
Elizabeth Thompson Gowdy	John H. Gowdy	1930	New Hampshire AC	China Central Conference
Jinying Hao	Chih Ping Wang	1930	China	China
Mary Jane Eaton Blake	Edgar Blake	1920	New Hampshire	Paris Episcopal Area
Maude Estella Hammond Cushman	Ralph Spaulding Cushman	1932	New England and New York State	Denver Episcopal Area

Spouse	Bishop	Year Elected	Elected From	First Episcopal Assignment
Minnie E. Gattinoni	Juan Ermete Gattinoni	1932	Uruguay and Argentina	Bolivia, Argentina, Uruguay
Harriet Ammie Keeler Magee	Junius Ralph Magee		USA	St. Paul
Ruth Robinson Pickett	Jarrell Waskom Pickett	1935	Texas, India	Bombay
Lisa Elphick	Roberto Valenzuela Elphick	1936	Latin America	Panama, Peru, and Chile
Clara Yetta Flint	Charles Wesley Flint	1936	USA	Atlanta
Willamine Weihrauch Hammaker	Wilbur Emery Hammaker	1936	USA	Nanking (China)
Hanna Melle	F.H. Otto Melle	1936	President, Frankfurt Theological Seminary	Germany Central Conference
Ruth Fisher Oxnam	Garfield Bromley Oxnam	1936	Southern California AC	Omaha
Lottye Blanche Simon Shaw	Alexander Preston Shaw	1936	USA	New Orleans
Helen Emily Springer	John McKendree Springer	1936	USA, Africa	Africa
Mildred May Worley Ward	Ralph Ansel Ward	1937	USA, China	Chengtu, China

From The Methodist Episcopal Church, South

Spouse	Bishop	Year Elected	Elected From	First Episcopal Assignment
Mary Nicholson Ainsworth	William Newman Ainsworth	1918	South Georgia AC	probably southern and south central conferences
Virginia Bourne Darlington	Urban Valentine Williams Darlington	1918	West Virginia AC	North and South Carolina

Spouse	Bishop	Year Elected	Elected From	First Episcopal Assignment
Gertrude Vaughn Amis Dubose	Horace Mellard Dubose	1918	USA	California
Bessie Harris Moore	John Monroe Moore	1918	Secretary Home Missions	Brazil
Ada Blanche Whitehurst Beauchamp	William Benjamin Beauchamp	1922	USA	Europe
Carolyn Odalie Browne Boaz	Hiram Abiff Boaz	1922	President, Southern Methodist University	Asia
Mary Jessie Munroe Dickey	James Edward Dickey	1922	North Georgia AC	___
Lessie Rush Jackson Dobbs	Hoyt McWhorter Dobbs	1922	North Alabama AC	Brazil
Margaret Matilda Gulick Hay	Samuel Ross Hay	1922	Texas	China
Lucy Gordhall Campbell Kern	Paul Bentley Kern	1930	Tennessee Annual	China
Martha J. McDonald Moore	Arthur James Moore	1930	USA	Pacific Coast Area
Bess Patience Crutchfield Smith	Angie Frank Smith	1930	North Texas AC	Missouri & Oklahoma
Helen Myrtle Hawley Mcallum Cannon	James Cannon Jr	1918	Virginia AC	Latin America & Africa
Bertha Whitley Decell	John Lloyd Decell	1938	Mississippi AC	southern conferences
Leland Burks Holt	Ivan Lee Holt	1938	USA	Texas & New Mexico

Spouse	Bishop	Year Elected	Elected From	First Episcopal Assignment
Sally Katherine Beene Martin	William Clyde Martin	1938	USA	Pacific Coast
Elizabeth Lytch Peele	William Walter Peele	1938	Western North Carolina AC	at large
Ida Bernice West Purcell	Clare Purcell	1938	North Alabama AC	Charlotte
Bess Kyle Beckner Selecman	Charles Claude Selecman	1938	President, Southern Methodist University	Oklahoma
Frances Edith Hancock Watkins	William Turner Watkins	1938	North Georgia AC	Columbia

From The Methodist Protestant Church

NOTE: The Methodist Protestant Church did not have bishops but elected two in 1939 in preparation for the next year's union, bringing two new spouses into the Bishops' Wives' Fellowship.

Spouse	Bishop	Year Elected	Elected From	First Episcopal Assignment
Moselle Mar Donaldson Broomfield	John Calvin Broomfield	1939	Pittsburgh AC	St. Louis
Clara Morgan Straughn	James Henry Straughn	1939	President, West Lafayette College	Pittsburgh

Reflections and Personal Stories

Helen Emily Springer's Story

Bishop John McKendree Springer's book, *I Love the Trail: A Sketch of the Life of Helen Emily Springer* (Nashville: The Parthenon Press, 1952), offers an in-depth view of the life of missionaries and the role of bishops' spouses in these transitional years. Based on diaries kept by his wife, as well as his own memories and knowledge, his book describes the formative experiences of Helen's childhood on a farm near New Sharon, Maine, and her experience of a call to serve Christ at the age of 16. Helen joined a local Methodist Church, taught church school, and, in 1889, at the age of 21, responded to a call for missionaries made by William Taylor, a missionary bishop of The Methodist Episcopal Church. Early in her service, she met and married William Rasmussen, also a missionary, and they served together in the Congo until his death from a fever in 1895. After a period of time in the United States, recovering from fever and exhaustion herself, Helen returned to Africa, this time to Rhodesia. She married John in 1905, and together they served at mission stations and throughout the African countryside. They were in the United States on furlough in 1936, traveling across the country to talk about Africa, soliciting financial support for missions there, and recruiting missionaries for service. The General Conference meeting in Columbus, Ohio, needed to elect a missionary bishop for Africa, to replace one who was retiring. In his book, John shared the following excerpts from Helen's diary:

May 9: "Well, we have put the case in God's hands. If He wants John for that work, good and well. If not, we don't want him to have it."

May 15: "The third ballot gave John 411 votes, a clear majority, and he was elected. Bishops Johnson and Gowdy were asked to escort him to the platform, and Mr. Swan of Chicago shouted, 'And Mrs. Springer too.' So we both had to go, Bishop Johnson taking me and John Gowdy my John. It was almost the last straw for me. I had not the slightest emotion up to that time, but it rolled over me amid the roar of applause like a tidal wave" (Springer, 132).

John went on to comment that two "firsts" took place that day. "We were seated in the front row in the gallery at the left of the stage. When my election was announced, I leaned over and kissed my wife right there, in public though it was. The applause which had arisen increased into a roar with shouts of approval. I felt most definitely that in thus placing upon me the responsibility for administration and leadership in Africa, the confidence which the Church had come to have in me had been built up in no small measure through the devoted cooperation of my wife. In their voting, some of the delegates may have been influenced by the inspiring personality and influence of Mrs. Springer. And I wished, to the extent that the act of kissing her there in public would declare it, to make known publicly my view of the matter. We never heard of a precedent of that act on such an occasion. And then, was she not the first wife of a bishop to be escorted with her husband to the platform? It has happened since. Did this set a precedent?" (Springer, 133).

John went on to note: "Needless to say, Helen greatly enjoyed the fellowship of the additional group into which this election placed her. The Bishops' wives were naturally drawn into an intimacy of common interests and of occasional activities and responsibilities. They had as much of an organization as was need, and communications passed around occasionally" (Springer, 133).

In July, before they returned to Africa, Helen wrote in her diary, "I realized today how impossible it would be for me to stay in my home while John was out for months holding conferences" (Springer, 134). She faced a somewhat different role now, after years of arduous work on the front lines, traveling from village to village on foot or carried by natives in a hammock, leading worship, teaching, providing health care, learning native languages and translating materials into them, writing articles, and sharing the love of Christ in every way possible. She continued to serve with distinction in Angola and Liberia and other places in Central Africa, returning to the United States for the Uniting Conference in 1939. On May 10, Helen wrote in her diary, "This was the Great Day, the Historic Day of the Conference when Bishop Hughes gave a most masterly closing address on 'The Methodists Are One People.' Then he with Bishop John M. Moore and Bishop Straughn solemnly announced and confirmed the Unification of the three Methodist Churches, followed by the 'Hallelujah Chorus.' Then as the great audience of about 10,000 began to leave, we said our good-byes to so many of our dear friends. I felt especially sad at parting with the Bishops' wives who had become very dear to me" (Springer, 142).

Not Everyone Was Happy with the 1939 Merger

Sarah Antoinette Curtright Candler's husband, Bishop Warren A. Candler, elected in 1898 in The Methodist Episcopal Church, South, opposed the reunification of the Northern and Southern Methodist churches. He had to retire when proponents of reunification persuaded the 1934 General Conference to establish a rule requiring bishops to retire at age 72 (http://www.georgiaencyclopedia.org/articles/arts-culture/warren-akin-candler-1857-1941).

Lucy Chase Chapman Denny's husband, Bishop Collins Denny, who was elected in 1910 from the Baltimore-Washington Conference of The Methodist Episcopal Church, South, retired in 1932 and did not attend the 1939 meetings because he did not wish to be regarded as a bishop of the new church (Short, 13). He and their son, Collins Denny Jr, challenged reunification all the way to the US Supreme Court, which ruled that it had no jurisdiction in the case, thus ending all challenges to the 1939 reunification. Collins Denny Jr, became a pro-segregation lawyer in Virginia (https://en.wikipedia.org/wiki/Collins_Denny).

Chapter 5

1940–1944

Spouses Who Joined the Episcopal Family 1940–1944

Detailed profiles and citation information can be found in Part 5, beginning on page 251.

Jurisdiction or Central Conferences	Spouse	Bishop	Year Elected	Elected From	First Episcopal Assignment
Western	Martha Harrold Baxter	Bruce Richard Baxter	1940	President, Williamette University	Portland (Oregon) & Territory of Alaska
Central	Louise Marie Watts King	Lorenzo Houston King	1940	Atlanta AC, M.E. Church	Atlantic Coast Area
Central Conferences	Juanita Rodriguez Recarey De Balloch Gowland	Enrique Carlos Balloch Gowland	1941	Paraguay, Uruguay, and Argentina	Pacific (Chile, Perú, Panama, and Costa Rica)
Central Conferences	Harriett Lang Boutelle Lacy	George Carleton Lacy	1941	USA, China	Foochow

Jurisdiction or Central Conferences	Spouse	Bishop	Year Elected	Elected From	First Episcopal Assignment
Central Conferences	Carolyn Belle Osburn Mondol	Shot Kumar Mondol	1940	India	Hyderabad
Central Conferences	Helen Cady Rockey	Clement Daniel Rockey	1941	India	North India
Central Conferences	Wife name unknown	Wen Yuan Chen	1941	China	Chungking
Central Conferences	Wife name unknown	Z. T. Kuang	1941	China	Peiping

NOTE: The *Discipline* also lists the following other bishops elected in this quadrennium: William Alfred Carrol Hughes (1940) and Fred Dennis (1941).

Highlights of Our Life Together: 1940–1944

For the most part, the spouses' life together has taken place within the context of the bishops' Council meetings. Unless otherwise noted, the information in "Our Life Together" segments is based on the memory and personal notes of the author and information found in the episcopal spouses' scrapbooks and minutes stored at the Archives and History Center on the campus of Drew University in Madison, New Jersey. The earliest scrapbook appears to have been created around 1952. Noted here are only those meetings about which we found information involving the spouses or during which the Council took actions directly or indirectly affecting the spouses.

Council Meeting, December 3–5, 1940—Atlantic City, NJ

During this meeting, a group of women gathered to organize themselves as the Methodist Bishops' Wives Fellowship. According to "A Brief History" handwritten by **Frances B. Corson**, "This group was organized to meet a need and a desire of the bishops' wives to know each other better and to find strength in fellowship for their unique task." **Mrs. Francis J. McConnell**, wife of the bishop of the New York Area, was elected president for the quadrennium. Other officers elected included **Mrs. E. L. Waldorf**, wife of the bishop of the Chicago Area (secretary and treasurer), and **Mrs. James Straughen**, wife of the bishop of the Pittsburgh Area (second treasurer). (The minutes reflect the practice at that point in time of referring to wives by their husband's names.)

Council Meeting, May 7–9, 1941—Nashville, TN

Social activities were curtailed and the Council gave most of its attention to the Committee on War Emergency and Overseas Relief (Oden & Williams, 58).

Council Meeting, December 9–12, 1941—Sea Island, GA

As Council members arrived at this idyllic resort on December 7, 1941, news of the Japanese attack on Pearl Harbor broke, and those present all gathered around radios to listen to President Roosevelt's address to the nation (Oden & Williams, 58).

Council Meeting, December 15–17, 1943—Princeton, NJ

During this meeting, the Council created a plan for quadrennial overseas visitations by active bishops, realizing that none of them still living had served an episcopal area overseas (as did many of the earlier bishops) and that all bishops need some understanding of the global church (Short, 34).

Council Meeting and General Conference, April 26–May 6, 1944—Kansas City, MO

The Bishops' Wives Fellowship elected **Bess Smith**, wife of the bishop of the Houston-San Antonio Area, president for the next quadrennium, along with vice president **Clara Flint** of the Washington Area, secretary **Willamine Hammaker** of the Denver Area, and treasurer **Sally Martin** of the Omaha Area (Spouses' Scrapbooks, 1949–1964).

Reflections and Personal Stories

Window on History: World War II

A bishop's spouse often experiences a unique window on historical events because of the bishop's role and the area to which he or she is assigned or, in some cases, because of where they were before election. In addition to the drama of the 1939 union, some spouses of bishops who served during this time period experienced an "up close and personal" view of World War II. Methodists had established churches, schools, and hospitals in countries that were considered our enemies, and well-trained Methodist nationals carried on these ministries.

Maria Straube Wunderlich, born in Germany in 1910, married Friedrich Wunderlich in 1930 and raised her children amidst the horrors of World War II (*Biographical Directory*, 1984; http://www.emk-frauen.de/pdfs/Lebensbild_M-Wunderlich.pdf).

When **Gerlinde Minor**, born in Germany in 1938, was growing up, churches and schools were being destroyed by bombing, and often her family had nothing to eat. She attended school under the socialist system of the German Democratic Republic. The grandchild of Methodist preachers and a fourth-generation Methodist herself, she found faith at an early age (*Biographical Directory*, 2012–2016; email communication with Gerlinde Minor, January 2018).

Annegret Klaiber, born in Tübingen, Germany, in 1938, was only one year old when her father was drafted to serve as a soldier on the front line. He came home seven years later, after serving time as a prisoner of war. During those years, Annegret often heard that the fathers of her friends were killed or missing in action. She remembers many bomb alarms and spending many nights in an air-raid shelter (Annegret Klaiber, written in 2017).

In 1941, when the Japanese attacked the Malay peninsula, **Celeste Amstutz** and Hobart Amstutz were serving as missionaries there. Celeste escaped to India, where their children were attending the Woodstock School, and for two years she taught classes at Woodstock and assisted with administration. In 1943, they returned to the United States, where the children enrolled in American universities. Hobart, who had remained in Singapore in 1941, became a prisoner of war for three and a half years (Amstutz Mission Biographical Files [UM Archives–GCAH, Madison, New Jersey]).

Otto Melle, resident bishop of the Germany Central Conference in Berlin, 1936–1946, refused to go west for safety, because he "did not want to leave the Berlin Methodists alone in the day of darkness." In spite of the fierce warfare during those years, his wife, **Hanna Melle**, and their daughter Edith stayed with him in Berlin (September 8, 1958 letter in Spouses' Scrapbooks, 1948–1964).

In 1943, **Mary Luella Leonard**'s husband, Adna, was asked by President Roosevelt to tour the American forces in Europe and Africa as a representative of the Commission on Chaplains of the Federal Council of Churches. During this mission, he died in an airplane crash over Iceland and was buried there (http://catalog.gcah.org/publicdata/gcah2396.htm).

Mildred Ward endured what must have been three particularly difficult years when Bishop Ralph Ansel Ward was imprisoned by the Japanese 1942–1945 and was not allowed to write to her (Nolan B. Harmon, ed., *Encyclopedia of World Methodism, vol. II* [Nashville: The United Methodist Publishing House, 1974], 2450–51).

No information was found about the **wife of Z. T. Kaung** (also known as Jiang Changchuan), although it is known that he had a daughter and six grandchildren. If his wife was living at the time, one can imagine her feelings when her husband, elected bishop of North China in 1941 and assigned to the Peiping Episcopal Area, found himself under constant surveillance by the Japanese, who occupied China 1937–1945. He was under suspicion because of his close ties with the Sung family and Chiang Kai-shek, whom he had baptized in 1930 (http://methodistmission200.org/jiang-changchuan-z-t-kuang-1884-1958/).

In California, **Lucile and Mel Wheatley** moved into the home of a Japanese-American family, who had been sent to an internment camp, to protect it from vandals ("A Service of Remembrance and Resurrection, November 4, 2018" program book for the Council of Bishops of The United Methodist Church).

Chapter 6

1944–1948

Spouses Who Joined the Episcopal Family 1944–1948

Detailed profiles and citation information can be found in Part 5, beginning on page 251.

Jurisdiction or Central Conferences	Spouse	Bishop	Year Elected	Elected From	First Episcopal Assignment
NC	Julia Estelle Merrill Brashares	Charles Wesley Brashares	1944	USA	Des Moines
NC	Lola Mabel Stroud Garth	Schuyler Edward Garth	1944	USA	Wisconsin Episcopal Area
NE	Frances Blount Beamon Corson	Fred Pierce Corson	1944	New York East AC	Philadelphia
NE	Helen Marion Nutter Hartman	Lewis Oliver Hartman	1944	Editor, The Zion's Herald	Boston
NE	Mary (Lida) Iszard Ledden	Walter Earl Ledden	1944	Southern New Jersey AC	Syracuse
SC	Mildred Helen Fryer Martin	Paul Elliott Martin	1944	North Texas AC	Arkansas-Louisiana

Jurisdiction or Central Conferences	Spouse	Bishop	Year Elected	Elected From	First Episcopal Assignment
SC	Bess Owens Smith	William Angie Smith	1944	USA	Oklahoma-New Mexico
SE	Edith Genevive Crogman Brooks Brown	Robert Nathaniel Brooks	1944	Professor, Gammon Theological Seminary	New Orleans
SE	Orina Winifred Kidd Garber	Paul Neff Garber	1944	Dean, Duke Divinity School	Geneva
SE	Amy Patten Walden Harrell	Costen Jordan Harrell	1944	SE USA	Birmingham
Central Jurisdiction	Oma A. Burnett Kelly	Edward Wendall Kelly	1944	USA	St. Louis
Central Jurisdiction	Emma C. Arnold King	Willis Jefferson King	1944	USA	Liberia
Central Conferences	Consuelo Garcia Alejandro	Dionisio Deista Alejandro	1944	Philippine Islands AC	Manila
Central Conferences	Esma Rideout Booth	Newell Snow Booth	1944	Massachusetts, Congo	Congo
Central Conferences	Basilia Baltazar Gutierrez	Benjamin R. Gutierrez	1944	Philippines	Davao
Central Conferences	Dorothy Sinclair Day Subhan	John Abdus Subhan	1945	North India AC	Bombay
Central Conferences	Beatrice Dibben Sommer	Johann Wilhelm Ernst Sommer	1946	Germany Central Conference	Frankfort-on-Main

NOTE: The *Discipline* also lists the following other bishop elected this quadrennium: August Theodor Arvidson (1946).

Joining by Marriage This Quadrennium

Spouse	Year Married	Bishop	Where Serving
Luisa Teresa Bissio Wesley	1945	Arthur Frederick Wesley	Atlantic (Argentina, Uruguay, and Bolivia)
Helen Newton Everett Springer	after 1946	John McKendree Springer	Retired

Highlights of Our Life Together: 1944–1948

Unless otherwise noted, the information in "Our Life Together" segments is based on the memory and personal notes of the author and information found in the episcopal spouses' scrapbooks and minutes.

Council Meeting, July 24–27, 1944—Chicago, IL

Council discussion centered on race relations and racism, following intense debate on that issue during the General Conference and reports that African American delegates had experienced discrimination (Oden & Williams, 59–62).

Council Meeting, February 20–25, 1946—Atlantic City, NJ

The Council of Bishops decided to meet twice a year (Short, 55).

Council Meeting, May 1–6, 1947—Riverside, California

The Council discussed and decided to appeal the Judicial Council's ruling on a General Conference action stating that retired bishops may speak but are not allowed to vote in Council proceedings. This appeal failed. This means they are completely disenfranchised, since all bishops, active and retired, have no vote in an annual conference or in a local church (Short, 53–56; Oden & Williams, 63–64).

Spring Council Meeting and General Conference, April 28–May 8, 1948—Boston, MA

The wives enjoyed a luncheon at a tea room and were guests, along with the bishops, at a breakfast at the Old Wayside Inn. Two receptions were held, one at the home of Boston University President Daniel and Mrs. Marsh and the other at the home of Mrs. Howard Selby, whose husband was a renowned Methodist leader in the Boston Area (*Official Minutes of the New England Conference, The Methodist*

Church, 1954, 751; also see https://archive.org/stream/journalboston00meth/journalboston00meth_djvu.txt).

The group elected **Ruth Oxnam** as president, **Amy Harrell** as recording secretary, and **Mildred Martin** as treasurer. **Lida Lidden** "graciously consented to act as corresponding secretary." **Amy Harrell** resigned as recording secretary, and **Willamine Hammaker** wrote the minutes of that meeting. Some of the spouses' first names appeared in the minutes.

Reflections and Personal Stories

Window on History: World War II, Continued

Harriett Lacy had been married to George Carleton Lacy, an American missionary in China, for 23 years when he was elected bishop of the China Central Conference in 1941. They had a son and a daughter, both born in China. During World War II, while her husband was supervising the church behind enemy lines, she worked with the American Bible Society in New York. She returned to China in 1947 but was forced to return to the United States in 1949 because of the Communist takeover of China. In 1950, when all foreign missionaries were forced to leave China, George was the only Westerner in that area denied an exit permit. He was detained under house arrest and died soon after (https://www.revolvy.com/main/index.php?s=George%20Carleton%20Lacy).

Orina Garber moved from the U.S. to Europe with her husband, Paul, when he was elected in 1944 and assigned to the Geneva Episcopal Area (North Africa, Switzerland, Belgium, Spain, Yugoslavia, Hungary, Austria, Bulgaria, Poland, Czechoslovakia, and the Madeira Islands). She accompanied him on visitations to churches struggling to recover from the destruction of World War II: properties in ruins, pastors who had been imprisoned, and families that had been separated. They graciously accepted limited accommodations and shared their resources with pastors and church members (*Journal of the North Carolina Annual Conference of The Methodist Church 1960,* 136–137).

When **Eunice and Ralph Dodge** were serving as missionaries in Angola (1936–1950), there was a period of three years when they were unable to return to Africa from furlough in the United States because of travel restrictions during World War II (*Biographical Directory,* 2004–2008).

In 1944, when **Consuelo Garcia Alejandro**'s husband, Dionisio Deista Alejandro, was elected bishop in the Philippines, no other Methodist bishop could go there to consecrate him because of the Japanese occupation. He served, but was not consecrated until 1946, after the islands were liberated (https://www.geni.com/people/Dionisio-Alejandro/6000000001356579724).

Chapter 7

1948–1952

Spouses Who Joined the Episcopal Family 1948–1952

Detailed profiles and citation information may be found in Part 5, beginning on page 251.

Jurisdiction or Central Conferences	Spouse	Bishop	Year Elected	From	First Episcopal Area Assignment
NC	Florence Engle Northcott	Harry Clifford Northcott	1948	Rock River AC (Illinois)	Wisconsin
NC	Mary Esther Kirkendall Reed	Marshall Russell Reed	1948	Detroit AC	Detroit
NC	Lucille Marguerite Arnold Raines	Richard Campbell Raines	1948	USA	Indianapolis
NC	Catherine Stewart Werner	Hazen Graff Werner	1948	Detroit AC, professor, Drew University	Ohio

Jurisdiction or Central Conferences	Spouse	Bishop	Year Elected	From	First Episcopal Area Assignment
NE	Margaret Farrington Ratcliffe Lord	John Wesley Lord	1948	Newark AC	Boston
NE	Gertrude Jane Allen Wicke	Lloyd Christ Wicke	1948	Pittsburgh AC	Pittsburgh
SC	Delma A. Millikan Dawson	Dana Dawson	1948	SC USA	Kansas-Nebraska
SE	Ruth Tuck Franklin	Marvin Augustus Franklin	1948	Alabama-West Florida AC	Jackson (Mississippi)
SE	Louise Clay Baird Short	Roy Hunter Short	1948	Louisville AC	Jacksonville (Florida)
W	Mary Leeper Kennedy Archipley	Gerald Hamilton Kennedy	1948	western USA	Portland (Oregon)
W	Ruth Estella Clinger Phillips	Glenn Randall Phillips	1948	California	Denver
W	Ruth Lena Underwood Tippett	Donald Harvey Tippett	1948	Colorado	San Francisco
Central Jurisdiction	Margaret Davis Bowen	John Wesley Edward Bowen Jr	1948	USA	Atlantic Coast
Central Conferences	Edna Priscilla Caye Archer	Raymond Leroy Archer	1959	Pittsburgh AC, Southeast Asia CC	Singapore
Central Conferences	Odette de Olivereira Barbieri	Sante Uberto Barbieri	1949	Latin American CC	Argentina, Bolivia, and Uruguay
Central Conferences	Manuela Lorenzana Lardizabal Valencia	José Labarrete Valencia	1948	Philippines	Philippines

NOTE: The *Discipline* also lists the following other bishop elected this quadrennium: David Thomas Gregory (1950).

Joining by Marriage This Quadrennium

Spouse	Year Married	Bishop	Where Serving
Mable Edna White Mason Selecman	1945	Charles Claude Selecman	Dallas
Katherine Boeye Ward	1948	Ralph Ansel Ward	Shanghai, China
Starr Carithers Holt	1950	Ivan Lee Holt	Missouri

Highlights of Our Life Together: 1948–1952

Unless otherwise noted, the information in "Our Life Together" segments is based on the memory and personal notes of the author and information found in the episcopal spouses' scrapbooks and minutes.

Spring Council Meeting, April 26–30, 1949— Atlantic City, NJ

The Philadelphia Area hosted a dinner honoring "The Bishops of The Methodist Church and Their Wives" at Chalfonte-Haddon Hall (Spouses' Scrapbooks, 1948–1964).

Spring Council Meeting, April 23–27, 1951— Grand Canyon National Park, AZ

The Council of Bishops met at the El Tovar Hotel in the park. The Women's Guild of the Community Church in Grand Canyon invited the bishops' wives to a tea hosted by Mrs. H. C. Bryant, wife of the superintendent of the park, at her home near the hotel (Spouses' Scrapbooks, 1948–1964).

Spring Council Meeting and General Conference, April 26–May 3, 1952—San Francisco, CA

During General Conference, the bishops' wives, many wearing hats, enjoyed a Hawaiian luncheon ($3.50 a plate, including gratuity), complete with Hawaiian leis, at the Sir Francis Drake Hotel, chaired by **Bess Owens Smith** of the Oklahoma-New Mexico Area. **Ruth Tippett** of the San Francisco Area hosted a tea at her home, assisted by the wives of the district superintendents and officers of the Ministerial Wives' Association of the

California-Nevada Conference. The General Conference booklet notes a reception for "Bishops, Members of the Judicial Council and Wives" at the Palace Hotel. Newspaper clippings from that event show the spouses in formal gowns. The Chinese Methodist Church of San Francisco entertained the Council of Bishops at the Far East Café, and "women visitors" were offered tours to San Francisco's Chinatown, Methodist churches and residences for young business women and Chinese business girls, the Pacific School of Religion, and other Methodist institutions, as well as to Muir Woods and other scenic destinations. Officers elected for the quadrennium were **Lucille Raines**, president; **Louise Short**, vice president and recording secretary; **Ruth Tippett**, corresponding secretary; **Gertrude Wicke**, treasurer; **Bess Smith**, historian (Spouses' Scrapbooks, 1948–1964).

Reflections and Personal Stories

Remembering Frances Corson (by Dr. Frederick E. Mason)

"My memories of Bishop Corson are closely tied with my memories of the beautiful woman, **Frances Corson**. At first, I saw her only from a distance. However, I agreed with my new assistant at St. James Church who was sitting next to me when he first saw her. He half arose from his seat and then, sinking back, said, 'Who is that beautiful woman?' 'That,' I said, 'is the bishop's wife.' 'It can't be,' he said softly. 'No Methodist bishop would be allowed to have a wife that beautiful.' But beauty is not Mrs. Corson's only virtue. She is an intelligent, compassionate woman, a community leader in her own right and a very witty person. Once, when the New Jersey Conference was honoring Bishop Corson, a youth leader arose to give his presentation. He said that though Bishop Corson often preached too long, the young people loved him, and they were glad he had been re-assigned to the area. Mrs. Corson followed on the program almost immediately. She said, 'I agree with the young man who thinks the bishop preaches too long, and I want to announce to the bishop now that I hope we all get out of here by 9:30 o'clock.' The Methodists, who loved her frank wit and charm, applauded loudly; but, as you might expect, the meeting did not end until about 10:30.

A bishop's spouse remembers seeing Mrs. Corson sitting at the piano wearing a lace collar, hair perfectly groomed, the essence of perfection even in the heat of July.

"No one was ever able to cut down the length of Bishop Corson's speeches. He explained his position to me. 'Fred,' he said, 'there are things that need to be said, and I'm going to say them no matter how long it takes.' It usually took quite long. Certainly by her charm, sagacity, and community leadership, Mrs. Corson had as much to do with making the wheels go 'round as did the bishop" (Dr. Frederick E. Mason, 'Bishop Fred Pierce Corson: A Personal Recollection,' [*The United Methodist Reporter for Eastern Pennsylvania*, May & June, 1985], 53; https://tinyurl.com/y3ar3ne9).

Bishop Peggy Johnson recalls hearing a retired leader in the Eastern Pennsylvania Conference comment that when Bishop Corson was going to visit a church, he would ask that his wife be given a corsage to wear when they arrived for worship. Gwen White would later comment that because they were traveling so much, sometimes the only thing in their refrigerator would be a corsage, prompting her to speak of someday writing a memoir titled "A Corsage in the Refrigerator."

Remembering Louise Short

Louise met Roy while he was in seminary and she was a student at the University of Louisville in Kentucky. Louise often accompanied him on his many travels and helped with missionary work. She made friends from all walks of life. "She loved everybody," her son, Pastor Riley Short, said. "She accepted you for who you were, and I think it had to do with her Christian faith. She believed the love of Christ was for everyone."

Although widowed in 1994, Louise remained active in Council activities and traveled the world. She routinely went to gatherings of the Council of Bishops, the Southeastern Jurisdiction, and the Tennessee Annual Conference. She also took on the responsibility of welcoming new bishops and their spouses to the

Council. "Sometimes we tend to talk about the bishops and not their spouses, but Mrs. Short had a ministry all her own," said Bishop Lindsey Davis, who met Mrs. Short and her husband when he was a teen Methodist youth leader in Kentucky. He noted that his wife, Jennifer, once introduced Mrs. Short as the "Queen Mother of Methodism in the Southeastern Jurisdiction." It was a title Louise liked, he said. "She was well-known as a teacher and a speaker all on her own," Davis said. "She wasn't overshadowed by Bishop Short" (email communication with Bishop Davis, October 2016).

At the age of 90, she rode a camel in the ancient city of Petra. At 95, she walked on the Great Wall of China. At 100, she visited Cambodia to see Angkor Wat. The following year, at 101, she balanced on a surfboard in Costa Rica for a family photo. Her last trip was to the General Conference in 2012, at the age of 106. Jo Ann McClain, administrative assistant with the Council of Bishops, recalled greeting her with a wheelchair to take her through the hotel and convention center to the plenary hall. Louise said, "Jo Ann, I can walk," but finally agreed to be wheeled to the gathering with a reluctant, "Fine." They were no sooner in the plenary space than she jumped out of the chair and started greeting people (interview with JoAnn McClain, May 2012). Louise died in 2016 at the age of 110, having attended every General Conference of The Methodist Church and The United Methodist Church from 1939 to 2012 (http://www.legacy.com/obituaries/tennessean/obituary.aspx?pid=180499782).

Remembering Manuela Lorenzana Lardizabal Valencia

Manuela grew up in the Philippines as a devout and faithful Roman Catholic. When she was in the seventh grade, a blind and spiritually powerful preacher from the United Brethren Church came to her town. Her cousins, whose family had converted to that church, invited her to the service, and she was deeply touched by the message, realizing that Christ is the only one who saves, not the church, as she had been taught as a child. Although members of her family resented her conversion, they were moved by the changes they saw in her and they reconciled with her. While still a student, Manuela was active in the church, and later, as a teacher, she taught Sunday school and often went into the barrios to teach and preach to the people there. She transferred her membership to a Methodist Church, where José was pastor. After their marriage, she gave up her teaching job to serve the church full time, accompanying José on visitations, maintaining a gracious home in which visitors felt welcome, and serving in the Women's Society of Christian Service.

When José became a district superintendent, she was elected district president of the Women's Society. Before the outbreak of World War II made travel difficult, she was particularly active in promoting tithing and stewardship. In 1948, José was elected as a delegate to the General Conference in Boston, Massachusetts. Friends and co-workers raised money for Manuela to accompany him, and they spent time before and after General Conference speaking at churches across the United States. While in Boston, Manuela represented the women of the Philippines in the organization of the World Federation of Methodist Women and became vice president of the East Asia Area for a term. She was also the first national president of the Women's Society of Christian Service of The Methodist Church in the Philippines, an office she held for eight years.

When José was elected bishop in 1948, once again Manuela stepped up to expand her ministry, organizing pastors' wives' associations and institutes, which helped to develop supportive relationships, strengthen the spiritual lives of the parsonage families, and provide practical support for those who were ill or struggling financially. She also organized the first National Pastors' Children Association to foster closer relationships among them, to deepen their spiritual lives, and to help them fulfill their role in home, church, and community. For 20 years she traveled with José, while also pursuing ministries of her own, preaching and teaching widely. Bishop Lloyd Wicke once said of her, "This lady is one of the best preachers I have ever heard" (José Labarrete Valencia, *After Thy Will: Story of the Life of Manuela Lardizabal-Valencia (Handmaiden of God)* [Board of Women's Work, United Methodist Church in the Philippines, 1987], 74).

Manuela traveled widely. When José went to Denver, Colorado, in 1960 for General Conference, she spent more than a month in Mindanao preaching two or three times a day and visiting rural churches. In 1961, she served as a delegate to the World Federation of Methodist Women and the World Methodist Conferences held in Oslo, Norway, an experience she describes eloquently in one of her personal writings included by her husband in his book about her life

(Valencia, 56–61). She also went to Okinawa to visit churches established there after World War II and wrote a report of the needs she saw, challenging churches in the Philippines to respond (Valencia, 48–51). José concludes his biography of Manuela with these words: "Manuela lived 'After the Will of God' and was God's *handmaiden in this life*" (Valencia, 77). Her favorite hymn, not surprisingly, was "Have Thine Own Way, Lord" (*UMH*, 382).

Chapter 8

1952–1956

Spouses Who Joined the Episcopal Family 1952–1956

Detailed profiles and citation information can be found in Part 5, beginning on page 251.

Jurisdiction or Central Conferences	Spouse	Bishop	Year Elected	Elected From	First Episcopal Assignment
NC	Margaret Havens Coors	D. Stanley Coors	1952	USA	St. Paul
NC	Eunice LeBourveau Ensley Wicke	Francis Gerald Ensley	1952	Columbus, Ohio	Iowa
NC	Eleanor Hemstead Dodge Voigt	Edwin Edgar Voigt	1952	USA	Dakota
NE	Emily Louise Lewis Newell	Frederick Buckley Newell	1952	New York East AC	New York
SC	Minnie Euphemie Keyser Watts	Henry Bascom Watts	1952	south central USA	Nebraska

Jurisdiction or Central Conferences	Spouse	Bishop	Year Elected	Elected From	First Episcopal Assignment
SE	Elizabeth Keller Branscomb	John W. Branscomb	1952	Florida AC	Florida and Cuba
W	Doris K. Malin Grant	Alsie Raymond Grant	1952	North Central and Western USA	Portland (Oregon)
Central Jurisdiction	Ethel Christian Smith Clair	Matthew Walker Clair	1952	USA	St. Louis
Central Jurisdiction	Virginia L. Ross Love	Edgar Amos Love	1952	Washington AC	Baltimore
Central Conferences	Ruth Marthine Larsen Hagen	Odd Arthur Hagen	1953	Principal, Methodistkyrkans Nordiska Theologiska Seminarium, Göteborg, Sweden	Northern European
Central Conferences	Juana Puch Sabanes	Julio Manuel Sabanes	1952	Latin American Central Conference	Santiago Episcopal Area (Chili, Peru, Panama, and Costa Rica)
Central Conferences	Alice Mumenthaler Sigg	Ferdinand Sigg	1954	Central and Southern Europe	Geneva
Central Conferences	Maria Straube Wunderlich	Friedrich Wunderlich	1953	President, Methodist seminary, Frankfurt-am-Main	Eastern and Western Germany

NOTE: The *Discipline* also lists the following other bishop elected in this quadrennium: Lyle Lynden Baughman (1954).

Joining by Marriage This Quadrennium

Spouse	Year Married	Bishop	Where Serving
Catherine Fae Luster Lane Franklin	1953	Marvin Augustus Franklin	Jackson (Mississippi)
Frances Novella Grant Kelly	1955	Edward Wendall Kelly	Retired

Highlights of Our Life Together: 1952–1956

Unless otherwise noted, the information in "Our Life Together" segments is based on the memory and personal notes of the author and information found in the episcopal spouses' scrapbooks and minutes.

Fall Council Meeting, November 17–21, 1952—Atlantic City, NJ

One day was given to orientation for newly elected bishops by the full Council. Because so many bishops wanted to give advice to their new colleagues, the Council appointed a committee to handle orientation in the future (Oden & Williams, 74–75).

Spring Council Meeting, April 28–May 1, 1953—Omaha, NE

The Council, which previously divided itself into two standing committees (the Committee on Reference and the Committee on Law and Administration), restructured, assigning just one bishop from each jurisdiction to each committee, to serve for one quadrennium only (Oden & Williams, 75).

Fall Council Meeting, December 8–11, 1953—St. Simon's Island, GA

The Council of Bishops' first meeting at a retreat center was held at Epworth-by-the-Sea, on St. Simon's Island in Georgia. According to a clipping in the scrapbook, the bishops "relaxed their dignity" for a shore dinner provided by 1,000 Georgians. **Fae Franklin**, the new bride of Bishop Marvin Augustus Franklin, received a camellia corsage (Spouses' Scrapbooks, 1948–1964).

Fall Council Meeting, November 18–21, 1954—Chicago, IL

The Council attended the opera *Tosca* at the Miniature Grand Opera Theatre (Spouses' Scrapbooks, 1948–1964).

Spring Council Meeting, April 1955—Seattle, WA

The Council was honored at a banquet.

Spring Council Meeting and General Conference, 1956—Minneapolis, MN

During General Conference, an Order of the Day called for the "Presentation of the Bishops' Wives," during which President **Mildred Martin** spoke briefly, expressing appreciation for the thoughtful courtesies extended to the wives and offering prayers for the conference and the tasks before it. The women wore long gowns for an evening reception honoring the bishops and their wives, along with members of the Judicial Council and their wives, during which they were photographed in small groups. A Bishops' Wives Luncheon ($3.00 per person) was held at the Woman's Club in Minneapolis, and the Ministers' Wives' Association of the Minnesota Conference hosted a May Day Luncheon at Lake Harriet Methodist Church. The bishops' wives also toured Methodist institutions nearby. **Bess Owens Smith** wrote a brief poetic Historian's Report for this session (see below). Officers elected for the next quadrennium included **Mildred Martin** as president, a treasurer, a recording secretary, a corresponding secretary, and an historian.

Reflections

Historian's Report by Bess Owens Smith

"The shades of 1952 falling quite quickly have finally enveloped the years to 1956. If the scenes behind the years could be unfolded today, we would relive sunshine and shadow, laughter and tears, victories and defeats. But we have come from all parts of the earth to meet in beautiful Minneapolis to live as devoted sisters for a short three weeks. We will share our joys and sorrows, then we will depart to have thousands of miles separate our human voices. But our abiding love, our deepest sympathetic understanding and our ever increasing appreciation will continue as the ebb and flow of the vast ocean never eases in our world.

"When in the morning of the coming tomorrows we find ourselves in the loneliness of faraway places or crushed by the demands of ever increasing obligations, these days of delightful fellowship and inspiring affection will enable us to be even more effective witnesses for our Lord. Our strength will be equal to our task and our horizons will be extended to include that which is. . . . Today we welcome new voices which will add to the melody of our symphony and our lives are richer because they are a part of our fellowship.

"We miss some whose presence have [*sic*] enabled and blessed our lives. They are absent now but the memories of yesteryear cause them to be bound to us by spiritual ties. . . . May we be worthy of the high honor and trust in which we live as leaders of the church. We are truly grateful for the manifold blessings of our life as we live it in an Episcopal Residence."

—Bess Owens, 1956 (Spouses' Scrapbooks, 1948–1964)

Chapter 9

1956–1960

Spouses Who Joined the Episcopal Family 1956–1960

Detailed profiles and citation information can be found in Part 5, beginning on page 251.

Jurisdiction or Central Conferences	Spouse	Bishop	Year Elected	Elected From	First Episcopal Assignment
SC	Wilma Alice Sedoris Frank	Eugene Maxwell Frank	1956	Kansas AC	Missouri
SE	Rebecca Lamarr Harmon	Nolan Bailey Harmon	1956	Book Editor, The Methodist Church	Charlotte
SE	Mary Brown Buckshaw Hodge	Bachman Gladstone Hodge	1956	North Alabama AC	Birmingham
Central Conferences	Celeste Thelma Bloxsome Amstutz	Hobart Baumann Amstutz	1956	Illinois, Singapore	Singapore
Central Conferences	Eunice Elvira Davis Dodge	Ralph Edward Dodge	1956	Dakota, Angola	Rhodesia (now Zimbabwe)

Jurisdiction or Central Conferences	Spouse	Bishop	Year Elected	Elected From	First Episcopal Assignment
Central Conferences	Rajabai Ruth Peters Sundaram	Gabriel Sundaram	1956	Southern Asia Central Conference	Hyderabad (India)
Central Conferences	Annie Belle Thaxton Taylor	Prince Albert Taylor Jr	1956	Central Jurisdiction	Monrovia (Liberia)

NOTE: The *Discipline* also lists the following other bishops elected in this quadrennium: John Gordon Howard (1957), Hermann Walter Kaebnick (1958).

Joining by Marriage This Quadrennium

Spouse	Year Married	Bishop	Where Serving
Ellen Louise Stoy Lowe	1957	Titus Lowe	Retired

Highlights of Our Life Together: 1956–1960

Unless otherwise noted, the information in the "Our Life Together" segments is based on the memory and personal notes of the author and information found in the episcopal spouses' scrapbooks and minutes.

Winter Council Meeting, December 10–13, 1956—Pasadena, CA

The Council met at the Huntington Sheraton Hotel. **Mary Kennedy** hosted a tea at the episcopal residence in Hollywood Hills, and another tea honored the wives of the newly elected bishops. Cecil B. DeMille spoke at the Bishops' Banquet, and the wives attended a luncheon at the Hollywood Brown Derby, followed by a tour of Paramount Studios and a private viewing of the film *The Ten Commandments.*

Spring Council Meeting, April 23–26, 1957—Cincinnati, OH

Twenty-eight wives assembled on the mezzanine of the Netherland Hilton. Treasurer **Mary Esther Reid** gave a welcoming speech and introduced the newcomers. Members then shared humorous stories from their experiences, as well as helpful tips. **Lucille Raines** reported that, at her first reception, a "dear old lady reached for her hand and said, 'So sorry, new wife of Bishop.'" **Myrtle Wade** told of an experience in Finland when a man greeted her with "I am so sorry you have come" (a translation error) followed by "I hope you will be glad you have come." **Bess Smith** shared her joy in being a bishop's wife.

Fall Council Meeting, November 1957—Gatlinburg, TN

The Council met at the Mountain View Hotel.

Spring Council Meeting, April 8–10, 1958—Miami Beach, FL

During this meeting at Roney Plaza, the wives enjoyed a special bus ride the length of Miami Beach and over a causeway to Coconut Grove and Coral Gables. They also visited a new church and the Wesley Foundation at Miami University, where they had tea. Some went on a boat ride around the islands and some to Parrot Island. Wednesday evening, they attended the Council meeting to hear visitation reports.

Spring Council Meeting, April 14–17, 1959—Washington, DC

The itinerary for the wives included visits to the National Gallery of Art, the Grant Memorial, Wesley Theological Seminary (for dedication of the chapel), Jefferson Memorial, Lincoln Memorial, the Tidal Basin, the Iwa Jima Memorial, Tombs of the Unknowns, Mount Vernon, Christ Church, and other sites in Alexandria, Virginia, along with drives by the Capitol, Library of Congress, Supreme Court, Methodist Building, and other famous landmarks.

Fall Council Meeting, November 17-20, 1959—Phoenix, Arizona

The Council focused mainly on the 1960 General Conference Episcopal Address, which would give considerable time to racial and ecumenical concerns (Oden & Williams, p. 74).

Spring Council Meeting and General Conference, April 28–May 9, 1960—Denver, CO

The Bishops' Wives Luncheon was held in the Gold Room of the Denver-Hilton Hotel. Iliff President and Mrs. Harold Carr hosted a tea with other Iliff faculty, followed by a short drive around the city. The wives toured the Denver U.S.

Mint, enjoyed a dinner hosted by Chancellor and Mrs. Chester M. Alter of the University of Denver, and toured the U.S. Air Force Academy as guests of Chaplain and Mrs. Charles L. Carpenter, with a tea at the Officers' Club. A reception at the hotel called for "formal dress," and the Denver Area Ministers' Wives hosted a luncheon at Park Hill Methodist Church. **Mary Kennedy** was elected president for the 1960–1964 quadrennium. Other officers elected were two vice presidents, a recording secretary, a corresponding secretary, a treasurer, and an historian.

Reflections

Ethel Clair, historian, noted in her report that during the past quadrennium the group had met in Minneapolis, MN; Pasadena, CA; Cincinnati, OH (twice); Gatlinburg, TN; Miami Beach, FL; Washington, DC; Phoenix, AZ; and Denver, CO. "We have been guests at receptions, luncheons, banquets, coffees, teas, tours, boat rides, and a film premier." She noted that the "golden cord" that binds us is composed of links of friendship, fellowship, and mutual concern for the church, its constituency, and the families of the episcopal residences (Spouses' Scrapbooks, 1948–1964).

Chapter 10

1960–1964

Spouses Who Joined the Episcopal Family 1960–1964

Detailed profiles and citation information can be found in Part 5, beginning on page 251.

Jurisdiction or Central Conferences	Spouse	Bishop	Year Elected	Elected From	First Episcopal Assignment
NC	Marian Bannon Black Alton	Ralph Taylor Alton	1960	Northeast Ohio AC	Wisconsin
NC	Edith Heritage Garrison	Edwin Ronald Garrison	1960	North Indiana AC	Dakotas
NC	Frances M. Mahaffie Nall	Torney Otto Nall Jr	1960	North Central Jurisdiction	Minnesota
NE	Winifred Maxwell Jackson Holloway	Fred Garrigus Holloway	1960	Dean, Drew Theological Seminary	West Virginia
NE	Eunice Treffry Jones Mathews	James Kenneth Mathews	1960	Associate General Secretary of Global Mission	Boston

Jurisdiction or Central Conferences	Spouse	Bishop	Year Elected	Elected From	First Episcopal Assignment
NE	Miriam Kathleen Horst Middleton	William Vernon Middleton	1960	Eastern Pennsylvania AC	Pittsburgh
NE	Arleen Burdick Ward	William Ralph Ward Jr	1960	Pittsburgh AC	Syracuse
SC	Catherine Andrews Copeland	Kenneth W. Copeland	1960	Southwest Texas AC	Nebraska
SC	Elizabeth Louise Boney Galloway	Paul Vernon Galloway	1960	Arkansas, Oklahoma	San Antonio
SC	Kate Sayle Pope	William Kenneth Pope	1960	Texas	Arkansas
SC	Eva B. Richardson Slater	Oliver Eugene Slater	1960	West Texas AC	Kansas
SC	Mildred Henry Walton	Aubrey Grey Walton	1960	Arkansas	Louisiana
SE	Mary Lucille Hendrick Gum	Walter Clarke Gum	1960	Virginia AC	Louisville
SE	Dorothy Elizabeth Reel Hardin	Paul Hardin Jr	1960	Alabama-West Florida AC	Columbia
SE	Huldah Jo Chapin Henley	James Walton Henley	1960	Tennessee	Florida
W	Florence Ruth Wales Palmer	Everett Walter Palmer	1960	California	Seattle
Central Jurisdiction	Ida Elizabeth Smith Golden	Charles Franklin Golden	1960	Associate General Secretary, National Division Board of Missions	Nashville-Birmingham
Central Jurisdiction	Geneva Magnolia Nelson Harris	Marquis LaFayette Harris	1960	USA	Atlanta

Jurisdiction or Central Conferences	Spouse	Bishop	Year Elected	Elected From	First Episcopal Assignment
Central Jurisdiction	Carolyn Lee Moore	Noah Watson Moore Jr	1960	Delaware AC	Gulf Coast
Central Jurisdiction	Mildred Brown Smith	John Owen Smith	1960	South Carolina	Atlanta
Central Conferences	Vera Loudon Stockwell	Bowman Foster Stockwell	1960	USA, teacher, Union Seminary in Argentina	Pacific
Central Conferences	Agnes Elphick Dunstan Zottele	Pedro Roberto Zottele	1962	Chile	Chile, Peru, Panama, and Costa Rica

Joining by Marriage This Quadrennium

Spouse	Year Married	Bishop	Where Serving
Nina Fontana Garber	1963	Paul Neff Garber	Richmond

Highlights of Our Life Together: 1960–1964

Unless otherwise noted, the information in "Our Life Together" segments is based on the memory and personal notes of the author and information found in the episcopal spouses' scrapbooks and minutes.

Fall Council Meeting, November 15–17, 1960—Chicago, IL

The spouses posed for a group picture in the sanctuary.

Spring Council Meeting, April 24–26, 1962—Mexico City, Mexico

This was the first Council meeting held outside the U.S.

Fall Council Meeting, November 13–15, 1962—St. Louis, MO

Wilma Frank and **Ethel Clair** hosted a luncheon at Wilma's home, assisted by the ministers' wives of the St. Louis North District. Decorations and food at this luncheon were typical of St. Louis: a miniature lighted riverboat, autumn flowers, German coffee cake, French and English pastry, and American apple butter. Before the luncheon, the visitors enjoyed a tour of the St. Louis riverfront, Jefferson Memorial, Washington University, and area churches. The area also hosted a reception and dinner at the Statler-Hilton Hotel. A note in the scrapbook describes the Barnes Hospital Medical Center, which opened in 1914 "under the auspices of the Methodist Episcopal Church South or its successor." Although Mr. Robert Barnes, who made the original bequest, attended another church, and his wife still another, he made this designation in his will because he thought Methodists were doing the best job of all caring for the sick and injured (Spouses' Scrapbooks, 1948–1964).

Spring Council Meeting, April 1963—Oakland, CA

The Council was honored at a banquet and presentation of a play, "The Breaking of a Ripple," which was commissioned by the Women's Society of Christian Service for the Sixth Assembly of the Women's Division in May 1962, written and directed by Don Mueller, and produced by a group known as Methodist Actors Serving the Church.

Fall Council Meeting, November 12–14, 1963—Detroit, MI

The Michigan Area hosted a dinner for the bishops and spouses in the Fountain Room of the Masonic Temple.

Spring Council Meeting and General Conference, April 1964—Pittsburgh, PA

The Western Pennsylvania Area held a dinner for the bishops and spouses in the ballroom of the Penn-Sheraton Hotel and a reception in same hotel. A Bishops' Wives' Luncheon at the Carleton House featured a Polynesian theme, including orchid leis for all the women, flown in from Hawaii. **Bess Smith** was elected president for the next quadrennium, along with two vice presidents, a recording secretary, a corresponding secretary, a treasurer, and an historian. The Pittsburgh Area Night program during General Conference, titled "The Trumpet of Time," commemorated historic milestones of Methodism, including "20th century Methodism in Action through Pittsburgh's Inner-City Program"

(Spouses' Scrapbooks, 1948–1964). The election of Bishop Prince Taylor as president-designate of the Council of Bishops, the first African America to hold this office, indicated the growing awareness of civil rights and a growing desire to act for justice.

Reflections and Personal Stories

Eunice Mathews Remembers

Eunice Mathews, in a 2009 interview, recalled that after Jim's election and assignment to the Boston Area in the summer of 1960, they discovered that they would be hosting the spring meeting, already scheduled for their new home city. Knowing nothing about Boston themselves, they pulled together a committee to plan. Since the wives' schedule generally focused on pleasurable outings, they arranged for a visit to a museum and for some sightseeing. Jim asked, "Don't you ever study anything?" Later, when Eunice was president, she and **Mary Ella Stuart** invited someone to come and speak to the group, which was something of a surprise to the older members. She also recalled shocking the group by proposing a rotation of the president's office every year or two years, instead of each quadrennium.

Eunice also recalled how kind the older spouses have always been to the newer spouses, although there were no formal "big sister" arrangements then. **Julia Brashares**, whose husband would retire in 1964, was especially kind to Eunice. The wives often sat in on Council worship and business, except, of course, when the bishops went into Executive Session. She also noted that, because people are busier now, meetings are not as relaxed. —interview with Eunice Mathews, 2009

Remembering Eunice Jones Mathews

On her ninetieth birthday, when presented to the General Conference in Pittsburgh, **Eunice Mathews** spoke with assurance, "I need not be defined by being the daughter of a renowned evangelist, nor as the wife of a bishop. I am free to be myself . . . a freedom I have in Jesus Christ" (Martha Gunsalus Chamberlain, *A Love Affair with India: The Story of the Wife and Daughter of E. Stanley Jones* [General Commission on Archives and History, 2009], 151). Her words rang in the hearts of those of us who have sought to balance who we are with the role into which we have married. She modeled for us the possibility of being a faithful, supportive episcopal spouse without giving up our own identity and calling. Yet with her characteristic modesty, when **Martha Chamberlain** began to discuss with her the book she wanted to write, Eunice insisted that it should be about her mother, Mabel Jones. Fortunately, Martha persuaded her to share her story too, providing us with an understanding of their deep connection and the formative influence of Mabel Jones on her daughter.

Eunice was born in Sitapur, India, about 50 miles north of Lucknow, to American missionaries E. Stanley and Mabel Jones. As an only child, she loved to read. Her mother, who allowed her to read for a half hour each night in bed, in her mosquito-netted sleeping quarters on the rooftop, before extinguishing her lamp, likely realized that moonlight provided for surreptitious reading beyond the permitted time (Chamberlain, 35). Mother and daughter shared long, but blessed times together while her father was absent. In 1928, while on an extended preaching and fund-raising trip in the United States, Dr. E. Stanley Jones was elected a bishop by the General Conference of The Methodist Episcopal Church. Eunice promptly wrote out 14 reasons why her father should not be a bishop. Her mother "pulled a sheet over her head and indulged in a very feminine cry" (Chamberlain, 58). They were soon relieved to learn that he had resigned before his scheduled consecration.

Years later, in 1960, shortly after returning from a family camping trip to California, Jim, then associate general secretary of Global Missions, was away from their New Jersey home making speeches, including a brief one at the Northeastern Jurisdictional Conference. After he left there, the conference elected him to the episcopacy. Because officials could not reach Jim, they called Eunice and gave her the news. When Jim returned home, he was "greeted with less than enthusiasm. Daughter Anne was crying, and son Stan would not even speak to him. Who died? What happened? Whatever is wrong? To his utter shock, Eunice replied, 'They've elected you a bishop'" (Chamberlain, 140). Several years earlier, Jim had turned down an election to the episcopacy by the Central Conference of Southern Asia, meeting in Lucknow, India, because he believed that Indian Methodism, at 100 years old, was mature enough to elect indigenous bishops (James K. Mathews, *A Global Odyssey: The Autobiography of James K.*

Mathews [Abingdon Press, 2000], 233–34). This time, however, after conferring with Eunice, Jim decided to accept. That night they left for Washington, DC, the site of the Jurisdictional Conference, arriving at 3:00 a.m. Later that morning at Metropolitan Memorial Church, they were presented to the conference and learned of his assignment to the Boston Episcopal Area. Eunice prepared herself and the children for another big move and a new life (Chamberlain, 140).

While working for her father before her marriage, Eunice had typed and edited 25 of her father's books. When Bishop Mathews' memoirs were published in 2000, he credited her with deciphering his handwriting and for seeing it through so many revisions that he suggested the memoirs be called "We Did It Together" (Chamberlain, 146). Jim wrote, "They say that some marriages are made in heaven and I tend to believe it." Describing Eunice, he confessed, "I write these words more than half a century later and am still as excited by her sparkle and vivacity as when we first met" (Mathews, 152).

Although Jim and Eunice certainly served together, Eunice also made her own mark. In 1960, the assistant commissioner for drug rehabilitation in Massachusetts asked Eunice to write "Drug Abuse: Summons to Community Action." First published in the *Boston Globe,* 50,000 copies of the book were later distributed from New England to Florida (Chamberlain, 140). In the spring of 1989, at a dinner held by the UMW of Metropolitan Memorial Church in Washington, DC, Eunice presented a history of UMW, titled *Recollections on Our Heritage as United Methodist Women.* In this address, later put into print, she "showcases women as change-agents, holding hands around the globe" (Chamberlain, 146), describing the work of saints like Isabella Thoburn, Clara Swain, Mary McCloud Bethune, and dozens more. She was elected vice president of the United Methodist General Commission on Archives and History in 1981 and again in 1985, the first woman to hold this position, and she worked on fund-raising for the UM Archives and History Center on the campus of Drew University in Madison, New Jersey (Chamberlain, 142).

With Jim, Eunice traveled the world. In Rome, she received from the hand of Pope Paul VI a gold medallion of St. Peter and Saint Paul. In London, she met with Queen Elizabeth II and Prince Philip. She flew to Honolulu with Hillary and Bill Clinton on Air Force One, sat with President George and Barbara Bush at the dedication of the interfaith chapel at Camp David, and was asked by Martin Luther King Jr to step out of line at his Nobel Peace Prize gathering so that he could tell her that her father's book, *Gandhi: Portrayal of a Friend,* had clarified and mobilized his understanding of nonviolent resistance (Chamberlain, 144–45).

In the Bishops' Spouses' Association of the Council of Bishops, her sweet presence, kindness, and interest in others helped many a newcomer feel welcomed and loved. On occasion, she spoke up for the needs of India and Methodist institutions there, for which she advocated in other arenas as well. In a document composed by her children from notecards she had probably prepared for one of her many presentations or writing projects, Eunice reflected on what she had observed in developing countries moving from colonial rule to independence. She quotes a visitor to India, who said, "All the proof I'd ever need that missions are worthwhile is to walk one day through an Indian village and the next through Isabella Thoburn College." Eunice pointed out that girls from all over India came to that college because of its high educational, moral, and ethical standards; and she credits such schools for the fact that over 45 women were then serving in India's houses of Parliament, in addition to two female governors and a prime minister. She also spoke of gains in the fields of medicine, agriculture, industry, and technology, all greatly influenced by the fine work of mission institutions.

When we look at the amazing life and accomplishments of Eunice Jones Matthews, we should not minimize the strength of faith and character it must have taken for her to balance the roles of daughter, wife and partner, mother, and Christian servant in the world. When her husband, at age 82, announced that, after serving 20 years in two areas as an active bishop and three years in two others after retirement, he was ready and available for yet another assignment, Eunice's voice from the back of the room soared over the gathering, "No way!" Yet a few months later, Bishop James K. Mathews was indeed reactivated and reassigned, and so, in effect, was Eunice.

Window on History: The Assassination of John F. Kennedy

Sally and William Martin were at home in Dallas on November 22, 1963. William went to his office building on Main Street to watch the parade. Sally had gone ahead to the site of the luncheon that was scheduled to follow the parade. Five minutes after the president's car passed William's office, he heard the news and hurried home, where he and Sally spent the rest of the day watching the television reports. During the next days and weeks, William was caught up in responding to an uproar generated by the sermon of one of his pastors, who called the city of Dallas and its citizens to take responsibility for creating a climate of hate in which such an act could happen (James E. Kirby, *Brother Will: A Biography of William C. Martin* [Nashville: Abingdon Press, 2000], 424–28).

Window on History: Conflict in Africa

In 1956, Ralph Dodge, a white American missionary serving in Angola with his wife, **Eunice Dodge**, also a missionary, was elected bishop by the Africa Central Conference and assigned to the Rhodesia (now Zimbabwe) Episcopal Area. After he had served there for eight years, Prime Minister Ian Smith, considering him a threat to the white government's control over the black majority population, expelled him. Ralph and Eunice's daughter Lois was to be married to a British man in the Old Mutare Methodist Center, two weeks after the deadline for both Ralph and Eunice to leave the country. Bishop Dodge made an appeal that gained permission for Eunice to stay through the wedding and a permit for him to return to Rhodesia "for the sole purpose" of attending it (https://tinyurl.com/yy93keuc, 261).

Marilina DeCarvalho first met Emilio DeCarvalho in 1963, when he came to serve the church she attended. He had just been released from prison after spending two and a half years there, suffering greatly. Angola's struggle against colonialism and Portuguese control had resulted in horrendous persecution of those advocating for independence. Many persons, including large numbers of pastors, were executed or thrown into prisons, where they suffered beatings and other abusive treatment. Marilina and Emilio married three years later and served at a mission station until he was elected bishop in 1972. Angola was still fighting for its independence, and, as bishop, Emilio often traveled in dangerous areas. Marilina, at home with their three children, felt at peace only when he returned (interview with Marilina DeCarvalho, 2016).

Chapter 11

1964–1968

Spouses Who Joined the Episcopal Family 1964–1968

Detailed profiles and citation information can be found in Part 5, beginning on page 251.

Jurisdiction or Central Conferences	Spouse	Bishop	Year Elected	Elected From	First Episcopal Assignment
NC	Alice T. Kearns	Francis Enmer Kearns	1964	North Central Jurisdiction	Ohio East
NC	Mildred Shay Loder	Dwight Ellsworth Loder	1964	President, Garrett Theological Seminary	Michigan
NC	Mary Elizabeth Hunt Webb	Lance Webb	1964	North Central Jurisdictional Conference	Illinois
NC	Alice Wuerfel Pryor	Thomas Marion Pryor	1964	Detroit and Michigan ACs	Chicago

Jurisdiction or Central Conferences	Spouse	Bishop	Year Elected	Elected From	First Episcopal Assignment
SC	Twila Stowe Bryan	William McFerrin Stowe	1964	Texas and Oklahoma	Kansas Episcopal Area
SE	Mamie Lee Ratliff Finger	Homer Ellis Finger Jr	1964	Mississippi AC	Nashville
SE	Martha Ann Ogburn Goodson	Walter Kenneth Goodson	1964	North Carolina AC	Birmingham
SE	Mary Ann Hunt	Earl Gladstone Hunt Jr	1964	Holston AC	North Carolina Episcopal Area
SE	Lois May Sheppard Pendergrass	Edward Julian Pendergrass Jr	1964	Florida AC	Jackson
W	Mary Ella Stuart	Robert Marvin Stuart	1964	California-Nevada AC	Denver
Central Jurisdiction	Sarah Charles Adams Allen	Lineunt Scott Allen	1967	Central Jurisdiction	Gulf Coast
Central Jurisdiction	Ruth Naomi Wilson Thomas	James S. Thomas	1964	Central Jurisdiction	Iowa
Central Conferences	Lilly Waag Andreassen	Harry Peter Andreassen	1964	Norway, Angola	Angola
Central Conferences	Janaki John Panikar Balaram	Prabhakar Christopher Benjamin Balaram	1965	India	Bengal and Lucknow
Central Conferences	Emilia Ramos Guansing	Benjamin I. Guansing	1967	professor, Union Theological Seminary, Philippines	Manila
Central Conferences	Elizabeth Frances Hall Lundy	Robert Fielden Lundy	1964	Tennessee	Malaysia, Singapore
Central Conferences	Melvena M. Morris Nagbe	Stephen Trowen-Weati Nagbe	1965	Liberia	Liberia

Jurisdiction or Central Conferences	Spouse	Bishop	Year Elected	Elected From	First Episcopal Assignment
Central Conferences	Heidi Niederhauser Schäfer	Franz Werner Schäfer	1966	Switzerland AC	Geneva
Central Conferences	Evelyn Mary Michael Shaw	Alfred Jacob Shaw	1965	India	Bombay
Central Conferences	Louise Lutshumba Shungu	John Wesley Shungu	1964	Central Congo AC	Congo
Central Conferences	Thelma E. Zunguze	Escrivao Anglaze Zunguze	1964	Mozambique	Mozambique

Also Joining This Quadrennium

Anna Maude Sullivan Dennis, widow of Bishop Fred L. Dennis of the United Brethren Church.

Joining by Marriage This Quadrennium

Spouse	Year Married	Bishop	Where Serving
Modena McPherson Rudisell Holt	1966	Ivan Lee Holt	Retired
Henrietta Gibson Ledden	1964	Walter Earl Ledden	Retired

Highlights of Our Life Together: 1964–1968

Unless otherwise noted, the information in "Our Life Together" segments is based on the memory and personal notes of the author and information found in the episcopal spouses' scrapbooks and minutes.

Fall Council Meeting, November 1964—Chicago, IL

The wives enjoyed a luncheon at the Chicago Art Institute and tea at the home of **Alice Pryor**, the hosting bishop's wife (Spouses' Scrapbooks, 1948–1964).

Spring Council Meeting, 1965—Houston, TX

A tea for the wives was hosted at Blaine Memorial Japanese Church and a luncheon was held at the Warwick Hotel. During a dinner for the bishops and their wives at the Shamrock Hilton Hotel, Texas Governor John B. Connally, a Methodist layman, spoke, calling for support of state and national initiatives to address problems in education, morality, and law and order (Spouses' Scrapbooks, 1965–1968).

Fall Council Meeting, 1965—Seattle, WA

The Council met at the Olympic Hotel, where a dinner was held to honor the bishops and their wives. Thirty-six of the wives rode the monorail to the Seattle Center, where they enjoyed lunch at the Space Needle's revolving restaurant "with its picturesque view of the city, its surrounding lakes, Puget Sound and mountains" (Historian's report by Florence Palmer, in Spouses' Scrapbooks, 1965–1968).

Spring Council Meeting, 1966—Louisville, KY

The wives enjoyed a tea hosted by **Louise Short**, wife of the hosting bishop; brunch in the executive mansion; tours of the state capital and of "My Old Kentucky Home;" a visit to the graves of Bishop Darlington and Daniel Boone; a film about Abraham Lincoln and visit to his birthplace and childhood home; and tours of a horse farm and Ashland, the home of Henry Clay in Lexington.

Fall Council Meeting and Special Session of General Conference, November 1966—Chicago, IL

The bishops and their wives stayed at the Hilton Hotel. Discussion had been underway for some time regarding merger with the Evangelical United Brethren Church. An article in the *Wives' Scrapbook* (1965–1968) quotes EUB Bishop Mueller expressing concern that the race issue might threaten the proposed merger. The conference voted to set 1972 as a non-mandatory target date for desegregation of all its annual conferences, including an end to the all-Negro [*sic*] Central Jurisdiction.

A special service was held to dedicate the new hymnal, a joint project of the Commission on Worship and The Methodist Publishing House, with a threefold purpose: 1) to draw upon the rich heritage of ecumenical hymnody, including Wesleyan tradition, 2) to provide resources for a diversity of religious experiences, and 3) to meet the needs of the next generation.

Spring Council Meeting, 1967—Buffalo, NY

Host Bishop Ralph and **Arlene Ward** offered two events for the Council family: a visit to and tour of Niagara Falls and a reception at Kleinhans Music Hall. Regarding the reception, the Wards wrote, "Either clericals or business suits will be quite in order. The ladies may want to wear long dresses since we will be seated on the platform." A list of gifts given to those attending included candies, a desk folder, Niagara Frontier Note Paper, maps and brochures, a crystal bowl and pickle fork from Oneida Silversmiths, and a "Madonna and Child" from Buffalo Center City Churches.

Fall Council Meeting, November 13–16, 1967—Miami Beach, FL

The Council family rode buses to the airport to observe the arrival of a "freedom flight" from Cuba, followed by a "Cuban lunch." When the Council of Bishops of The Methodist Church and the Board of Bishops of the Evangelical United Brethren gathered for a convocation on Wednesday, corsages for the ladies were delivered in advance to their hotel rooms, and a musical program featured the Bethune-Cookman and Florida Southern College Choirs. The wives also enjoyed a cruise on Biscayne Bay; toured Villa Vizcaya, the estate of James Deering built in 1914; and had coffee at the Miami District parsonage.

Spring Council Meeting, April 15–20, and General Conference, April 23–May 4, 1968—Dallas, TX

During this Uniting Conference, the wives enjoyed a luncheon and meeting at Southern Methodist University, a tour of suburban areas of Dallas, tea at the Owen Fine Arts Center at Southern Methodist University, an area dinner honoring bishops' wives and widows in the grand ballroom of Sheraton-Dallas, orchid corsages, luncheon at the Great Hall of the Apparel Mart, and a style show of past fashions titled "Do You Remember?" by the Dallas Goodwill Industries Auxiliary. Ann Landers spoke, and Marion Downs sang at the Yellow Rose of Texas Luncheon for all women attending the Uniting Conference. Bishops, bishops' wives, and bishops' widows were honored at a Texas-style luncheon with fashions by Neiman-Marcus at the Statler Hilton Hotel and a formal reception in the grand ballroom of the Sheraton-Dallas Hotel, including orchid corsages for the ladies again. The wives' organization began electing officers for two-year terms, instead of four, as in previous quadrennia. **Eunice Ensley** was elected president.

The Texas night presentation at the Moody Coliseum of Southern Methodist University included a musical dance-drama "The New Wilderness," tracing the history of "the sons and daughters of Wesley, Asbury, Otterbein and Albright—from the shores of Western Europe in the seventeenth century to the secular society of the late twentieth century." On another occasion, a dramatic musical presentation titled "Climbing Jacob's Ladder" depicted "the founding, development, and contribution of schools and colleges for the education of Negro [*sic*] youth, established and supported by The Methodist Church." A May 4 Dallas newspaper, summing up the conference actions, noted, "They took militant stands against discrimination and for the practice of civil disobedience of the law if conscience demands it" (*Spouses' Scrapbook*, 1965–1968).

Reflections and Personal Stories

Window on History: A Context of Change

During this era of civil unrest and protest, Methodist women provided significant leadership in the quest for justice. Cora Rodham Ratliff, the mother of **Mamie Ratliff Finger**, was an active member and leader in the Women's Missionary Society of The Methodist Episcopal Church, South, and the Women's Society of Christian Service after the 1939 merger. She worked courageously for civil rights during the tumultuous years of the early to mid-nineteenth century. Alice G. Knotts, in her 1996 book, *Fellowship of Love: Methodist Women Changing American Racial Attitudes, 1920–1968* (Nashville: Abingdon Press), describes Methodist women's work for civil rights as "one of the largest, longest, most far-reaching and underreported aspects of the civil rights movement in the United States, involving an organization of 1.2 million members. From 1920 through 1968 and beyond, this work has been underreported because the organization was denominationally based and female in a time when, by and large, neither church business nor women's activities made news" (19). Mamie later wrote of her mother, "Cora Ratliff's abiding and basic principle was always to help those who were deprived by society, either racially, economically, or personally. This was her response to having to achieve on her own at uneven odds against her" (Mamie Lee Ratliff Finger, "Cora Rodman Ratliff, 1891-1958: A Woman of Courage and Vision," [1989], private collection of Mamie Lee Ratliff Finger. The original manuscript is in the Heritage Center at Lake Junaluska, NC).

According to Knotts,

> Methodist women found that their Christian responsibility engaged them in pressing for social change on two fronts simultaneously, toward breaking down barriers of race and gender. Torn by the difficulties of working interracially, some white women chose to work separately through their missionary societies and the Association of Southern Women for the Prevention of Lynching (ASWPL). At the same time, through their experiences in summer Christian Leadership Schools and local Bible-study/community organizing groups for African American women, white southern Methodist women realized the need to work *with* African American women if their Christian beliefs were to be practiced. (Knotts, 70)

Knotts profiles Cora Rodham Ratliff and four other Methodist women as key leaders in anti-lynching efforts; in building community across racial lines; and in advocating for fair trials, equal access to public facilities, desegregation in church and community, and full inclusion of African Americans within church structures and activities. Mamie Ratliff Finger and many other episcopal spouses advocated and worked for equality in their communities. Rose Stokes, for example, was the only white teacher to show up for the first day at her newly desegregated elementary school in Atlanta in 1961.

Meanwhile, our church struggled with its own racial divide, as we moved toward the merger of The Methodist Church and the Evangelical United Brethren, which would finally bring to an end the racially segregated Central Jurisdiction in the United States. At the same time, growing nationalism and global self-determination movements around the world stimulated increasing fervor for autonomy. In Cuba, and in other nations struggling for independence and freedom from foreign control, Methodism was seen by some, unfortunately, as an arm of the United States government.

In 1893, Bishop James Thoburn, an early missionary to India, had written, "We may accept it as certain, beyond any shadow of a doubt, that in every nation under the sun our Christian converts will want to assume the management of their own affairs as soon as they are permitted to do so. . . . Accepting, then, a fact so obvious as this, it requires the highest wisdom on the part of all missionary managers to co-operate with the natural tendency of events on the mission field, and to develop our indigenous government of every Christian church as rapidly as possible" (Philip Wingeier-Rayo, "A Momentous 50th Anniversary: The Work of the Commission on the Structure of Methodism Overseas," [*United Methodist Insight*, February 8, 2018], 1; https://um-insight.net/in-the-church/umc-global-nature/the-work-of-the-commission-on-the-structure-of-methodism-ove/).

The 1964 General Conference established a Commission on the Structure of Methodism Overseas (COSMOS) to study The Methodist Church's work outside the United States. In 1968, COSMOS recommended autonomy for the Methodist churches in Argentina, Bolivia, Costa Rica, Chile, Panama, Peru, Malaya, Sarawak, and Uruguay, in addition to the churches in Mexico and Brazil, which had become autonomous in 1930, and in Cuba, which elected its first bishop in February 1968 (Wingeier-Rayo, 3).

Ruth Thomas's Story

Ruth met Jim Thomas at a family gathering when she was in high school and he in college. They immediately struck up a lively friendship, and nine years later, when they realized they were not biologically related, that friendship deepened into courtship. They married in 1945. In her "Faith Journey," written in the spring of 2005, she says, "Our life together has been a journey of faith, far exceeding our hopes and dreams. We have laughed, cried, worked, prayed, and praised our way through many stages of life. Throughout our journey together, which has been fraught with both challenges and rewards, I deliberately endeavored in every situation to put my best foot forward in a manner both appropriate and natural for the authentic me."

Ruth was a certified teacher, working in North Carolina public schools then, and Jim was a college chaplain. Following their marriage, he served as a pastor, then as a professor at Gammon Theological Seminary in Atlanta, then earned his

PhD at Cornell University. In 1953, he was called into the position of associate secretary of the Division of Higher Education of The Methodist Church, requiring them to move to Nashville, Tennessee, where Jim served for 11 years.

Ruth and Jim faced a significant adjustment in Nashville. "It was a time of great civil unrest. The world as we had known it, a world of racial hierarchy, segregation, and humiliating discrimination, was about to change in dramatic ways—but not without passionate, even frightening, resistance. We participated in Monday night mass meetings at churches, in small group community meetings, and in other gatherings representing various aspects of our society trying to work through these changes."

Ruth continued, "Previously we had lived, learned, worshipped, and otherwise existed within the Black community, but the Division of Education was integrated and open to all. Its policies were radical for this time and in this environment of entrenched segregation.... This was not the first time that we had lived or worked with people of another race. At Gammon, the faculty was integrated, as were homes and classrooms, within the iron fence of the seminary campus. As much as I regretted leaving Atlanta, I appreciated how the people of Nashville welcomed and endeared themselves to us. It was a great opportunity for growth and development of soul and spirit for all of our family, individually and collectively."

After the birth of their fourth daughter in 1957, Ruth returned to teaching. "Because Nashville was the seat of much of the national work of the then Methodist (now United Methodist) church, many meetings were held there. My husband's portfolio included overseeing the Black Colleges affiliated with the Methodist Church.... Because the pervasive policies of segregation that ruled hotels, restaurants, and all other institutions—including churches—denied public accommodations to people of color, many individuals with whom my husband worked stayed at our home when they visited Nashville on business. In addition, ... white colleagues who had become friends with my husband stayed with us by choice when they came to town. In this way, our children learned early that people—regardless of race, class, titles, gender, etc. —are people; and this ongoing experience taught them a great deal about the power of the individual spirit, about the folly of prejudice, about the beauty of diversity, and, as they would laughingly put it today, about the relative importance of good table manners....

"We spent 11 very good years in Nashville, making lifelong friends and seeing to the upbringing of our four daughters. . . . We left Nashville in 1964 for the happiest of reasons: my husband was elected to the highest position in the church, the episcopacy. When elected, he was the youngest bishop with the youngest children in the church. I found myself the helpmate of a man who had been very active in working for oneness in church and society, now an official trailblazer for the church."

Jim was one of the first bishops elected from the Central Jurisdiction and assigned to a different Jurisdiction. Ruth described the culture shock they experienced when they moved to Iowa: "Culture, race, geography, demographics, and climate, among other elements, were completely new to us. Our youngest girls, for example, fresh from the segregated school systems of the South, were two of only three children of color in their school in Des Moines."

She went on to note, however, "As we were making the transition from 'goodbye' in Nashville to 'hello' in Des Moines, we felt love that defies description from both directions. While in Nashville, we had participated in the struggle for desegregation of church and society by going to group meetings, sharing experiences, working for reconciliation, taking part in boycotts. Des Moines was to be a very different situation. Before we moved to Iowa, many people there wrote welcoming letters to us, even to the children. Upon our arrival, we lived in a hotel for a few days, as the episcopal residence, our new home, was being redecorated. We were invited out for meals and sightseeing. In spite of occasional hate mail and calls, it became evident that we were respected and welcomed by an overwhelming majority of the Methodists in Iowa.

"Having young children posed a challenge. . . . Luckily for us, the bishop who preceded us had children at home when he was assigned to Iowa. His wife took care of their children and accompanied him only when she could. I was grateful that this precedent had been set, stilling constant inquiries about the absence of the bishop's wife. . . . I did decide, however, that since I really did not yet understand much about the structure and workings of Methodism, I would make it a point to attend Annual Conference sessions, Jurisdictional Conferences, and General Conferences, and to participate in mission trips abroad. . . .

". . . We now lived in a virtually all-white society, almost a complete reversal of our earlier years. I sought out experiences and activities for the children to involve them in the small African American community in Des Moines, as well as in the larger white community. . . .

"When I resigned my teaching position in Nashville upon Sammye's election to the episcopacy, I chose not to continue employment outside the home. . . . Volunteerism, however, had always been a part of my life, and I continued to be active in church and community activities. Although I did not travel much with my husband in those earlier days, I often went with him after our last child left for college. I learned so much about The United Methodist Church, different cultures, human nature, and about life itself, especially about balancing independence with interdependence. The Iowa people did so much to support us, standing between us and any rejection that attempted to impose itself upon us. For example, before we moved into the new episcopal residence, we later learned, supporters had scouted the neighborhood to check the pulse of the community to be sure that our living there would not create any significant tension or anxiety for us.

". . . I was invited to many group functions and programs during those years. When three conferences—North Iowa, South Iowa, and Evangelical United Brethren—merged in 1968, I felt signally honored to be invited as keynote speaker for the first annual meeting of the UMW and to be presented a mission recognition pin with nine tiny ruby stones in the shape of a cross."

"The time we spent in Iowa was a time of great civil unrest. Not only did we have to meet the challenges of new environment, culture, and schools for the children, not to mention enduring sub-freezing weather; we were also enmeshed in the throes of an era that, in the effort to break free from old ways, showed strong resistance to authority. . . .

"In 1976, after the maximum 12 years in one place allowed by church policy, we were assigned to the East Ohio Episcopal Area. By now all of the girls had left home . . . [and] I became even more involved in traveling, speaking, and participating in group meetings and other spirit-fulfilling activities. One of my most bittersweet non-church involvements took place in East Ohio. . . . I became certified as a lifeguard, and I said 'Yes' when asked to volunteer to help in the Y's program for non-ambulatory children and youth. The first day I had a difficult time avoiding tears. . . . I grew to find peace and joy in the fact that for that time, each week, I was helping some precious child to be happy and to enjoy water play.

"Although it is impossible for me to chronicle all the many instances when we felt unity of spirit with the people we served, first in Iowa, then in East Ohio, I will mention one that always warms our hearts when we remember it. During the mid-eighties, while we were in East Ohio, the Board of Church and Society supported a demonstration against apartheid in South Africa. Bishops and other leaders were among those invited to participate. My husband responded to the invitation and to his inner compulsion to go to Washington, DC, to demonstrate in front of the South African Embassy. It so happened that the date of the demonstration was the same as that of a . . . cabinet meeting. . . . The meeting continued as usual, in his absence.

"When the cabinet adjourned for lunch, they went out and bought lunch 'to go' for themselves and me, bringing it to our home to eat and pray with me in a singular show of support. It was heartwarming to sit around the table with those dear people and invoke God's blessings on a demonstration for the freedom of disenfranchised people in a deplorable situation. . . .

"Upon retirement from the episcopacy in 1988, my husband held the position of Distinguished Visiting Professor of Theology at Perkins School of Theology at Southern Methodist University in Dallas. Four years later, we again retired to the familiar ground of Atlanta, where he taught both at Clark Atlanta University and at Candler School of Theology at Emory University. . . . We still receive calls, letters, and visits from friends, close and casual, from both Iowa and Ohio. . . . God has been so good to us, through so many people, as we have tried to do His will in working with others to help all people get a glimpse of Heaven on Earth."

Twila Stowe Bryan's Story

Twila Stowe Bryan's first husband, William McFerrin Stowe, was elected to the episcopacy in 1964. Twila recalled that there were no nominations of episcopal candidates or interviews or organized meetings with delegations before the election then. Bishop Stowe died on Thanksgiving Day in 1988, eight years after retirement and after several years of living with leukemia. Bishop Monk Bryan's wife, Cornelia, died the next spring. When Monk came to Dallas to visit his daughter, he and Twila went out together for Mexican food. They married in 1992.

Twila recalled that the bishops' spouses met for fellowship, dressed in their best clothes, and talked about their trips and shopping finds, such as purses they bought in Hong Kong. Although none of other spouses had careers, Twila had worked as a Christian education director before marriage. She was somewhat disappointed in the spouses' association, as she had anticipated that such a talented group might do something interesting. **Eunice Mathews** agreed with her. Early on, when Twila asked another spouse for ideas and tips about being a bishop's spouse and about mission trips, she was told that if she was smart enough to be a bishop's wife, she was smart enough to figure it out. She was glad to see the association change through the years. As new members brought fresh ideas and vision to the association, it became much more rewarding and meaningful for her. Twila remained active through the years, teaching at Schools of Christian Mission, leading retreats, and speaking at various meetings.

Twila also shared that, for a period of time, the bishops made quadrennial visits to mission sites in other countries, sometimes journeying by boat for two or three months. The spouses often went along, too, paying their own expenses. Twila remembers spending a month traveling to India, Japan, Isle of Borneo, East Malaya, and Singapore. She and William were deeply gratified to visit with missionaries in Africa, Liberia, Congo, Nigeria, Kenya, and Sierra Leone. They often traveled with Dwight and **Mildred Loder** and took a cruise around Norway with them before their official trips, to get to know each other better. Twila recalls a visit to a Nigerian agricultural mission on her birthday, where the wife of a missionary planned a birthday meal for her. Although all the other women sat around the walls, the hostess, eager to empower women, seated Twila at the table with the men. Twila said it felt strange to her, but no one else seemed to mind. She also remembers flying over mountains to deliver 500 baby chickens. They were supposed to bring equal numbers of male and female chicks, but no one could figure out which was which. On another occasion, they had a wonderful experience visiting with a missionary couple, Richard and Sylvia Smythe, in New Delhi, India, who had "adopted" five native children, raised them, and paid for their schooling. After losing track of the Smythes for a while, Twila later found them through the UMW Prayer Calendar and located them at the Brooks Howell home for retired missionaries in Asheville, North Carolina. Twila also remembers meeting an outstanding Indian woman who went to Methodist schools. Sadly, she reported, because there were no Methodist boys' schools then, there were no Christian boys for the girls to marry. —interview with Twila Bryan, October 2010

Twila's obituary notes that she "will be remembered for her faith, intelligence, creativity, integrity, charm, and grace. Twila's life was committed to being the hands of God through church work, volunteer work, music, missions, teaching, and as a devoted mother, wife, and friend. Up to her last days she was busy keeping up on social issues, donating to missions, and writing encouraging notes to friends and family" (http://www.legacy.com/obituaries/dallasmorningnews/obituary.aspx?pid=173393181).

Remembering Mamie Lee Ratliff Finger

"For me, perhaps the most important consequence of Dad's being elected for Mother and for all of us was that we left Mississippi," wrote **Mamie Lee Ratliff Finger**'s son Bill in 2017. "Mother was a real Mississippi girl, but in some ways, like her mother before her, she was more of a global person. Her time in Atlanta and New York City before getting married clearly whetted her appetite, but then she was thrown back into 20 years or so of dealing with the intensity of Mississippi. Moving to Nashville and later to Knoxville helped her, I think, to spread her wings in many ways—with her work raising money for and supporting Ewha University being perhaps her most important public work, at least the highest profile" (email communication with Bill Finger, June 2017).

Mamie's daughter, Elizabeth, added, "One of the things I remember most about my mother as a bishop's spouse is that she was very supportive of her husband and also had her own interests and goals. She was very involved with community causes and particularly involved in raising money for Ewha University in South Korea. In 1986, she was awarded an honorary doctorate from Ewha, and she and my father traveled to South Korea for my mother to receive this award. My father noted that on this trip, he was 'Mrs. Finger's husband, not Bishop Finger.' I also heard from other bishops' wives that my mother helped them to remember that they were a bishop's wife, but they were also their own person and it was important to pursue their own interests. Several bishops' wives commented on this to me and how much they appreciated the support and encouragement of my mother. She was like a mentor for many younger bishops' wives" (email communications with Elizabeth Finger, February 2017).

In 2002, Mamie prepared a devotional booklet titled *Mysteries and Verities.* She explains, "Last winter my early morning mental and spiritual energy went to rereading all my speeches to retreats, churches, conferences. These excerpts you may find life strengthening taken either as a one-a-day vitamin or all together in one big gulp. Instead of giving you predigested daily devotions, I'm suggesting thoughts to stimulate your own meditation for the day." Brief quotations address such themes as simplicity, grace and gratitude, power and authority, listening and receptivity, mission and service. She advises, "Find and accept the core of your being and know the joy of being your own self" (*Bishops' Spouses' Association Scrapbook,* 2000–2004).

Mamie summed up her feelings about her role: "Recently a young minister's wife at Annual Conference asked if I didn't get tired of always being referred to as 'the Bishop's Wife.' This question helped me articulate my own feelings as I said, 'Let's look at that; I wouldn't be here now if I weren't that. So that's an important part of my identity and my being. But ah! It's not all!'" (Mamie Lee Finger, *The Kaleidoscope Turns Through Nearly a Century of America, 1918-2000* [place of publication and publisher not identified, 1986?], 137).

Remembering Mary Ann Hunt

James C. Logan, in his biography of Bishop Hunt (*A Charge to Keep: The Life of Earl Gladstone Hunt Jr* [Nashville: Abingdon Press, 2000]), states that Mary Ann was "at ease in the role of wife of pastor, president, and bishop" (33) and describes her thus: "She was gifted with exciting exuberance for life, undergirded by a long-nurtured, deep Christian piety" (31). She and Earl met when she was in the fifth grade, and their families both participated in the life of First Church in Johnson City, Tennessee, where they married in 1943 (30–31). Earl later dedicated his second book to her with these affectionate words: "To Mary Ann whose love, faith, and life have lightened my load and brightened my way" (Earl Gladstone Hunt, *I Have Believed: A Bishop Talks About His Faith* [Nashville: Upper Room, 1980], 5).

During his years as a pastor, she "quietly ministered" alongside him, and when he became president of Emory and Henry College, she "endeared herself to the college students as counselor, confidante, and even at times matchmaker. . . . She was an avid supporter of the football and basketball teams and never missed a game, always seated in the front row of the cheering section. Old-timers recall with relish how Mary Ann acquired the habit of correcting the officials when they called certain plays about which she had a differing opinion." Hunt, as president of the college, deemed it "inappropriate to sit with such a vocal partisan." She entertained various speakers who came to the college, even while caring for her husband's aging mother, and enjoyed stimulating conversations with the guests. Later, Earl would refer to her as the "family liberal." When he was elected to the episcopacy in 1964, she became active in local churches in each of the three areas he served, while also traveling with him to England, Ireland, Sweden, Germany, Austria, Kenya, and Hawaii. **Rebecca Harmon**, wife of Bishop Nolan B. Harman, described Mary Ann with approval as "an independent soul" (Logan, 32–33). During a celebration of Earl's retirement during his last session presiding at the Florida Annual Conference, a video interview with Mary Ann was shown. Its title, "A Bishop's Wife Speaks Her Mind," was no doubt a play on the title of Earl's book published in 1987, *A Bishop Speaks His Mind.*

Their son Stephen recalled, "Virginia was a very Southern state, and my father's attempts to invite distinguished visitors and performers to campus ran up against segregation in its most blatant forms. Even the Martha Washington Inn, which the college owned in those days, would not permit African-Americans to stay due to Virginia's strict accommodations rules. My father's creative solution was to invite guests to stay at the President's residence, which as a private home was exempt from the draconian race laws of the era. As a consequence, my mother (who supported this solution enthusiastically), my grandmother, and I had the high privilege of visiting in person with stars such as Marian Anderson, Dorothy Maynor, Lord Caradon (the British Ambassador to the United Nations) and others. I believe that it was the personal experience of the human cost of segregation and the attitudes in Virginia that caused my father to become a staunch supporter of integration in the church and a deep admirer of Dr. Martin Luther King Jr.

"My mother completely supported my father's beliefs, and one example bears this out. 1968 was the deadline set by the General Conference for the end of segregation and the merger of the former Central Jurisdiction with white conferences. My father, anticipating this, had already named Rev. James 'Pete' Peters, a prominent black North Carolina Methodist pastor, to his cabinet. Judge James Satterfield, the Mississippi Conference lay leader [known to be opposed to integration], was fearful that my father would be assigned to the Mississippi Episcopal Area and started a rumor to that effect. I was working at Lake Junaluska Assembly that summer and was manning the sound booth in Stuart Auditorium on the day, [with] my father presiding, that the vote was to be taken by the Southeastern Jurisdictional Conference. Before the session started, he took me aside and told me that he was stationing ministers at the bottom of the stairs leading to the sound booth in case someone tried to attack the booth, and then he told me, 'When I give this sign from the dais, I want you to immediately cut off the microphone feed to the Mississippi delegation.'

"When I went over to the Terrace Hotel to escort my mother to Stuart Auditorium, a group of obviously irate Mississippi lay delegates blocked our path to the elevator and would not let us pass. Even though I, quite a bit more radical in those days than my mother, wanted to challenge them, my mother silenced me and confronted the ringleader. She told him that my dad was presiding that morning and would immediately notice our absence and that we knew we were being reassigned to Western North Carolina and that rumors to the contrary were lies spread by Judge Satterfield to mislead them. The Mississippians reluctantly parted and let us get on the elevator.

"While my father was a lifelong evangelical preacher and did indeed refer to my mother affectionately as the "family liberal," he was quite capable of breaking with evangelical orthodoxy and embracing progressive positions, especially on race, science and economics. Before the end of his life he switched his political registration from Republican to Democrat because, as he told me, 'I no longer recognize these people.' My mother, of course, had been a lifelong Democrat! My dad was even, near his death, having second thoughts about his position on gays, musing to me in one memorable conversation that 'perhaps it was nature and not nurture after all.'

"My mother was by my father's side at both of his retirements, from the Episcopacy and from the Foundation for Evangelism. She helped to nurse him through the neuropathy, near-blindness, and intestinal issues that combined to cause his final illness, but the experience took a heavy toll. Upon my father's death, my mother suffered a breakdown, and just as therapy got her through that, she began to show signs of onset dementia. She is still going strong at age 97, although she is largely bedridden and has trouble forming complete sentences or carrying on a conversation; but she still remembers faces and people, and always has a cheerful smile."

—email and telephone communications with Stephen Hunt, July 2017

Lois Pendergrass's Window on History: Racial Turmoil in the USA in the 1960s

A few days after Bishop Pendergrass and Lois arrived in Mississippi in 1964, the bodies of three murdered civil rights workers were discovered, bringing national attention to the racial problems there. Edward worked diligently to bring together the Black and White conferences in the area and to help with the process of desegregation. Their granddaughter, living with them at this time, recalled they often found KKK literature on their lawn. One night, a truckload of men came to their home and tried to erect a cross on the front lawn. Edward went out and persuaded them to leave (*Florida Annual Conference*, *1996*, 388).

Louise Shungu's Window on History: Conflict in Africa

During the tumultuous early days of the Republic of Congo, after it gained independence from Belgium in 1960, Bishop John Wesley Shungu, shortly after his election in 1964, made a heroic trip to rescue his wife, Louise, and 11 of their 13 children from behind rebel lines near Lodja (http://archives.gcah.org/bitstream/handle/10516/4179/article34.aspx.htm?sequence=2).

Mary Ella Stuart's Story: Dealing with Depression

In 1977, Abingdon Press published Mary Ella's book *To Bend Without Breaking: Stress and How to Deal with It,* based on her experiences with depression and what she learned in trying to heal from it. In an addendum written in 1996, Mary Ella commented, "I have known intellectually for a long time that there is no cause for guilt about depression. Still, appropriating that insight emotionally has been very difficult. I agonized for years because I believed my faith was not strong enough. Why would a person who really believed in God and affirmed Christ's loving care be depressed after all? . . . Knowing that I have a clinical depression has been a great relief" (Mary Ella Stuart, *To Bend Without Breaking: Addendum* [1996], 4). She describes the multiple challenges that overwhelmed her: a miscarriage and the death of two babies, ill health, thyroid imbalance, her mother's failing memory, a move to a new home with a new school situation for her child, her husband's new job with much greater responsibilities (1977, 21). In her search for healing, she was helped most by three things: 1) psychological insight, self-awareness, and mindfulness techniques; 2) medication to correct chemical imbalances in her body, and 3) spiritual disciplines such as prayer, study of the Scriptures, and worship (1996, 3)—and especially the Twelve Steps, which she discovered through Al-Anon (1977, 23–24). Her book is still used as a resource in the field of stress management. Mary Ella lectured widely and led seminars, workshops, and retreats in California and seven other states (*Biographical Directory*, 2000–2004).

Interview with Wilma Frank and Magdalene Mueller

A Dallas newspaper reporter interviewed **Wilma Frank** and **Magdalene Mueller** in the spring of 1968, following the election of their husbands as president and president-designate of the Council of Bishops. Wilma, who had moved from the Kansas Annual Conference to the Missouri Episcopal Area when her husband was elected in 1956, described the change from being the wife of a minister to being the wife of a bishop as very traumatic: "It means leaving the close fellowship of a congregation whom you can serve and to whom you are devoted to go into a relationship in which you really don't have any close personal ties." A bishop spends much time traveling throughout the area, and Wilma was unable to travel with him when their four children were young. She described St. Louis as "a very challenging" place to live and work because "it seems far ahead of most cities in the wonderful spirit between the races. . . . I feel the Christian imprint on the community makes this spirit possible."

The article notes that the Franks had three married daughters and a younger son, Tom, a sophomore at Harvard, planning to work in a church-sponsored inner-city mission project during the coming summer. After describing Wilma's history of working with youth and women's groups in the churches her husband served, the article speaks of her interest in organizing spiritual-life retreats for ministers' wives and laypeople and shares several other observations she made: "I truly believe that women are the strongest spiritual force in the world"; "I agree that the church needs to be renewed—but not destroyed"; "I still believe that the church, with all its imperfections, is the only hope of making an impact which can bring a solution to society's racial and international problems."

The article reports that Bishop Mueller served EUB churches in Minnesota and Indiana for 17 years, then served as general secretary of Christian education for the Evangelical United Brethren Church in 1942. He was elected bishop in the EUB church in 1954, and the Uniting Conference of 1968 made him a bishop of The United Methodist Church. The article asserts, "This was a big change for **Mrs. Mueller**, who had worked with children's and youth groups in their parishes and 'missed contacts with people of the church. So often the young people would just stop off at our house on their way home from school and I certainly missed their coming by.'"

The article continues, "The bishop's wife has travelled with him throughout his jurisdiction and on church business throughout the world. They visited Germany and Switzerland when he had charge of EUB work in those countries, and Nairobi, Kenya, and Crete when he served as EUB delegate to the World Council of Christian Education. She was unable to accompany him on two Easter trips to visit U.S. servicemen . . . as president of the National Council of Churches from 1963 to 1966. Mrs. Mueller admits that she was 'somewhat concerned' when her husband traveled by helicopter to visit battle areas in Vietnam on his 1966 tour. He also went to Thailand in 1966 and to Korea in 1965. The woman considers a visit to Nigeria 'the most rewarding trip we made.' The couple's son-in-law and daughter, Mr. and Mrs. Arin C. Hoesch, were missionaries in the country for 13 years. 'We actually saw the conditions under which they lived, the zeal with which they did their work and the love that they extended to those people.' Bishop and Mrs. Mueller plan to go to Europe this summer to attend the World Council of Churches meeting and the uniting conference of EUB and Methodist churches established in Europe by American missionaries. The church official's wife expects 'a busy year as we get started with the big new church we have.'"

—"News of Women" (*Dallas Morning News*, 4/26/1968)

Part 3

BISHOPS' SPOUSES IN THE UNITED METHODIST CHURCH

1968–2000

Chapter 12

1968–1972

Spouses Who Joined the Episcopal Family 1968–1972

Detailed profiles and citation information can be found in Part 5, beginning on page 251.

From Evangelical United Brethren Church Past Elections

NOTE: The women listed below in order of their husbands' year of election were still living in 1968 and may or may not have been active in the new organization.

Spouse	Bishop	Year Elected	Elected From	First Episcopal Assignment
Ada May Visick Warner	David Warner	1929	California	Pacific Coast
Justina Lorenz Showers	John Balmer Showers	1945	faculty, Bonebrake Theological Seminary	Eastern (Harrisburg)
Erma Irene Martin Heininger	Harold Rickel Heininger	1954	USA	Northwest (Illinois, Wisconsin, Minnesota, North Dakota, South Dakota, northwestern Canada)

Spouse	Bishop	Year Elected	Elected From	First Episcopal Assignment
Magdalene Stauffacher Mueller	Reuben Herbert Mueller	1954	Minneapolis and Indiana	Canada, Germany, Indiana, Michigan, Switzerland)
Ruth Porter Herrick	Paul Murray Herrick	1956		Central Area
Katherine Higgins Shannon Howard	Paul E. V. Shannon	1957		Pittsburgh
Blanche May Frank Sparks	W. Maynard Sparks	1958		Western Area
Mary Francis Noblitt Milhouse	Paul William Milhouse	1960	Illinois AC	Southwestern

Newly Elected in The United Methodist Church in 1968–1972

Jurisdiction or Central Conferences	Spouse	Bishop	Year Elected	Elected From	First Episcopal Assignment
NC	Phyllis Jeanne Shaeffer Armstrong	Arthur James Armstrong	1968	Florida, Indiana	Dakotas
NC	Kathryn Elizabeth Fischer Washburn	Paul Arthur Washburn	1968	Illinois	Minnesota
NE	Ruth Richardson Nichols	Roy Calvin Nichols	1968	California, New York City	Pittsburgh
NE	Betty Rowe Wertz	D. Frederick Wertz	1968	Central Pennsylvania AC	West Virginia
SC	Artha Blair Crutchfield Carleton	Alsie Henry Carleton	1968	North Texas AC	Northwest Texas-New Mexico
Central Conferences	Martha Rygge Borgen	Ole Edvard Borgen	1970	Norway AC	Norway
Central Conferences	Emilia V. Rosario Ferrer	Cornelio M. Ferrer	1968	Philippines AC	Manila

Jurisdiction or Central Conferences	Spouse	Bishop	Year Elected	Elected From	First Episcopal Assignment
Central Conferences	Socorro Mella-Granadosin	Paul Locke A. Granadosin	1968	Philippines	Baguio
Central Conferences	Anneliese Fritzsch Härtel	Armin E. Härtel	1970	German Democratic Republic	German Democratic Republic
Central Conferences	Agnes Karan Singh Joshi	Ram Dutt Joshi	1969	India	Bombay
Central Conferences	Sushila Sentu Lance	Joseph R. Lance	1969	India	Lucknow
Central Conferences	Wife name unknown	Eric Algernon Mitchell	1969	Bengal AC	Hyderabad
Central Conferences	Maggie Muzorewa	Abel Tendekayi Muzorewa	1968	Africa	Zimbabwe
Central Conferences	Wife name unknown	Federico Jose Pagura	1969	Argentina	Panama and Costa Rica
Central Conferences	Klara Auguste Beatrice Schuchardt Sommer	Carl Ernst Sommer	1968	Southwest Germany AC	Frankfurt

NOTE: The *Discipline* also lists the following other bishop elected in this quadrennium: William Ragsdale Cannon (1968).

Joining by Marriage This Quadrennium

Spouse	Year Married	Bishop	Where Serving
Margaret Hollis Henley	1970	James Walton Henley	Florida Episcopal Area

Highlights of Our Life Together: 1968–1972

Unless otherwise noted, the information in "Our Life Together" segments is based on the memory and personal notes of the author and information found in the episcopal spouses' scrapbooks and minutes.

Fall Council Meeting, November 1968—Chicago, IL

The Council met at the Conrad Hilton Hotel in Chicago. The wives gathered in the "Lower Tower" for fellowship and business; visited Old Town for browsing and shopping, followed by tea at "The Bakery"; toured the inner-city area and the Circle campus; and visited Newberry Center.

Spring Council Meeting, April 1969—Charleston, WV

The Council met at the Charleston House in Charleston, West Virginia. A "Program for the Wives" lists a tour to the Blenko Glass Company in Milton, West Virginia; a tea at the Governor's Mansion hosted by his wife, Mrs. Arch A. Moore Jr; a dinner hosted by the West Virginia Episcopal Area ("Dress optional"); and a luncheon and fashion show at Morris Harvey College hosted by **Betty Wertz**.

Fall Council Meeting, November 1969—Columbus, OH

The Council was hosted for dinner at Ohio State University. Participants received gifts of "buckeye" cookies.

Spring Council Meeting and Special Session of General Conference, 1970—St. Louis, MO

The invitation for a banquet at the Sheraton-Jefferson Hotel noted "Dress for women: short formals." The spouses toured the Riverfront, attended a St. Louis Symphony concert, had lunch at the St. Louis Club and at a tea room, and toured an azalea garden and the historic Sappington House. The photo album snapshots for this meeting are in color, reflecting the new technology. **Margaret Lord** was elected president for two years.

Fall Council Meeting, November 17–19, 1970—Portland, OR

Senator Mark O. Hatfield spoke at a dinner at the Portland Hilton for bishops and spouses. A note posted in the scrapbook reads: "We're missing you, and wishing you were here. No special news. Our bride, **Margaret Henley**, is making a wonderful impression. She fits into the group perfectly and Jimmy is radiant. Lunch today and area dinner tonight will be the high spots socially."

Special Meeting, March 1–4, 1971—New York, NY

This special meeting of the Council, which was convened to celebrate the 25th anniversary of the United Nations, featured a tour and program about the United Nations and the musical *1776* at the St. James Theater. Someone noted in the scrapbook: "through sleet and storm—bishops and wives—it was worth it."

Spring Council Meeting, April 13–15, 1971—San Antonio, TX

A handwritten letter from **Eva B. Slater** notes that "There will be a special room at the St. Anthony Hotel for our meeting and visiting. **Margaret Lord** is suggesting that each one bring a 'sample' of her hobby. There will be space enough for 'show' and hopefully, time enough for 'tell.'" An enclosed card listed fellowship time for Monday evening and a business meeting Tuesday morning, followed by a "Riverboat Fiesta" in the evening ("informal, bring a sweater"). A buffet luncheon was held on Wednesday at Bishop and Mrs. Slater's home. Coffee and a visit to the McNay Art Institute were scheduled for Thursday.

Fall Council Meeting, 1971—Des Moines, IA

A card written by **Ruth Thomas**, wife of the hosting bishop, read "Weather is capricious at that time of year. Lightweight winter attire is advisable." Activities included fellowship, business, a luncheon at Simpson College, a tour of the Des Moines Art Center, dinner at Hotel Fort Des Moines (with speaker Senator Harold E. Hughes), a meeting and brunch at the episcopal residence (with Attorney Mrs. Luther Glanton speaking). The spouses also enjoyed a tour of Tiferth Israel synagogue, led by the rabbi's wife, and a Festival of Israeli Art.

Spring Council Meeting, April 10–13, 1972—Epworth-by-the-Sea, St. Simon's Island, GA

A letter from **Mamie Lee Finger** announced a beach party to be held on the patio of the Sea Palms Beach Club, "very casual clothes" for walking on the beach, if desired. Activity options included visiting art galleries, antiquing, shopping at the Lighthouse Museum, and a dramatic presentation of Eugenia Price's *Lighthouse*. The bishops and their wives enjoyed a bus tour of the Wesley sites on St. Simon's Island and dinner at the Aquarama on Jekyll Island ("dressy clothes, not formal"). Overseas visitation reports were given by bishops Lance, Muzorewa, Pickett, and Nall. On Thursday, the wives went to a luncheon at the Cloister on Sea Island and toured three gardens there. The wives voted to elect officers for one-year terms, instead of two, as in the previous quadrennium.

General Conference, April 17–29, 1972—Atlanta, GA

The spouses enjoyed a pre-General Conference luncheon at the episcopal residence followed by a reception at the governor's mansion, hosted by Mrs. Jimmy Carter. They also participated in a city tour and a luncheon featuring a "One Work" Fashion Show at the Marriott Motel ballroom. The spouses elected **Mamie Lee Finger** president for a one-year term.

Reflections and Personal Stories

Donna Wertz Ream Remembers Betty Wertz, Her Mother

Betty Rowe Wertz was born in 1919 in Newport, Pennsylvania. After graduating as valedictorian of her high school class, she went on to study at Juniata College in Pennsylvania. After two years of separation from Fred, who had been the love of her life since second grade, she left school to marry him and move to Boston, Massachusetts, where he was attending seminary. She put her aspirations aside at that time to support him. Probably she would tell you that her greatest claim to fame in her life was rearing her four children. One child was born at each of Fred and Betty's pastoral assignments in Pennsylvania: Bob while they were in Doylestown, Joanne while in Stewartstown, Donna while in Harrisburg, and finally, Beth, in Carlisle. Fred always said he became a district superintendent to stop those babies from coming!

During those years, Betty's time was pretty well taken up with the family. Other activities centered on music. She was an incredible musician, with a lovely alto voice and the ability to play anything on the piano. Her gifts ranged from accompanying at many of Dad's early churches to playing piano for the square-dance calling he loved to do. When the children were raised, however, Betty began to spread her wings and use the God-given talents she had put on the shelf. She was a poet! She wrote over 100 poems about her family, her travels with Dad, her beloved pets, and her ever-deepening relationship with God. It was during these years that Mother was able to fully embrace her spiritual life. She became a sought-after speaker for women's retreats and was known for loving and embracing people of different sexual orientations. One of her most beautiful poems, "What a Difference," reflects this. She bravely spoke out on this issue long before it was the thing to do. Throughout all these years, Betty also enjoyed her hobby of needlework. She never knew how to operate a sewing machine, but she could knit and crochet incredible treasures. Every one of her grandchildren has a blanket or sweater or Christmas stocking from Nanny!

At the Northeastern Jurisdictional Conference in 1968, Fred was confident that he was being sent to Pittsburgh and had already met with the Episcopacy Committee from that area. When Roy Nichols was elected, however, the only vacancy was in West Virginia; and the Jurisdictional Committee did not feel they could send an African American bishop there because of potential discrimination. Betty was back in her room packing, happily dreaming of remaining in her beloved Pennsylvania for this next phase of their lives. Fred had to return to the room to tell her that they were going to West Virginia. Needless to say, Betty was initially disappointed. However, after they had been in West Virginia for a few months, Betty, easily won over by the beauty of the mountains and the love of the people, said to Fred, "I have been talking to God about it and this is definitely where we were meant to be! This really is 'almost heaven'!"

Betty was diagnosed with cancer in her seventies. She fought bravely and suffered greatly, but she modeled for her family and friends the strength of faith during those years. She never complained and always said what a blessed life she had had and how she could never be ungrateful for the way it ended. After a 10-year battle, she died in August of 1999 at the age of 80. She loved nature, flowers, the West Virginia hills, music, and her children and grandchildren with a passion! She served God right up to the very end, and she was deeply loved by many people.

The following poems are published by permission of Donna Wertz Ream:

What a Difference!

By Betty Rowe Wertz

What a difference it would make if he were your son!
The strident calls of "sinner" would be hushed;
The possibility of change would be questioned;
Judgment would be reserved for God alone.
Your lifetime of love and nurture would not be in vain;
Your encouragement of gifts and talents would be enhanced through God's grace;
And his reverence and respect for life
Would continue to be deeply apparent.
Unconditional love, and accepting what we cannot change
Are not mere words or theories;
They are here, and now call for open minds;
Knowing what a difference it would make if he were your son!!

My Turn

By Betty Rowe Wertz, February 1997

Many years ago it was my turn to be a child;
My turn to enjoy simple pleasures . . .
Skipping down a small hometown street,
Roller skating around the square,
Gathering violets for a local clergyman,
Sharing friendships with young and old,
And it was GOOD!

Later, it was "my turn" at being a youth;
Discovering the joys of learning,
The satisfaction of athletic skills,
The awareness of the world of music and its disciplines,

Finding early in my life the attraction of young love and its mystery,
And it was GOOD!

Later still, it was "my turn" to become a wife and mother;
Love maturing into total commitment, accepting both faults and delights,
Motherhood awakening in me bonds that would last a lifetime,
From cuddly babies to independent young people,
And it was GOOD!

Then it was "my turn" to be an adult;
Children grown and gone and a husband who needed me in ministry,
Hobbies to pursue, grandbabies to welcome and miles to travel, at home and abroad,
Retirement years to discover farming skills
And always friendships, new and old, along the way,
And it was GOOD!

Now it is "my turn" to grow old;
To become more fully aware of my mortality,
To sense the slowing of physical prowess,
To recognize a growing generational gap,
To love the quiet, and the need to take my time,
Still, the love of family, friends and my Lord remain constant,
And it is VERY, VERY GOOD!

Chapter 13

1972–1976

Spouses Who Joined the Episcopal Family 1972–1976

Detailed profiles and citation information can be found in Part 5, beginning on page 251.

Jurisdiction or Central Conferences	Spouse	Bishop	Year Elected	Elected From	First Episcopal Assignment
NC	Helen Eloise Graves Clymer	Wayne K. Clymer	1972	north central USA	Minnesota
NC	Annamary Horner DeWitt	Jesse Robert Dewitt	1972	Detroit AC	Wisconsin
NC	Lois Dixon	Ernest T. Dixon Jr	1972	north central USA	Kansas
NE	Dorothy Barnhart Ault	James Mase Ault	1972	Wyoming AC	Philadelphia
NE	Phenola Valentine Carroll	Edward Gonzalez Carroll	1972	Baltimore-Washington AC	Boston

Jurisdiction or Central Conferences	Spouse	Bishop	Year Elected	Elected From	First Episcopal Assignment
NE	Annie Owings Sansbury Warman	John Boyle Warman	1972	Pittsburgh AC	Harrisburg
NE	Lois Josephine Yeakel	Joseph Hughes Yeakel	1972	Central Pennsylvania AC; General Secretary Board of Evangelism	New York West
SC	Benja Lee Bell Crutchfield	Finis Alonzo Crutchfield Jr	1972	Oklahoma AC	New Orleans
SC	Thelma Goodrich	Robert E. Goodrich Jr	1972	Texas AC	Missouri
SC	Isabelle Elliott Holter	Don Wendell Holter	1972	President, Saint Paul School of Theology	Nebraska
SE	Mary Jeanne Everett Blackburn	Robert McGrady Blackburn	1972	Florida AC	Raleigh
SE	Milah Dodd Gibson McDavid	Joel Duncan McDavid	1972	Alabama-West Florida AC	Florida
SE	LuReese Ann Watson Robertson	Frank Lewis Robertson	1972	South Georgia AC	Louisville
SE	Eleanor Lupo Sanders	Carl Julian Sanders	1972	Virginia AC	Birmingham
SE	Ada Rose Yow Stokes	Marion "Mack" B. Stokes	1972	North Georgia AC	Jackson
SE	Mary Jane Tullis	Edward Lewis Tullis	1972	Kentucky AC	Columbia
W	Grace Ying Hom Choy	Wilbur Wong Yan Choy	1972	California-Nevada AC	Seattle

Jurisdiction or Central Conferences	Spouse	Bishop	Year Elected	Elected From	First Episcopal Assignment
W	Marjorie Ida Tuell	Jack Marvin Tuell	1972	Pacific Northwest AC	Portland (Oregon)
W	Lucile Elizabeth Maris Wheatley	Melvin E. Wheatley Jr	1972	California-Pacific AC	Denver
Central Conferences	Ekoko L. Onema	Fama Onema	1972	Democratic Republic of Congo	Congo
Central Conferences	Marilina Stella De Jesus Figueiredo DeCarvalho	Emilio J. M. DeCarvalho	1972	Angola AC	Angola
Central Conferences	Navamani Peter	Mamidi Elia Peter	1972	India	Southern Asia
Central Conferences	Anna Harmon Warner	Bennie de Quency Warner	1973	Liberia AC	Liberia

Joining by Marriage This Quadrennium

Spouse	Year Married	Bishop	Where Serving
Marion Thompson Garrison	1973	Edwin Ronald Garrison	Retired

Highlights of Our Life Together: 1972–1976

Unless otherwise noted, the information in "Our Life Together" segments is based on the memory and personal notes of the author and information found in the episcopal spouses' scrapbooks and minutes.

Fall Council Meeting, September 22–25, 1972—Cleveland, OH

The spouses enjoyed a tour of the city, a luncheon at the Canterbury Country Club, a theatre party at the Cleveland Playhouse, and a spiritual life retreat led by Kenneth Mitchell. After a group picture was taken for *Together* magazine, the spouses discovered that, somehow, an unknown woman had joined them!

When they retook the picture, some of the spouses had already left (Tuell Diary). A page of "General Suggestions" added to the bylaws and duties of officers indicates a desire to make sure certain things happen. For example, the secretary of the Council of Bishops was to be asked to send two copies of the address list of bishops and wives to each bishop, so both could have a copy (this was before digital messaging and home copiers); both the president and the corresponding secretary were to write letters to spouses of newly elected bishops; and the wife of the jurisdictional president of each College was to inform the corresponding secretary of the Bishops' Wives Association of illnesses within the jurisdiction. The treasurer was responsible for collecting and keeping records of dues paid, $1.00 per year payable at the spring meeting. Such detailed documents suggest the difficulty of maintaining a well-organized association with only two meetings a year and geographic distance between members, as well as the extremely busy lives led by persons trying to balance family life with the bishops' schedules.

Spring Council Meeting, April 24–27, 1973—Washington, DC

Among the political leaders who made presentations was Senator Ted Kennedy, speaking about health care. **Henrietta Ledden** and Earl Ledden hosted the Council at a Kennedy Center symphony one evening. Visits to the State Department and the White House and a luncheon at Mt. Vernon Place Church were hosted by the Baltimore and Peninsula Conferences. The invitation to the area banquet indicates that dress would be informal, "long dress optional." The spouses elected **Ida Golden** president.

Fall Council Meeting, November 12–15, 1973—Nashville, TN

The spouses toured Andrew Jackson's Hermitage, McKendree Manor Retirement Home, the United Methodist Publishing House, Edgehill Mission, and neighborhood centers. Grand Old Opry star Minnie Pearl, who lived next door to the episcopal residence, came to **Mamie Finger**'s home to entertain the spouses, including a skit titled "The Bishop Comes to Grinder's Switch."

Spring Council Meeting, April 15–18, 1974—Los Angeles, CA

The spouses toured the Burbank Studios and the Music Center, enjoying lunch at a Mexican market on Olvera Street. **Marji Tuell** recalls introducing **Marilina DeCarvalho**, from Angola, to her first Mexican food (Tuell Diary). **Eva B. Slater** was elected president.

Fall Council Meeting, November 10–14, 1974—Lake Junaluska, NC

The Charlotte Episcopal Area hosted the spouses with a bus tour to Asheville, where they visited the Biltmore Estate and the Governor's Mountain Residence and had lunch ($2 each) at the Brooks-Howell Home for Retired Deaconesses and Missionaries. They also drove by the home of author Thomas Wolfe. The Area also hosted a banquet in Asheville.

Spring Council Meeting, March 31–April 4, 1975—Minneapolis, MN

Justice Blackman spoke to the council, and the spouses enjoyed a backstage tour of Guthrie Theater and a tour of the Twin Cities. **Mildred Loder** was elected president.

Fall Council Meeting, November 10–14, 1975—New Orleans, LA

Bishop Finis Crutchfield provided a lavish Mardi Gras theme. The spouses enjoyed a Garden District Walking Tour.

Spring Council Meeting April 20–25, 1976, and General Conference—Lincoln City, OR

The Tuells entertained the Council for its spring meeting with Senator Frank Church of Idaho as a dinner speaker and an Alaskan-themed spouses' luncheon. **Eunice Mathews** was elected president. The spouses' organization began the practice of naming a president designate to serve on the Executive Committee the year before serving as president (Tuell Diary).

Reflections and Personal Stories

Dorothy Ault's Story

Dorothy Ault remembers that she and Jim did not really expect that he would be elected. Jim was president of the seminary at Drew and loved what he was doing.

Wayne Clymer, also elected that year, was serving as president of the EUB seminary near Chicago. Wayne and his wife, **Helen Clymer**, spent a week together with Jim and Dorothy fishing before the Jurisdictional Conference, discussing how hard it would be to leave work that they enjoyed so much and wondering what they would be getting themselves into if they were to be elected. Dorothy and Helen anticipated that they would probably not want to go to Council of Bishop meetings, but then they went in order to see each other and kept going back because of the deep friendships they formed with the other spouses and because of the richness of their experiences. Through the years, Dorothy noted that an increasing number of spouses held jobs of their own. She saw the Bishops' Spouses' Association become more organized and offer a greater variety of activities. Dorothy especially appreciated the seminars offered to help the spouses grow spiritually and develop leadership skills. She recalls **Gwen White** teaching them how to lead spiritual-growth experiences and encouraging them to do so back in their conferences.

During their first quadrennium on the Council of Bishops, she and Jim traveled to Rhodesia and Zambia for their first Global Visitation. Later they visited India, with a delightful side trip to Nepal, and still later visited South Korea. She and Jim showed slides of their travels and provided mission interpretation at district meetings around the conference. The Eastern Pennsylvania Episcopal Area at that time included the Philadelphia and Wyoming (northeastern Pennsylvania and part of New York State) conferences and Puerto Rico, where they visited twice a year. Jim learned enough Spanish to be able to read the liturgy for some services there. They loved the people and encouraged their efforts to become an autonomous church. Dorothy had been working as a speech therapist in Morristown, New Jersey, when Jim was elected. Afterward, she volunteered at a school for the hearing impaired, which gave her a wonderful opportunity to use her training and skills and still be free to travel with Jim. In spite of their reluctance during the election process, Jim's election provided her with great opportunities and deep friendships she might never have experienced otherwise. —interview with Dorothy Ault

Marilina DeCarvalho's Story

"I first met Emilio in 1963, when he came to serve as pastor of the church I attended. Angola had come through a horrible time of persecution because of our struggle against colonialism. We wanted to be free of the Portuguese domination but did not achieve our independence until November 11, 1975. Many people were executed, others were thrown into prisons where they were beaten and suffered the worst possible treatment, similar to that experienced in Nazi concentration camps. Many pastors—of whom the majority were Methodists—were killed or imprisoned. When Emilio came to serve our church, he had just been released after two and a half years in prison, where he had suffered greatly.

"We were married in August 1966 and lived in Dondi, a mission station located in Central Angola, for six years. In 1972, he was elected a bishop 'in absence' during the Africa Central Conference meeting in Limbe, Malawi. He was working then as dean and teacher at the Emanuel Theological School, an ecumenical project. We had two children and, in addition to my role as wife and mother, I was teaching Pedagogy in the girls' school.

"There were no telephones then, only letters and telegrams for sharing information. When Emílio brought home a telegram, looking at me very seriously without saying a word, I thought that my mother must have died. After reading the message, both of us cried, we prayed, we laughed, as it brought very good and unexpected news: 'Pastor Emílio, you have been elected a bishop.' From that moment on, everything changed. We moved back to the capital, my home place. Besides my responsibility with the family, I had a job in a program that kept me actively involved: organizing meetings with women and pastor's wives, visiting churches in the districts, and directing a social program with children. Since Emilio was often away traveling around the conference and attending meetings inside and outside the country, I often cared for our three children by myself. Because of the ongoing war in Angola, I could feel at peace only when he arrived back home. Most of the time he drove on bad roads through dangerous areas. Sometimes I accompanied him, leaving the children with my mother.

"In 1988, the Angola Annual Conference was divided into two Episcopal Areas, and Emílio was appointed to supervise the West Angola Episcopal Area. Serving a smaller area made life easier for us, and we could see the spiritual growth and improved lives of our people. I continued to coordinate the church social program for children and work with the Angolan Methodist Women's Organization. I was elected as a member of the Africa Church Growth and

Development Committee, which was organized by the World Division of the Board of Global Ministries of The United Methodist Church. I served as its president for seven years. Later I served for seven years as a member and vice president of the General Council on Ministries of The United Methodist Church. I learned and grew from working with and relating to all kinds of people, not only in our conference but also in the United States and countries in Europe and Africa, attending meetings, some of which I chaired. In 1995, I became the first African to be chosen as president of the Bishops' Spouses' Association. I have enjoyed my friendships with bishops and their spouses since 1974, when I first attended the Council meetings, right up to the present. I have special friends of different colors and from different countries.

"I feel that I am a blessed daughter of God to have Emílio as my spouse, our three children, 13 grandchildren, and one great grandchild. Retirement has been good, giving me opportunities to be with my family and friends, to do things that I love to do, to encourage younger women, and to help where I am needed."

—written 2016

Lucile Wheatley's Window on History: The Struggle for Inclusion

After the 1968 merger that created The United Methodist Church, a special task force was assigned to rewrite the social principles statements of The Methodist Church and the Evangelical United Brethren into one cohesive statement for The United Methodist Church. Included in the proposal brought before the General Conference in the spring of 1972 was a statement affirming the "sacred worth of all persons," regardless of sexual orientation. Following a passionate floor debate, an amendment was made and passed, adding "we do not condone the practice of homosexuality and consider this practice incompatible with Christian teaching." This first mention of homosexuality in Methodist policy led to intense efforts by some to strengthen and enforce this position and by others to eliminate and reverse it.

During a meeting in Colorado Springs in 1978, as the Council of Bishops considered a statement in support of the denomination's negative statements regarding homosexuality, Bishop Mel Wheatley delivered an impassioned address to his colleagues in which he came out as the parent of a gay son and indicated his strong opposition to the direction the church was taking regarding its gay and lesbian members. Some years later, Lucile remembered how the behavior of some of the bishops and their wives changed toward them after that. "I knew it took a lot of courage for him to do that and I knew from the way people were just kind of slightly uncomfortable around us that, even at the dinner and everything, that all the men probably had gone home and told their wives immediately, when it was supposed to be assumed that this was a matter behind the closed doors of the bishops' room" (Mark Bowman interview with Bishop Mel and Lucile Wheatley in their California home on October 10, 1994, part 4, https://www.lgbtran.org/Interview.aspx?ID=15).

During the 1980 General Conference, the Episcopal Address expressed support for the "incompatibility" statements about homosexuality. Because he objected to that portion of the address, Mel clearly requested that his name not be included with the list of all the bishops when the address was published. When his name did, in fact, appear there, Mel insisted on the publication of a statement indicating that he did not support the opinion about homosexuality expressed in the Episcopal Address, which brought public attention to their position, resulting in a flood of responses, some hostile, some grateful.

In PFLAG (Parents and Friends of Lesbians and Gays), the Wheatleys experienced the kind of acceptance and loving support found among only a few of their episcopal colleagues, and they began to accept invitations to speak at many United Methodist churches in their area. It became apparent that some of these invitations were made not to learn more about the issue or to understand the Wheatleys' support of gay and lesbian persons, but with the intention of "crucifying" them because of their stance. Mel and Lucile began to take gay persons along with them on speaking engagements in order to put a human face on the issue. During the 1984 General Conference, Lucile sat with members of Affirmation: United Methodists for Gay and Lesbian Concerns, instead of with the other bishops' wives. In 1982, when Mel appointed an openly gay pastor to a local church, he was brought up on heresy charges, but absolved. That experience was very painful for both Mel and Lucile, "like a knife through the heart." Lucile and Mel sang with the Gay and Lesbian Association of Choruses and were honored with PFLAG's Lifetime Achievement Award in 1999.

In June 2017, the Methodist Federation for Social Action of the California Pacific Annual Conference presented Lucile with the annual Mildred Hutchinson award. The program for that event noted that she "was a mentor to an entire generation of LGBTQI+ persons in the UMC; she was a valuable and life-saving resource to those who did not know where to turn. In addition to their ground-breaking work with LGBTQI+ persons, the Wheatleys were also known for their work in interfaith and cross-cultural dialogue and reconciliation." Lucile, who had just turned 100 years old in March, was presented to the annual conference session in that same June and spoke briefly.

—email communication with son Jim Wheatley, August 2017–February 2018

Chapter 14

1976–1980

Spouses Who Joined the Episcopal Family 1976–1980

Detailed profiles and citation information can be found in Part 5, beginning on page 251.

Jurisdiction or Central Conferences	Spouse	Bishop	Year Elected	Elected From	First Episcopal Assignment
NC	June Ammons	Edsel Ammons	1976	Rock River (Northern Illinois) AC	Michigan
NC	Corneille Bacon Downer Bryan	Alonzo Monk Bryan	1976	Texas and Missouri	Nebraska
NC	Polly Anne Martin Hodapp	Leroy Charles Hodapp	1976	South Indiana AC	Illinois
NE	Gwendolyn Ruth Horton White	C. Dale White	1976	New England AC	New Jersey
SC	Lila Elaine Goodwin Hicks	Kenneth William Hicks	1976	Nebraska AC	Arkansas
SC	Bonnie Faye Pressley Lovern	James Chess Lovern	1976	Oklahoma AC	San Antonio

Jurisdiction or Central Conferences	Spouse	Bishop	Year Elected	Elected From	First Episcopal Assignment
SC	Virginia Maude Late Shamblin	J. Kenneth Shamblin	1976	Texas, Arkansas	Louisiana
Central Conferences	Angelina Joaquim Garrine Penicela	Almeida Penicela	1976	Mozambique AC	Mozambique
Central Conferences	Lisa Henzler Sticher	Hermann Ludwig Sticher	1977	southern Germany	Federal Republic of Germany and West Berlin
Central Conferences	Kasongo Maria Ngolo Wakadilo	Ngoy Kimba Maurice Wakadilo	1976	Central Africa AC	Shaba (now Katanga)

NOTE: The *Discipline* also lists the following other bishops elected in this quadrennium: LaVerne D. Mercado (1976) and Shantu Kumar A. Parmar (1979).

Joining by Marriage This Quadrennium

Spouse	Year Married	Bishop	Where Serving
Jewell Louise Fannin Haddock Blackburn	1978	Bishop Robert McGrady Blackburn	Raleigh Episcopal Area
Ernestine Gray Clark Dixon	1979	Bishop Ernest T. Dixon Jr	Kansas Episcopal Area

Highlights of Our Life Together: 1976–1980

Unless otherwise noted, the information in "Our Life Together" segments is based on the memory and personal notes of the author and information found in the episcopal spouses' scrapbooks and minutes.

Fall Council Meeting, November 16–19, 1976—Philadelphia, PA

The Council met for one session in historic Congress Hall, and a worship celebration took place at Tindley Temple United Methodist Church. A Quaker woman spoke to the spouses about her faith and her church. A separate list of suggestions for General Conference was added to the bylaws, including that the bishops' wives would present a hymnal to the usher for their section and that the president and executive committee would appoint "Big Sisters" across jurisdictional lines. In the list of officers and their duties, it was now the corresponding secretary who was designated to write to wives of newly elected bishops.

Spring Council Meeting, April 12–15, 1977—Williamsburg, VA

Spouse activities included tours of historic Williamsburg, Jamestown, Yorktown, and a plantation. **Marji Tuell** recalls wearing her hair pinned up with a curly piece on top for a banquet there. **Eunice Mathews**, who was president that year, recalled that she and **Mary Ella Stuart** decided to invite someone to come and speak to the group, which seemed to be something of a surprise to older members. From then on, the spouses often had some kind of study or learning experiences in addition to social events and tours. **Martha Goodson** was elected president.

Fall Council Meeting, November 14–18, 1977—Milwaukee, WI

This meeting, hosted by Jesse and **Annamary Dewitt**, was held at the Red Carpet Inn, with the "Family Dinner" and opening Communion service at Whitefish Bay United Methodist Church. Announcements included the election of Bishop Bennie de Quency Warner, who was present, as vice president of Liberia, and the election of Bishop Abel Tendelkayi Muzorewa to high office in Zimbabwe (Oden & Williams, 127). On Tuesday, the spouses were bussed to Wingspread, home of the Johnson Foundation, for a luncheon and program co-sponsored by the Wisconsin Conference and The Johnson Foundation. Rita Johnson, vice president in the area of programs for The Johnson Foundation, spoke about foundations in the United States and about The Johnson Foundation's creative initiatives for individual, community, and national growth and well-being. Following the program, First United Methodist Church in Racine presented president **Martha Goodson** with a Betty Crocker cookbook and a Wisconsin calendar. That afternoon, **Gwen White** led a workshop on "Parsonage Families and the Emerging Issues of American Family Life," including discussion of "The New Assertive Woman."

Wednesday morning, Gwen led a second workshop on "Developing Support Systems for Clergy Families," followed by a luncheon with the bishops at Wesley

Park Retirement Center. That evening, the bishops and spouses enjoyed a dance performance by members of the United Methodist Indian Congregation of Milwaukee. On Thursday, the "Bishops' Wives and Bishops' Widows" were served a luncheon at Wauwatosa United Methodist Church, and transportation was provided for shopping and sightseeing, including a visit to Mitchell Park Conservatory in Milwaukee. —Spouses' Scrapbooks, 1977–1979

Spring Council Meeting, March 27–31, 1978—Oklahoma City, OK

The Council met at the Sheraton Century Center, beginning with a Family Western Dinner and a tour of the National Cowboy Hall of Fame. The first two days of this meeting focused on a "Family and Morals" seminar chaired by Bishop Dale White and open to the spouses, during which leaders in the field of marital counseling spoke, and concern was expressed for the growing divorce rate among clergy families (Oden & Williams, 127–128). Dale and **Gwen White** were certified leaders through the Association for Couples in Marriage Enrichment, founded by David and Vera Mace, an organization that worked closely with our General Board of Discipleship for many years.

Host spouse **Francis Milhouse** gave as favors beaded cross-and-flame logos made by her family through the Cookson Hills Center, in Cookson, Oklahoma, a General Board of Global Ministries project. The Memorial Service in W. Angie Smith Chapel at Oklahoma City University was followed by a reception at the home of University President and Mrs. Dolphus Whitten Jr. On Wednesday, the bishops and spouses attended a luncheon forum sponsored by the Oklahoma City Chamber of Commerce, and on Thursday the spouses attended a special luncheon at Oklahoma City University, followed by a visit to nearby St. Luke's UMC and Heritage House. The area committee, composed of members of the Oklahoma and Oklahoma Indian Missionary Conferences, also planned a Farewell Dinner for the Council Thursday evening at the Petroleum Club. **Twila Stowe** was elected president. —Spouses' Scrapbooks, 1977–1979

Fall Council Meeting, November 24–28, 1978—Colorado Springs, CO

The Council met at the Antlers Plaza Hotel "at the foot of Pike's Peak," gathering for opening Communion in the United States Air Force Academy Cadet

Chapel, followed by dinner at the nearby Flying W Ranch. The spouses enjoyed a scenic ride on Tuesday to the Broadmoor Hotel for a luncheon, followed by their business meeting. The next day, the "bishops' wives and widows" gathered for a retreat day at the John Wesley Cabin belonging to First Church, Colorado Springs. Dr. Jean Miller Schmidt, Iliff Assistant Professor of Modern Church History, joined them to guide the sharing, which included a panel of bishops' wives discussing the various community services and volunteer activities in which they were involved. Among those sharing were **Thelma Goodrich**, who had been researching ethnic hymns for a new hymnal; **Gwen White**, who presented workshops, sometimes with her husband, on family life and marriage enrichment; **Marji Tuell**, who led workshops on hymnology, wrote a leaflet on how to teach hymns, and led singing at General Conference; **Mary Ella Stuart**, who used her book *To Bend Without Breaking* for leading stress-management workshops; and **Twila Stowe**, who served as a volunteer with Contact, a nationwide telephone ministry for people in crisis situations. The Executive Committee also arranged for the spouses to meet at the El Pomar Retreat with Sister Helen Flaherty, a highly respected Roman Catholic with a world perspective on women and the church. During the Denver Episcopal Area Night banquet and program, for which the bishops and spouses were seated by Jurisdiction, the Council enjoyed a concert by the Adams State Choir from Alamosa, Colorado.

During that same Council meeting, reports on overseas Global Visitations were given by a panel that included Jack and **Marjorie Tuell**, Dale and **Gwen White**, Paul and **Kathryn Washburn**, Ralph and **Marion Alton**, Monk and **Corneille Bryan**, and Bishop Warner from Liberia.

—Spouses' Scrapbooks, 1977–1979

Marji Tuell broke tradition by leading singing at Council worship, the first time a spouse was invited to provide such leadership (Tuell Diary).

Spring Council Meeting, April 17–20, 1979—Boston, MA

The Council celebrated its fortieth birthday at this meeting, which was held at the Copley Square Hotel in Boston. Following the opening Communion service at Boston University, bishops and spouses enjoyed dinner at the New England Aquarium. Host spouse **Phenola Carroll** wrote in her welcoming letter to the spouses, "Dress for the evening banquet will be as formal as you wish.

I will wear a long skirt." The program included a speech by the Right Honorable George Thomas, MP, PC, Speaker of the House of Commons; an oratorio "New Land, New Covenant" by Howard Hanson with text by Howard Clark Kee; and an historical narrative litany. After breakfast at Cricket's Restaurant in Quincy Market and a viewing of "Where's Boston," a multimedia presentation of the city and its people, the spouses browsed in the Market and then went to Heritage United Methodist Church for a luncheon. The Memorial Service was held at Trinity Episcopal Church. The next day, the spouses went to Boston University for a time of sharing. Professor Lyn Rhodes of the Boston University School of Theology and Professor Jean Carey Peck of Andover Newton, along with several female ministerial candidates, led a discussion of issues related to women in ministry—past, present, and future. The spouses enjoyed a luncheon at the home of Boston University President and Mrs. John Silber. The following day, the spouses boarded buses for Concord, Massachusetts, for the Patriot's Day parade and a scenic tour of Lexington, followed by a luncheon at Sudbury UMC. **Mary Ella Stuart** was elected president.

Fall Council Meeting, 1979—Albuquerque, NM

The Council stayed at the Albuquerque Inn and held their meetings in the adjacent Convention Center. The Council gathered for opening Communion at First UMC on Monday evening, then for dinner at Central UMC. The next morning after worship with the Council, the spouses boarded buses for a tour of Santa Fe, including the kiva-shaped Capitol Building; the La Fonda Hotel (known for its location at the end of the Santa Fe Trail); the Santa Fe Plaza; the Palace of the Governors (the oldest public building still in continuous use in the United States, built in 1610 when the village of Santa Fe was established by the Spanish governor); the Fenn Galleries; and the Famous Stairway of Our Lady of Light Chapel. The buses took them for lunch at The Compound, a modern-day joining of six tiny adobe houses in the artists' section, followed by tea at the home of Governor and Mrs. Bruce King. Wednesday, the spouses rode buses to the Old Town area of Albuquerque for a Mexican luncheon at La Placita Restaurant, located in a building originally owned by the relatives of a flamboyant Spanish governor, according to host spouse **Artha Blair Carleton** in her welcoming letter. The luncheon included a program by Indian artist and author

Pablita Velarde and was followed by a tour of the Old Plaza and San Felipe de Neri Church, established in 1706, and shopping. On Thursday, according to Artha Blair's "Schedule for Ladies' Activities," they visited the Indian Pueblo Cultural Center and toured the museum there. After a luncheon at the Center, they rode to the other side of Albuquerque to visit Isleta Indian Pueblo. The Northwest Texas-New Mexico Episcopal Area Night dinner and program included entertainment by the Frances Bustamante Dancers, a presentation on area history by local pastor Dr. Harry Vanderpool, and Broadway music by Gene Ives and Kathy Ives Clawson. —Spouses' Scrapbooks, 1977–1979

During that same fall meeting, the spouses listened to a panel discussion by spouses who had visited China and a presentation by **Anneliese Härtel** from East Germany. Because the East German government resisted letting both of the Härtels leave the country at the same time, fearing they might never return, Armin had suggested that the spouses send Annalise an official invitation, on Council stationery, to speak to them on the subject of "The Role of Women in East Germany." She was allowed to accompany her husband this one time. Her talk did indeed provide interesting information, but even more important was the fact that she was able to relax and enjoy the rest of the week getting acquainted with the other spouses and seeing a bit of America. —Tuell Diary

Spring Council Meeting (Nashville, IN) and General Conference (Indianapolis, IN)—April 15–26, 1980

The Council met in Nashville, Indiana, at the Brown County Inn, which offered tennis, swimming in an indoor-outdoor pool, hiking, and shopping in Nashville. The spouses visited Columbia, Indiana, to tour buildings designed by premier American architects and were entertained by an Indiana artist, Jerry Buam, during lunch at Indiana University in Bloomington. During their last evening before General Conference, hosts **Mary Ella Stuart** and Marvin Stuart planned a game-playing party for relaxation and fun. **Ruth Nichols** was elected president.

Bishop Bennie Warner and his wife, **Anna Warner**, were in the United States for this Council meeting and the General Conference. Anna made a presentation to the Bishops' Spouses' Association. During that time, Bishop Warner, who had been elected vice president of Liberia three years earlier, learned that the military had taken over the government of his country.

Reflections and Personal Stories

Gwen White's Window on History: The Iranian Crisis

In December 1979, **Gwen White** wrote in her journal, "Dale has been asked to be part of a seven-man team going to Iran over the Christmas holidays on a peace mission. This seems almost unbelievable, so it must be ordained that he go. This also means that he will miss Christmas, to which he had been looking forward so much, with everyone coming home, and especially little two-year old Matthew being here for a week. But in the light of 50 other families being separated because the Iranian militants are holding their loved ones hostage, how can we honestly complain?"

Gwen shared this experience with me (Jane Ives) in the summer of 2016, thumbing through her journal and reading selected sections aloud. She explained that the idea for this peace mission came out of an ecumenical clergy demonstration at the Statue of Liberty in New York City. The gathering was intended as an appeal—in the name of a God of compassion and mercy—to the Iranian militants and especially to the Ayatollah Khomeini to release the 52 Americans who had been taken hostage. A copy of the words spoken that day were sent to the Iranian Embassy, along with a request for a team of clergy to go to Iran on a peaceful mission to listen and to learn. The seven clergy chosen for the team went to Washington, DC, to meet with the Iranian ambassador and a United Nations official to negotiate arrangements for their trip. The two-hour meeting began on Friday, December 21 at 5:30 p.m. The next morning, they learned that their visas were ready and that they were to depart at 6:00 p.m. that evening. Dale, Gwen, and their daughter Lisa spent Saturday morning packing and preparing. Gwen remembers hurrying to shop for necessary items, getting money from the bank, and taking Dale's shoes in for new soles. Lisa clipped newspaper articles for her father to read during the flight. In the early afternoon, fighting tears, Gwen and Lisa walked out with Dale to the car that would take him to the airport. Dale joked that getting to Kennedy would probably be the most difficult part of the trip. When Gwen asked him what role he thought he would play, he grinned and said that he thought they might let him carry the tickets.

Gwen recalls this as the hardest good-bye she had ever experienced. The sadness of separation, humility mixed with pride that Dale had been chosen to play this important role, all jumbled together with sorrow that he would not be with the family for Christmas. Daughter Lisa went back into the house. Gwen, with a huge lump in her throat, walked over to the mailbox to get the mail, then went inside. She sat at the table to sort the mail and decided to open only the envelope with the return address of a dear friend. Inside she found a beautiful blue card with gold letters spelling out "Shalom" in Hebrew on the front and then in English inside. Her friend had added in her own handwriting: "Peace, the oldest wish and the newest hope."

Gwen later wrote in her journal, "I didn't quite know what to do with my mixed feelings. I was stunned that this message, a symbol of Dale's calling to this mission of peace and justice, should come just when I needed to move from private self-pity to a broader understanding of God's mission. The entire experience began to hit me," she said, "and I didn't even know how to pray. I called a trusted friend, Dean Lanning. Stunned to hear what was happening, he offered to call the other cabinet members in the New Jersey Conference [where we were serving]. I recalled Dale's sermon from the Sunday before, in which he recalled being in war-torn Beirut, so close to the place where Jesus was born, coming into a world very similar to the one in which we live now, bringing a message of peace and reconciliation. 'When will it ever end?' Dale asked. 'When will we ever learn the ways of peace? When will we ever drive a wedge of love and reconciliation into the spiraling circle of hate?' How little did he realize, when preaching those words, that he would soon be called to do just that."

Gwen described the arrival of their children later that day. They were shocked when they heard that their father was on the way to Iran. Saturday evening, they saw a television news clip showing the group at Kennedy airport preparing to depart, the reporter noting that the Iranian government had not invited them. They could see Dale in the background of the picture, tending to the luggage.

Just before Dale left, he had shown Gwen the switch for the lights he had put on a little Christmas tree in the yard. Christmas Eve they all put on coats and went out to see the surprise Grandpa had left. They stood under the stars singing carols. "Silent night" brought them to tears. They finally went to bed around

11:00 p.m. but were wakened at midnight by a friend who called to tell them to turn on the television to see a news report about the group being received by Khomeini. The family talked until 1:00, then crawled back in bed. Lisa crawled in bed with her mother, who recalls praying constantly, filled with gratitude for the dear presence of her family and for the support coming from so many others.

At 8:00 a.m. on December 26, the phone rang, and Gwen heard the words "Tehran calling," then Dale's voice loud and clear saying "Merry Christmas." He reported that the team had been told they would have five minutes with Khomeini but were allowed to stay 30. Khomeini gave permission for them to travel freely without harassment. What a joy and relief to hear Dale's voice so clearly, as if he were in the next room. Dale called again later to tell her that they had moved out of one hotel into another to escape the press, which was swarming all over the place. He also asked Gwen to make some telephone calls for him as he urgently needed to talk with some specific persons. Gwen relayed messages, puzzled as to what was happening. Things obviously were moving fast. Dale wanted someone stateside to keep him informed about what was being reported in the news. Gwen recalls the television playing all day and especially watching the 11:00 p.m. news. Friends brought over two more television sets so they could watch all three major news channels at once. They caught a brief report that two of the team were allowed into the embassy, where they stayed for two hours. A reporter who asked if they had seen the hostages was told they had gone to speak with the militants. He asked, "About what?" but the response was "No comment."

Sunday and Monday, December 30 and 31, there was no news about the team. There were reports that Russia had invaded Afghanistan and that someone from the United Nations was traveling to Iran to try to settle the hostage problem. On New Year's Eve, Gwen noted, they sat in a vacuum, aware that Dale was due to return January 3rd. On New Year's Day, 1980, the family gathered for a Korean meal prepared by daughter Lisa. The phone rang and another series of messages were relayed. The family learned that the team had returned for a second visit with Khomeini and that they had seen the hostages. Their hopes for the release of the hostages rose, but it was not to be. Because of the Iranians' anger at President Carter for granting asylum to the Shah, the hostages were not released until he was out of office a year later. Dale and another member of the team later made a second trip to Iran, taking seven bags of mail that had accumulated for the hostages.

In April, Dale reported on his experience in Iran to the Council of Bishops in their meeting prior to General Conference in Indianapolis. The Council asked him to tell that story to the General Conference, which he did, receiving a standing ovation from those in attendance. On April 24, Dale and other United Methodist leaders went to the White House to meet with President Carter. While they were urging him not to use military force as a means to address the hostage situation, a staff person came in and placed a note on Carter's desk. The president excused himself, asking the group not to tell anyone about the meeting. The next morning's news reported the death of eight of our servicemen and one Iranian in a helicopter crash in the Iranian desert during a failed attempt to rescue the hostages.

It was a remarkable time in history, when the United States government allowed church leaders to try to solve, or at least to better understand a huge diplomatic crisis. Dale recalls his involvement as the highlight of his service as a United Methodist bishop. Gwen recalls the experience as a huge test of her faith and still treasures the memory of the exceptional support and care she and their family received at that time.

—as told to Jane P. Ives by Gwen and Dale White, January 2016

Maggie Muzorewa's Window on History: Conflict in Africa

During Zimbabwe's armed struggle for liberation in the 1970s, **Maggie Muzorewa** spent time in exile in Mozambique. There she volunteered at Maputo Hospital (Mozambique), where the wounded were brought from the war front. She then went to Nashville, Tennessee, for safety, returning to Zimbabwe in 1979. —Council of Bishops Memorial Booklet, November 2009

Chapter 15

1980–1984

Spouses Who Joined the Episcopal Family 1980–1984

Detailed profiles and citation information can be found in Part 5, beginning on page 251.

Jurisdiction or Central Conferences	Spouse	Bishop	Year Elected	Elected From	First Episcopal Assignment
NC	Betty Ann Fisher Boulton	Edwin Charles Boulton	1980	East Ohio AC	Dakotas
NC	Jane Elizabeth Curry Colaw	Emerson S. Colaw	1980	Northern Illinois, West Ohio	Minnesota
NE	Carolyn Ruth Baumgartner Bashore	George Willis Bashore	1980	Eastern Pennsylvania AC	Boston
NE	Mary Lou Grove	William Boyd Grove	1980	Western Pennsylvania AC	West Virginia
NE	Shirley Skeete	F. Herbert Skeete	1980	New York AC	Philadelphia

Jurisdiction or Central Conferences	Spouse	Bishop	Year Elected	Elected From	First Episcopal Assignment
SC	Ruth Odessa Robinson Handy	William Talbot Handy Jr	1980	Louisiana AC	Missouri
SC	Martha Carson Hardt	John Wesley Hardt	1980	Texas AC	Oklahoma
SC	Nancy Kelley Oliphint	Benjamin Ray Oliphint	1980	North Texas AC	Kansas
SC	Mary Jean Russell	John William Russell	1980	Oklahoma AC	Dallas-Fort Worth
SC	Ina Edmondson Schowengerdt	Louis Wesley Schowengerdt	1980	Missouri West AC	Northwest Texas-New Mexico
SE	Esther Mae Maddox Clark	Roy Clyde Clark	1980	Mississippi, Tennessee	Columbia (South Carolina)
SE	Louise Calhoun Duffey	Paul Andrews Duffey	1980	Alabama-West Florida AC	Louisville
SE	Mary Ann Minnick	Carlton Printess Minnick Jr	1980	Virginia AC	Jackson
W	Mary Carolyn Bamberg McConnell	Calvin McConnell	1980	Rocky Mountain AC	Portland (Oregon)
W	Ethelou Douglas Talbert	Melvin George Talbert	1980	Southern California, Arizona AC	Seattle
Central Conferences	Kashala Katembo	Kainda Katembo	1980	Southern Zaire AC	South Congo
Central Conferences	Violet Mamusu Sackie Kulah	Arthur Flumo Kulah	1980	Liberia AC	Liberia
Central Conferences	Angelina Baron del Rosario Nacpil	Emerito Pimental Nacpil	1980	Philippines AC	Manila
Central Conferences	Sabine Ngeza Ndoricimpa	John Alfred Ndoricimpa	1980	Burundi	Burundi

NOTE: The *Discipline* also lists the following other bishop elected in this quadrennium: Marjorie Swank Matthews (1980), the first female bishop in the denomination.

Also Joining This Quadrennium

Jurisdiction or Central Conferences	Spouse	Bishop	Year Elected	Elected From	First Episcopal Assignment
Central Conferences	Regina Leah Taylor Bangura	Thomas Syla Bangura	1979	Sierra Leone AC	Sierra Leone

NOTE: Thomas Bangura was elected bishop in 1979 in the autonomous Sierra Leone Methodist Church, which became part of The United Methodist Church in 1984 (http://sierraleoneumc.org/?page_id=259).

Joining by Marriage This Quadrennium

Spouse	Year Married	Bishop	Where Serving
Nancy Sueko Adachi-Osawa	1982	Wilber Wong Yan Choy	San Francisco Area
Elizabeth Greene Law Dodge	1983	Ralph Edward Dodge	Retired
Helen E. Jenkins Werner	1983	Hazen G. Werner	Retired

Highlights of Our Life Together: 1980–1984

Unless otherwise noted, the information in "Our Life Together" segments is based on the memory and personal notes of the author and information found in the episcopal spouses' scrapbooks and minutes.

Fall Council Meeting, November 11–14, 1980—Houston, TX

The bishops spent much time at this meeting formulating a response to recent murders of black persons in Buffalo, New York, and Atlanta, Georgia. They sent a letter to the cities and families involved, calling on all United Methodists and citizens of good will to work for better communication between black and white communities and to bring to justice those responsible for those deaths (Oden & Williams, 142).

The bishops and spouses enjoyed a meal at a fancy club for wealthy oil company men. Bishop Finis Crutchfield, according to his daughter-in-law, Karen, loved to tell about how he had arranged for bowls of rattlesnake meat to be placed on each table, but not identified until near the end of the meal. Since The Methodist Church of India was about to become autonomous, this was the last meeting of the Council in which the bishops from India would participate. Tears flowed during the farewell speeches and personal good-byes. The spouses visited Bayou Bend and other museums; the home of Miss Ima Hogg, daughter of the first native-born governor of Texas; the Galleria Shopping Mall, with such famous stores as Nieman-Marcus and Lord & Taylor; and "The Original Christmas Store." They also enjoyed a VIP tour of NASA, where a woman astronaut spoke to them, and a brief tour of Galveston (Tuell Diary).

Spring Council Meeting, April 27–May 11, 1981—Rapid City, SD

The bishops and spouses enjoyed an excursion to the Black Hills, Mt. Rushmore, Custer National Park, and the Statue of Crazy Horse, as well as to places frequented by Calamity Jane and Billy the Kid. **Mary Ann Hunt** was elected president.

Fall Council Meeting, November 16–20, 1981—Pittsburgh, PA

The wives toured one of the villages established by the Harmony Society, and the entire Council enjoyed a "Three Rivers" boat cruise.

Spring Council Meeting, April 26–30, 1982—Lake Junaluska, NC

The Memorial Service and Family Dinner were held at First United Methodist Church in nearby Waynesville. Governor Riley spoke at a luncheon for bishops and spouses at Spartanburg. The spouses received gifts of small baskets and pillow slips. They enjoyed a bus tour through the area and visits to the Greenville South Carolina Museum of Art, featuring a Wyeth exhibit, and a luncheon served by the UMW at Buncombe St. United Methodist Church. The luncheon featured dishes from recipes in their UMW cookbook, and a copy of the cookbook was given to each guest. This time, the minutes used the women's first names consistently. **Helen Clymer** was elected president.

Fall Council Meeting, November 15–19, 1982—Birmingham, AL

The spouses enjoyed a city tour of both modern and historic sites in Birmingham; a luncheon of "southern fixings" at Canterbury UMC; a morning visit to the offices of *Southern Living* magazine, including a tour of test kitchens and a candy-making demonstration; and visits to a restored village, Huntington College (a United Methodist school), and the home of Jefferson Davis.

Spring Council Meeting, May 3–6, 1983—Little Rock, AK

Governor Bill Clinton addressed the Council (Oden & Williams, 151). The Council spent much time discussing their leadership role, especially given the division among its members on various issues. Bishop Roy Short presented a paper on Corporate Leadership for discussion, highlighting the mandates dating back to 1785 to "travel through the circuits" and to direct the "spiritual business of the churches" (Oden & Williams, 152). The spouses visited the Hot Springs Arlington Hotel for a luncheon and some took hot bath treatments at the hot springs. A dinner was held at Hendrix College. **Corneille Bryan** was elected president.

Fall Council Meeting, November 14–17, 1983—Burlingame (near San Francisco), CA

The spouses toured Stanford University and enjoyed several Chinese celebrations. Choirs from Chinese, Filipino, Japanese, and Korean Churches sang for the Council.

Spring Council Meeting, April 24–28—Wilmington, DE, and General Conference, May 1–12, 1984—Baltimore, MD

The spouses visited the Dupont estate, and the Council took a bus tour to historic United Methodist sites in Baltimore, including Barrett's Chapel, Old New Salem, and Longwood Gardens. General Conference included two bi-centennial celebrations. **Marji Tuell** was elected president.

Reflections and Personal Stories

Window on History: Women Rising

As the spouses of Methodist bishops were beginning to experience, a major shift was taking place in our culture. One event pointing to that shift in the church was the Women's History Project. Following a recommendation from the National Seminar of UMW in 1975, the directors of the Women's Division of the Board of Global Ministries petitioned the 1976 General Conference for a special committee to be appointed "to research and publish a history of the contribution of women to The United Methodist Church." This action led to an enormous cooperative effort, culminating in a national conference titled "Women in New Worlds: Historical Perspectives on the United Methodist Tradition," held in Cincinnati, Ohio, February 1–3, 1980. Fifty-eight essays were presented on subjects ranging from Mary McCloud Bethune to inclusion of women in church polity to the temperance movement. Twenty of these essays were compiled into a book titled *Women in New Worlds: Historical Perspectives on the Wesleyan Tradition,* edited by Hilah F. Thomas and Rosemary Skinner Keller (Nashville: Abingdon, 1981). **Mamie Finger** is mentioned on page 11 as an active participant in this project: "The commission [Archives and History] is indebted to Rosemary Skinner Keller, chairwoman of its Women's History and Status Committee for 1980–84, and to **Mamie Ratliff Finger**, a member of that committee, for their leadership in carrying out the intent of the committee for the promotion of this volume" (Alice G. Knotts, *Fellowship of Love: Methodist Women Changing American Racial Attitudes 1920-1968* [Nashville: Kingswood Books, 1996]).

Mary Lou Grove Remembers

"My friendship with **Lucille Wheatley** illustrates why being part of the spouses' group was so important to me. We formed deep friendships with bishops and spouses who welcomed us when we arrived in 1980. Lucille was one of these for me. She was and is a gentle and elegant woman, a mentor, and dear friend." —email communication with Mary Lou Grove, October 2016

Eunice Mathews Remembers

"Some of you know that before the Indian church became autonomous, at General Conference Jim and I [**Eunice Mathews**] hosted in some local church facility an Indian dinner. This was originally for the India bishops, delegates, and missionaries. The bishops' wives from India would help me in this. Due to their culinary skills, this dinner became very popular and something people anticipated. Then at each succeeding General Conference others outside the India orbit asked to be included. At the last General Conference session in Indianapolis, 1980, before Indian Methodism became autonomous and the Methodist Church of India was born, we had over 300 present! Many people remember this with grateful recollection and real nostalgia for the privilege of fellowship with the Indian delegates. At almost every Council meeting, one of the older bishop's wives will speak to me about missing you ladies and how much they appreciated knowing you and learning from you."

—from a letter to newly elected bishops' wives in India, April 1995

Chapter 16

1984–1988

Spouses Who Joined the Episcopal Family 1984–1988

Detailed profiles and citation information can be found in Part 5, beginning on page 251.

Jurisdiction or Central Conferences	Spouse	Bishop	Year Elected	Elected From	First Episcopal Assignment
NC	Beverly Nadine Ellerbeck Job	Rueben Philip Job	1984	Dakotas AC	Iowa
NC	Martha Ellen Pegram Lawson	David Jerald Lawson	1984	Indiana AC	Wisconsin
NC	Jennie May "Kim" Tolson White	Woodie W. White	1984	Detroit AC	Central Illinois
NE	Inez Rossey Irons	Neil L. Irons	1984	West Virginia AC	New Jersey
NE	Phyllis Elizabeth Henry May	Felton Edwin May	1984	Peninsula AC	Harrisburg
NE	Josephine Mitchell Stith	Forrest C. Stith	1984	Baltimore Washington AC	New York West

Jurisdiction or Central Conferences	Spouse	Bishop	Year Elected	Elected From	First Episcopal Assignment
SC	Elizabeth Anne Connaughton Hearn	James Woodrow Hearn	1984	Louisiana AC	Nebraska
SC	Billye Kathryn Whisnand Underwood	Walter L. Underwood	1984	Texas	Louisiana
SC	Julia Kitchens Wilke	Richard B. Wilke	1984	Kansas	Arkansas
SE	Eva Rebecca Vines Eutsler	Kern Eutsler	1984	Virginia AC	Holston
SE	Sarah Frances Perry Fitzgerald	Ernest A. Fitzgerald	1984	Western North Carolina AC	Atlanta
SE	Mildred Hawkins "Tuck" Jones	Lewis Bevel Jones III	1984	North Georgia AC	Charlotte
SE	Edith Laney Strawn Knox	James Lloyd Knox	1984	Florida AC	Birmingham
SE	Martha Storey Morgan	Robert Crawley Morgan	1984	North Alabama AC	Mississippi
SE	Thelma Heard Newman	Ernest Wilbur Newman	1984	Florida AC	Nashville
W	Zoraida Freytes Galvan	Elias Gabriel Galvan	1984	Southern California-Arizona AC	Phoenix
W	Kathleen Ann Thomas–Sano	Roy Isao Sano	1984	California-Nevada AC	Denver
Central Conferences	Edita Bote Gamboa	José Gamboa Jr	1986	The Philippines	Davao
Central Conferences	Gerlinde Johanna Mueller Minor	Rüdiger Rainer Minor	1986	Middle German AC	Dresden

NOTE: The *Discipline* also lists the following other bishops elected in this quadrennium: Judith Craig (1984) and Leontine T. Kelly (1984).

Highlights of Our Life Together: 1984–1988

Unless otherwise noted, the information in "Our Life Together" segments is based on the memory and personal notes of the author and information found in the episcopal spouses' scrapbooks and minutes.

Fall Council Meeting, November 11–16, 1984—Orlando, FL

The spouses enjoyed a day at Epcot Center, hosted by the Florida Conference, and a visit to Bethune Cookman College. Uncomfortable about the cost to the church of such tours, the spouses discussed whether to insist on paying for their own entertainment. Others pointed out that it is an insult to refuse hospitality that has been offered. This is especially true in the African tradition.

Spring Council Meeting, April 27–May 3, 1985—Seattle, WA

During the spouses' meeting, presentations were made on color analysis and packing for travel. The spouses also enjoyed a bus tour and lunch at the University of Puget Sound and tours of Edelweiss Chalet, Boehm's Candy Factory, the city of Issaqua, Snoqualmie Falls, and Lookout Park. **Dorothy Ault** was elected president.

Fall Council Meeting, November 9–15, 1985—Wichita, KS

The spouses saw the premier of the movie *Papa Was a Preacher.* They visited Wichita State University and had a luncheon at the Wichita Club.

Spring Council Meeting, April 26–May 2, 1986—Morristown, NJ

The spouses enjoyed tours of the city of Princeton, the United Methodist Archives and History Building on the campus of Drew University, and a seeing-eye-dog training school. **Jewell Blackburn** was elected president.

Fall Council Meeting, 1986—Lake Junaluska, NC

The spouses visited Cherokee, and some sat in on presentations of the "In Defense of Creation" document.

Spring Council Meeting, March 20–27, 1987—Arlington, VA

The spouses visited several national sites in Washington, DC, including the Smithsonian. They also participated with the bishops in meetings with members of Congress. **Annamary DeWitt** was elected president.

Fall Council Meeting, November 16–20, 1987—Lake Junaluska, NC

Some spouses sat in on the report of Disciple Bible study, which Richard and **Julia Wilke** developed and authored.

Spring Council Meeting, April 16–22—Kansas City, KS, and General Conference, April 26–May 7, 1988—St. Louis, MO

The spouses enjoyed visits to the Truman Library and Hallmark Headquarters and a tea at the home of **Ruth Handy**, who was elected president. The General Conference established Africa University in Mutare, Zimbabwe (to which many of the spouses have traveled for episcopal visits and on mission work teams); accepted a new hymnal; and created a committee to study homosexuality (Oden & Williams, 162).

Reflections and Personal Stories

Anne Hearn's Window on History: Mother Theresa

"When we were in India for Woody's Episcopal Visitation, we met many wonderful and brave Christians. When we reached Calcutta, we visited several schools and then were taken to Mother Teresa's headquarters. Our guide insisted on taking us to the door, although we felt guilty about the number of people waiting outside. After the door was opened and we were introduced as Bishop and Mrs. Hearn from the United States, we were led upstairs. After a few minutes, Mother Teresa came in and greeted us with grace and hospitality, inviting us to go downstairs with her for tea and time to talk. Over tea and cookies, she inquired about our reasons for coming to India. She then began to talk about her work there and around the world. She expressed great concern about the AIDS epidemic, without condemnation, but with great love and care for those suffering and dying. She told the story of a young man in her hospice in the United States who had been on the verge of dying for many days. He told a young man who was sitting with him, 'I need to talk with my father. He is very angry at me, and I can't die until I talk with him.' Mother Teresa found his father's phone number and called him. The father, shocked and tearful at learning of his son's condition, said he would come.

That night he sat by his son's bed and they talked, even laughed together. That night the young man passed away peacefully, having reconciled with his father. Then Mother Teresa asked us if we would come and work with her sometime, maybe for a week or two or as long as we could. With a twinkle in her eye, she said to Woody, 'Because you are the bishop, you can do the laundry.' We will cherish the memory of this visit forever." —Anne Hearn, 2015

Chapter 17

1988–1992

Spouses Who Joined the Episcopal Family 1988–1992

Detailed profiles and citation information can be found in Part 5, beginning on page 251.

Jurisdiction or Central Conferences	Spouse	Bishop	Year Elected	Elected From	First Episcopal Assignment
NC	Charles E. Logsdon Christopher	Sharon Brown Christopher	1988	Wisconsin AC	Minnesota
NC	Marjorie Louise Clouse Duecker	R. Sheldon Duecker	1988	North Indiana AC	Chicago
NC	Janet Mae Dean Lewis	William B. Lewis	1988	Southern Illinois AC	Dakotas
SC	Karen Miers Blake	Bruce P. Blake	1988	Kansas West AC	Dallas
SC	Marilyn Brown Oden	William B. Oden	1988	Oklahoma AC	Louisiana
SC	Joy B. Solomon	Dan Eugene Solomon	1988	Southwest Texas AC	Oklahoma

Jurisdiction or Central Conferences	Spouse	Bishop	Year Elected	Elected From	First Episcopal Assignment
SE	Shirley Ann Cundiff Bethea	Joseph Benjamin Bethea	1988	North Carolina AC	Columbia
SE	Mariam Flora Crawford Hancock	Charles Wilbourne Hancock	1988	South Georgia AC	Alabama-West Florida
SE	Mera Gay Hughes	Harold Hasbrouck Hughes Jr	1988	Virginia AC	Florida
SE	Dorothy Stricklin Lee	Clay Foster Lee Jr	1988	Mississippi AC	Holston
SE	Carolyn Adele McKeithen Looney	Richard Carl Looney	1988	Holston AC	South Georgia
SE	Syble Mink Spain	Robert Hitchcock Spain	1988	Tennessee AC	Louisville
SE	Jean Stevens Stockton	Thomas Barber Stockton	1988	Western North Carolina AC	Richmond
W	Mae Marie "Mitzi" Eggers Dew	William W. Dew Jr	1988	California-Nevada AC	Portland (Oregon)
Central Conferences	Marta Bolleter-Zellweger	Heinrich Bolleter	1989	Switzerland-France AC	Central and Southern Europe
Central Conferences	Luciana da Silva Clementa Fernandes	Moises Domingos Fernandes	1988	Angola	Eatern Angola
Central Conferences	Annegret Klaiber	Walter Klaiber	1989	South Germany AC	West Germany
Central Conferences	Nocia Madonela Machado	Joao Somane Machado	1988	Mozambique	Mozambique
Central Conferences	Kaija-Riikka Växby	Hans Växby	1989	Finland Swedish Provisional AC	Baltic and Nordic

NOTE: The *Discipline* also lists the following other bishop elected in this quadrennium: Susan Murch Morrison.

Joining by Marriage This Quadrennium

Spouse	Year Married	Bishop	Where Serving
Velma Duell McConnell	1988	Calvin McConnell	Portland (Oregon)
Marie Schnake White Webb	1991	Lance Webb	Retired

Highlights of Our Life Together: 1988–1992

Unless otherwise noted, the information in "Our Life Together" segments is based on the memory and personal notes of the author and information found in the episcopal spouses' scrapbooks and minutes.

Fall Council Meeting, 1988—St. Simon's Island, GA

The spouses enjoyed a dramatic monologue based on *Beloved Invader,* a novel written by Eugenia Price and set on St. Simon's Island. They also enjoyed a luncheon at the Cloister and toured the Carley Zell and Portman Homes on Sea Island. Some traveled to Savannah to visit the Wesley sites there.

Spring Council Meeting, April 28–May 5, 1989—Raleigh, NC

The spouses were offered tours of the region, including Duke University and lunch at the North Carolina Museum of Art. A service dedicating the new 1989 edition of *The United Methodist Hymnal* provided proud moments for Bishops Job, Handy, and Bashore, and **Marji Tuell** and Mary Brooke Casad (daughter of Ben and **Nancy Oliphant**), all of whom had served on the revision committee. Some spouses sat in on Bishop Felton May's presentations on urban poverty. **Ethelou Talbert** was elected president.

Fall Council Meeting, November 7–10, 1989—Lake Junaluska, NC

During this meeting, **Marji Tuell** recalled, Bishop Minor, bishop of East Germany, came into the meeting room and announced in a stunned voice, "The wall is coming down!" (Oden & Williams, 167). **Zoraida Galvan** delighted the group by bringing her young son, Gabriel, to the meeting. **Sabine Ndoricimpa** spoke about events and conditions in Burundi.

Spring Council Meeting, April 28–May 4, 1990—Detroit, MI

The spouses visited Greenfield Village and the Henry Ford Museum, the General Motors Complex, and the Detroit Institute of Arts. They enjoyed tea at the episcopal residence. Some of them rode the People Mover, an automated elevated car system that loops around the downtown area. **Shirley Skeete** was elected president.

Fall Council Meeting, November 3–9, 1990—Fort Worth, TX

This meeting was held in conjunction with The National Gathering of the Fellowship of United Methodists, a bishops' initiative calling people together to share the joy of sharing Christ (email communication with Bishop Sherer-Simpson). The spouses enjoyed a visit to Harris Memorial Hospital for lunch and a talk by heart-transplant specialist Dr. DeBakey; a trip to the Omni Theater; and a tea at the episcopal residence hosted by **Mary Jean Russell**. **Marji Tuell** remembers **Mitzi Dew** and **Kathy Thomas-Sano** laughing as they sat fully dressed in the oversized bathtub at the episcopal residence. During high tea at the Worthington Hotel, hosted by the Bass family of Radio Shack and other fame, bishops' spouses were each asked to serve as a table host/hostess. During a tour of the North Fort Worth Stockyards, **Ethelou Talbert** and **Martha Borgen** took the opportunity to sit on the wooden horses (Tuell Diary).

Spring Council Meeting, April 27–May 3, 1991—Jackson, MS

The spouses enjoyed trips to Vicksburg National Park, the Good Shepherd Social Center, Old Capital Historical Museum, and the Smith-Robertson Museum, which is dedicated to Mississippi's civil rights struggle. They were invited to a dinner at Millsaps College, a tea at the episcopal residence, and coffee at the governor's mansion. **Frances Fitzgerald** was elected president. Discussion by the Council included updates on developments in the UMC in Germany, as impacted by the reunification of East and West Germany; developments in Russia, where political changes were providing new opportunities for church growth; and a consultation on racism (Oden & Williams, 174–175).

Fall Council Meeting, November 2–8, 1991—Lake Junaluska, NC

The spouses gathered at Lambuth Inn for a luncheon and style show. The Council held serious discussion about the Global Nature of the Church and prepared a proposal, which was on the General Conference agenda each quadrennium until it passed in 2008, but failed ratification by the annual conferences (Oden & Williams, 175–177).

Spring Council Meeting, April 27–May 1—Lexington, KY, and General Conference, May 5–16, 1992—Louisville, KY

The spouses visited Shakertown, the governor's mansion, and a country club, where they viewed the televised running of the Kentucky Derby. **Angelina Nacpil** brought her young son. **Charles Christopher** was elected president of the Spouses' Association. Jack Tuell brought concerns about the rioting and fires in the city of Los Angeles to the Council, resulting in a resolution referred to and passed by the General Conference (Oden & Williams, 178–179).

Reflections and Personal Stories

Nocia Madonela Machado: My Faith Journey

"I was born into a family of believers. My father was a pastor and my mother an active and very devoted believer. Since childhood I was taught to pray. I attended Vacation Bible School and also Sunday school. When I was 12 years old, I had to leave my parents to go to a girls' boarding school of the Methodist Episcopal Church. There, during a prayer session, I heard the voice of God calling me, telling me to give my life to Christ, who died and was resurrected for my salvation. I started to dedicate my life to the service of God and completed the Bible Course to become a Spiritual Leader, teaching the Bible to other girls, as well as teaching them to read and write. Later I enrolled in the nursing course in order to better serve my neighbors, both physically and spiritually.

"During this period, I met a youth, Joao Somane Machado, who is my husband today and one of the bishops of The United Methodist Church. We married and went to Brazil and later to Congo, preparing ourselves for pastoral ministry. I always felt the necessity to increase my knowledge in order to help women, not only those belonging to the church, but also all over our country. More than 65 percent of our women are illiterate and very poor. That is why I continue to answer the call to help women and youth in literacy and adult education, in the struggle against HIV/AIDS, and in other programs. I would like to do more, but God knows the challenges I face. . . .

"The United Methodist Church in Mozambique has two conferences (North of Save River and South of Save River) with 22 districts. The two conferences together have 35,228 active women members of the United Methodist Church Women's Society (UMCWS), [which] holds two conferences per year at the church and district level. At [the] central level, it holds an annual conference every two years. We promote seminars for the society's leadership, including pastors' wives, on disease prevention, especially HIV/AIDS, malaria, and tuberculosis. We also offer seminars about the various issues confronting women in their daily lives, both inside and outside the church. . . .

"The extreme poverty affecting all of Mozambique causes extreme poverty for our women, making it difficult for our centers to fully respond to such needs. The majority of our women live in rural areas, where HIV/AIDS disease is common and where the poverty rate is highest. Women in rural areas need assistance in the areas of literacy, human rights in their homes and families, and protection of their rights in the society as a whole.

"We believe the literacy program can empower women in the struggle for the self-sufficiency. . . . Such opportunities can change the present scenario whereby a widow is subject to appropriation of her family belongings, even her home, by the deceased husband's family—a situation that leaves her and her children in complete hopelessness. The United Methodist Church Women's Society in Mozambique promotes actions . . . to minimize and correct this social evil against women. However, in spite of much local effort, we lack adequate human and financial resources to eliminate this problem completely.

"I want to thank the General Board of Global Ministries and all the conferences of The United Methodist Church for their moral and material support. I thank God Almighty for the life and courage He gives me to work for UMCWS."

—Nocia Madonela Machado, general councilor of UMCWS, Mozambique, 2005

Dot Lee's Window on History: Racial Tensions

During the civil rights movement, the Ku Klux Klan burned a cross on the lawn of Clay and **Dot Lee**. When local restaurants refused to serve visiting FBI agents, Dot invited them to dinner at their home. This invitation was more than welcome, because she was known as an outstanding cook (https://www.umnews.org/en/news/2017-remembering-notable-church-members).

A Tribute to My Mama, Luciana Da Silva Clemente Fernandes

"Words are not enough to tell about my beloved Mom. In Proverbs 6:20-23 (NIV), God's Word tells us 'keep your father's command / and do not forsake your mother's teaching. / . . . / For this command is a lamp, / this teaching is a light, / and correction and instruction / are the way to life.' We were taught by our parents that when we keep and follow God's commandments, in return, we receive protection, teaching, guidance, lots of beautiful values and many blessings. My mother is our queen, our star because we learn from her many values that guide us in everyday life, edify us, and define us today.

"She is a brave mom, kind, patient and smart. My mom prays for us, and because of her prayers, I feel safe, confident and secure because I belong to her. Even though I live in a country different from her, I feel protected by God because my mother is always praying for me and my siblings. The Bible teaches us that we should honor our parents. God in divine perfection brought me into this world through my mother's womb. I thank God and I am very honored and proud to be one of my mom's children for many different reasons. My mama, **Luciana da Silva Clemente Fernandes**, is a mom with a generous heart. Her beauty comes from inside and out, extremely strong and humble, and she has great biblical values. She reflects the example of Queen Esther of the Bible, a loyal, wise and courageous queen. She raised eight children with discipline, lots of love, and affection. When my father was studying theology in Cuba for four years, my mother took care of us with her determination, faith, hard work, courage, and—above all—trust in God." —Isabel de Sousa, January 2018

Velma McConnell's Witness

On Human Relations Sunday, January 17, 2016, Velma spoke at her church, using as her text Proverbs 31:8 from the Common English Bible: "Speak out on behalf of the voiceless / and for the rights of all who are vulnerable." In her talk, she declared that the language in *The United Methodist Book of Discipline* amounts to discrimination against a certain group of people (the LGBTQIA+ community) and states that "this has become not only a *Religious* issue, but in our time a *Civil Rights*, a *Human Rights*, a *Family Rights* issue involving children, youth, adults, elders, of how we respond to Jesus' teaching to love God with heart, mind, and soul and to love our neighbors as ourselves!" Velma's remarks make clear why she declares herself to be a Reconciling United Methodist.

She describes herself as having been born to a mother of the first generation of women to vote, of being mentored by strong women teachers and clergywomen, Sunday school teachers, youth counselors, sisters, peers, our daughters-in-love, and strong gentle men . . . including our sons. . . .

"In college, a lesbian dorm-mate lived across the hall, and a gay friend, who aspired to become a Methodist pastor, was active in our Wesley Foundation. That is also where I met and married my first husband, Paul. With every job advancement, we transferred our church membership to a nearby Methodist Church, including Jason Lee UMC in Salem, and for the next 26 years we related to Willamette University.

"Both my husband, Paul, and Cal McConnell's wife, Mary, died of cancer; in 1988 my pastor, David Weekley, read our vows of marriage in the Jason Lee Sanctuary. . . .

"When Cal was assigned to serve as bishop of the Pacific Northwest Conference, based in Seattle, I stated my preference for placing my membership with a Reconciling Congregation and joined the Wallingford UMC, where I was active for eight years. In this wonderful congregation, I experienced the affirmation of gay, lesbian, and bisexual partnerships and the celebration of the adoptions and baptisms of their children, along with other young families seeking to rear their children in an inclusive, loving United Methodist community of faith.

"A memorable moment for me occurred when I was volunteering with the Multi-faith AIDS Project of Seattle (MAPS). During the final weeks of his life, a young Western Orthodox priest sought a Spiritual Companion. His partner, also a priest, relieved of congregational duties by their bishop, was appointed as caregiver. . . . Sometimes I could provide respite for his partner's hospital vigils. On my last visit with him, after our sharing meditations from his prayer book,

I asked if he had any requests. Without hesitation, Ken asked me to wash his feet. A nurse brought heated towels and warm water, rolling back the covers to reveal those painful, swollen, yellow-waxy feet. I wept in the knowledge that I was bathing the feet of Christ.

"The rest, shall we say, is history, as same-sex marriage and equal rights have become legal. Sadly, however, in our global UMC, the practice of homosexuality is the only act specifically named as a sin, which ignores the reality of homosexual experience, casts shame on homosexual persons, denies them support for committed relationships, and in some countries justifies execution. . . . I encourage you to open your eyes and hearts, to recognize the Christ in others, to acknowledge persons who need a hug, and encouraging word, a listening ear, a smile, or a thank you." —personal document shared with Jane Ives, May 2016

Annegret Klaiber's Story

"I was born August 10, 1938, the oldest of five children of my parents, Willi and Ruth Kaiser, in Tübingen, an old university city in the southwest of Germany. There I spent my childhood, my schooldays, and a part of my course of study in medicine. I live there now again, together with my husband, Walter Klaiber, in our retirement. During our years of study (Walter in theology and I in medicine) we learned to know and to love one another. We married in 1965 immediately after Walter's graduation.

"Our journey together led us to Nürnberg, Walter's first appointment, then for another two years to Tübingen, and after this for 18 years to Reutlingen, where Walter served as professor and dean of the Theological School. After Walter's election to the episcopacy in 1989, we moved to Frankfurt. During all these years, I worked part-time as a physician, partly as assistant in medical practices, partly as medical instructor in the education of pre-school teachers and youth care workers, and in Frankfurt as a medical consultant and counselor in a center for addicted persons. For two years, I served as head of this institution. In 2005, we both retired and came back to Tübingen.

"Three sons were born to us and grew up, learned professions, married and had children. Today we have seven grandchildren: three girls and four boys.

"Formative experiences in my life included:

"*World War II.* When I was one year old, my father was drafted, and during my whole childhood he served as a soldier on the front line. He returned seven years later from French war captivity, where many prisoners of war died from hunger and diseases. During those years, I was very often confronted with the news that the daddies of my friends were killed or missing in action, especially in Russia. There were many bomb alarms and we had to spend many nights in an air-raid shelter. Later I realized that the enemies were also daddies of children from another country. All of this was sad and painful and difficult to comprehend.

"I experienced much dying and death in my family, in our neighborhood, and among our circle of friends. I was especially challenged by the fact that even children and young people had to die. These experiences caused me to ask for help and later impressed on me that I myself should contribute to help other people, e.g. to give first aid and to care for people who are weak or sick. That was the reason I choose to become a medical doctor.

"*My Family.* Of special importance to me as a child were my four siblings, my brave mother, my grandparents, and especially my godmother. Later of course, I had my own family: my husband and our three sons. In both cases, I cherished the reliable togetherness and the love which carried us through even in difficult times.

"*The Church.* We belonged to a congregation of the Evangelical United Brethren in Tübingen, where I grew up taking part in the children's Sunday school and in the worship services. Later I became an active member, participating in the work with children, youth and women, and especially singing in the choir. Taking decisive steps in faith within the fellowship of the church has brought me to a place of lasting security and comfort, in relationship both to God and among people."

—written 2017

Chapter 18

1992–1996

Spouses Who Joined the Episcopal Family 1992–1996

Detailed profiles and citation information can be found in Part 5, beginning on page 251.

Jurisdiction or Central Conferences	Spouse	Bishop	Year Elected	Elected From	First Episcopal Assignment
NC	Margaret Crawford Jordan	Charles Wesley Jordan	1992	Northern Illinois AC	Iowa
NC	Janet Edith Pass Ott	Donald A. Ott	1992	Wisconsin AC	Michigan
NC	Blaine B. Rader	Sharon Zimmerman Rader	1992	West Michigan AC	Wisconsin
NE	Jane P. Ives	S. Clifton Ives	1992	Maine AC	West Virginia
NE	Wha-Sei P. Kim	Hae Jong Kim	1992	Northern New Jersey AC	New York West
SC	Raquel Mora Martinez	Joel Neftali Martinez	1992	Rio Grande AC	Nebraska

Jurisdiction or Central Conferences	Spouse	Bishop	Year Elected	Elected From	First Episcopal Assignment
SC	Etta Mae McClurg Mutti	Albert Frederick Mutti	1992	Missouri West AC	Kansas
SC	Mackie L. Harper Norris	Alfred L. Norris Sr	1992	Louisiana AC	New Mexico; Northwest Texas
SC	Lavelle Owen	Raymond Harold Owen	1992	Oklahoma AC	San Antonio
SC	Robert Glenn Sherer Jr	Amelia Ann Brookshire Sherer	1992	Texas AC	Missouri
SC	Zoe Strickland Wilson	Joe A. Wilson	1992	Texas AC	Fort Worth
SE	Linda Miller Carder	Kenneth Lee Carder	1992	Holston AC	Nashville
SE	Faye Thomas Fannin	Robert E. Fannin	1992	Florida AC	Birmingham
SE	Hannah Campbell Meadors	Marshall LeRoy (Jack) Meadors Jr	1992	South Carolina AC	Mississippi
SE	Mary Virginia Head Morris	William Wesley Morris	1992	Tennessee AC	Alabama-West Florida
W	Jeff Swenson	Mary Ann McDonald Swenson	1992	Pacific-Northwest AC	Denver
Central Conferences	Ruth Mandac Arichea	Daniel C. Arichea Jr	1994	Asia- Pacific Area United Bible Societies	Baguio
Central Conferences	Kerike Christiana Dabale	Done Peter Dabale	1992	Nigeria	Nigeria
Central Conferences	Nancy Mamie Humper	Joseph Christian Humper	1992	Sierra Leone AC	Sierra Leone
Central Conferences	Edith Munjoma Jokomo	Christopher Jokomo	1992	Zimbabwe AC	Zimbabwe

NOTE: The *Discipline* also lists the following other bishop elected in this quadrennium: Benjamin Gutierrez (1994).

Joining by Marriage This Quadrennium

Spouse	Year Married	Bishop	Where Serving
Marion Salisbury Hall Clark	1992	Roy Clyde Clark	Retired
Helen Fannings Ammons	1993	Edsel Ammons	Retired

Joining by Special Concordat This Quadrennium

Autonomous Affiliated Church	Maribel Bonilla Serrano	Victor L. Bonilla	1993	Puerto Rico	Methodist Church in Puerto Rico

(NOTE: The editors have been unable to determine what year the special concordat, bringing the bishop of The Methodist Church in Puerto Rico into the Council of Bishops, took place; Bishop Bonilla may have joined the Council at this time or later.)

Highlights of Our Life Together: 1992–1996

Unless otherwise noted, the information in "Our Life Together" segments is based on the memory and personal notes of the author and information found in the episcopal spouses' scrapbooks and minutes.

Fall Council Meeting, October 31–November 6, 1992—St. Simon's Island, GA

During the Spouses' Association meeting, new members were invited to share a few words about their faith journeys. **Ruth Thomas** (see p. 119) and **Etta Mae Mutti** (see p. 191) shared their stories in greater detail. A very moving worship service, with interpretive dance by **Jean Stockton**, addressed the challenges spouses face while transitioning into the episcopacy and moving to new areas. The Council meeting included retreat sessions for the bishops, during which times Janice Grana, World Editor and Publisher of The Upper Room, led the spouses in a study of Bonhoeffer's *Life Together*. The small group discussions helped us get to know and understand one another at a deeper level. Those of us from the US were especially moved and humbled by learning about the experiences of spouses from the Central Conferences. **Edith Jokomo** from Zimbabwe, for example, shared that she was sometimes asked to prepare for burial the bodies of deceased clergy spouses in their area (see p. 39).

Spring Council Meeting, April 30–May 7, 1993—San Diego, CA

The spouses enjoyed tours of Balboa Park, the San Diego Zoo, and several social service sites. **Anne Hearn** recalled being sure the group would not dress up for the trip to the zoo, but she turned out to be the only one wearing slacks (conversation with Anne Hearn, Summer 2015). Some spouses rode a streetcar to the Mexican border and walked over into Tijuana for some shopping. **Anne Hearn** was elected president.

Fall Council Meeting, October 30–November 5, 1993— Simpsonwood Retreat Center, Norcross, GA

A spouses' choir sang for Council worship one day. Spouses visited the Carter Center and Martin Luther King Jr's home and memorial. **Anne Hearn** later reported that, when she was president, she created a clear agenda for the business meeting and held the group to it, resulting in considerably less tension, speaking out, and arguing (conversation with Anne Hearn, Summer 2015). The members voted to pay their own way for outings, instead of allowing the hosting area to spend large amounts of money entertaining us. The members also voted to make a donation to a mission project chosen by the hosting bishop's spouse for each meeting.

Spring Council Meeting, April 30–May 6, 1994—Rochester, NY

Some spouses took a bus trip to Niagara Falls. Some visited and volunteered at mission sites: sorting clothing at a thrift shop, serving at a soup kitchen, and touring community centers. A group of spouses, seeing how much the bishops appreciated their covenant groups, decided to form one for themselves. Others soon formed as well. This turned out to be a vital experience for those who chose to participate, providing a setting for personal sharing, promoting mutual support, and deepening friendships. The confidentiality of such a group provided a place for exploring feelings and sharing struggles, helping many of us experience that we were not alone in trying to figure out how to live authentically in this new role. **Kathy Thomas-Sano** was elected president.

Fall Council Meeting, October 28–November 4, 1994—Lake Junaluska, NC

Gwen White led a spiritual retreat on "Integral Spirituality" and shared about her experiences participating in and leading covenant groups. **Marji Tuell** recalls being handed a small globe, with the suggestion to pray for the world while holding it (Tuell Diary).

Spring Council Meeting, April 29–May 5, 1995—Austin, TX

The spouses toured the San Antonio River Walk and the Alamo, visited the UMLAUF Statuary Park/Museum, and enjoyed a boat ride on the canal. Members of the class of 1992, wanting something more than the spouses' orientation we had experienced, had worked together to produce a "Thrival Kit" to present to the spouses of newly elected bishops during the fall meeting at Lake Junaluska. The Thrival Kit, a three-ring binder with sections for different topics, included statements and brief articles by various spouses sharing how they had coped with the challenges of transitioning to a new area and role, keeping in touch with their families, continuing their own professional life, entertaining, and so on. The theme for the Thrival Kit was *diversity*, affirming that there is no one right way to be a bishop's spouse, but that each individual needs to find a way to live out his or her personal calling in the particular area to which the bishop is assigned. The Thrival Kit work group presented its work to the Association for review and feedback and invited spouses to order copies for themselves. **Marilina DeCarvalho** was elected president.

Thrival: the ability to transcend survival. Thriving as a way of being. A state in which the circumstances do not dictate the outcome. Usually accompanied by highly effective self-care and other indicators of wellness. Transcends the actual doingness of things.

—Bill Cumming, School Solutions, Litchfield, Maine

During this Council meeting, some council members observed the hotel staff ignoring a table of people from Zaire, never even taking their orders, and followed up by reporting this snub to the restaurant and hotel manager (Tuell Diary).

Fall Council Meeting, October 28–November 3, 1995—Lake Junaluska, NC

Don Messer, theologian, author, and president of Iliff School of Theology was invited to lead a spiritual retreat.

Spring Council Meeting and General Conference, April 16–26, 1996—Denver, CO

Jack Tuell celebrated his recovery from double hip replacement by doing a few dance steps during the Council meeting prior to General Conference. The Association formalized the organization of covenant groups, polling the group to find out who would be interested in participating in the upcoming quadrennium. It was decided that after the upcoming elections, new groups would be formed in order to include the spouses of newly elected bishops and promote more diverse relationships. **Phyllis May** was elected president. During worship prior to the Episcopal Address at General Conference, a choir of bishops and spouses sang a hymn, which **Jean Stockton** interpreted with sacred dance. Hillary Clinton brought greetings to the General Conference and told about how her experiences in a Methodist youth group influenced her.

Reflections and Personal Stories

Etta Mae Mutti's Story

"In December of 1988, we received a call from our middle son, Fred, telling us he had the pneumonia that is associated with HIV/AIDS. At that time, this was definitely a death sentence, as there were very few drugs available to combat this disease. We had to absorb the reality that our son was going to die, and he was only 26 years old. Then our oldest son, Tim, called us in April of 1989 to tell us that he, too, was HIV positive. What a cruel blow to learn that we now had two sons with an incurable illness. Over the next three years, we watched our sons try to fight off the ravaging of their bodies caused by such infections as pneumocystis pneumonia, Kaposi sarcoma, pancreatitis, hepatitis, and tuberculosis. We traveled back and forth from our home in Kansas City to Atlanta and New York, where they were living, so we could be with them as much as possible. We saw them fight not only illness but also the stigma and discrimination that was so prevalent at that time. Death finally arrived for Tim in December of 1990, and Fred succumbed to the disease in September of 1991. Within a nine-month period, we lost two of our three sons.

"During all this, it was the sustaining presence of God that strengthened us. It was our assurance in the resurrection that enabled us to get through the worst of times. Later we shared our story by writing *Dancing in a Wheelchair: One Family Faces HIV/AIDS* (Nashville: Abingdon, 2001). Although writing the book helped us process our feelings and heal, it was never easy. As we wrote, 'We relived our anguish as we moved from chapter to chapter. Every day, as we sat at the keyboard composing, the memories forced up tears and sighs' (127).

"In some ways we began the grieving process when we first learned that both Tim and Fred were infected with HIV. At first we denied it, but then we admitted that AIDS is a terminal illness. Anger never got us down. We felt no need to blame our sons for getting sick. We did not blame God, who we always knew as a loving, sustaining presence. We prayed to God, begging for a cure, longing for the gift of more time. Probably we bargained with God, offering somehow to change our lives if these petitions could be answered. We accepted the realities of living with AIDS and counted on God, our family, loved ones, and friends to stand with us through the ordeal (92).

"We received overwhelming support from friends and colleagues throughout this ordeal: hugs, prayers, and remarkable offers of practical assistance, even though we were slow to share our sad news because we feared how people might react. We had suspected that Tim and Fred might be gay from the time they were in grade school, but they did not 'come out' to us until they were out of college. We were shocked and saddened when Fred and later Tim admitted that they were afraid to tell us because they feared we would reject them.

"We were quick to assure both boys of our love and acceptance, but sadly they—and we—did experience expressions of rejection and hatred from those with a limited understanding of homosexuality. The Westboro Baptist Church targeted Fritz with hateful signs and speeches during several conferences we attended. During the 1988 episcopal election process, a colleague told Fritz he should tell our sons that their homosexuality was a sin and that we could not accept their lifestyle. Fritz replied that we do not believe sexual orientation is a choice and that 'God surely would not condemn those who had no choice in the matter' (122). We thank God for those who opened their hearts to us, came to be with us at different times through this trial, offered financial and practical support to help us cope, and spoke up for us and our sons. . . .

"We continue to witness for AIDS sufferers and their families, working through the Global AIDS Fund project of our church."

Chapter 19

1996–2000

Spouses Who Joined the Episcopal Family 1996–2000

Detailed profiles and citation information can be found in Part 5, beginning on page 251.

Jurisdiction or Central Conferences	Spouse	Bishop	Year Elected	Elected From	First Episcopal Assignment
NC	Marsha Lynn England Coyner	Michael J. Coyner	1996	North Indiana AC	Dakotas
NC	Elaine M. Smithson Hopkins	John Lowry Hopkins	1996	South Indiana AC	Minnesota
NC	Beverly Keaton	Jonathan D. Keaton	1996	Northern Illinois AC	Ohio East
NC	Diane Sprague	C. Joseph Sprague	1996	Ohio West AC	Chicago
NE	Merrill Hassinger	Susan Wolfe Hassinger	1996	Eastern Pennsylvania AC	Boston
NE	Eleanor Lyght	Ernest S. Lyght	1996	Northern New Jersey AC	New York

Jurisdiction or Central Conferences	Spouse	Bishop	Year Elected	Elected From	First Episcopal Assignment
SC	Robert Wolff Huie	Janice Riggle Huie	1996	Southwest Texas AC	Arkansas
SE	Martha Elnor Gunsalus Chamberlain	Ray Willis Chamberlain Jr	1996	Virginia AC	Holston
SE	Jennifer Mink Davis	George Lindsey Davis	1996	Kentucky AC	North Georgia
SE	Linda Layfield Edwards Foster	Marion Mortimer Edwards	1996	South Georgia AC	Raleigh
SE	Dorothye Carithers Henderson	Cornelius Linton Henderson	1996	North Georgia AC	Florida
SE	Leigh Kammerer	Charlene Payne Kammerer	1996	Florida AC	Charlotte
SE	Margaret Fowler McCleskey	James Lawrence McCleskey	1996	Western North Carolina	Columbia
SE	Janene Deloris Pennel	Joe Edward Pennel Jr	1996	Tennessee AC	Richmond
W	Carol L. Paup	Edward W. Paup	1996	Rocky Mountain AC	Portland
Central Conferences	Nshimba Ntambo Nkula	Ntambo Nkulu Ntanda	1996	North Sheba AC	North Katanga

NOTE: The *Discipline* also lists the following other bishops elected in this quadrennium: Alfred Johnson (1996) and Peter D. Weaver (1996).

Joining by Marriage This Quadrennium

Spouse	Year Married	Bishop	Where Serving
Billie Jo Sanders	1997	Bishop Carl Julian Sanders	Retired
Katherine Crum Irwin Tullis	1997	Bishop Edward Lewis Tullis	Retired

Joining by Special Concordat This Quadrennium

Autonomous Affiliated Church	Iris Janet Rivera	Juan A. Vera Mendez	2009	Puerto Rico	Methodist Church in Puerto Rico

Highlights of Our Life Together: 1996–2000

Unless otherwise noted, the information in "Our Life Together" segments is based on the memory and personal notes of the author and information found in the episcopal spouses' scrapbooks and minutes.

Fall Council Meeting, October 26–November 1, 1996— St. Simon Island, GA

During the Association meeting, some spouses of retiring bishops shared their personal stories. **Velma McConnell** displayed T-shirts from her various adventures and involvements on an improvised clothesline. Retiring spouses from the Southeastern Jurisdiction sang a humorous song about the itineracy, making just a few changes to the wording of Ernest K. Emurian's "Don't Take the Pictures Off the Wall" (https://newspaperarchive.com/raleigh-register-jul-01-1957-p-4/).

Dr. Mackie Norris presented a program on Holistic Health. A number of spouses participated in the launch of the Council's Children and Poverty Initiative.

Spring Council Meeting, 1997—Des Moines, IA

The spouses went to visit the Dutch community of Pella, toured the state capitol, enjoyed a luncheon at which Lt. Governor Joy Cummins spoke, and attended a tea hosted by the warm and welcoming women of Walnut Hills United Methodist Church. The spouses also enjoyed luncheons at Wesley Acres Retirement Home and the Strawtown Inn. During the meeting, spouses of newly elected bishops shared their faith journeys. **Elaine Hopkins** presented a plan for creating spouse directories. **Martha Morgan** was elected president.

Fall Council Meeting, November 1–7, 1997—Lake Junaluska, NC

Marilyn Oden led a relationship-building retreat day for the spouses with the theme "Weave Us Together." A children's choir sang for the bishops and spouses during dinner one evening. The spouses' choir sang for worship one morning. **Phyllis May** shared with her covenant group the suffering she had observed during a visit to refugee camps in Rwanda, and in response the group enlisted the Association to make a churchwide appeal for shoes, which brought in thousands of pairs of shoes for the Rwandan children (see p. 200).

Spring Council Meeting, April 25–May 1, 1998—Lincoln, NE

The spouses enjoyed a tour of the capitol building; tea at the episcopal residence of **Raquel Martinez**; and a luncheon at the Cornhusker restaurant. **Kim White** was elected president.

Fall Council Meeting, October 30–November 6, 1998—
Simpsonwood Retreat Center, Norcross, GA

The spouses planned and led one of the Council worship services. This was a momentous change, given that 26 years earlier, the bishops had only reluctantly allowed the spouses to worship *with* them. Over time, when there was no bishop-pianist available, some were invited to play the piano for worship, and others were invited to read Scripture or liturgy. The invitation to fully plan and lead worship for the Council seemed to be a milestone. Spouse tours included visits to Martin Luther King Jr's home and the Carter Center. **Ruth Handy** taught the group how to make silk flowers, and **Faye Fannin** led a seminar on grandparenting.

Spring Council Meeting, May 1–7, 1999—Chattanooga, TN

The bishops and spouses enjoyed a dinner served at the Tennessee Aquarium. Other activities included a trip to Lookout Mountain and a ride on the Incline Railway there, a boat ride on the Chattanooga River, a visit to First Century Inner City Ministry, and a tour of a cave. Because a number of members had expressed concerns about a lack of inclusivity in our group, the Executive Committee of the Association assigned a team to plan and lead a workshop on community building during the fall 1999 meeting. **Marilyn Oden** was elected president.

Fall Council Meeting, October 30–November 5, 1999—
Lake Junaluska, NC

Hannah Meadors, deeply moved by a June 1999 visit with her husband to camps for Kosovo refugees in Macedonia, recruited a team of bishops' spouses to visit Kosovo in the fall of 1999 at their own expense. Traveling with an UMCOR team, Hannah, **Mitzi Dew**, **Leigh Kammerer**, and **Jane Ives** visited four different schools, delivering school kits and sports equipment to children and teachers who had survived the war there. During the fall Council meeting, those who had traveled to Kosovo shared highlights of that experience with the full Council.

As directed by the Executive Committee during the last Council meeting, a team of spouses, including **Margaret Jordan**, **Helen Ammons**, **Margaret McCleskey**, and others led a community-building workshop. After listening to a panel of four spouses sharing their experiences of feeling excluded, small group conversations and large group discussion focused on identifying actions to take to foster a stronger feeling of community within the Episcopal Spouses' Association (email communication from Margaret Jordan, 6/18/18). Participants signed a covenant listing 10 such actions to take at future meetings, such as intentionally sitting with persons we don't know, participating in personal sharing and community-building activities, and giving and receiving hospitality without judgment and with consideration for the uniqueness of each person's journey. It was decided to put the covenant in the Thrival Kit notebook as reminder of this intent (Thrival Kit Notebook, 13, in Bishops' Spouses' Collection, UM Archives and History Center).

During this Council meeting, the spouses also enjoyed a Bible study led by Dr. Evelyn Laycock. A group of spouses met to begin establishing a network to support UMCOR in its work with children and mothers in crisis.

Spring Council Meeting April 25–May 2, and General Conference, May 2–12, 2000—Cleveland, OH

The spouses toured Stan Hywet Hall and Gardens, had lunch at Tangier Restaurant, and enjoyed a tea in Akron. The covenant groups that had been meeting for the quadrennium held their last session. Eileen Carey, wife of the Archbishop of Canterbury, guest of the Council, spoke to the Association, emphasizing similarities between her experiences and relationships and ours. Staff from UMCOR held a day-long training workshop for the spouses about Community Based Primary Health Care and discussed ways to help promote mission education and support.

Mitzi Dew and other spouses organized mission sharing sessions called "Global Enrichment Presentations" for delegates and guests during General Conference. Among those who presented were spouses from Africa, Europe, the Philippines, and the United States. **Mitzi Dew** was elected president.

Window on History: A Slavery Museum

When the Council of Bishops asked Cliff to go to Angola to preside over the episcopal election at the West Africa Central Conference in the fall of 1996, I (**Jane Ives**) decided to accompany him. During our time there, we joined a bus tour to the National Slavery Museum about an hour away from Luanda. We were the only white people in the group, a fact that became increasingly uncomfortable as we filed somberly through the small white building perched on a bluff at one end of a wide stretch of white sandy beach. We could easily imagine slave ships anchored there, awaiting their cargo. Inside the museum, we saw shackles and chains and a few other artifacts, photographs, and maps. An interpreter pointed out the baptismal font, where, after being branded like cattle, the captives were baptized and given new names, then led through "the door of no return" to the ships. I hid my eyes from the others in the group and wept.

Window on History: Conflict in Africa

In 1984, after the assassination of the first democratically elected president of Burundi, to whom Bishop Ndoricimpa served as a spiritual advisor, he and **Sabine** were forced to leave Burundi, where he had served since his election in 1980. They lived in Kenya while he continued to work with the church in Burundi and expanded mission into Kenya, Tanzania, Uganda, and Sudan, areas that are now part of the East Africa Conference. John and Sabine returned to Burundi in 2000, by which time the conflict between Hutu and Tutsi tribes had claimed some 200,000 lives. He served there until his death in 2005 (http://archive.wfn.org/2005/08/msg00006.html).

Irene Innis and family were severely impacted by the Liberian Civil War, which began in 1989. (See p. 38 for her story.) In 1997, at the end of the civil war in Liberia, **Violet Kulah** and Arthur Kulah adopted 27 homeless and parentless children to raise along with seven children of their own (*Biographical Directory*, 2004–2008).

In 1990, fighting and pillaging in the Democratic Republic of Congo destroyed the training center where **Kasongo Maria Ngolo Wakadilo** taught sewing and other skills to pastors' spouses, needy, and handicapped persons (*Biographical Directory*, 1992; email communication with son Steve Wakadilo, July 2017).

Window on History: Phyllis May

As noted above and in chapter 3, **Phyllis May** joined a volunteers-in-mission team that went to Uvira, in the Democratic Republic of Congo or former Zaire, to work in camps for refugees from Rwanda in 1995. She remembers madness, killings, destruction, insanity, death. Hundreds of thousands fled to Goma and other towns of what was formerly Zaire. Millions of men, women, and children were killed. In a 2016 personal note to the author, she wrote: "Thanks be to God for allowing me, in some small way, to bring hope and healing and to share God's love for one month as a part of the Board of Global Ministries outreach. Along with many other United Methodists from around the world, we established housing, clinics, food stations, education centers, and opportunities for the young ones to share in play and socialization. We established a 'Refuge' for women, children, and men who had lost everything and in some cases everyone to whom they were related. 'All of God's children have shoes,' we used to sing, but no! These children had worn, bloody, blistered, cut feet with open sores. As I returned to my sisters and brothers in the Council of Bishops, I pled for shoes. In response, thousands of shoes were sent to Goma and distributed to the many refugee camps. God is so good! We are all His children, bone of His bone, flesh of his flesh. Called to help in time of need, we seek to live by the great commandment, to love God with our whole heart, mind, soul, and strength, and to love our neighbors as ourselves. To God be the Glory!"

Phyllis wrote eloquently about this experience for *New World Outlook* magazine, in an article titled "O God, Deliver Them! Deliver Us!" and published in the January/February 1995 issue. In the fall of 1997, during a Council meeting at Lake Junaluska, she told her covenant group about the experience. In response, the covenant group enlisted the spouses' organization to make a churchwide appeal for shoes. Impressed by the generous response and the effectiveness of the spouses' networking, the United Methodist Committee on Relief (UMCOR) encouraged and supported the development of a Mission Support Network for the Bishops' Spouses' Association.

Window on History: Aftermath of War in Kosovo

Hannah Meadors, deeply moved by a June 1999 visit with her husband to camps for Kosovo refugees in Macedonia, recruited a team of bishops' spouses to visit Kosovo in the fall of 1999. Traveling with an UMCOR team, they visited four different schools, delivering school kits and sports equipment to children and teachers who had survived the war.

Leigh Kammerer recalls: "I remember well the trip with **Hannah Meadors** and **Mitzi Dew** and **Jane Ives** to Kosovo and Macedonia in fall of 1999. They were so gracious and welcoming to me. I have never forgotten that. It was the first time I ever traveled out of continental North America. I vividly recall giving out school kits and how overwhelming and humbling it was to experience the excited response of the school children to such mundane items. I remember the speeches some of the students prepared and presented to us. I remember trying to drink the very strong tea we were served. I remember the very generous hospitality shown to us, and the evening we ate in a restaurant. When we used the facilities, the men's and women's were right next to each other with a very thin wall between. I could hear the women discussing the hole-in-the-floor toilet, and I yelled over to Mitzi not to fall in. Our laughter lightened the difficulties of this challenging journey as we witnessed the suffering of the people in Kosovo."

Jane Ives recalls: "We were overwhelmed by the greeting we received at the schools. Children who had suffered unspeakable horrors handed us huge bouquets of wildflowers, formed receiving lines to greet us, and opened their school kits with glee. 'Look what I got!' they exclaimed, holding up pencils, erasers, and other precious school supplies. We also toured areas that had been bombed and met with persons working to help the people recover from the devastation of the war. This experience inspired us to seek ways to promote mission education and support."

PART 4

UNITED METHODIST BISHOPS' SPOUSES IN A NEW CENTURY

2000–2018

Chapter 20

2000–2004

Spouses Who Joined the Episcopal Family 2000–2004

Detailed profiles and citation information can be found in Part 5, beginning on page 251.

Jurisdiction or Central Conferences	Spouse	Bishop	Year Elected	Elected From	First Episcopal Assignment
NC	Lamarr V. Gibson	Linda Lee	2000	Detroit AC	Michigan
NC	Charlene Ann Feldner Ough	Bruce R. Ough	2000	Iowa AC	West Ohio
NC	Cynthia Palmer	Gregory Vaughn Palmer	2000	East Ohio AC	Iowa
SC	Joye Fay Stokes Chamness	Benjamin Roy Chamness	2000	Texas AC	Fort Worth
SC	Kay Arcille Hutchinson	William Wayne Hutchinson	2000	New Mexico AC	Louisiana

Jurisdiction or Central Conferences	Spouse	Bishop	Year Elected	Elected From	First Episcopal Assignment
SC	Jewell Lena Wells Moncure	Rhymes H. Moncure Jr	2000	Missouri East AC	Dallas
SC	Valerie Vaughn Whitfield	David Max Whitfield	2000	North Arkansas AC	Northwest Texas-New Mexico
SE	Deborah Phoebe Cox Goodpaster	Larry Martin Goodpaster	2000	Mississippi AC	Alabama-West Florida
SE	Margaret Rosetta Hayden King	James R. King	2000	USA: Alabama, California, Tennessee	Louisville
SE	Margaret Lee Watson	Benjamin Michael Watson	2000	Alabama-West Florida AC	South Georgia
SE	Melba Jarvis Whitaker	Timothy W. Whitaker	2001	Virginia AC	Florida
W	Minnie Jones Brown	Warner H. Brown Jr	2000	California-Nevada AC	Denver
Central Conferences	Lucrécia Manual Alexandre Domingos	Gaspar João Domingos	2000	Angola	West Angola
Central Conferences	Irene Janjay Zeon Innis	John G. Innis	2000	Liberia	Liberia
Central Conferences	Elizabeth Justo	Benjamin A. Justo	2000	Northeast Philippines AC	Baguio
Central Conferences	Toril Olsen	Øystein Olsen	2001	Norway AC	Nordic and Baltic
Central Conferences	Laurinda Vidal Quipungo	José Quipungo	2000	East Angola AC	East Angola
Central Conferences	Dania Aben Soriano	Leo A. Soriano	2000	Mindano (Philippines) AC	Davao
Central Conferences	Alegria Hembrador Toquero	Solito K. Toquero	2001	Bulacan (Philippines) AC	Manila

NOTE: The *Discipline* also lists the following other bishops elected in this quadrennium: Beverly J. Shamana (2000) and Violet L. Fisher (2000).

Joining by Marriage This Quadrennium

Spouse	Year Married	Bishop	Where Serving
Virginia Schoenbohm Clymer	2000	Bishop Wayne K. Clymer	Retired
Marilyn Ruth Williams Magee Talbert	2000	Bishop Melvin G. Talbert	Retired
Susan Thomas	2002	Bishop Neil L. Irons	Harrisburg Episcopal Area
Walter Woods	2002	Bishop Beverly J. Shamana	San Francisco Episcopal Area

Highlights of Our Life Together: 2000–2004

Unless otherwise noted, the information in "Our Life Together" segments is based on the memory and personal notes of the author and information found in the episcopal spouses' scrapbooks and minutes.

Fall Council Meeting, November 5–10, 2000—St. Simons Island, GA

During the business meeting, the spouses of newly elected bishops wore matching T-shirts that they had designed. Spouses of the class of 1996 presented a humorous skit about the life of bishops' spouses based on Dr. Seuss's *Oh, the Places You'll Go*! The Association voted to change the job of the historian to a quadrennial position, instead of annual, in order to provide more continuity for this role.

President **Mitzie Dew** gave "verbal bouquets" to three spouses who had made major leadership contributions in missions in their areas and around the world: (1) **Phyllis May** founded the Congress Heights UMC Academy for children in pre-school and elementary grades, worked in drug rehabilitation and homeless programs, and worked with women and children in refugee camps in the former country of Zaire, starting a school that met under a tree until the United Nations gave her a tent. (2) **Karen Blake** served on the Board of Trustees of Lydia Paterson Institute, a mission school of the UMC in El Paso, Texas and raised $500,000 for an endowment campaign. (3) **Hannah Meadors** worked with the state of Mississippi to strengthen education for children; traveled to refugee camps in Palestine, Macedonia, and Kosovo; recruited a team of bishops' spouses to visit and distribute school kits to children in Kosovo; spearheaded the organization of the Mission Support Network; and worked closely with the Children and Poverty Campaign.

Small groups, each including a new member, shared responses to the question, "What causes or concerns do you feel passionate about?" Later in the week, **Martha Chamberlain** offered a workshop on writing memoirs, and many enjoyed a sightseeing boat trip on the river. **Mary Morris** distributed new covenant group assignments and these groups met, as did the Mission Support Network (initially named Mother/Child Survival) and the task forces for the Spouses' Directory and for the Thrival Kits.

Spring Council Meeting, May 1–4, 2001—Scottsdale, AZ

Annual conference chancellors and some of their spouses participated in this meeting. The spouses visited the Heard Museum, where they learned about Native American and southwestern history and art. Tanya Griffith, a clergy spouse from the Desert Southwest Conference, entertained at a luncheon with several short monologues telling the stories of famous women. The bishops and spouses enjoyed the demonstrations of a Sidewalk Sunday School Mobile Ministry and other examples of United Methodist outreach ministries.

During the business meeting, **Charlene Ough** and **Deborah Goodpaster** shared their faith journeys. A master list of Big Brother/Sister assignments was shared, and members were invited to attend a meeting of the Mission Support Network (MSN). **Kashala Katembo** was elected president.

The MSN reviewed results of a survey through which spouses indicated different ways they might participate in the Mission Support Network. **Martha Chamberlain** gave a report of her recent trip with UMCOR to India, where she visited Jamkhead and learned more about Comprehensive Community-based Health Care. A number of other members reported on mission involvements in their areas. Prayer was offered for **Jo Stith**, who was traveling with UMCOR in Latin America.

Fall Council Meeting, November 4–9, 2001—Lake Junaluska, NC

During this meeting, the Council held sessions to prepare bishops and spouses for upcoming Global Visitations. During the spouses' meeting, **Marji Tuell** led a program using hymns from around the world. Since President **Kashala Katembo** was unable to attend, **Raquel Martinez** presided. The group decided that the jurisdictional representatives would send a personal note along with the minutes to spouses not present at the meeting. Guidelines for the historian were added to the bylaws/job descriptions. The historian will display photos from previous meetings throughout each quadrennium and two years into the next before they are sent to the archivist at the UM Archives and History Center. The historian will also call the UM Archives and History Center to clarify requirements for material submitted.

Elaine Hopkins distributed directories to those who had not yet received theirs, and **Jane Ives** reported for the Mission Support Network, encouraging spouses to work with their annual conferences to promote the One Great Hour of Sharing. **Char Ough** requested volunteers to work on the Thrival Kit updates for the upcoming class of 2004. Raquel requested volunteers to work on an update of our Spouses' Directory.

On Thursday, **Janene Pennel** and **Melba Whitaker** offered a workshop on Ways to Enrich Clergy Families. Janene shared the Thrival Kit for clergy spouses, which she helped the Virginia Conference develop. Paul Dirdak from UMCOR met with the spouses interested in the Mission Support Network. **Jo Stith** reported on her trip to Latin America, and others shared mission concerns and experiences.

Spring Council Meeting, April 28–May 3, 2002—Minneapolis, MN

The business meeting opened with a program by **Kay Hutchinson**, who led songs from *The Faith We Sing*, weaving together her faith journey and music. **Kashala Katembo**, president, brought dresses she had had made for the officers. (In Africa, wearing uniform dresses affirms the equality and shared commitment of all women.) In response to a letter from **Eunice Mathews**, the Association voted to give $500 from the treasury to the Clara Swain Hospital in India.

Many of the spouses went on a trip to LARK Toys; enjoyed shopping in Red Wing, Minnesota; and had lunch at the St. James Hotel. **Elaine Hopkins** led a workshop for the spouses on "The Impact of Stress on the Communications Process." The group visited the episcopal residence, where they enjoyed a musical program, and the Mall of America, which was near the hotel. **Jane Ives** was elected president.

Lamarr Gibson shared the first edition of "Global Mission News," a newsletter sharing news of the Mission Support Network, including background information on the network, recommended resources, and part of **Jo Stith**'s report on her trip to Latin America. Jo's report included these words: "This was no ordinary journey for me. Though not a novice to missions, I could not have imagined how I would be stretched. Though not an easy journey, I would recommend it to each of you. And YES, I WOULD VOLUNTEER to do this again." The group worked on a mission statement and continued to discuss how to balance support of UMCOR with other mission projects in which members are already involved. The group considered organizing by geographical areas they have visited or where they have missional connections and began drafting a chart of such areas.

Fall Council Meeting, November 3–8, 2002—San Juan, Puerto Rico

The Council met in a lovely hotel right on the water, with a nice swimming beach and pool. The spouses enjoyed tours of the island, the El Yunque Rainforest, and the old city of San Juan, with the old Spanish fort nearby.

During the meeting on November 5, **Joye Chamness**, **Margaret Watson**, and **Lamarr Gibson** shared their faith journeys. An Executive Committee motion passed, which stated that "requests for money for special projects or concerns should be brought to the Executive Committee in writing before the meeting." Other changes to the bylaws included a note that the work of a jurisdictional representative could be shared by more than one person. The group discussed suggestions **Kashala Katembo** had made to help them be more global, noting that **Raquel Martinez** serving as "host" to Central Conference spouses during this meeting—making sure they had the schedule, answering questions, and encouraging them to participate in activities—had been very helpful. Appreciation was expressed for the translator who came to the meeting to help with communication. The hope is that the Mission Support Network will help provide a more global focus. **Valerie Whitfield** and others volunteered to do the data input for an updated Directory after the next set of episcopal elections. Another group is updating the Thrival Kit, and members were encouraged to share what they have learned that has been helpful to them as bishops' spouses. **Mackie Norris** will serve as liaison with the General Commission on the Status and Role of Women, which is beginning a Clergy/Spouse Task Force project to strengthen denominational support of clergy families and spouses. **Margaret Watson** will chair a committee for assigning members to and coordinating covenant groups for the next quadrennium.

Spring Council Meeting, April 27–May 2, 2003—Dallas, TX

During the Association meeting, **Minnie Brown** shared her faith journey through song and story. Updates to bylaws and duties of the officers were approved. Members willing to serve as Big Brothers/Big Sisters to spouses of bishops elected next year were asked to sign up. Progress reports were given on the updating of the Directory and the Thrival Kits, on the work of the Mission Support Network, and by those planning the mission presentations to be made during General Conference.

During the Mission Support Network meeting, **Melba Whitaker** reported on her trip to East Angola with two other persons from the Florida Annual Conference, describing her visit to **Laurinda Quipungo**'s clinic and emphasizing the need for medications there. The group discussed ways to raise money to send medications to East Angola, and a number of spouses made donations to a fund for that purpose. **Jane Ives** shared a letter from Mozambique describing ministries with persons infected with and affected by HIV/AIDS. **Dania Soriano** shared pictures and updates on her work with Community Based Primary Health Care in the Philippines. **Lamarr Gibson** spoke about his recent trip to Haiti, with which the Detroit Annual Conference has a relationship.

Spouses participated in hands-on mission experiences at social service agencies and in visits to the Bridwell Library and the Meadows Museum at Southern Methodist University. **Marilyn Oden** hosted a tea at the episcopal residence with entertainment by a local storyteller, Rosemary Rumbley. **Lamarr Gibson** published and shared another issue of the spouses' Global Mission Newsletter. **Mary Morris** was elected president.

Fall Council Meeting, November 3–7, 2003—Washington, DC

The Council met at the Doubletree Hotel in Arlington, Virginia. The spouses were offered a tour of the National Cathedral, an ethnic luncheon, a bus trip to Baltimore to visit Lovely Lane and Old Otterbein United Methodist historic sites. Bishops and spouses were bussed to Capitol Hill to visit with legislative leaders from their home states. The spouses were also hosted for lunch at Hyattsville UMC, in Baltimore, where the Deaf Church choir performed.

At the Association meeting, vice president **Annegret Klaiber** presided, leading us in prayer for **Mary Morris**, who was ill, and in devotions. **Lucrécia Domingos** spoke briefly about their work in West Angola, thanking the group for their prayers and Bob and **Faye Fannin** for the sewing machines and supplies their conference provided.

The Mission Support Network (MSN) met with Paul Dirdak, chief executive of UMCOR, who explained the importance of the One Great Hour of Sharing offering and encouraged the spouses to promote it in their annual conferences. **Mitzi Dew** reported on the involvement of persons from Arizona in mission to Kosovo. **Melba Whitaker** reported that, thanks to funds raised by a half dozen annual conferences, along with donations made by members of the MSN, Stop Hunger Now was able to ship a container of medicine to Angola in September. **Jane Ives** distributed a Fact Sheet about the MSN and reported that the Thrival Kit project had been handed over to the spouses on the Orientation Committee for the next class of newly elected bishops and their spouses. **Melba Whitaker** reported on the trip she led to Guatemala for spouses from the Florida Annual Conference and her plans for another such trip to Peru. **Eunice Mathews** distributed calendars from the Clara Swain Hospital in India. **Mitzi Dew** issued a challenge and collected $1,150 from the members present for the hospital.

Spring Council Meeting, April 23–26, and General Conference, April 27–May 7, 2004—Pittsburgh, PA

Spouses toured the Western Pennsylvania Conference headquarters and enjoyed a program presented there. **Mitzi Dew** and a number of other spouses again organized mission presentations titled "God at Work Around the World" during the first week of General Conference. Presenters included three African spouses, one from the Philippines, one from Europe, and one from the United States. Approximately 90 persons attended the two events. Twenty-five evaluation forms were returned, unanimously affirming the events as informative and inspiring and recommending that more such events be offered in the future

President **Mary Morris** presided at the Association meeting on April 25. **Elaine Hopkins** reported on the results of a survey of the membership regarding how the group might function and what kinds of activities are most important. This led to two bylaws additions: "When all spouses of any jurisdiction and the Central Conferences have served as president, their turn will be bypassed" and "All spouses of bishops who are interested in serving as officers shall be considered by the Nominating Committee." We heard reports on the new covenant groups to start at the fall meeting and on new interest groups to be offered: journaling, book reviews, sewing/needlepoint, sharing ideas, and discussions of social problems and world affairs. The final meeting of current covenant groups was scheduled for April 26. **Melba Whitaker** and **Toril Olsen** shared their faith journeys. **Elaine Hopkins** was elected president.

Reflections and Personal Stories

Valerie Whitfield: Guillain–Barre Syndrome, the Episcopacy, and Me

"My journey with Guillain-Barre Syndrome and the episcopacy started in May 2000. Max had put his name forward for consideration for the episcopacy and had completed interviews with most of the areas. On the weekend before he was to leave for General Conference in Cincinnati, Ohio, we worked in the yard putting out 38 bags of mulch. Afterward, although we were both very tired, we dressed and went out to a restaurant for dinner. During our meal, I began to have trouble breathing and I felt itchy all over. Max took me to the emergency room, where they said I was probably having an allergic reaction to something in the mulch. They gave me medications, and we went home. Very early Monday morning, I took Max to the airport to catch his flight to Cincinnati for General Conference. During that week I experienced debilitating pain and paralysis. Our family took me back to the hospital, where I was admitted. After many tests,

MRIs, CAT scans, and blood work, I was diagnosed with Guillain-Barre Syndrome. None of us had ever heard of it before. Max came home.

"Guillain-Barre Syndrome (GBS) is an autoimmune condition in which the body attacks its own nerve endings. It usually begins in the extremities and progresses throughout the body, causing pain and paralysis. GBS can result in total paralysis, including the diaphragm, but I was fortunate enough not to have to endure being on a respirator. My paralysis affected my eyelids, the muscles of my eyes, lips, legs, and hands. I was unable to walk, write, smile, brush my teeth, or do so many of the things we usually take for granted. After several weeks in the hospital and a rehabilitation facility, I was released to go home. I could barely stand and had to be in a wheelchair, but I was home. Max decided he would withdraw his name from the election, but after much prayer and discussion, we decided that he would continue his journey to the episcopacy. In July, he was elected. We were so excited and pleased to be assigned to the Northwest Texas/New Mexico Episcopal Area.

"We arrived in Albuquerque on September 1 to find a home on four levels, a huge challenge for me. Not to be stopped, I went up and down the stairs almost any way one could imagine. While Max and his superintendents visited each church and parish in the area, I stayed at home, but I had a tremendous backup system. The entire area staff was there to help me. I could not drive, but if I needed anything, Max's administrative assistant and council director were available for me at all times.

"Our first Council of Bishops' meeting, at Epworth-by-the-Sea on St. Simons Island in Georgia, was a wonderful experience. I was welcomed by the other episcopal spouses and immediately felt loved and included, even though I could not join the spouses' excursions. I was amazed by the instant care and concern. During Council meetings, I have been able to get to some of the meals and worship services. Sometimes individuals or small groups of spouses visit me in my room. If our room is near the elevator, I leave my door open so that people can drop by to visit. Just before I became ill, Max gave me a tiny Pomeranian puppy. Emmi became my constant companion and kept me from feeling so lonely when Max was traveling. She traveled with me to Council meetings, too, where bishops and spouses greeted her and asked us how she was doing. We lost her in November 2016 and miss her so much.

"The class of 2000 has been a great support to me, as they are for each other as well. We have class meals and social gatherings, and special friends from that group have shared ideas, offered encouragement, prayed for me, and given me the help I needed in understanding my role as an episcopal spouse. For this I am so grateful. The way I had worked with our district spouses back in Arkansas wasn't possible in our new geographically extensive episcopal area. Being part of the bishops' spouses' fellowship has enabled me to grow, develop, and heal. Without the support of these special people, I don't believe I could have recovered my health to the extent I have today. The episcopal family is truly a church for those of us fortunate enough to enter this unique ministry.

"Guillain-Barre has given me many challenges, but it has not defeated me. I meet each day with the hope I can get out of bed and do normal things, but the reality is that each day begins with pain, depression, and low energy. With God's help and the love of those around me, I face each challenge with prayer, hope, and determination. Amen." —written 2016

Eleanor Lyght's Window on History: 9/11

"The experiences of September 11, 2001 are etched in my memory for a lifetime. We were living in New Rochelle, New York, then, and on that terror-filled day, I had gone to work as usual in Paterson, New Jersey, while Ernest, the resident bishop of the New York Annual Conference, stayed at home to complete preparation for an upcoming conference event. Our son Eric, who was at work in Weehawken, New Jersey, could actually see the World Trade Center from the vantage point of his office building, which was located on the Hudson River. Eric's wife, Rose, was at work in Manhattan. Erwyn, our youngest son, at that time was living in Maryland, not far from Washington, DC.

"The school day started out quite typically for me, teaching music and having fun with my students. All of a sudden, the classroom TV monitor came on with the news that a plane had hit one of the Twin Towers in New York City, followed by the announcement that another plane had hit the other Tower. We soon learned that a third plane had hit the Pentagon in Virginia. The students and I, stunned, watched the TV, switching between scenes in New York and Washington. As we tried to figure out what was going on, the TV went off as abruptly as it had come on. Apparently, someone realized that some of the students might have family members working in the Towers. As soon as the class ended, I hurried over to the school's TV Studio to see what was happening. As I watched, I could see smoke, fire, and people jumping out of windows from the burning buildings. I actually saw the Towers collapse. It was unbelievable.

"Our son Eric, knowing that his father often traveled into the city, called me to find out where Ernest was that day. Some people's cell phones were not working because of the loss of antennas housed on top of the towers. It was kind of chaotic because people were trying to reach family and friends and family and friends were trying to reach them. People whose phones were working were kind enough to share [with] others. A few hours after the collapse of the Towers, one of my former students came to me, deeply shaken, reporting that he had just left one of the Towers shortly before it collapsed. Friends told me of people they knew who got up to go to work at the Towers, but for a variety of reasons, did not go to work that day. Since all the tunnels and bridges were closed except for the Tappan Zee Bridge, my trip home, which usually took 40 minutes, took more than two hours.

"September 14 was our son Erwyn's wedding. He and his fiancée were stressed because they knew people who worked in the Towers. Many family members and friends from the South and the West Coast, including some who were to participate in the wedding ceremony, were not able to come because all air flights had been cancelled. One family member, who was in the air when the Towers were struck, was diverted to Canada.

"A few days later, Ernest and four of his pastors went to Ground Zero. An alarm sounded while they were there, and they were told to run because the site was so unstable. Like so many who were near the scene during and after the attack, Ernest has suffered mysterious health problems that may be related to contaminants in the air. In the aftermath, the annual conference and UMCOR were on the scene and helped in many different ways. Many of the New York churches opened their doors so that people could come in and pray. The conference held a memorial service at Park Avenue United Methodist Church the next week, and later, the City of New York hosted a Memorial Service at Yankee Stadium. We will never forget this tragic day and the heroic efforts of so many to rescue persons from the Towers and to heal the emotional and physical trauma."

—written 2016

Marilyn Magee Talbert's Window on History: African Americans in The United Methodist Church

In her book, *The Past Matters: A Chronology of African Americans in the United Methodist Church* (Discipleship Resources, 2003), **Marilyn Magee Talbert** carefully and clearly chronicles significant events and persons related to the history of African Americans in our church, juxtaposing them with world history events. Marilyn says:

"I wrote *The Past Matters* because I see such a need to educate our people, to correct distortions, to fill in missing information, and to own the role of African Americans in The United Methodist Church and its predecessor bodies. Amazingly, a number of whites continue to believe that African Americans came into the church in 1968, when the Central Jurisdiction was dissolved. Younger generations of African Americans have no understanding of their heritage in the church. I designed the book to show the history of African Americans in our church in the context of the culture at that time and in relationship to other events in our country's history. I hope that this book is being used as a resource for understanding the history of our church and that confirmation classes, orientation sessions for new members, and other groups all make it an essential part of their learning.

"When we were preparing to celebrate the 200th anniversary of Methodism in this country, I was curious about the contributions of African Americans and began a timeline to which I kept adding nuggets of information. An editor at Discipleship Resources saw the timeline on my conference table and challenged me to write the book. I think it is important because 'there is no escaping the profound impact of slavery on this nation, the role it had on the developing Methodist Church, and the residual effect on all of the life of Black people in this country' (p. 21). The development of America, with the issue of slavery and its residual effects, and the development of Methodism seem to be so inextricably interwoven, one could draw the conclusion that this nation is not a melting pot, maybe not even a salad, but a braided nation." —written 2016

Chapter 21

2004–2008

Spouses Who Joined the Episcopal Family 2004–2008

Detailed profiles and citation information can be found in Part 5, beginning on page 251.

Jurisdiction or Central Conferences	Spouse	Bishop	Year Elected	Elected From	First Episcopal Assignment
NC	Kenneth P. Ehrman	Sally Dyck	2004	East Ohio AC	Minnesota
NC	Im Hyon Jung	Hee-Soo Jung	2004	Wisconsin AC	Chicago
NC	Bradley Kiesey	Deborah Kiesey	2004	Iowa AC	Dakotas
NE	Sally Bickerton	Thomas J. Bickerton	2004	West Virginia AC	Pittsburgh
NE	Prema Devadhar	Sudarshana Devadhar	2004	North Central New York AC	Greater New Jersey Episcopal Area
NE	Barbara Walker Matthews	Marcus Matthews	2004	Baltimore Washington AC	Philadelphia

Jurisdiction or Central Conferences	Spouse	Bishop	Year Elected	Elected From	First Episcopal Assignment
NE	Jack Dale Middleton	Jane Allen Middleton	2004	New York AC	Harrisburg
NE	Elizabeth (Lisa) Hyeja Park	Jeremiah Jungchan Park	2004	Greater New Jersey AC	New York
NE	Beverly Anne Schol	John R. Schol	2004	Eastern Pennsylvania AC	Washington, DC
SC	Karen Jenkins Crutchfield	Charles N. Crutchfield	2004	New Mexico AC	Arkansas
SC	Deliliah "Dee" Bernard Hayes	Robert E. Hayes Jr	2004	Texas AC	Oklahoma
SC	Mary Lou Reece	Scott J. Jones	2004	North Texas AC	Kansas
SC	Esther W. Schnase	Robert C. Schnase	2004	Southwest Texas AC	Missouri
SE	Joyce Hannah Gwinn	Alfred W. Gwinn Jr	2004	Kentucky AC	Raleigh
SE	Delphine Yvonne Ramsey Swanson	James E. Swanson Sr	2004	South Georgia AC	Holston
SE	James "Rusty" Russell Taylor	Mary Virginia (Dindy) Kilgore Taylor	2004	Holston AC	Columbia
SE	Michael E. Ward	Hope Morgan Ward	2004	North Carolina AC	Mississippi
SE	Patricia Parker Willimon	William Henry Willimon	2004	South Carolina AC	Birmingham
SE	Eileen W. Wills	Richard "Dick" J. Wills Jr	2004	Florida AC	Nashville
W	Greta Goo Hoshibata	Robert T. Hoshibata	2004	Pacific Northwest AC	Portland (Oregon)

Jurisdiction or Central Conferences	Spouse	Bishop	Year Elected	Elected From	First Episcopal Assignment
W	Thomas Lucas Spaniolo	Minerva Garza Carcaño	2004	Oregon-Idaho AC	Phoenix
Central Conferences	Berthe Ngbesso Odombo Boni	Benjamin Boni	2004	Côte d'Ivoire	Côte d'Ivoire
Central Conferences	Jessica Mavula	Kefas K. Mavula	2007	Nigeria AC	Nigeria
Central Conferences	Greater Taremeredzwa Munesi Nhiwatiwa	Eben K. Nhiwatiwa	2004	Zimbabwe East AC	Zimbabwe
Central Conferences	Heidi Albrecht Streiff	Patrick Phillip Streiff	2005	Switzerland-France-North Africa AC	Central and Southern Europe
Central Conferences	Betty Wandabula	Daniel A. Wandabula	2006	East Africa AC	East Africa
Central Conferences	Tobias Wenner	Rosemarie Beisel Wenner	2005	Germany South AC	Germany
Central Conferences	Henriette K'Untu Yemba	David K. Yemba	2005	Central Congo AC	West Congo

Joining by Marriage This Quadrennium

Spouse	Year Married	Bishop	Where Serving
Sherrie Boyens Dobbs Johnson	2005	Bishop Alfred Johnson	Retired
Linda Sells Weaver	2006	Bishop Peter D. Weaver	Boston
Princilla Smart Evans Morris	2006	Bishop William Wesley Morris	Retired
Marcia Ann Stamm Solomon	2004	Bishop Dan Eugene Solomon	Retired

Highlights of Our Life Together: 2004–2008

Unless otherwise noted, the information in "Our Life Together" segments is based on the memory and personal notes of the author and information found in the episcopal spouses' scrapbooks and minutes.

Fall Council Meeting, October 30, 2004—St. Simon's Island, GA

At the Association meeting, vice president **Marsha Coyner** and **Char Ough** welcomed the new class of spouses with the song, "Getting to Know You" and personal introductions. Marsha led us in a get-acquainted activity, and **Bob Huie** shared his faith journey. **Brad Kiesey** volunteered to organize a spouses' choir. An updated list of Big Brother/Big Sister assignments was shared. **Margaret Watson** presented a list of five covenant groups that had been formed for those who had indicated interest, and others were invited to join. Although different groups used different devotional resources, they all provided a setting for sharing joys and concerns and committing to pray for one another.

Some of the spouses took a bus trip to Savannah, touring highlights of that city. Those who did not go were offered the opportunity to make beaded bracelets. Bishops and spouses enjoyed a lecture, demonstration, and dessert presented and prepared by the chef who had served the G-8 summit meeting a few weeks earlier. The spouses also enjoyed a program on Wesley and a humorous talk on parsonage life.

Spring Council Meeting, May 1–6, 2005—Washington, DC/Arlington, VA

The Council met at the Sheraton National Hotel in Arlington, Virginia. At the Association meeting, **Carol Paup** distributed copies of the 2004 Episcopal Spouses' Directory, and the group expressed thanks to her and **Valerie Whitfield** for their work. **Jane Ives** distributed printed copies of the faith journey that **Ruth Thomas** had shared verbally at the fall 1992 meeting and invited others who were willing to write theirs to do so. Following a get-acquainted activity, spouses met in small groups to share their faith journeys. Since **Brad Kiesey** was unable to attend, the planned choir rehearsal was canceled. **Raquel Martinez** was elected president.

Fall Council Meeting, October 30–November 5, 2005—Lake Junaluska, NC

Minnie Brown, president designate, presided in Raquel's absence. The members voted to extend the term of the current Executive Committee by one year because there would be no spring meeting in 2006, only the fall meeting in Mozambique. New officers would be elected in the spring of 2007. **Delphine**

Swanson read **Valerie Whitfield**'s faith journey, since she was not able to be present. Delphine also led a get-acquainted activity, and the Ghost of Lake Junaluska (**Margaret McCleskey**) visited and shared a "teeny tiny tale." **Jane Ives** distributed copies of faith journeys by **Etta Mae Mutti** and **Nocia Machado** and encouraged others to share theirs as well. The following interest groups were scheduled: journaling, book group, Mission Support Network, Spanish language group (canceled because the leader was not able to be present), and a music/choir group. The spouses' covenant groups met each morning at separate tables in the plenary room, while the bishops were meeting with their own covenant groups. Spouses were invited to sign up for a visit to Givens Retirement Home, and **Julia Wilke** invited everyone to her house on Wednesday afternoon. During the Mission Support Network meeting, **Melba Whitaker** shared about the trip she led to Peru with UMCOR, taking pastors' spouses from her area.

Spring 2006

No Council meeting was scheduled because of the additional time and expense needed for the fall meeting in Mozambique.

Fall Council Meeting, November 1–6, 2006—Maputo, Mozambique

"Seventy bishops, plus 45 family members (38 spouses, 3 children, 3 grandchildren, and one niece) attended this first Council of Bishops meeting held in Africa. We greatly appreciated the 'radical'/sacrificial hospitality of Bishop Machado and his team. The president of Mozambique, as well as the minister of Justice (a United Methodist woman), greeted us at opening worship. Several local choirs sang Handel's 'Hallelujah Chorus' a cappella in Portuguese.

"Family members enjoyed an excursion to Tsalala school and an AIDS respite center, then Malanga UMC, where the UMW cooked our lunch. During worship, the UM women wore matching outfits to signify their spiritual state: black skirts (former sinful life), red jackets (Jesus' blood), and white hats (pure life and the Holy Spirit). The hats are earned over a period of three years—an impressive achievement. A second day-trip took us north of Maputo, where we were greeted by local officials at Xai-Xai. Then on to Tinga-Tinga school and the Janene Pennel Primary School, which was a gift from the Virginia Annual

Conference when Bishop Pennel retired in 2004. On the way back south, we visited the HIV-AIDs orphanage and women's training center, dancing to the drums and walking under a flower arch made by the children. The Xai-Xai church fed us lunch, even though we were hours late in arriving. Throughout the day, UM women had joined us to sing for us on the long bus rides. Such joy! On our final bus trip, we had a police escort to the city craft market. The vendors were friendly, the crafts were delightful—but the police escort was worrisome (and necessary).

"On our last evening there, a buzz went through the dining room: a special guest might appear. No name yet, just 'special.' Finally, Nelson Mandela and his wife, Graça Machel, entered the room. Ms. Machel spoke first, informing us that she and Nelson were both 'Methodist children,' educated by Methodist missionaries. The widow of Mozambique's first president, she had served as minister of Education in Mozambique. She spoke eloquently about her work helping women and children, about education and literacy and opportunity. She claimed Bishop Machado as her spiritual father. Then Nelson Mandela addressed us, recounting his early experiences with the Methodist Church and emphasizing the importance of religion. He added comments about the usefulness of women and the importance of listening to them, eliciting 'Amen's from several of us. Bishop **Janice Huie**'s closing comment that night expressed what we all felt; we had been in the presence of saints.

"During a two-day extension to the meeting, we visited beautiful coastal areas. The Bahule church, where we worshiped, showered us with bougainvillea blossoms and filled our pockets with peanuts for the journey home. We were blessed by their generosity, joy, and faith." —written by Karen Crutchfield, 2016

Spring Council Meeting, April 29–May 4, 2007—Myrtle Beach, SC

The Council met in a hotel right on the beach. The spouses traveled to the Brookgreen Gardens to view flowers and statuary. During the Association meeting, **Joyce Gwinn** and **Walter Woods** shared their faith journeys and distributed printed copies as well. **Jane Ives** reported that the spouses' trip to the Philippines, which the Mission Support Network had planned, was canceled due to the unrest there. **Carol Paup** volunteered to continue updating the Directory.

Times and places for the book, journaling, and covenant group meetings were announced. The book group discussed Timothy Tyson's *Blood Done Sign My Name: A True Story* and wrestled with the reality of racist violence. Bishop Hope Morgan Ward joined the discussion because the author is her brother-in-law. He joined the book discussion by telephone. **Minnie Brown** was elected president.

Fall Council Meeting, November 4–9, 2007—Lake Junaluska, NC

At the Association meeting, we learned about upcoming activities. Tuesday afternoon the spouses were offered a tour of the McCleskey and Carder homes, with transportation by trolley. Wednesday morning, spouses were invited to gather for a car caravan to Barber's Orchard, followed by a scenic drive on the Blue Ridge Parkway to enjoy the fall colors and to Maggie Valley UMC, where box lunches were served. On Thursday, **Margaret McCleskey** entertained the spouses at the Bethea Center with a play she had written about Susannah Wesley. The book, journaling, and Mission Support Network (MSN) groups met. The MSN prepared a bulletin board where bishops and spouses could post their greeting cards, sent out a group Christmas card from those who participated, and collected $8,721.56 for UMCOR.

Spring Council Meeting, April 19–23, and General Conference, April 23–May 6, 2008—Fort Worth, TX

At the Association meeting, members discussed the need for clearer communication regarding meals for which the spouses have to pay or eat elsewhere. The group approved a non-binding resolution stating that "The Bishops' Spouses would like to be invited to participate with voice in the Council of Bishops' discussion on racism." **Mary Lou Reece** agreed to take charge of the book club. **Joye Chamness** hosted a tea at the episcopal residence, with entertainment by a pianist. Spouses participated in several social service projects. **Greater Nhiwatiwa** was elected president. **Minnie Brown** reminded the group to always include widows and widowers in communications about activities. Earlier this year, **Edith Jokomo** sent an email to all the surviving spouses, inviting them to become part of an email and regular mail covenant group. She expressed how much she missed seeing other bishops' spouses and hoped they could provide support for one another and perhaps even make plans to attend some of the Council meetings. Several other surviving spouses expressed interest, but shortly after this, email service in Zimbabwe failed for a time and communication about this project discontinued.

Sally Bickerton's Story

In 1991, Sally married a marine corps aviator, and during the next few years they lived in three different duty stations around the U.S. After her husband died in a helicopter crash in 1996, leaving her with two young children, Sally returned to West Virginia to live near family. She met Tom Bickerton at a charge conference when he was a district superintendent overseeing the merger of three churches in New Martinsville. She loves to say, "You never know what might happen at a charge conference!" Those churches take great pride in the fact that because they merged, Tom and Sally got together.

Her experiences as a military wife prepared her well for being a clergy and episcopal spouse. She was well acquainted with the expectation of moving as a fact of life. She knows well the importance of connecting to not just the community in which you live but also other spouses who are having similar experiences. She commented, "Relating to local military wives' groups was essential, because we never knew when we would need their support. Whether struggling with a difficult assignment, parenting challenges, or personal health issues, no one else knows what you are going through as well as another military or clergy spouse. While we were in Western Pennsylvania, I helped revive clergy spouse retreats because I know how important those relationships are. I enjoyed working on joint retreats with **Elaine Hopkins** in East Ohio. No one really knows what it is like to be an episcopal spouse except another episcopal spouse, and it is a great gift to be understood without having to explain."

Sally told the author that she was reading the book *First Women: The Grace and Power of America's Modern First Ladies*, by Kate Andersen Brower. She noted that while their husbands are in office, first ladies have a title, an office and a staff, plus expectations, of course, but no salary. When the president leaves office, he keeps his title, but she loses hers. While some spouses of retired bishops may feel a similar loss of a role, most report great joy in reclaiming family life and couple time. —interview with Sally Bickerton, March 11, 2017

Mary Lou Reece: Juggler

"My journey as a bishop's spouse has been rich and full, but not without its challenges. I own and am the CEO of a third generation construction company. We build concrete structures for highways in a four-state area. Technology has been very good to me, and I learned early, while married to an itinerant Methodist minister, to run my business from anywhere. For many years, I worked mostly from an office, commuting from wherever my husband was appointed. When he was elected a bishop, I knew that things were changing and my 'office' would need to be wherever I am. I am fortunate that technology has allowed me to do both my jobs. I often say that I really have two full-time jobs and that as long as I have a cell phone and a computer, I can do my 'day job.' Now that I have become a grandmother as well as the daughter of an aging mother, I've added about a half-time additional job to that challenge.

"Admittedly, I haven't done everything well. I have too many balls in the air. It is hard to be a full-time executive while I'm trying to listen to General Conference actions, for instance. I find myself drawn into the discussions because I care about this church that is my home. And yet issues in my company require my attention. Oops, I dropped a ball somewhere, I am sure.

"In addition, I am an extreme extrovert. I LOVE the gatherings with my friends in the episcopal spouse group. Then I find I want to go on 'side trips' with the other spouses, who are lovely, smart, well-read, interesting, and very fun people from all over the world. It is such a rich group of men and women. Being the spouse of a bishop can be very lonely, and it feeds my soul to spend time with these friends who share the same experiences. So here I am again today and at least twice a year—trying to work, trying to play with my friends, and trying to be the best possible support for my husband. It might be a bit much. I drop a few balls. I'm not the best I could be at anything. But I am blessed to do as much as possible—as well as possible—given these arduous constraints.

"In order to survive the potential loneliness of this position, I have established a couple of helpful disciplines. First, I found myself a small accountability group of laypeople with whom I meet each week, which was not easy to accomplish. We practice accountability based on the Emmaus Reunion Card, asking ourselves each week where we have answered God's call and denied God's call and when we have felt closest to Christ. This wonderful group enriched my life for our entire 12 years in the Great Plains Conference. Second, in the church where I placed my membership, I found a strong Sunday school class that allows me to participate in their social events, even though I do not get to the class. This has been extraordinarily life-giving for both Scott and me. These are our friends. We ride bikes with them, go to parties, eat dinners with them both out and in, and generally have a real and sustained friendship group apart from the clergy in our area. What a joy this has been. I recommend it to any extroverted (read 'I need friends') person in this position.

"This has been a wonderful journey with many challenges and gifts. I have bid jobs from Panama. I have walked in the rainforest. I have experienced UMW in Mozambique providing radical hospitality. I have seen amazing fruits of this blessed connection. I pray for its continuing fruitfulness in the centuries to come." —written in 2016

Mike Ward's Window on History: Hurricane Katrina

"Hurricane Katrina made landfall in Mississippi in late August 2005, a year to the day after Hope and I moved there for her first assignment as bishop. We'd come from North Carolina, where I'd just wrapped up two terms as state superintendent of Public Instruction and where Hope had served as director of Connectional Ministries and as district superintendent. We'd dealt with hurricanes in our work—but none like Katrina.

"We were on the coast in the days following the storm and returned regularly during the months and years that followed. I figured I could be most useful in the recovery efforts by sweating it out alongside other volunteers. I had put myself through college doing maintenance at an apartment complex, which means that I know a little about a number of construction tasks and not a lot about any single one of them. That said, I could haul relief supplies; and in the recovery stage I could handle a shovel, clean out muck, tear out wet insulation, and spray down gutted frameworks with disinfectants. And I'm not bad with sheetrock. So we spent a lot of time on the coast helping with home repair.

"The blessings came in multiple forms. We spent time with incredible people. There were pastors who set aside their own losses as they worked tirelessly with their congregations and their communities. There were faithful and determined folks who moved us by their witness as they reassembled their lives. There were heartbroken folks who just could not recover, at least not in those environs, and who left for new lives elsewhere. People offered hospitality even though they seemed in no position to do so. One couple, as we gutted and re-walled their home, made us a different bayou feast every night—prepared in their FEMA trailer! And there were volunteers from EVERYWHERE. They came and they kept coming. Methodist volunteers helped over 75,000 households.

"My contributions seemed modest compared to those of folks who really knew how to handle tools, but I found that I could also be useful in other ways. I was a faculty member in the College of Education and Psychology at The University of Southern Mississippi. The RAND Gulf States Policy Institute gave us a grant to study the impact of Katrina on schools. We dug into lessons learned about preparation and response for schools in disasters. We inquired about the impact on teachers and school services. But for me, the most meaningful research occurred when I looked at the storm's impact on displaced students. The results weren't surprising: displaced kids had lower achievement, were more likely to drop out, and behaved worse than their non-displaced peers. Sadly, these problems persisted—and even increased—in the years following Katrina.

"We've returned to North Carolina, and as I write this, we're engaged with the response to Hurricane Florence. I'm hopeful that, with God's help, the lessons we gleaned from the experiences of students, educators, and families after Katrina will make response and recovery a little easier in the wake of this storm."

—written in 2016

Chapter 22

2008–2012

Spouses Who Joined the Episcopal Family 2008–2012

Detailed profiles and citation information can be found in Part 5, beginning on page 251.

Jurisdiction or Central Conferences	Spouse	Bishop	Year Elected	Elected From	First Episcopal Assignment
NC	Racelder Grandberry-Trimble	Julius Calvin Trimble	2008	East Ohio AC	Iowa
NE	Michael C. Johnson	Peggy Olver Johnson	2008	Baltimore Washington AC	Philadelphia
SC	Leslie Jean Bray Bledsoe	Wilbert Earl Bledsoe	2008	Texas AC	Dallas
SC	Barbara Langley Dorff	James E. Dorff	2008	North Texas AC	San Antonio
SC	Jolynn Lowry	John Michael Lowry	2008	Southwest Texas AC	Fort Worth
SE	Janet Elaine Dowell Leeland	Paul Lee Leeland	2008	North Carolina AC	Alabama-West Florida

Jurisdiction or Central Conferences	Spouse	Bishop	Year Elected	Elected From	First Episcopal Assignment
W	Janet Hagiya	Grant J. Hagiya	2008	California-Pacific AC	Seattle
W	Clinton Stanovsky	Elaine J. Woodworth Stanovsky	2008	Pacific Northwest AC	Denver
Central Conferences	Elisabeth Flinck	Christian Alsted	2009	Denmark AC	Nordic and Baltic
Central Conferences	Lurleen Lapuz Juan	Rodolfo A. Juan	2008	Philippines AC	Baguio
Central Conferences	Eugenio Tomas	Joaquina Filipe Nhanala	2008	Mozambique AC	Mozambique
Central Conferences	Millicent Yambasu	John Kpahun Yambasu	2008	Sierra Leone AC	Sierra Leone

NOTE: The *Discipline* also lists the following other bishop elected in this quadrennium: Lito Cabacungan Tangonan (2008).

Joining by Marriage This Quadrennium

Spouse	Year Married	Bishop	Where Serving
Julia Nolen Knox	2009	Bishop James Lloyd Knox	Retired
Wayne Eldon Simpson	2009	Bishop Ann Brookshire Sherer	Nebraska Episcopal Area.

Joining by Special Concordat This Quadrennium

Autonomous Affiliated Church	Rosemarie Jackson	Rafael Moreno Rivas	2009	Puerto Rico	Methodist Church in Puerto Rico

Highlights of Our Life Together: 2008–2012

Unless otherwise noted, the information in "Our Life Together" segments is based on the memory and personal notes of the author and information found in the episcopal spouses' scrapbooks and minutes.

Fall Council Meeting, November 2–6, 2008—St. Simon's Island, GA

Vice president **Cynthia Palmer** led the spouses in greeting and celebrating the new spouses with balloons, flowers, banners, and the song "This Is the Day."

Gerlinde Minor also introduced **Heidi Streiff**, who was present for the first time. **Jane Ives** distributed an updated fact sheet for the Mission Support Network, noting that the UMCOR Christmas project raised almost $13,000 last year. Jane also reported good progress on efforts to obtain email and "snail mail" addresses for all the spouses and to recruit "snail mail buddies" to send along electronic information for those without email access. Those who had signed up to be in covenant groups were assigned to six groups, with 10 to 12 spouses in each, for this quadrennium. The Council's secretary, JoAnn McClain, had set up a listserv for the spouses, and **Mackie Norris** was maintaining the database. **Clint Stanovsky** invited anyone interested in a kayaking trip to let him know. **Rose King**, host bishop's spouse, announced details for a trip to Jekyll Island.

Spring Council Meeting, May 3–8, 2009—Bethesda, MD

During the Association meeting, after some discussion, the members voted to expand the duties of the vice president to include coordinating with the various interest group leaders, the host conference, and the Executive Committee. The Mission Support Network coordinator was added to the list of officers to serve on the Executive Committee for the quadrennium. Bishops and spouses were bussed to Capitol Hill to meet with legislators. Later in the week, the spouses enjoyed tours of the White House and of Hillwood, the elegant estate and gardens of Marjorie Merriweather Post. **Linda Weaver** was elected president.

Fall Council Meeting, November 1–5, 2009—Lake Junaluska, NC

Activities offered to the spouses included serving and sharing a meal with homeless persons in Waynesville, visiting the Biltmore Estate in Ashville, shopping in Waynesville and Maggie Valley, and going to an apple farm. During the Mission Support Network meeting, **Mary Lou Reece** reported on a trip being planned by the Zoe Ministry, in which she planned to participate, inviting other spouses to join her. The group discussed sending out occasional email reports of the missional involvements of members. The book group discussed **Martha Chamberlain**'s *A Love Affair with India* and *Double Bind*, by Chris Bojhanian. The six covenant groups met.

Spring Council Meeting, May 2–7, 2010—Columbus, OH

Bishops and spouses were hosted for dinner at the Ohio State House. The spouses visited several social service agencies sponsored by the conference. We enjoyed lunch at a restaurant called The Refectory, located in a building that used to be a church, which was run by the husband of one of our translators, Linda Boulos (correspondence with Linda Boulos, February 4, 2017; https://refectory.com/the-restaurant/).

The Association voted to amend the bylaws by adding a person to the Executive Committee to maintain the Spouses' Directory and Listserv and possibly manage the assignment of jurisdictional representatives. **Barbara Dorff** was elected to fill this position. **Joyce Gwinn** was elected president.

Following the business meeting, **Mary Lou Reece** shared about her trip to Kenya and Rwanda through the Zoe Ministry. The book club reviewed and discussed *The Help*, by Kathryn Stockett, and **Marilyn Magee Talbert**'s recently published book *The Past Matters: A Chronology of African Americans in the United Methodist Church* (Nashville: Discipleship Resources, 2003; see Marilyn's story on p. 217). During the book discussions, one African American woman reported that she could not read *The Help*, because the experiences in it were so close to what her mother had experienced. When a southern white woman asked why we have to even see color, another African American stated that she wants to be known as a Black woman, because that is who she is.

Fall Council Meeting, November 2–6, 2010—Panama City, Panama

One evening during this meeting, the bishops and spouses and other guests took a boat trip through the canal locks. No spouse activities or group meetings had been planned because not many spouses had indicated they were coming, but after worship the first day they met in the hall and decided to get together to hear from some of those present. The spouses gathered by the hotel pool on Tuesday, where **Leslie Bledsoe** talked about the technology available for persons with vision disabilities. **Laurinda Quipungo** and **Lucrécia Domingos** shared about their lives in East and West Angola, with assistance from translator Isa Arez. Funds were collected for the UMCOR Christmas project. The spouses shopped for *molas*, which are beautiful works of cloth art created by the

Kuna Indians. Later in the week, **Barbara Dorff**, through her son's connections, arranged for the former first lady of Panama, Vivian Torrijos, to speak to the spouses. She spoke about her work with "Aid for AIDS Panama" and for disabled children. Vivian also promotes breast cancer awareness.

Spring Council Meeting, May 2–6, 2011—St. Simons Island, GA

The Executive Committee of the Association recommended that former presidents, and others interested in helping, review the bylaws and consider what kind of document is needed to guide the organization. The book club discussed *In the Sanctuary of Outcasts: A Memoir*, by Neil White. **Cynthia Palmer** was elected president.

Fall Council Meeting, October 30–November 4, 2011—Lake Junaluska, NC

On Tuesday, the spouses had lunch at the Maggie Valley Country Club, where they were entertained by singer and story-teller Charles Maynard. On Wednesday, they visited the Cherokee Museum and Gift Shop and the Cherokee UMC on the nearby Indian Reservation, then had lunch at Granny's restaurant there. Covenant groups met in the Susan Todd Lounge; and the book club discussed *Sarah's Key* by Tatiana de Rosnay and *Married to a Bedouin*, by Marguerite van Geldermalsen. The journaling group enjoyed **Jo Stith**'s readings from her journal and discussed the importance of keeping records for future generations. **Barbara Dorff** shared about archiving family records. The spouses were also reminded of the UM Archives and History Center on the campus of Drew University, which is eager to obtain writings, journals, and sermons by bishops and other church leaders. The Mission Support Network coordinated the UMCOR Christmas project again. Some spouses toured the World Methodist Museum and the Heritage Museum in the Harrell Center there at Lake Junaluska. The spouses were also offered the opportunity to take a bus to the Biltmore Estate in nearby Asheville or to sign up for a massage or pedicure.

Spring Council Meeting, April 18–20, and General Conference, April 24–May 4, 2012—Tampa, FL

During the business meeting on April 19th, President **Cynthia Palmer** read a litany written by **Marilyn Brown Oden** titled "A litany of celebration in honor of the spouses of retiring bishops." Cynthia suggested this become a regular part of the last meeting in each quadrennium. A motion was made and approved to explore having a website. The group enjoyed a program that included music led by **Kay Hutchinson** and **Karen Crutchfield** and a skit by the "Off Key Players" (**Jolynn Lowry**, **Clint Stanovsky**, **Linda Weaver**, and **Marsha Coyner**), which was a parody of the Song of Solomon. **Jane Ives** reported that she was gathering material for a history of the bishops' spouses and invited members to share stories and experiences with her. **Jolynn Lowry** was elected president for the next year; and since the full council would not be meeting in the spring of 2013, **Henriette Yemba** was elected for 2013–2014.

Reflections and Personal Stories

Carol Paup's Story

"In 2009, three years before my husband Ed died, he was diagnosed with a very aggressive brain tumor. The tumor was located in the area that controls decision-making, and it was cancerous. Soon he went through surgery, radiation, and chemotherapy. After he died, it was difficult for me to think about our last few years with positive thoughts. Those years were unlike anything I could have imagined. My heart was broken. One day, however, I started thinking about all of the many special times we had together through the years, with our daughters, our extended family, and the dear friends we made in the churches we served during our 47 years of marriage. I decided that from then on, I would focus on happy memories and picture them as additions to a blank latchhook rug. Whenever I recall a happy event, I welcome and treasure that memory and mentally pull it up through my new latchhook rug. This process has been such a blessing to me personally. I must admit, as I picture my new rug in my mind, it is an awesome sight! And I am grateful." —written September 2017

Karen Crutchfield Remembers: Three Adventures

"1) Spouses' Outing in Panama. Spouses who attended the 2010 Council meeting in Panama will forever remember the canoe trip to a local Indian village. . . . We traveled by bus to the northern coast, then back inland to meet the villagers. Because their four canoes could not hold all of us, some spouses waited at the bus while the rest of us traveled up the shallow river. . . . [O]ne canoe grounded on a sandbar. Four of the spouses in that canoe got out and waded across the sandbar, despite warnings about crocodiles. . . .

"[Each] trip to the village took about 30 minutes. We enjoyed demonstrations of dancing, crafts, tribal stories, and a lunch made from local foods. The young leader of the tribe informed us that the tribe had lived in Colombia but moved recently to Panama to escape the drug wars of Colombia. River skills were new to them!

"At the end of our visit, spouses filled the four canoes, and 10 of us volunteered to wait for a second trip. During the hour of waiting, the skies grew quite dark, and two more spouses wandered back from the village. Now we were 12, plus a cooler of canned drinks we had not consumed. When one lone canoe came back for us, we crowded in and hoped for the best. Water came up to the edge of the canoe, and then the rains began. Not sweet and gentle rain, but rather a hard driving rain that blinded all of us and slowed our journey on the river. By the time we reached the bus, we were completely drenched and glad to disembark! Cheers for our arrival reached us as we climbed onto the bus. That night at dinner with the Council, **Cynthia Palmer** gave a rousing report of our aquatic adventure. The translator was heard to say he was relieved to have delivered us all safely back to the hotel.

"2) The Democratic Republic of the Congo. In the summer of 2009, I accompanied my husband on his second trip to the North Katanga Annual Conference in the Democratic Republic of Congo. For 15 days we were in Kamina, DRC, observing and teaching and being inspired by the Lord's work in that area. For me, it was transformational. Such joy, such hardship, such faith, such potential! And what a privilege for me to enjoy the UMC global fellowship, acting as one with people who live in circumstances so different from my own. . . . I met twice with clergy spouses, visited with war orphans, and helped **Mrs. Ntambo ('Mama Nshimba')** deliver fabric to clergy widows. We visited many of the church's other projects in the area: a feeding program for children, the 'sanitary market,' schools, a teaching college and a university, a model farm, medical facilities, and water wells. The work of the church in this area is multi-faceted, often chaotic, and glorious. We witnessed the incredible vitality and growth of the UMC in an area where civil war was recent history, where violence often intruded, where life was hard but love prevailed. . . .

"3) Visiting Military Chaplains. United Methodist chaplains who serve on US military bases around the world share a strong bond with one another and with the United Methodist Endorsing Agency, which is part of the General Board of Higher Education and Ministry. Retreats for the chaplains and their spouses provide time for renewal and fellowship. . . . I attended two such retreats with my husband Charles and with Tom Carter from the General Board of Higher Education and Ministry.

"In February 2010, we went to a retreat in Ettal, Germany, with Air Force chaplains from northern Italy and southern Germany. We also visited US military bases at Aviano, Italy, and near Heidelburg, Germany. . . . I learned that the chaplains are 'all military and all clergy,' having to maintain relationships with and requirements for both. Their spouses are a very special lot: fully committed to moving where sent, raising children away from supportive family, helping each other when chaplains are deployed. The opportunity to retreat briefly from such responsibilities is vital to their sense of community and connection to the global denomination. . . .

"In October 2011, we found ourselves again on US military bases, this time on Okinawa and Hawaii. . . . Again, I witnessed the devotion of chaplains and spouses to both the military and the church. Sessions of the retreats addressed PTSD, Bible study, UMC pensions, and the like. Worship was simple and deeply felt. My time spent in the presence of chaplains and their spouses was richly rewarding. My gratitude for such willing service is profound."

—written September 2016

Chapter 23

2012–2016

Spouses Who Joined the Episcopal Family 2012–2016

Detailed profiles and citation information can be found in Part 5, beginning on page 251.

Jurisdiction or Central Conferences	Spouse	Bishop	Year Elected	Elected From	First Episcopal Assignment
NE	Barry Steiner Ball	Sandra Steiner Ball	2012	Peninsula-Delaware AC	West Virginia
NE	Joy Diane Brockway Webb	Mark J. Webb	2012	Central Pennsylvania AC	Upper New York
SC	Joan Craig McKee	Michael McKee	2012	Central Texas AC	Dallas
SC	Dean Harvey	Cynthia Fierro Harvey	2012	Texas AC	Louisiana
SE	Felecia Brown Holston	Lewis Jonathan Holston	2012	North Georgia AC	Columbia

Jurisdiction or Central Conferences	Spouse	Bishop	Year Elected	Elected From	First Episcopal Assignment
SE	Pamela Carter	Kenneth H. Carter	2012	Western North Carolina AC	Florida
SE	Kiok Chang Cho	Young Jin Cho	2012	Virginia AC	Richmond
SE	Lynn Barkley McAlilly	William T. McAlilly	2012	Mississippi AC	Nashville
SE	Lee Padgett	Debra Wallace-Padgett	2012	Kentucky AC	Birmingham
Central Conferences	Restetita Francisco	Ciriaco Francisco	2012	Philippines AC	Davao
Central Conferences	Joyce Orpilla Torio	Pedro M. Torio Jr	2012	Northwest Philippines AC	Baguio
Central Conferences	Victoria Nogay Khegay	Eduard Khegay	2012	Central Russia AC	Eurasia
Central Conferences	Asmau Yohanna	John Wesley Yohanna	2012	Mungo Dosso area of Nigeria	Nigeria

NOTE: The *Discipline* also lists the following other bishops elected in this quadrennium: Martin McLee (2012), Gary Mueller (2012), and Gabriel Yemba Unda (2012).

Highlights of Our Life Together: 2012–2016

Unless otherwise noted, the information in "Our Life Together" segments is based on the memory and personal notes of the author and information found in the episcopal spouses' scrapbooks and minutes.

Fall Council Meeting, November 4–9, 2012—St. Simons Island, GA

Racelder Grandberry-Trimble reported for the committee that had worked on an update of the bylaws and job descriptions. The changes were adopted, with the recommendation that this group continue to work to be sure the bylaws continue to reflect what the Association does. The Mission Support Network coordinated the UMCOR Christmas project again. The spouses were invited for lemonade at the Arthur J. Moore Museum. Some of the spouses traveled to Savannah to visit Wesley Monumental UMC, hear a presentation about a ministry called Operation Hungry Child, enjoy lunch at Paula Deen's The Lady & Sons Restaurant, and shop a little.

Spring Meeting, May, 2013 (active bishops only)

Positive reports from the fall orientation session for spouses of newly elected bishops emphasized the focus on building team spirit and caring community and led to discussion of how to create a new vision for the spouses' organization.

Fall Council Meeting, November 10–15, 2013—Lake Junaluska, NC

During the Association meeting, a motion was made and passed to designate at least $2,000 of the UMCOR Christmas 2013 offering to the Advance Special for the Philippines for recovery from Typhoon Haiyan. Announcements included plans for book club and covenant groups meetings and a request for volunteers to help pack meals for Stop Hunger Now. Members broke into small groups for a discussion of how the Bishops' Spouses' Association should function in the future. **Margaret McCleskey** presented a program demonstrating how to go from very casual to very elegant using scarves. **Henriette Yemba** was installed as president.

Also, during this fall meeting, Peggy Sewall, assistant general secretary of Episcopal Services at the General Commission on Finance and Administration (GCFA), offered a workshop for the spouses on "Being Prepared When a Member of an Episcopal Couple Dies." She shared very helpful information from GCFA about who should be notified of such a death and protocols to be followed regarding funeral arrangements, benefit adjustments, moving, and the like.

Spring Meeting, 2014 (active bishops only)—San Diego, CA

Spouses attended a baseball game, visited the San Diego Zoo, and participated in a communion service at the Mexican border.

Fall Council Meeting, November 2014—Oklahoma City, OK

The Council met at the Skirvin Hilton Hotel. Bishops and spouses participated in an act of repentance led by clergy and laity of the Oklahoma Missionary

Conference with exemplary graciousness and hospitality. The spouses were sobered and moved by the Oklahoma City bombing memorial and delighted by the Chihuly glass display at the art museum and Native American art at the Oklahoma Supreme Court Building, where they also heard from Dr. Henrietta Mann, currently serving as the founding president of the Cheyenne and Arapaho Tribal College in Weatherford, Oklahoma. The spouses had lunch at the Oklahoma History Center, where they enjoyed a dance presentation, led by Zack Morris, of the Sac and Fox, Potawatomi, Pawnee, and Kickapoo tribes. During a tour of the Native American Museum at the History Center, they learned more about the tragic removal of tribes to Oklahoma, known as the Trail of Tears. **Barbara Matthews** was installed as president.

In an effort to facilitate communication and improve connection, **Lee Padgett**, historian, announced that he had established a Facebook page, Association of Bishop Spouses, where he posts pictures and comments about our activities. **Mary Lou Reece** commented, "A Great Plains clergy spouse page like this has been a useful forum for discussions among people with similar concerns."

At this meeting, a proposal was made and approved to change the organization's structure to a fellowship for a two-year trial period (see "A New Way of Functioning" in chapter 3).

The first leadership team of the Bishops' Spouses' Fellowship (BSF), elected to serve for one or two years on a staggered rotation, included **Barbara Matthews** (Northeastern Jurisdiction), **Rose King** (Southeastern Jurisdiction), **Greta Hoshibata** (Western Jurisdiction), **Joan McKee** (South Central Jurisdiction), **Char Ough** (North Central Jurisdiction), **Greater Nhiwatiwa** (Central Conferences/Africa), and someone to be named to represent the Central Conferences/Europe and the Philippines. Leaders were named for interest groups: book group—**Jolynn Lowry**; missions—**Leslie Bledsoe**; covenant groups—**Janet Leeland**; journaling—to be named. Four covenant group leaders were named for the remainder of the quadrennium: **Mike Johnson, Elaine Hopkins, Barbara Dorff**, and **Lisa Park**.

Spring Council Meeting, May 1–7, 2015—Berlin, Germany

The spouses gathered on the morning of May 2 for their meeting. After a hymn, Scripture reading, and prayer, **Tobias Wenner** and **Gerlinde Minor** welcomed the group. Reports were shared about the previous meeting in Oklahoma, the treasury, interest groups, the welcome table, sightseeing opportunities, and mission opportunities. Sixty-three spouses of both active and retired bishops signed the attendance register. **Mike Johnson**, treasurer, reported a total UMCOR offering of $7,660 for 2014 and a treasury balance of $2,998.26. The meeting ended with some games and then a closing prayer. Spouses were offered the opportunity to visit local ministries with children.

Fall Council Meeting, November 1–5, 2015—Lake Junaluska, NC

Only active bishops and spouses participated in this meeting and Fall Learning Forum. Spouses were offered the opportunity to make nativity sets out of precut wood and cloth, supplies provided for a small fee, with any money left over to be donated to UMCOR. Other activities included book club, covenant groups, and fellowship.

Spring Council Meeting, May 3–9, and General Conference, May 10–20, 2016—Portland, OR

The Council of Bishops convened in Portland, Oregon, the week before General Conference was to begin. Three tours were offered: a United Methodist history tour of the Salem area; a tour of the Pacific Coast; and a tour of the Columbia Gorge and Mt. Hood. The spouses learned to use the city's modern transit system to travel between the hotel and the Convention Center, visited the city's Japanese and Rose Gardens, Powell Book Store, and other places of interest. The spouses gathered at First Methodist Church in Portland for lunch, fellowship, an informational meeting, and a workshop on phone apps. The theme of the meeting was "Bishops' Spouses Love Circle Gathering and Sharing." The group held a service of celebration remembering the spouses who died during the past quadrennium and a litany of celebration to honor the spouses of bishops retiring this year. A lovely program book included lists of the active bishops and their spouses, retired bishops and their spouses, and surviving spouses. The Council of Bishops voted to include retired bishops in all future meetings.

Reflections and Personal Stories

At the fall 2014 meeting, the spouses decided to completely revamp their way of functioning. A shift that had taken place in the tone and experience of the spouses' orientation, part of the quadrennial retreat provided for newly elected bishops and their spouses that year, may have contributed to that happening.

Ken Ehrman explains: "It is my impression that prior to 2012, orientation for spouses of newly elected bishops assumed that the career of the person elected to the episcopacy defined the life of the spouse of that person. For example, in 2004, when I went to the orientation, the focus was on what I would have to deal with as the spouse of a bishop, what I would need to know in order to be a good bishop's spouse, and what I would need to know when accompanying my spouse to meetings in the United States and around the world. However, even in 2004, a significant number of spouses of those elected identified primarily with their own vocation/career, rather than with that of their bishop-spouse. In fact, because of their own careers, a significant number of spouses did not move to where their bishop was assigned. The majority of those who did move continued to participate actively within their own professions.

"In 2012, when Sally Dyck and I were invited to help lead the orientation session, we decided to focus on the spouses as individuals in their own right and what they were experiencing, their concerns and hopes, and their needs, instead of on what someone thought they needed to know. We acknowledged that they were dealing with the disruption of their careers, leaving families and friends behind, and entering into situations probably not of their choosing. We recognized that they were the ones who knew what they needed during the week of orientation and that they could provide support and insight to one another by sharing their stories. **Barbara Dorff** gave wonderful leadership by initiating activities that started conversations without dictating the direction of the conversation. We focused on three questions: 1) What gifts do you bring us; 2) What do you need? 3)What do you want to do? I know that the participants appreciated the time they spent together, the friendships that developed, and the support they received."

Joan McKee's Reflections

"I was hesitant about Mike becoming a bishop because of the transition and uncertainty for me and for our family. As the election process progressed at the conference, I too was caught up in the competitive spirit of winning but would have loved for him to graciously decline.

"When I came to the orientation session for new bishops and their spouses in Carefree, Arizona, I was anything but carefree. I was grateful that the sessions for spouses focused on each of us as individuals in transition and how to move forward in this new situation. We were given the book *Good Grief* by Granger E. Westberg, which was very helpful. We talked about caring for ourselves and for each other along this journey, forming a strong supportive relationship.

"At my first Council meeting, I was delighted to see these friends again and to make new friends, but I was very disappointed by the [Association's] business meeting, which I found to be very divisive. Bylaws and the treasury seemed to stand in the way of fellowship, which set a negative tone. At the next meeting, I became part of a conversation group working to eliminate the bylaws and shift from a formal organization to a more supportive fellowship." —written 2016

Janene Pennell's Reflections

"As I reflect on my eight years as an active bishop's spouse, my head is flooded with memories of so many interesting and wonderful experiences. After Joe was elected to the episcopacy, we attended workshops and training sessions that we called 'Charm School.' At our first Council meeting, the spouses were divided into covenant groups. It happened that I was placed with the most amazing group of spouses: **Eunice Mathews**, **Mary Morris**, **Jennifer Davis**, **Marion Clark**, and others. These women were wonderful mentors and role models for me. We served the Virginia Conference for eight wonderful years, surrounded by strong lay and clergy leadership, diversity, and people who loved the UMC. We were privileged to travel to Africa, Asia, the Baltic Region, Europe, Hawaii, and Russia to experience the ministry and mission of our beloved UMC. Since 1996, the COB has become our 'church family.' We have been so blessed and are very grateful." —written March 2017

Chapter 24

2016–2018

Spouses Who Joined the Episcopal Family 2016–2018

Detailed profiles and citation information can be found in Part 5, beginning on page 251.

Jurisdiction or Central Conferences	Spouse	Bishop	Year Elected	Elected From	First Episcopal Assignment
NC	Julie B. Bard	David A. Bard	2016	Minnesota AC	Michigan
NC	Melissa Kay Riffell Beard	Frank J. Beard	2016	Indiana AC	Illinois
NC	Gary Haller	Laurie Haller	2016	West Michigan AC	Iowa
NC	Derrick Malone	Tracy S. Malone	2016	Northern Illinois AC	Ohio East
NE	Marion Easterling	LaTrelle Easterling	2016	New England AC	Washington
NE	Raphael K. Koikoi	Cynthia Moore-Koikoi	2016	Baltimore-Washington AC	Pittsburgh
SC	Susan R. Farr	Robert Farr	2016	Missouri AC	Missouri

Jurisdiction or Central Conferences	Spouse	Bishop	Year Elected	Elected From	First Episcopal Assignment
SC	Mary Louise Nunn	James Gregg Nunn	2016	Northwest Texas AC	Oklahoma
SC	Maye Saenz	Ruben Saenz Jr	2016	Rio Texas AC	Great Plains
SE	Sherrill O. Cooper Bryan	Lawson Bryan	2016	Alabama-West Florida AC	South Georgia
SE	Nancy Graves	David W. Graves	2016	Holston AC	Alabama-West Florida
SE	Allen Johnson	Sue Haupert-Johnson	2016	Florida AC	North Georgia
W	Robin Ridenour	Karen P. Oliveto	2016	California-Nevada AC	Mountain Sky
Central Conferences	Julienne Dembo Lunge	Daniel Onashuyaka Lunge	2017	Central Congo AC	Central Congo
Central Conferences	Blandine Mujinga Ngoy	Mande Muyombo	2017	North Katanga, Tanganyika, and Tanzania AC's	North Katanga (DRC)
Central Conferences	Richlain K. Quire	Samuel J. Quire	2016	Liberia AC	Liberia
Central Conferences	Silvia Rückert	Harald H. Rückert	2017	Germany South AC	Germany

NOTE: The *Discipline* also lists the following other bishops elected in this quadrennium: Sharma Lewis (2016) and Leonard Fairley (2016).

Joining by Marriage This Quadrennium

Spouse	Year Married	Bishop	Where Serving
L. Cecile Adams	2016	Bishop Donald A. Ott	Retired
Gloria Doe Kulah	2016	Bishop Arthur Flumo Kulah	Retired
Karen Goodman Mueller	2016	Bishop Gary E. Mueller	Arkansas Episcopal Area
Manafundu Diandja Marie-Claire Unda	2017	Bishop Gabriel Yemba Unda	East Congo Episcopal Area
Dawn Sparks Fairley	2018	Bishop Leonard Fairley	Louisville Episcopal Area

Joining by Special Concordat This Quadrennium

Autonomous Affiliated Church	Alma Y. Varela Dieppa	Hector F. Ortiz Vidal	2016	Puerto Rico	Methodist Church of Puerto Rico

Highlights of Our Life Together: 2016–2018

Unless otherwise noted, the information in "Our Life Together" segments is based on the memory and personal notes of the author and information found in the episcopal spouses' scrapbooks and minutes.

Fall Council Meeting, October 30–November 2, 2016— St. Simon's Island, GA

The spouses gathered to tend to necessary business followed by an ice-cream social. The spouses of newly elected bishops were introduced, and all members were reminded of the new plan of organization introduced in 2014. The group voted to continue as the Bishops' Spouses' Fellowship. The team names the conveners for the meetings or for the year. The group closed the treasury, sending the remaining funds ($2,968.58) to UMCOR. Future activities will be paid for in advance or by taking a free-will offering. Interest groups, which anyone is free to initiate, were discussed. These will be coordinated through **Joan McKee**.

Jane Ives reported on progress updating the email list for the spouses, hoping that in the future bishops will take responsibility for updating their spouses' email addresses for the list the Council Office has agreed to include with the roster. The Fellowship is working with the Council office to make sure spouses also receive the personal notices and prayer requests sent to the bishops. Jane expressed concern for the surviving spouses, some of whom need a "Snail Mail Buddy" in order to receive emailed information. Also discussed was the fact that there is no provision in the new structure for recording or storing minutes. Jane volunteered to coordinate a report of this current meeting and to discuss with someone at the UM Archives and History how best to submit such records. Because cards are not being signed as a group to send to those who cannot attend or who are experiencing illness, births, or deaths, spouses were encouraged to send cards on their own.

The leadership team members at this time were: **Greta Hoshibata** (Western Jurisdiction, 2016–2017); **Joan McKee** (South Central Jurisdiction, 2017); **Char Ough** (North Central Jurisdiction, 2017); **Greater Nhiwatiwa** (Central Conferences/Africa, 2017; **Michael Johnson** (Northeastern Jurisdiction, 2018; **Sherrill Bryan** (Southeastern Jurisdiction, 2018); and someone to be named from Central Conferences/Europe and The Philippines

On Tuesday, the spouses enjoyed a fun-filled day at Jekyll Island, including a luncheon at Harry's Oceanside Restaurant, where the amazing view and sound of the waves soothed and relaxed them. Before dining, they joined together in an icebreaker to learn more about one another. After lunch, the spouses ventured out to the village to shop or visited the Georgia Sea Turtle Center to learn about the rehabilitation of turtles there. Some of them enjoyed riding the trolley to tour the historic landmarks of magnificent Millionaires Village and Cottages. This Spouses' Day Apart was hosted by **Sherrill Bryan**, bishop's spouse of the South Georgia Annual Conference. Although she was unable to attend because of a fall, Sherrill had prepared beautiful sea-themed decorations and gift bags for the group. The book club met to discuss *All the Light We Cannot See* by Anthony Doerr and *Waiting for Snow in Havana* by Carlos Eire.

—written by **Delphine Swanson**, December 2016

Spring Council Meeting, April 30, May 5, 2017—Dallas, TX

The Council met at the Fairmont Dallas Hotel. The Fellowship convened at First UMC in Dallas Monday afternoon. New spouses were introduced and the host spouse, **Joan McKee**, welcomed the group and explained upcoming activities and options. **Greta Hoshibata** explained the new functioning as a fellowship, no longer an association. **Mike Johnson** reported that the last balance of treasury, $2,576.89, had been paid to UMCOR and the account is now closed. **Leslie Bledsoe** shared information about the American Foundation for the Blind in Dallas, encouraging spouses to visit while in town. **Jane Ives** reported on her book progress (*They Also Serve: Methodist and United Methodist Bishops' Spouses, 1940–2018*). Wednesday morning, we visited the George W. Bush Presidential Library and Museum for a tour and for tea and photos with Laura Bush. The book club met on Wednesday afternoon to discuss *When Breath Becomes Air* by Paul Kalanithi, and *The 100-Year-Old Man Who Climbed Out the Window and Disappeared* by Jonas Jonasson.

Fall Council Meeting, November 5–7, 2017—Lake Junaluska, NC

The Fellowship convened Monday afternoon in the Susan Todd Lounge in Harrell Auditorium. **Mike Johnson** invited the members to stand by jurisdictions and introduce ourselves. After announcements and clarifications of plans for the week, Mike invited the spouses to engage in conversation around our tables by responding to three prompts: 1) Share your greatest joy since we last gathered; 2) Share your greatest challenge since we last gathered; 3) Pray for one another. This was a very rich time of sharing and a wonderful bonding experience.

Lee Padgett reminded the spouses to join the Facebook group he set up: Association of Bishop Spouses. The new leadership team starting November 2017 included **Mike Johnson**, **Julie Bard**, **Robin Ridenour**, **Karen Goodman**, **Millie Yambasu**, and **Nancy Graves**. After the meeting, the book group convened to discuss *The Underground Railroad* by Colson Whitehead, and *Hillbilly Elegy* by J.D. Vance.

On Tuesday, spouses participated in an outing, about which **Karen Mueller** reported: "We would like to thank the Western North Carolina Conference for their extravagant generosity in hosting our spouses' day trip. We visited the John C. Campbell Folk School, which was established to preserve the arts heritage of the area. We observed many different craft workshops and tried to outdo each other in the craft store. We won't name the winner, but let's just say the 'winning total' had close to three zeroes behind it. We were especially blessed to have lunch at the Hinton Rural Life Center. An excellent chef prepared our delicious meal and then was inundated with recipe requests! The day was filled with laughter and camaraderie and everyone agreed it was a fun-filled and informative outing. Thank you to **Janet Leeland** and her team for planning and hosting a great trip!" **Lee Padgett** arranged a great hiking trip to Cataloochee in the Great Smoky Mountains National Park for those spouses of active bishops staying for the learning retreat.

Spring Council Meeting, April 29–May 4, 2018—Chicago, IL

The Council met at the Hilton Rosemont. Sixty-two spouses registered. After the meeting, the book club met to discuss *The Wright Brothers* by David

McCullough and *A Gentleman in Moscow* by Amor Towles. Since no activities had been planned for the spouses, several groups rode into downtown Chicago by train or Uber to visit the Field Museum of Natural History, the Art Institute of Chicago, Millennium Park with its reflective "Bean" sculpture, and other places of interest. Some of the spouses met together in one large covenant group and shared around the circle, focusing on ways to communicate with each other in spite of language differences.

Fall Council Meeting, November 4–7, 2018—St. Simon's Island, GA

The spouses gathered in the Pioneer Room in Turner Lodge at Epworth-by-the-Sea on Monday afternoon. **Mike Johnson** convened the Fellowship and announced that, after this meeting, the new leadership team will consist of **Maye Saenz** (South Central Jurisdiction), **Raphael Koikoi** (Northeastern Jurisdiction), **Robin Ridenour** (Western Jurisdiction), **Julie Bard** (North Central Jurisdiction), and **Nancy Graves** (Southeastern Jurisdiction) who will also act as convener for the team. No one from the Central Conferences has been named yet. Mike announced that, instead of minutes, he was keeping a journal to pass along to the next leadership team. **Delphine Swanson** explained a plan to make donations to Epworth-by-the-Sea and Lake Junaluska, where the spouses have spent much of their time together, by buying a memorial brick for each. The spouses were invited to contribute. **Mackie Norris** spoke up for Gulfside Assembly in Waveland, Mississippi, another significant United Methodist site, which was significantly damaged when Hurricane Katrina destroyed every building there. The group decided to collect donations for Gulfside at the next meeting. **Lee Padgett** invited those interested in a bike ride to meet after lunch on Wednesday. A sign-up sheet was circulated for those interested in forming covenant groups. Mike then invited members to each share a few personal words, especially prayer concerns and joys. The book club discussed *Paul: A Biography* by N.T. Wright and *The Orphan's Tale* by Pam Jenoff. On Tuesday the spouses enjoyed an outing arranged by the South Carolina Annual Conference: luncheon in the River Room at the Coastal Kitchen Restaurant and shopping in downtown Brunswick for those who did not choose to return to Epworth right after lunch.

Author's Note—

Our organization has changed many times through the past 77 years, and it will likely change again in response to what happens in our church and in our culture and in response to the personal inclinations of our bishops' spouses. Although the practice of taking minutes was dropped for a while, the new leadership team is working on a way to resume record-keeping and communication with members not present at our meetings. The recent shift in our way of functioning has freed us up to experience a more relaxed and genuinely supportive fellowship. I am grateful for the friendships and learning opportunities our fellowship has offered me and for all who have given leadership as our organization has evolved. I pray for all those whose lives have been and will be turned upside down by the words, "We have an election." May they be blessed, as I have been, by this amazing experience.

Part 5

PROFILES OF METHODIST AND UNITED METHODIST BISHOPS' SPOUSES: 1940–2018

The following profiles are as complete and correct as possible, given the difficulty, in some cases, of reaching a living person or relative or finding source information on others. The loss of electrical power and internet access in Puerto Rico caused by Hurricane Maria in 2017 added to this difficulty. Some individuals requested that particular information not be published. Dates were taken from the list of bishops in the current edition of *The Book of Discipline of The United Methodist Church* (Nashville: The United Methodist Publishing House, 2016); William B. Oden and Robert J. Williams' book, *The Council of Bishops in Historical Perspective* (Nashville: Abingdon, 2014), and other sources, including archival documents at the United Methodist Archive and History Center in Madison, New Jersey. Unless otherwise noted, citations to annual conference journals and minutes are from The United Methodist Church. A question mark in or after a date indicates that sources gave conflicting information or that the date was estimated based on other information provided, such as year married and number of years married at time of death. To the best of our ability, we verified all facts through December 31, 2018, and we have not included events (meetings, births, deaths, marriages) that took place after that date.

Spouses are listed in alphabetical order by surname. If the bishop has a different surname, it is listed in brackets after the name of the spouse.

All links in this book were functional at the time of writing. However, some links may no longer be active at the time of publication.

Nancy Sueko Adachi-Osawa [Choy] (b. 1936)

In 1982, Nancy married Wilbur Wong Yan Choy (b. 1918). He was elected bishop in 1972 out of the California-Nevada Conference and served the Seattle Episcopal Area (1972–1980) and the San Francisco Episcopal Area (1980–1984), then retired. Nancy and Wilber settled in Seattle, Washington. Wilbur has four children from his marriage to Grace Ying Hom Choy, who died in 1977. Nancy has two children and three grandchildren.

Nancy was ordained a deacon in the Pacific Northwest Conference in 1979 and elder in the California-Nevada Conference in 1983. She served churches in both conferences, was elected delegate to the 1992 General and Western Jurisdictional Conferences, and also served as associate council director for the Pacific Northwest Conference. She retired in 1998.

—*Biographical Directory*, 2012–2016

L. Cecile Adams [Ott] (b. 1943)

In 2016, Cecile married retired Bishop Donald A. Ott (b. 1939). Don has two children and seven grandchildren with his first wife, Jan, who died in 2015. Cecile has two children and two grandchildren, plus another couple with three children that Cecile considers family.

Cecile is a long-time friend of Don and Jan. She has worked in direct service with children and families at risk through the church and other nonprofit institutions for 45 years. A retired licensed local pastor, Cecile served as a Christian educator in several local churches in the North Georgia and North Mississippi Annual Conferences, as associate council director for the North Mississippi Annual Conference (1977–1981), as director of Elementary Children's Ministries for the General Board of Discipleship (1981–1991), as associate council director for the Detroit Annual Conference (1991–1995), and then as council director (1995–1998). An avid birder and landscaper, she has written for *Alive Now* and *The Upper Room Disciplines* and is a certified leader of the RealTime CoachingTM Seminar.

—email communication with Cecile Adams, February 2017, September 2018

Mary Nicholson Ainsworth (d. 1964)

In 1893, Mary married William Newman Ainsworth (1872–1942). William was elected out of the South Georgia Annual Conference of The Methodist Episcopal Church, South, in 1918. His episcopal responsibilities included conferences and missions in Texas, Mississippi, Alabama, Tennessee, Virginia, Georgia, Cuba, China, Japan, and Korea. He also represented the church in many national and international conferences. He retired in 1938. Mary and William had two children and at least one granddaughter.

Mary served as national president of the Wesleyan College (Macon, Georgia) Alumnae Association.

—https://www.findagrave.com/cgi-bin/fg.cgi?page=gr&GRid=54419687; https://findingaids.library.emory.edu/documents/P-MSS283/printable/; https://archive.org/stream/1943November/1943_November_djvu.txt

Consuelo Garcia Y Zaragosa Alejandro (1894–1957)

In 1915, Consuelo married Dionisio Deista Alejandro (1893–1972). Dionisio was elected in 1944 out of the Philippine Islands Annual Conference, the first Filipino elected bishop in The Methodist Church. Because the Philippines were occupied by the Japanese at that time and no other Methodist bishop could go there to consecrate him, he was not consecrated until 1946, after liberation. He served the Manila Episcopal Area (1944–1948), was re-elected in 1960, served until 1964, and then retired. Consuelo and Dionisio had eight children and some grandchildren.

Consuelo was a deaconess, a graduate of Harris Deaconess Training School.

—*Philippine Islands Mission*, 2016, 33–34; https://www.facebook.com/FilipinoMethodistHistory/photos/a.330853530291656.73273.141716852538659/561246023919071/; https://library.syr.edu/digital/guides/a/alejandro_dd.htm; https://en.wikipedia.org/wiki/Dionisio_Deista_Alejandro; *Encyclopedia of World Methodism, Vol. 1*, 83–84; https://www.geni.com/people/Consuelo-Zaragosa-Garcia-Alejandro/6000000001356712033; online correspondence with Luther Jeremiah Oconer, October 2017, and with Eileen Alejandro Aguhar, November 2018

Sarah Charles Adams Allen (d. 2010)

In 1942, Sarah married Lineunt Scott Allen (1918–2004). Scott was elected in the Central Jurisdiction in 1967. He served the Gulf Coast Area (1967–1968), the Holston Episcopal Area (1968–1976), and the Western North Carolina Episcopal Area (1976–1984), then retired. Sarah and Scott had at least one daughter and one granddaughter.

Sarah was born in Covington, Georgia, and received an AB from Clark College in Atlanta, where she met Scott. "This meeting of minds and hearts led to a union of love and dedication that lasted for more than six decades. This union spanned many miles and service to humanity and the church. . . . Remembered for her love for her husband, family and others, Sarah Allen has been described as an ideal helpmate who shared her financial resources, personal influence and support with family and friends." (Council of Bishops Memorial Booklet, May 2011). Sarah later took special studies at Gammon Theological Seminary. She taught public school in Savannah, Georgia, and in New Orleans, Louisiana, and was active in UMW.

—*Biographical Directory*, 2000–2004; https://www.findagrave.com/memorial/131615212/lineunt-scott-allen; http://archives.gcah.org/bitstream/handle/10516/7423/article22.aspx.htm?sequence=2&isAllowed=y

Marian Bannon Black Alton (b. 1909)

In 1931, Marian married Ralph Taylor Alton (1908–1994). Ralph was elected out of the Northeast Ohio Annual Conference in 1960 and served the Wisconsin Area (1960–1972) and the Indiana Area (1972–1980), then retired. He was reactivated to serve the Indiana Area again (Nov. 1983–Sept. 1984). Marian and Ralph had two children.

Marion loved music and worked as a public school music supervisor and a professional soloist. She was active in Church Women United and enjoyed knitting and reading. After retirement, she continued her interest in music and volunteer work.

—*Biographical Directory,* 1984;
http://catalog.gcah.org/DigitalArchives/memoirs/Alton-Ralph-Bishop.pdf

Helen Fannings Ammons (b. 1933)

In 1993, Helen married Edsel Ammons (1924–2010). Edsel was elected by the North Central Jurisdiction in 1976 and served the Michigan Episcopal Area (1976–1984) and the West Ohio Episcopal Area (1984–1992), then retired. Edsel had six children and two granddaughters with his first wife, June, who died in 1990. Helen has three adult children.

Helen was director of Student Life at Garrett-Evangelical Theological Seminary, where Edsel served as bishop-in-residence in retirement. She is a graduate of the University of Illinois (Champaign campus), and prior to joining the staff of Garrett-Evangelical Theological Seminary, she worked as a social worker in Adoption and Foster Care. She has held many offices and positions of leadership in local congregations as well as in the Northern Illinois Annual Conference. She has been elected delegate to four Jurisdictional and General Conferences, and she served for 16 years as a member of general agencies of the church (eight years on the General Council on Finance and Administration and eight years on the General Board of Higher Education and Ministry). Her commitment to the ecumenical witness of the church is evident in her years of association with and membership on the General Assembly of the National Council of Churches. For many years, Helen has been a volunteer in community organization work and has received several awards to mark the importance of that work.

—*Biographical Directory*, 2004–2008;
email communication with Margaret Jordan, 6/17/18

June Ammons (1928–1990)

June married Edsel Ammons (1924–2010). Edsel was elected in 1976 out of the Rock River (Northern Illinois) Annual Conference and served the Michigan Episcopal Area (1976–1984) and the West Ohio Area (1984–1992), then retired. June and Edsel had six children and two grandchildren.

June, who was born in Chicago, attended Wilson Junior College and Northwestern University, majoring in business management and accounting. She worked as a business manager and accountant in the Board of Global Ministries Health and Welfare Division offices in Evanston, Illinois, during the 1960s and 1970s. Later she worked as "council liaison" for the Ohio Job Training Coordinating Council in the Ohio Bureau of Employment Services.

—*Biographical Directory*, 2004–2008; Council of Bishops Memorial Booklet, May 2011; *Minutes of the West Michigan Annual Conference*, 1991, 249

Celeste Thelma Bloxsome Amstutz (1901–1988)

In 1923, Celeste married Hobart Baumann Amstutz (1896–1980), a pastor in Illinois. In 1926, shortly after the birth of their first child, they moved to Singapore to serve as missionaries of The Methodist Church. Hobart was elected bishop in 1956 and assigned to the Singapore Area, where they served until his retirement in 1964. He was reactivated to serve in Pakistan, where they lived for the quadrennium. In 1968, they settled in Claremont, California and continued to be active in The United Methodist Church. Celeste and Hobart had two children.

Celeste graduated from Northwestern University with BL and MA degrees. She traveled for some time in Lyceum and Chautauqua as a dramatic reader and musician. She also assisted Hobart in his ministry as pastor, teacher, and editor. In Singapore, she taught at the Theological College and began the first course in Public Speaking in English in Singapore and Malaya. Celeste also served as president of the Women's Christian Temperance Union, vice president of the YWCA, and conference president of the Women's Society of Christian Service. She was a gracious hostess to hundreds of visitors to Southeast Asia. When Malayan Methodism celebrated its semi-centennial anniversary in 1935, Celeste directed the presentation of the 400-person pageant, "The Morning Light," depicting that history. In 1941, when the Japanese attacked the Malay peninsula, she escaped to India where their children were attending the Woodstock School. For two years, she taught classes and assisted with administration at Woodstock. In 1943, they returned to the United States, where the boys enrolled in American universities. Hobart, who had remained in Singapore in 1941, became a prisoner-of-war for three and a half years, then when released, returned to the U.S. After their return to Singapore and his election to the episcopacy, she continued as his helpmate in the role of bishop's wife.

—*Biographical Directory*, 1984; Amstutz, Mission Biographical Files [UM Archives–GCAH, Madison, New Jersey]; https://www.findagrave.com/memorial/94381542

Jennie Lulah Ketcham Anderson (1862–1950)

In 1887, Jennie married William Franklin Anderson (1860–1944). William was elected in The Methodist Episcopal Church in 1908 after serving in the New York area and was assigned to the Chattanooga Episcopal Area (1908–1912), the Cincinnati Episcopal Area (1912–1924?), and the Boston Episcopal Area (1924–1932), then retired. From 1915 through 1918, he also supervised missions in Italy, France, Finland, Norway, North Africa, and Russia, making five trips to Europe during World War II. Jennie and William had seven children and 15 grandchildren.

Jennie, the daughter of a Cincinnati minister, was a classmate of William's at Ohio Wesleyan University. She was instrumental in establishing several organizations, such as Esther Hall, Mother's Memorial Friendship Home, and the Home for the Aged, all in Cincinnati. Throughout her life, she devoted herself to church and welfare work. In 1938, she published a book titled *Bible Trails for Children with Holiday By-Paths.*

—https://en.wikipedia.org/wiki/William_F._Anderson_(bishop); http://catalog.gcah.org/publicdata/files/4642/Done/anderson-bishop-william.pdf (p. 7); information sent by family September 2017; https://www.facebook.com/Bishop-William-Franklin-Anderson-Jennie-Lulah-Ketcham-Descendants-315115341978746/

Lilly Waag Andreassen

In 1949, Lilly married Harry Peter Andreassen (1922–2010). Harry was elected bishop in 1964, after serving in Norway and as a missionary in Angola, at the Africa Central Conference. He was assigned to the Angola Episcopal Area. Lilly and Harry had four children.

Lilly was a graduate nurse.

—*Encyclopedia of World Methodism, Vol. 1,* 106

Edna Priscilla Caye Archer (1891–1950)

In 1916, Edna married Raymond Leroy Archer (1887–1970). Raymond, a missionary out of the Pittsburgh Annual Conference of The Methodist Episcopal Church, was elected in 1950 by the Southeast Asia Central Conference, the first westerner elected bishop out of that conference. He served the Singapore Episcopal Area (1950–1956), then retired. Edna and Raymond moved back to Pittsburgh. Having no children of their own, they delighted in their nieces and nephews.

Edna graduated from Chicago Evangelical Institute (now Vennard College). For several years, while awaiting her missionary appointment, she worked as a teacher for the YWCA, particularly among the immigrants living in the Westinghouse Valley. After Raymond returned from missionary service in Java, they married and returned to Java, then to Sumatra, Borneo, and Singapore, for 40 years of service in the foreign mission field. A missionary in her own right, Edna was active in teaching and leading music, especially in Christian Education with children. She was a gracious hostess to the local congregations as well as the many visitors from the United States who came to observe the work of the church in the Singapore area. A gifted speaker, Edna traveled throughout the United States making presentations about the work of the Board of Missions.

—*Encyclopedia of World Methodism, Vol. 1*, 126; https://en.wikipedia.org/wiki/Raymond_LeRoy_Archer; http://prabook.com/web/person-view.html?profileId=282625; *The Official Journal and Yearbook*, the Western Pennsylvania Conference, 1973, 318

Mary Leeper Kennedy Archipley [Kennedy] (1906–2000)

In 1928, Mary married Gerald Hamilton Kennedy (1907–1980). He was elected in 1948 and assigned to the Portland (Oregon) Episcopal Area (1948–1952) and the Los Angeles Area (1952–1972), then retired.

Mary and Gerry attended high school together and went on to the Pacific School of Religion. She is quoted in *TIME* magazine (May 8, 1964) as saying, "We have a hard time advising young people against early marriage." Mary was by Gerald's side during both his active years and his long illness at the end of his life, absolutely selfless in her devotion to him. In 1981, Mary married Paul Archipley and continued to live in California. She was always neatly dressed and wore her hair in a trademark bun until she changed her hairstyle because of the ravages of Parkinson's disease, which was diagnosed in 1986.

—*Biographical Directory*, 1984; *A Celebration of Ministry, California-Pacific Annual Conference*, 2001, 22

Ruth Mandac Arichea (b. 1940)

In 1963, Ruth married Daniel C. Arichea Jr (b. 1934). Danny was elected in 1994 while serving in Hong Kong as Regional Translation Coordinator for the Asia-Pacific Area United Bible Societies. He served the Baguio Episcopal Area (1994–2000), then retired. Ruth and Danny have three children and four grandchildren.

Ruth attended Philippine Christian College, Union Theological Seminary (BA-Religious Education, Major in Sacred Music, 1960; DMin, 2001, major in History of Methodism in the Philippines); Duke University Divinity School (MRE, 1965), and Philippines Women's University (BA-Music, 1974). She has taught music at Harris Memorial College and Union Theological Seminary. When her husband joined the United Bible Societies, she and the rest of the family moved to where he was assigned, first in Thailand (1972–1974), where she taught music at a Thai high school, then in Indonesia (1975–1987), where she taught at Jakarta International School, and in Hong Kong

(1987–1995), where she worked with the Filipino ministry at the English-speaking Methodist Church, directing two choirs and acting as adviser to the Filipino Methodist Fellowship. In addition to helping her husband in the episcopal office, Ruth was (and continues to be) executive director of KAGAWAD, a nonprofit, non-stock foundation established in 1995 to assist church workers and their families. She is also involved in the Ligo Land ministry of Central UMC in Manila (*Ligo* is the Tagalog word for "bath"). Ligo Land is a ministry to street children in the vicinity of Central Church, funded primarily by honorariums received by Bishop Arichea. Ruth has recently been consecrated by Bishop Rodolfo A. Juan as music minister of the Philippines Annual Conference.

—*Biographical Directory*, 2004–2008;
email communication with Bishop Arichea, June 2017

Dorothy Barnhart Ault (b. 1924)

In 1943, Dorothy married James Mase Ault (1918–2008). He was elected bishop out of the Wyoming Annual Conference in 1972 and served the Philadelphia Episcopal Area (1972–1980) and the Pittsburgh Episcopal Area (1980–1988), then retired. Dorothy and Jim have three living children (a fourth died in infancy), four grandchildren, and one great-granddaughter.

Dorothy earned a BS from Montclair State College in 1970. She then worked professionally as a speech therapist with emotionally disturbed children. After Jim's election to the episcopacy, she continued to do volunteer work in this field, finding it a very gratifying and important part of her life. She is also fond of gardening, quilting, and antiquing.

Favorite Scripture: Micah 6:8 / Favorite Hymn: "God of Our Life" by Hugh Thomson Kerr

—*Biographical Directory*, 2000–2004;
email communication with Dorothy Ault, 5/15/2017, 9/3/2018

Mary Putnam Stearns Badley (d. 1946)

In 1903, Mary married Brenton Thoburn Badley (1876–1949). Brenton, born to missionary parents and raised in Bombay, India, served there as a missionary himself. He was elected in The Methodist Episcopal Church in 1924 and assigned to Bombay and later to Delhi, retiring in 1944. Mary and Brenton had three children.

Mary was born in New Hampshire and graduated from the College of Liberal Arts at Boston University. She taught high school for two years in Massachusetts and then offered her services to the Women's Foreign Missionary Society. Isabella Thoburn, on furlough in the United States, invited Mary to teach at the Women's College that is now Isabella Thoburn College in India. There Mary met Brenton, a professor of English at what is now Lucknow Christian College. They founded a home filled with

Christian love and hospitality. Her obituary describes her as "a sincere friend, patient, understanding and helpful." She was an active member of the North India Women's Foreign Missionary Society Conference, even after Brenton was elected bishop and they moved to Bombay, hundreds of miles away. While in Bombay, she served as a member of the Managing Committee of the Missionary Settlement of University Women and of the Bombay Presidency Women's Council, through which she connected with women of the Hindu, Muslim, and Parsee communities. Although she was not well, she is credited with contributing substantially to framing the Constitution of the Women's Society of Christian Service, and she served as first president of the conference WSCS.

—*Indian Witness* (May 23, 1946), 1–2, and other documents in Brenton Badley's administrative file at the UM Archives and History Center; https://www.ancestry.com/genealogy/records/mary-putnam-stearns_41356104; *Encyclopedia of World Methodism, Vol. 1*, 194

Lena Sarah Benson Baker (d. 1966)

In 1901, Lena married James Chamberlain Baker (1879–1969). James was elected in 1928 out of the Illinois Annual Conference of The Methodist Episcopal Church and was assigned to supervision of Japan, Korea, and Manchuria (1928–1932), the San Francisco Episcopal Area (1932–1948), and the Los Angeles Episcopal Area (1948–1952), then retired.

Lena was born in Missouri. She studied music while James was studying at Boston University. They returned to Illinois and served a little country church for two years; then he was appointed to the University of Illinois. They opened their home to students and founded the first Wesley Foundation. According to a memoir written by Bishop Gerald Kennedy, she was as eager to go to Asia as her husband was: "She filled the role of first lady of our Area with dignity and respect. In the words of the book of Proverbs, 'A good wife is the crown of her husband.' And if I may say so, his comfort and his hope." A memorial from the bishops' wives' meeting noted that "She was an unrelenting rebel against sham and any form of tyranny."

—*Encyclopedia of World Methodism, Vol. 1*, 198–199; *Journal of the Southern California-Arizona Annual Conference, The Methodist Church, 1967*, 265; Spouses' Scrapbooks, 1949–1964

Janaki John Panikar Balaram

In 1934, Janaki married Prabhakar Christopher Benjamin Balaram (1906–1968). Prabhakar, born in India, was elected in 1965 by the Central Conference of Southern Asia after serving in India and with the Board of Missions in the United States, where he also studied for five years. He was assigned to the Bengal and Lucknow Annual

Conferences but died before completing the quadrennium. Janaki and Prabhakar had three children.

—*Encyclopedia of World Methodism, Vol. 1*, 200–201

Barry Steiner Ball (b. 1961)

In 1987, Barry married Sandra Lynn Steiner (b. 1962). Sandra was elected out of the Peninsula-Delaware Conference in 2012 and assigned to the West Virginia Episcopal Area. Barry and Sandra have two daughters.

Barry graduated from the Citadel in Charleston, South Carolina, and from Duke Divinity School, where he and Sandra met. He recently completed his DMin from Wesley Theological Seminary. He is an ordained elder with membership in the Peninsula-Delaware Conference. Barry is also an endorsed military chaplain with the Air Force Reserves. In 2017, he retired from his position with Maryland Department of Natural Resources and Drug Enforcement Agency. Barry currently is working with local churches in West Virginia, helping them find ways to respond to the opioid epidemic. Barry is also the primary caretaker of the episcopal canine, Oscar.

—*Biographical Directory*, 2012–2016; personal letter, December 17, and email communication with Barry Ball, January 2018

Regina Leah Taylor Bangura (1925–2005)

In 1952, Regina married Thomas Syla Bangura (1925–2006). In 1979, Thomas was elected out of the Sierra Leone Annual Conference, then an autonomous Methodist church. In 1984, it became part of the West Africa Central Conference of the United Methodist Church. Thomas served the Sierra Leone Episcopal Area until 1992, then retired. Regina and Thomas had four children and two grandchildren.

Regina, daughter of a Christian father and Muslim mother, attended Harford School for Girls and Nurses' School, graduating with SRN and SCM certificates. She worked for the Sierra Leone government and then for the Kissy Clinic of The United Methodist Church. She took training in Planned Parenthood at the Margaret Sanger Institute in New York and earned a diploma in Practical Nursing from the Philadelphia School of Practical Nursing. "Regina Bangura loved people and she was loved by people. . . . She had a gift for cultivating friendships among the poor. She attended the poor, she walked with the poor, she fed the poor and provided clothing for the poor. She believed in service and Christian discipleship. She once said, 'Christian discipleship calls for sharing our money, time and love. The demands of discipleship seem to be severe at times, and yet those who make the sacrifice testify to the rewards that they receive.'" Her hobbies were reading and singing.

—*Biographical Directory*, 2000–2004; *Council of Bishops Memorial Booklet*, Spring 2007; http://sierraleoneumc.org/?page_id=259

Odette de Olivereira Barbieri (1899–1983)

In 1924, Odette married Sante Uberto Barbieri (1902–1989), who was born in Italy, raised Roman Catholic, and brought to Brazil at the age of eight. After converting, becoming a Methodist minister, and serving churches in Brazil and Argentina and as a seminary professor and dean, Sante was elected bishop in 1949 by the Latin American Central Conference. He served an episcopal area including Argentina, Bolivia, and Uruguay and was reelected for four consecutive quadrennia. After that, he was invited by the Council of Bishops of The United Methodist Church to continue as a bishop for one year, after which he was appointed bishop of The Methodist Church in Peru. He retired as an active bishop in 1970 but continued presiding over the organization of the Methodist churches in Argentina, Bolivia, Costa Rica, Panama, Peru, and Uruguay as they became autonomous; as well as preaching, lecturing, and writing. Odette and Sante had four children, 14 grandchildren, and 12 great-grandchildren.

Odette, born in Brazil, was a schoolteacher when she met Sante, who converted from his Catholic upbringing. She was influential in his joining The Methodist Church and becoming a minister.

—https://en.wikipedia.org/wiki/Sante_Uberto_Barbier; *Biographical Directory*, 1984; *Encyclopedia of World Methodism, Vol. 1*, 222–223

Julie B. Bard (b. 1960)

In 1982, Julie married David A. Bard (b. 1959). David was elected bishop in 2016 out of the Minnesota Annual Conference and assigned to the Michigan Episcopal Area. Julie and David have three children.

Julie graduated from the University of Minnesota with a BAS in Kindergarten, Elementary, and Special Education. She has worked as a public school teacher and currently teaches first grade. She is also a volunteer tutor for refugee children in Lansing, Michigan, and serves as a docent at the Michigan History Museum. Julie enjoys spending time with her family, traveling, walking, reading, and sewing.

Favorite Scripture: 1 Corinthians 16:13-14 / Favorite Hymn: "We Are Called" (*TFWS*, 2172)

—email communication with Julie Bard, July 2017

Carolyn Ruth Baumgartner Bashore (b. 1933)

In 1957, Carolyn married George Willis Bashore (b. 1934). George, ordained in the former Evangelical United Brethren Church in 1958, was elected bishop in 1980 out of the Eastern Pennsylvania Annual Conference. He served the Boston Episcopal Area (1980–1988) and the Pittsburgh Episcopal Area (1988–2000), then retired.

Carolyn and George settled in Pittsburgh. They have three children and seven grandchildren.

Carolyn graduated from the Westminster Choir College in Princeton with a BA in music in 1956. She traveled with the Westminster Choir on a six-month world tour and sang numerous concerts in Carnegie Hall with the New York Philharmonic Orchestra.

—*Biographical Directory*, 2000–2004

Martha Harrold Baxter (1897–1980)

Martha married Bruce Richard Baxter (1892–1947). Bruce was elected in 1940 by the Western Jurisdiction of The Methodist Church while serving as president of Willamette University since 1934. He served the Portland Episcopal Area, which included Oregon, Idaho, Washington, and the Territory of Alaska, from 1940 until his death in 1947.

Born in Ohio, Martha studied at Mount Union College in Alliance, Ohio, and later studied music and Italian at Radcliffe College. She was active in the educational settings where Bruce worked and had opportunities to travel overseas. She was known for her "zest for selfless service," and after Bruce's death, Martha devoted herself to the care of Bruce's mother and sister. She also continued to be active in The Methodist Church.

—*Journal 13th Session of the Oregon-Idaho Annual Conference, 1981*, 97–98; https://www.findagrave.com/cgi-bin/fg.cgi?page=gr&GRid=101954378; http://library.willamette.edu/archives/history/presidents/baxter/

Melissa Kay Riffell Beard (b. 1957)

In 1981, Melissa married Frank J. Beard (b. 1953). Frank was elected in 2016 out of the Indiana Annual Conference and assigned to the Illinois Episcopal Area. Melissa and Frank have two daughters and three grandchildren.

Melissa, born in Indiana, completed undergraduate degrees in Biblical Literature at Bethel College-Mishawaka and Nursing at Ball State University and an MA in social work at Indiana University. She worked for over 30 years in the field of mental health before becoming a hospice social worker. Her hobbies include sewing and crafts, collecting buttons, and antiques.

—https://www.sj-r.com/news/20160723/new-methodist-bishop-likes-to-engage-people; email communication with Melissa Beard, February 2018

Ada Blanche Whitehurst Beauchamp (1876–1957)

Ada married William Benjamin Beauchamp (1869–1931). William was elected in The Methodist Episcopal Church, South, in 1922, after serving churches in Virginia and Kentucky. He served the 12th Episcopal District, comprising Missions in

Europe (1922–1926), then Georgia and Mexico. Ada and William had four (or eight) children.

—https://www.findagrave.com/memorial/92829490; https://prabook.com/web/william.beauchamp/1100722

Shirley Ann Cundiff Bethea (1931–1992)

In 1958, Shirley married Joseph Benjamin Bethea (1932–1995). Joseph was elected in 1988 out of the North Carolina Annual Conference and assigned to the Columbia Episcopal Area, where he served until his death. Shirley and Joseph had one daughter.

Shirley graduated from Bennett College in Greensboro, North Carolina. After teaching in public schools in Scotland County, Reidsville, Greensboro, Rockingham, and Raleigh in North Carolina and in Richmond, Virginia, Shirley retired from teaching to become a full-time volunteer in a variety of ministries of The United Methodist Church and community organizations. She was active in the life and work of I. DeQuincey Newman United Methodist Church. She participated with the UMW at the local church, district and conference levels. Shirley served on a number of boards and agencies including Epworth Children's Home, Columbia Urban League, Bethlehem Center, and Killingsworth Home. She gave unselfishly of her time, talent and resources. As a daughter, a sister, wife and mother, she was passionate about and loved her family, which was evident at every family gathering. The following words speak to her life that was rooted in her love of God and guided by her passion to serve: "If I can help somebody as I pass along, if I can cheer somebody with a word or song, if I can show somebody he's traveling wrong, then my living will not be in vain" (Martin Luther King Jr, in a sermon preached at Ebenezer Baptist Church and replayed at his funeral).

—*Biographical Directory*, 1992; email communication with daughter Josepha Bethea Wall, July 2017; http://kevinstilley.com/martin-luther-king-quotes/

Sally Bickerton (b. 1965)

In 2003, Sally married Thomas J. Bickerton (b. 1958). Tom was elected in 2004 out of the West Virginia Annual Conference. He served the Pittsburgh Episcopal Area (2004–2016) and the New York Episcopal Area starting in 2016. Sally and Tom have four children.

Sally graduated from West Liberty State College in West Virginia with a BS in Business Administration and worked in accounting in the insurance industry and for a credit union. While Tom was serving in the Pittsburgh Episcopal Area, she worked in the finance department at the Western Pennsylvania Conference Center. She enjoys reading, baking, horseback riding and spending time with family.

Favorite Scripture: Philippians 4:6 / Favorite Hymn: "It Is Well with My Soul" (*UMH*, 377)

—*Biographical Directory*, November 2004–2008; email communication with Sally Bickerton, July 2017

Laura Close Birney (1868–1963)

Laura married Lauress John Birney (1871–1937). Lauress was elected in 1920 after serving churches in Ohio and Massachusetts and serving as dean of Boston University School of Theology. He served the Shanghai Episcopal Area in China (1920–1932), then retired in ill health. Laura and Lauress had one daughter and two grandchildren.

His memoir notes that Laura was his "constant companion over roads that were pleasant and roads that were hard." Together they "made the episcopal residence in Shanghai a home of refuge and comfort to all missionaries going through this port of entry to China, when disturbed in mind, weakened in body, or impoverished in purse. Here these two ministered gladly to every need as though each newcomer who crossed their threshold was among their nearest kin."

—*Official Record of the 5th United and 37th Annual Session Eastern Swedish Conference, The Methodist Episcopal Church 1937*, 139–14; https://www.findagrave.com/cgi-bin/fg.cgi?page=gr&GRid=136760170; https://www.findagrave.com/cgi-bin/fg.cgi?page=gr&GRid=136760171; http://catalog.gcah.org/publicdata/files/4642/bishop-lauress-j-birney.pdf

Jewell Louise Fannin Haddock Blackburn (1922–2018)

In 1978, Jewell married Bishop Robert McGrady Blackburn (1919-2002), who was serving the Raleigh Episcopal Area (1972–1980). He served the Richmond Episcopal Area (1980–1988), then retired. Robert had three children with his first wife, Mary Jeanne Everett Blackburn, who died in 1977. Together Robert and Jewell had six children, eight grandchildren, five step-grandchildren, and one step-great-grandson.

Jewell, born in Florida, was the widow of Judge L. Page Haddock, with whom she had three children. Jewell was awarded honorary life memberships in both the Florida and National Parent-Teacher Association for her outstanding leadership and service in this organization. She was also active in the local church, academic institutions, and civic programs. In 1969, she was appointed by Governor Claude Kirk to the Advisory Board of the Florida Division of Youth Services. She was also a trustee of Florida State College at Jacksonville, serving during the critical first decade of that institution. She was a licensed lobbyist for the State and National PTAs, in both the Florida Legislature and Congress.

—*Biographical Directory*, 1984; http://www.legacy.com/obituaries/timesunion/obituary.aspx?n=robert-m-blackburn&pid=262186; obituary posted by the Council of Bishops' office, March 22, 2018

Mary Jeanne Everett Blackburn (1922–1977)

In 1943, Mary Jeanne married Robert McGrady Blackburn (1919–2002). Bob was elected in 1972 out of the Florida Annual Conference and served the Raleigh Episcopal Area (1972–1980) and the Richmond Episcopal Area (1980–1988), then retired. Mary Jeanne and Robert had three children.

Mary Jeanne graduated from Georgia State College for Women and did graduate work at Candler School of Theology, Emory University. She taught Social Studies at the high school level and later did social work with the American Red Cross. Mary Jeanne was a vital part of her husband's ministry from the beginning of his first appointment. As one of their parishioners wrote, "When Bob Blackburn became your preacher, you had two people ministering to the needs of the church. She knew everyone in the church by name as well as by family and had a special talent for making each person feel important and needed. Her role seemed to come easy to her because of her love of Christ and His church and her devotion to Bob. . . . When her husband was elected bishop, she was unaffected. She began forthwith to learn her new constituents by name, along with their families, their personal joys, frustrations, and anticipations. . . .She organized the ministers' wives. Understanding their frustrations with the itinerant system, she directed the development of a compendious collection of scrapbooks (one for each district) with professional pictures of each parsonage, a floor plan, a listing of all furnishings provided. . . . The depth of genuineness of Mary Jeanne's faith became more apparent as her illness became more obviously acute to her and her family. . . . During the long, tedious days of the months prior to her death she manifested the same calm assurance, the same profound faith, the same adorable devotion, the same fearless discipleship which had characterized her during her most active days when she went among the people she loved."

—*Journal of the Florida Annual Conference* [May 30–June 2, 1978], 377–378; http://www.legacy.com/obituaries/timesunion/obituary.aspx?n=robert-m-blackburn&pid=262186; *Biographical Directory*, 1984

Karen Miers Blake (b. 1939)

In 1957, Karen married Bruce P. Blake (born 1938). Bruce was elected in 1988 out of the Kansas West Annual Conference and served the Dallas Episcopal Area (1988–1996) and the Oklahoma Episcopal Area (1996–2004), then retired. Karen and Bruce settled back in Kansas. They have three sons, four grandchildren, and three great-grandchildren.

Karen attended Friends University. She served as personal secretary to Drs. David and Vera Mace, authors of marriage and family resources and programs, and as administrative secretary at Woodlawn United Methodist Church. She has served on the Board of Trustees of Lydia Patterson Institute, El Paso, Texas, a mission project of the South Central Jurisdiction of The United Methodist Church. In retirement, Karen is very active in community work, which includes serving on the Board of Directors of the Winfield Meals on Wheels program and being involved in her local church, Grace United Methodist Church in Winfield, Kansas. Her hobbies include growing plants and flowers, doing volunteer work, walking, doing needlework, and traveling.

—*Biographical Directory,* 2000–2004; https://www.unitedmethodistbishops.org/person-detail/2463407; email communication with Karen Blake, July 2017

Mary Jane Eaton Blake

In 1930, Mary Jane married Edgar Blake (1869–1943). Edgar was elected in The Methodist Episcopal Church in 1920 after serving churches in New Hampshire. He served the Paris Episcopal Area (1920–1928) and the Indianapolis Episcopal Area (1928–1940, including the Detroit Episcopal Area after the 1939 merger), then retired. Edgar had two sons and two daughters by his first wife, Charlotte Woodman Blake, who died in 1925.

Mary Jane, from Circleville, Ohio, served as a missionary under the Women's Foreign Missionary Society for 11 years. She met Edgar while she was in Europe, in charge of the Crandon Institute, a girls' school in Rome. She also worked with the Women's Home Missionary Society in Ohio. She is noted for her genuine friendship, leadership skills, and speaking ability and was sometimes assigned by her husband to fill in for him on important occasions.

—http://catalog.gcah.org/publicdata/files/4642/blake-bishop-edgar.pdf; "Tribute to Mrs. Edgar Blake, A Woman of Service," by Mrs. Walter R. Fruit, *Michigan Christian Advocate* [June 20, 1940], 7

Leslie Jean Bray Bledsoe (b. 1947)

In 1985, Leslie married Wilbert Earl Bledsoe (b. 1950). Earl was elected in 2008 and assigned to the Dallas Episcopal Area, then to the New Mexico/Northwest Texas Episcopal Area in 2012. Leslie and Earl have a blended family of six children, 12 grandchildren, and two great-grandchildren.

Leslie started college at Prairie View A&M University in Texas. After the first semester, she joined the Marine Corps and then went to work for the Veterans Administration in New Jersey. She returned to Texas and went to work for the Social Security Administration, then returned to Prairie View to finish her BA. She became a licensed social worker and worked at nonprofit crisis centers for battered women and homeless persons. She then received a call to ministry, earned her local pastor's license, and was appointed to a local church. While serving there, she also began working at another job at a college near her home.

In 2002, after experiencing severe headaches, she suddenly woke up in the hospital, totally blind. This was an extreme shock, and she was completely overwhelmed by fear and worry about how she would be able to live her life. She went through a period of grieving and depression, during which she was supported by members of churches Earl had served. One group offered their companionship, comfort, and encouragement and helped her begin to function again. She was very afraid of going out in the public because, although she saw bright colors, she could not recognize objects. They took her outside and helped her with mobility skills. Another group came for an hour every Wednesday and prayed with her. That was when she began to function again. She started in her kitchen, getting things organized so she could find them, and then gradually began to go places and do more things to overcome her fear. Earl encouraged and supported her through all these difficult adjustments.

Meeting and talking with other people helped get her mind off the challenges she faced. Visiting churches as the bishop's wife, talking and praying with people, helped her overcome her fear. It was hard coming to the Bishops' Spouses' meetings at first, but she was lovingly received, and she made herself speak up, reach out to people, and help others understand how best to support her. The Commission for the Blind provided her with technology and tools, computer software and cassette tapes, to help her adapt to being blind. Although she still struggles with fear sometimes, especially in new situations, Leslie likes to tell individuals and groups about the supports available for the blind and even for those with low vision. For example, the American Council of the Blind (www.acb.org/), which has a center in Dallas where Leslie sometimes volunteers; the National Federation of the Blind (https://nfb.org/); and the American Foundation for the Blind (www.afb.org/) all provide technology, training, and other supports to remove barriers, create solutions, and expand possibilities for persons with vision loss.

—*Biographical Directory*, 2012–2016;
interview with Leslie Bledsoe, 5/3/17, and telephone interview, 8/6/17

Carolyn Odalie Browne Boaz (1869–1963)

In 1894, Carrie married Hiram Abiff Boaz (1866–1962). Hiram was elected in The Methodist Episcopal Church, South, in 1922, while serving as president of Southern Methodist University, having been deeply involved in the founding and early years of that institution. He served in Asia (1922–1926), overseeing church work in Japan, China, Korea, Manchuria, and Siberia. They returned to the United States, and he served the Arkansas and Oklahoma Conferences of The Methodist Episcopal Church, South (1926–1930). For the next eight years, he served several other conferences within Texas and New Mexico, retiring in 1938. Carrie and Hiram settled in Dallas, and he became a trustee of Southern Methodist University. They had three daughters, four grandchildren, and six great-grandchildren.

Carrie, the daughter of a preacher who was the first Methodist missionary to the Indians, met Hiram while they were both attending Sam Houston Normal School in Texas. They both taught in public schools in Texas until he received his call to ministry. Although she questioned that call at first, she continued to work while he went back to school. In 1906, after several years in the pastorate, he was elected president of Polytechnic College in Fort Worth. They lived in an apartment in a girls' dormitory, and she enjoyed being housemother to the female students and helping Hiram turn the struggling college into a thriving institution. Later, while he was studying in New York City, she audited courses at Columbia and took advantage of the city's library, museums, and concerts, while focusing on raising their children. During his first four years as a bishop, she traveled with him in Asia, separated from her child, family, friends, and all that was familiar to her, but she remained "steady, true, and cheerful." During their years living in Little Rock, Arkansas, she was happy to be near their grandchildren, and she also enjoyed living in Houston, Fort Worth, and finally Dallas.

—*Annual Journal Central Texas Conference of The Methodist Church, 1963*, 184–186; https://en.wikipedia.org/wiki/Hiram_Abiff_Boaz; https://www.findagrave.com/memorial/136205470/caroline-odalie-boaz; http://www.lib.utexas.edu/taro/smu/00068/smu-00068.html

Marta Bolleter-Zellweger (b. 1937)

In 1966, Marta married Heinrich Bolleter (b. 1941). Heinrich was elected in 1989 out of the Switzerland/France Annual Conference by the Central Conference of Central and Southern Europe. He was elected again for life in 1993. He served the Central and Southern Europe Episcopal Area (1989–2006), then retired. Marta and Heinrich have three children and five grandchildren.

Marta was involved with the women's groups that were key to the revitalization of local churches through the period of political changes (1991–2004), which brought about new mission opportunities in Eastern Europe and the Balkans. She encouraged and supported them by organizing and leading women's seminars throughout the area. She taught creative ways to do Bible study and supported the mediation and reconciliation efforts between the ethnicities and national groups, which were needed for an authentic Christian witness in the society. In the local church in Switzerland, she led the committee to organize breakfast meetings for women. Marta trained as a teacher for creative design. She loves sewing and crafting, and reading is still at the center of her interests.

Favorite Scripture: Psalm 73:28 / Favorite Hymn: "Come Let Us with Our Lord Arise" (*TFWS*, 2084)

—*Biographical Directory*, 2000–2004 and 2004–2008; email communication with Bishop Bolleter and Marta Bolleter-Zellweger, February 2018

Berthe Ngbesso Odombo Boni

In 1979, Berthe married Benjamin Boni (b. 1952). Benjamin, who was President of the Annual Conference of The Methodist Protestant Church of Côte d'Ivoire, was elected bishop of the newly established Annual Conference of the United Methodist church in Côte d'Ivoire in 2004. Berthe and Benjamin have six children.

Berthe pursued her elementary education in Côte d'Ivoire and received training in Family Education at the School of Parents and Educators in Strasbourg, France. She is a member of the Retired Clergy/Surviving Spouses Chaplaincy Team, an Advisor to the Association of Spouses of the Clergy, a Member of the Episcopal Visitation Team, and a Member of the Jubilee Women's Choir.

—*Biographical Directory*, 2008–2012; http://ee.umc.org/bishops/bishop-benjamin-boni

Esma Rideout Booth (1902–1988)

In 1925, Esma married Newell Snow Booth (1903–1968). Newell was elected in 1944 after serving churches in Massachusetts and then as a missionary in the Congo. He served the Congo Episcopal Area (1944–1964). When the Belgian Congo became an independent nation, he was assigned to the Harrisburg Episcopal Area, serving there until his death. Esma and Newell had three children, one who died at the age of two, and five grandchildren.

Esma was born in Maine and grew up in Massachusetts. She graduated from Boston University, where she met and married Newell, and taught high school. She later earned an MA in pre-school education from Hartford Seminary in 1936. In 1928, she went to Africa with Newell, where she did teaching and translating and worked with literacy programs. During World War II, she stayed in the United States with their children, separated from her husband. She especially enjoyed writing and published many children's stories based on her experiences in Africa in efforts to "raise our consciousness of a world community."

—*Encyclopedia of World Methodism, Vol. 1*, 299; https://prabook.com/web/newell_snow.booth/1096449; *Official Journal 1989 Central Pennsylvania Conference*, 465

Martha Rygge Borgen (1928–2003)

In 1949, Martha married Ole Edvard Borgen (1926–2009). Ole was elected in 1970 out of the Norway Annual Conference, while serving as European secretary of the World Methodist Council; he served the Norway Episcopal Area (1970–1989), then retired. In retirement, he served as bishop-in-residence at Asbury Theological Seminary in Wilmore, Kentucky (1989–1992), after which they returned to Lillestrøm, Norway. Martha and Ole had two children.

Martha was a member of the National Board of UMW in Sweden and in Norway and also of the Norwegian Ecumenical Women's Council. In 1996, she was a delegate to the World Federation of Methodist Women Assembly in Rio de Janeiro, as well as to the World Methodist Council in the same city, representing the Northern Europe Central Conference. She also served as president of the Women's Association of the Norway Annual Conference.

—*Biographical Directory*, 2000–2004, 2004–2008

Betty Ann Fisher Boulton (b. 1931)

In 1949, Betty Ann married Edwin Charles Boulton (1928–2000). Ed was elected bishop in 1980 out of the East Ohio Annual Conference. He served the Dakotas Episcopal Area (1980–1988) and the East Ohio Episcopal Area (1988–1996), then retired. Betty Ann and Ed have four children, three grandchildren, and one great-grandchild.

Betty Ann studied organ as a special student at the University of Dubuque, University of Iowa, St. Olaf College, Eastman School of Music, and Duke University. She earned her BM in organ performance from Concordia College in Moorhead, Minnesota, in 1986 and her MM in organ performance from The University of Akron in 1993. She taught organ and piano for 53 years and retired in 2011 after being organist for Emmanuel United Church of Christ for nine years. She also taught in public schools and gave private piano lessons. Her special interests include music, reading, time with family, and time in the sun. She now lives at Copeland Oakes Retirement Community in Sebring, Ohio, in independent living since 2015.

Favorite Hymn: "When in Our Music God Is Glorified" (*UMH*, 68)

—*Biographical Directory*, 2000–2004; email communication, July 2017

Margaret Davis Bowen (1894–1976)

In 1921, Margaret married John Wesley Edward Bowen Jr (1889–1962). John, grandson of former slaves, was elected in 1948 by the Central Jurisdiction of The Methodist Church and served the Atlantic Coast Area (1948–1960), then retired. Margaret and John had one son.

Margaret received her MED from the University of Cincinnati in 1935. An educator, she led the Gilbert Academy, a leading private Black college in New Orleans, in the late 1930s. After John's election, she resigned from Gilbert and moved to Atlanta, where she became the first president of the neighborhood association of Just Us, the first Black-owned constructed subdivision in the city of Atlanta, where a small park has been dedicated to her. She was a religious leader and civil rights activist, as well as being active in the church. She traveled with her husband to Liberia, Angola, and the Belgium Congo, after which she put on an outstanding week-long display of African art in the West Hunter Branch of the Atlanta Public Library.

—https://www.findagrave.com/cgi-bin/fg.cgi?page=gr&GRid=147533656; https://en.wikipedia.org/wiki/Margaret_Davis_Bowen; *Encyclopedia of World Methodism, Vol. 1*, 309–310; *The Central Christian Advocate* [November 29, 1951]

Elizabeth Keller Branscomb (1906–1991)

In 1928, Elizabeth married John W. Branscomb (1905–1959). John was elected in 1952 out of the Florida Annual Conference and served the Florida Episcopal Area and Cuba until his death. Elizabeth and John had two children, five grandchildren, and six great-grandchildren.

In each of John's pastorates, Elizabeth was loved and admired. Bishop Robert M. Blackburn shared these thoughts: "Although she maintained a low profile in the local and general church, she was nonetheless a strong and effective personality in many areas of the church's life. . . . [and] moved into the role of a bishop's wife with true dignity and grace. . . . Bishop Branscomb's sudden and untimely death in 1959 came as a great shock to the Florida Area and to the entire church. With quiet poise and Christian courage, Elizabeth made the adjustment as a widow and continued to live in the Florida area. . . . Elizabeth always played a supportive role in life: for her husband, her family and her church. Never one to be conspicuous, she was always there to be a companion, mother, and a loyal friend. . . . We will remember her as a delightful, cheerful individual, always witty, possessing a keen sense of humor which was evident to her very last days."

—*1992 Journal of the Florida Annual Conference*, 452; *Biographical Directory*, 1984; https://www.findagrave.com/cgi-bin/fg.cgi?page=gr&GRid=111599781

Julia Estelle Merrill Brashares (1892–1974?)

In 1916, Julia married Charles Wesley Brashares (1891–1982). Charles was elected in 1944, after serving churches in Massachusetts, Maine, Ohio, and Michigan, and served the Des Moines Episcopal Area (1944–1952) and the Chicago Episcopal Area (1952–1964), then retired. Julia ("Susie") and Charles had three sons, 11 grandchildren, and four great-grandchildren.

Julia was born in Kansas, but grew up in Somerville, Massachusetts, and graduated from Wellesley College. She was always looking for people she could help and enjoyed friendships wherever Charles served. She also traveled with Charles to Japan, China, India, Africa, and South America.

—https://en.wikipedia.org/wiki/Charles_Wesley_Brashares;
Journal and Yearbook of the Northern Illinois Conference [1975], 351–352

Moselle Mar Donaldson Broomfield (1860–1951)

In 1898, Moselle married John Calvin Broomfield (1872–1950). John was elected in 1939 out of the Pittsburgh Conference of The Methodist Protestant Church, of which he had been president since 1924. The Methodist Protestant Church elected its first two bishops that year in preparation for the next year's union. He was assigned to the St. Louis Episcopal Area and retired in 1944.

Born in West Virginia, Moselle "exercised great influence in the life of her husband. She was deeply religious, devoted to her church, and faithful to every responsibility. She possessed a very gracious personality and administered her domestic duties with untiring patience."

—*Official Journal and Yearbook Pittsburgh Annual Conference, 1951*, 896;
https://www.findagrave.com/cgi-bin/fg.cgi?page=gr&GRid=89643371; https://en.wikipedia.org/wiki/John_Calvin_Broomfield; https://www.revolvy.com/main/index.php?s=John%20Calvin%20Broomfield&item_type=topic; http://catalog.gcah.org/publicdata/files/4642/broomfield-bishop-john-c.pdf

Edith Genevive Crogman Brooks Brown [Brooks]

In 1919, Edith married Robert Nathaniel Brooks (1888–1953). Robert was elected in 1944, while serving as professor of church history at Gammon Theological Seminary. He served the New Orleans Episcopal Area from 1944 until his death in 1953.

Edith traveled with her husband to Africa, April 15–September 15, 1947, when he was sent by the Council of Bishops to review and appraise Methodist work there, and to South America, June 25–September 13, 1948, when he was sent by the Department of Foreign Missions of the Board of Missions and Church Extension. She said that the trip to Africa was the most rewarding experience of her life and that being asked to accompany her husband to South America was "a great honor." Some years after Robert's death, she married Richard S. Brown.

—*Biographical Directory*, 1984;
http://catalog.gcah.org/publicdata/files/4642/brooks-bishop-robert-n.pdf

Gertrude Virgil Brown (1875–1970)

In 1899, Gertrude married Wallace Elias Brown (1868–1939). Wallace was elected in The Methodist Episcopal Church in 1924 after serving churches in New York State. He served the Helena Episcopal Area (1928–1932) and the Chattanooga Episcopal Area (1932–1939), then was assigned to Portland, Oregon in 1939 to help with the merger in the three northwest states and Alaska. He died 11 days after arriving there. Gertrude and Wallace had five sons, 13 grandchildren, and 29 great-grandchildren.

Gertrude was born in New York State and graduated from Syracuse University, where she met Wallace. In college, she was a member of Kappa Alpha Theta sorority and a senior honorary member of Eta Pi Upsilon. She became known as "a warm, friendly and businesslike pastor's wife." After Wallace's death, she returned to Syracuse to find the new Women's Society of Christian Service struggling for acceptance. She was elected the first president of the Central New York Conference Women's Society, and "through her dynamic leadership it became a virile and supportive fellowship in nearly every charge in the conference. She was medium of stature and mild of manner, but no one misjudged her quiet style as a sign of weakness, for she was exceedingly firm, and as those who even now well remember, she could 'talk turkey' to any minister with instant results." She eventually gave up her leadership role to focus on her growing family.

—*Central New York Annual Conference . . . Official Minutes of the 104th Session, 1971*, 147–148; https://www.findagrave.com/cgi-bin/fg.cgi?page=gr&GRid=68827830; http://prabook.com/web/person-view.html?profileId=283246; http://catalog.gcah.org/publicdata/files/4642/brown-bishop-wallace-e.pdf

Minnie Jones Brown (b. 1947)

In 1982, Minnie married Warner H. Brown Jr (b. 1946). Warner was elected bishop in 2000 out of the California-Nevada Annual Conference and served the Denver Episcopal area (2000–2008) and the California-Nevada Episcopal Area (2008–2016), then retired. Minnie and Warner settled in Sacramento, California. They have three children and three grandchildren.

Minnie attended Cortez Peters Business School in Baltimore, where she was born, graduating as salutatorian of her class. She began work as a stenographer for the state of Maryland Regional Planning Council, then was promoted to secretary (I, II, and III). Her first husband, whom she married in 1967, died of cancer in 1971. She met Warner in 1981, and after their marriage, relocated with him to Oakland, California. Later she worked for the California-Nevada Annual Conference, where she gained most of her knowledge of the workings of the UMC. Minnie enjoys crafts, sewing, decorating their home, and music. She and Warner have enjoyed travels to Rome, Greece, Paris, Australia, New Zealand, Mexico, the Philippines, Africa, Korea, Figi, Tonga, Samoa, Israel, Puerto Rico, and other places.

Favorite Hymns: "I Love to Tell the Story" (*UMH*, 156), "Lord, I Want to Be a Christian" (*UMH*, 402)

—*Biographical Directory*, 2012–2016; https://www.unitedmethodistbishops.org/person-detail/2464111; email communication with Minnie Brown, September 2017

Corneille Bacon Downer Bryan (1911–1989)

In 1941, Corneille married Alonzo Monk Bryan (1914–2011). Monk was elected bishop in 1976, after serving churches in Texas and Missouri, and served the Nebraska Episcopal Area (1976–1984), then retired. Corneille and Bryan had three children and at least two grandchildren.

Corneille, born in Texas, attended Baylor University, where her father was a professor of Latin and Roman Mythology. Following his death, a few months before the end of her senior year, she taught one of his courses. She later earned an MA in education from the University of Missouri, Columbia. Corneille served as a volunteer at the University of Missouri Medical Center in Columbia and at a home for handicapped children. She was active in local church Christian education, P.E.O. (a philanthropic organization for women), and the American Association of University Women. Corneille and Monk led retreats on "Life in the Parsonage," even after his retirement. They settled at Lake Junaluska, North Carolina, and after her death, the Corneille Bryan Native Garden there was dedicated as a memorial to her.

—*Biographical Directory*, 2000–2004; *Missouri West Annual Conference Journal, 1990*, 199–200; http://www.lakejunaluska.com/activities/places_of_meditation/

Sherrill O. Cooper Bryan (b. 1949)

In 1973, Sherrill married R. Lawson Bryan (b. 1950). Lawson was elected in 2016 out of the Alabama-West Florida Annual Conference and assigned to the South Georgia Episcopal Area. Sherrill and Lawson have one son and one grandchild.

Sherrill attended both college and business school. She has worked in business and partnered with friends to run a ladies' apparel store. Her most rewarding position was as director of a performing arts center for inner city children in Mobile, Alabama. They brought children from public schools to the theater and taught them art, music, drama, and dance, then put on a performance for the community. As director, she chose themes that were faith-based and hopeful. She and Lawson met through the church, where she was serving as an adult youth leader. She loves to decorate, design, do flower arrangements, and shop for antiques; and she says, "I will paint anything."

Favorite Scripture: 2 Corinthians 4:7

—https://www.unitedmethodistbishops.org/person-detail/2463391; email communication with Sherrill Bryan, January 2018

Twila Stowe Bryan (1918–2014)

In 1943, Twila married William McFerrin Stowe (1913–1988). McFerrin was elected in 1964 after serving churches in Texas and Oklahoma. He served the Kansas Episcopal Area (1964–1972) and the Dallas-Fort Worth Episcopal Area (1972–1980), then retired. Twila and McFerrin had three children. McFerrin died in 1988, and, in 1992, Twila married retired Bishop Alonzo Monk Bryan. Monk had three children with his first wife, Corneille, who died in 1989.

Twila grew up in northwest Texas and majored in vocal music at Texas Tech. She served as chair of recruitment for Contact, a nationwide telephone ministry for people in crisis situations, took the training course, and served as a counselor herself. She is quoted as saying that her greatest satisfaction as the wife of a bishop "has been people and the opportunity to invest some of our lives in them and theirs in ours."

—*Biographical Directory*, 2000–2004; *The Texas Methodist*, Central Texas Conference Edition [November 3, 1978]

Laura P. Carson Burns (1878–1960)

In 1901, Laura married Charles Wesley Burns (1874–1938). Charles was elected bishop in The Methodist Episcopal Church in 1920, after serving churches in Massachusetts, Pennsylvania and Minneapolis. He served the Helena Episcopal Area (1920–1924), the San Francisco Episcopal Area (1924–1932), and was assigned to the Boston Episcopal Area in 1932. Laura and Charles had four children and eight grandchildren.

Laura was born in Philadelphia and graduated from Friends School there and from Goucher College in Baltimore. "With unbounded energy, she threw herself into the work of the church which she considered a minister's wife's field—an orphanage in Montana, an immigration station in California, a settlement house in Massachusetts. But at no time was her family neglected, for her leading role was that of wife and mother."

—*Official Journal and Yearbook of the Philadelphia Annual Conference of The Methodist Church, 1961*, 570–571; https://prabook.com/web/charles_wesley.burns/282648#

Helen Bartlett Graves Burt (1856–1946)

In 1881, Helen married William Burt (1852–1936). William transferred from the New York East Annual conference to the Italy Annual Conference in 1886 and was elected in 1904. He served as resident bishop of The Methodist Episcopal Church in Europe (1904–1912), residing in Zurich, Switzerland, and in Buffalo, New York (1912–1924), then retired. Helen and William had five children.

—https://www.findagrave.com/memorial/46610129/helen-bartlett-burt; http://catalog.gcah.org/publicdata/gcah1563.htm; http://prabook.com/web/person-view.html?profileId=282398; *Journal of the New York East Annual Conference of The Methodist Episcopal Church, May 28–June 1, 1936*, 800–801

Helen Myrtle Hawley Mcallum Cannon (1888–1974)

In 1930, Helen married James Cannon Jr (1864–1944). James was elected in 1918 out of the Virginia Annual Conference of The Methodist Episcopal Church,

South, and was in charge of mission work in Mexico, the Belgian Congo, Cuba and Brazil, as well as Alabama (1920–1922) and Pacific Coast work (1934–1938). He worked passionately for temperance and against the evils of alcohol and made 10 visits to Europe (1918–1922) to deal with issues related to the war and temperance. James had nine children with his first wife, Lura Virginia Bennet, who died in 1928. Helen was a widow who had been James's secretary.

—http://catalog.gcah.org:8080/exist/memoirs/memoirs.xql;jsessionid=v4irzfsdz8ii?start=21151&howmany=10; *Encyclopedia of World Methodism, Vol. 1*, 406–407; http://www.lva.virginia.gov/public/dvb/bio.asp?b=Cannon_James

Linda Miller Carder (b. 1939)

In 1961, Linda married Kenneth Lee Carder (b. 1940). Ken was elected in 1992 out of the Holston Annual Conference and served the Nashville Episcopal Area (1992–2000) and the Mississippi Episcopal Area (2000–2004), then retired and joined the faculty of Duke Divinity School. Linda and Ken have two children and five grandchildren.

Linda graduated from Emory and Henry College with a BA in religious education and did graduate study at Wesley Seminary. She worked for one year at East Tennessee State University, then accompanied Ken to Wesley Seminary in Washington, DC, where she worked for an Episcopal church. Linda has found great joy in family activities, handcrafts, decorating, and entertaining guests. Her Bible studies have given priority to the Sermon on the Mount and the writings of the Prophets. Among her most beloved hymns is "God of the Sparrow, God of the Whale" (*UMH*, 122), with its message of God's love for all creation and the human longing for home.

—*Biographical Directory*, 2000–2004; https://www.unitedmethodistbishops.org/person-detail/2464030; email communication with Bishop Carder, July 2017

Artha Blair Crutchfield Carleton (1913–2012)

In 1936, Artha Blair married Alsie Henry Carleton (1910–2002). Alsie was elected in 1968 out of the North Texas Annual Conference and served the Northwest Texas-New Mexico Episcopal Area (1968–1980), then retired. Artha Blair and Alsie had three children and one grandchild.

Artha Blair earned a BA and an MA from Southern Methodist University, where she was honored as the Outstanding Woman Graduate. She also pursued post graduate study at Boston University School of Theology. Artha taught in the Highland Park School System in Dallas and was involved in many church activities through the years. She was an accomplished musician and was known for her leadership in UMW and her support of the mission of the church, as well as her gracious manner, quick wit, and ready laughter. She loved adventure and enjoyed traveling in Europe, the Middle East, and Central and South America with her husband. Her hobbies included music, Texas and New Mexico history, and Spanish. She was also a member of Sigma Kappa sorority and of P.E.O.

—*Biographical Directory*, 2000–2004;
https://www.findagrave.com/cgi-bin/fg.cgi?page=gr&GRid=85559243;
http://amarillo.com/obituaries/2012-02-22/artha-blair-carleton

Phenola Valentine Carroll (1912–1999)

In 1934, Phenola married Edward Gonzalez Carroll (1910–2000). He was elected in 1972 out of the Baltimore–Washington Annual Conference and served the Boston Episcopal Area (1972–1980), then retired. Phenola and Eddie had two children and two grandchildren.

Phenola received her BS from Morgan College and did graduate work at Catholic University of America in personnel and guidance. During 1935 and 1936, Phenola and Eddie, along with Howard and Sue Thurman, were selected to represent the National Student Movement of the United States and Canada in a "Pilgrimage of Friendship" to India, Burma [*sic*], and Ceylon. Phenola worked as a teacher, economic analyst, editor, executive secretary, and social worker, as well as participating actively in church life. In 1978, she was honored by being selected as Massachusetts State Mother of the Year. Her interests included reading, walking, cooking, and traveling, especially "for the international contacts one makes."

—*Biographical Directory*, 1996–2000;
Baltimore-Washington Conference Journal, 2000, 602

Pamela Carter (b. 1955)

In 1981, Pam married Kenneth H. Carter (b. 1957). Kenneth was elected in 2012 out of the Western North Carolina Annual Conference and was assigned to the Florida Episcopal Area. Pam and Ken have two daughters.

Pam, born in North Carolina, graduated from Wake Forest University with a degree in religion and from Duke Divinity School with MAs of Religious Education and Theology. She and Ken met in seminary. Pam was ordained an elder in 1989 but took honorable location when their daughters were young. She has served in many areas of ministry: as an associate pastor, campus minister, education director, and more recently as a missions director. She has been very active in work with Haiti since 2006. Presently she serves in the Disaster Response Ministry of the Florida Annual Conference following Hurricane Irma.

Favorite Scripture: Psalm 16:5-6 / Favorite Hymns: "Be Thou My Vision" (*UMH*, 451), "Great Is Thy faithfulness" (*UMH*, 140)

—*Biographical Directory*, 2012–2016;
email communication with Pam Carter, January 2018

Martha Elnor Gunsalus Chamberlain (b. 1938)

In 1960, Martha married Ray Willis Chamberlain Jr (b. 1938). Ray was elected out of the Virginia Annual Conference in 1996 and served the Holston Episcopal Area until 2004, then retired. Martha and Ray have two sons, a daughter, a foster daughter, and six grandchildren.

Martha graduated from Sacred Heart Hospital School of Nursing at United Wesleyan College and practiced as a registered nurse both in Zambia, while Ray was serving as a missionary/ministerial school principal there, and in the U. S. She earned her BA and MA from George Mason University and received an honorary Doctor of Humanities from Liberia Methodist University. She teaches writing workshops and has published numerous articles and books, including: *Surviving Junior High* (1988), *Hymn Devotions for All Seasons: Fifty-two Favorite Hymns* (1989), *The Ultimate Flight* (1997), *365 Meditations for Grandmothers by Grandmothers* (with others, 2006), *A Love Affair with India: The Story of the Wife and Daughter of E. Stanley Jones* (2009), and *Satchel: A Cherokee Girl Tells All* (2016).

—*Biographical Directory*, 2004–2008; interview with Martha Chamberlain, 2017

Joye Fay Stokes Chamness (b. 1942)

In 1960, Joye married Benjamin Roy Chamness (1940–2018). Ben was elected in 2000 out of the Texas Annual Conference and served the Fort Worth Episcopal Area (2000–2008), then retired. He was reactivated to serve the Nashville Episcopal Area (2011–2012). Joye and Ben settled in Huntsville, Texas. They have two sons and six grandchildren.

Joye attended Centenary College in Shreveport, Louisiana, and Lamar College in Beaumont, Texas. She enjoyed a career as a secretary/administrative assistant at public schools and financial institutions. She has always been very supportive of Ben's ministry, being active in the churches and the conferences. At different times she played the piano, led the choir, assisted with Vacation Bible School, and played the handbells. She also helped organize two community handbell groups. Her heart for mission activities led her to work with UMARMY, Society of St. Stephen, Bear Creek Area Ministries, and UMW. At the Central Texas Conference one year, when Ben and Joye celebrated their 47th wedding anniversary, Joye announced that she would give $10 for every year of their marriage to the Imagine No Malaria campaign, suggesting there might be others who would like to do so also. The response was overwhelming. Approximately $100,000 was raised that day. Joye loves to travel and has done so, extensively with Ben, both within the U.S. and in 26 other countries. Since retirement, Joye has been engaged with UMW, P.E.O., Newcomers, a book club, and several bridge clubs. Her interests include her grandchildren, traveling, reading, bridge, and fishing.

—*Biographical Directory*, 2000–2004, 2012–2016;
https://www.umnews.org/en/news/bishop-chamness-calm-leader-dead-at-78

Wife of Wen Yuan Chen

No name or details were found for the wife of Wen Yuan Chen (1897–1968). He had a daughter living in the U.S. at the time of his death. He was elected in 1941 and served the Chungking Episcopal Area until the Communist takeover of China in 1949.

—*Encyclopedia of World Methodism, Vol. 1*, 426

Satyavati Violet Singh Chitambar (b. 1878)

In 1901, Satyavati married Joshwant Rao Chitamber (1879–1940). Joshwant, a member of the North India Annual Conference, was elected bishop in The Methodist Episcopal Church by the Central Conference of Southern Asia in 1930. He was assigned to an area including North India, Lucknow, the Central Provinces Conferences, and the Bhabua Mission. Satyavati and Joshwant had six children and at least three grandchildren.

Born in Beawar, India, Satyavati studied at Isabelle Thoburn College, where she met Joshwant, a fellow student. Bishop Brenton Badley said of her, "Satyavati Singh was one of the spiritual forces of our institution at Lal Engh. While her husband was a student in Bareilly Theological Seminary, the Chitambars lived the simple life. Their home has ever been one of the happiest and most beautiful I have ever known. The tiny, humble home is a center of rich Christian experience: love, devotion, and prayer. Here she showed those characteristics which throughout her life have been outstanding, namely, soul-winning, zeal for temperance and social purity, community uplift, and, above all personal Bible study and prayer." Satyavati attended the 1932 General Conference with her husband, touring camp meetings and speaking about India and its needs. In 1936, she was elected a lay delegate to General Conference. She also served as president of the National Woman's Christian Temperance Union of India (*The Christian Advocate* [January 23, 1936], 85). Eunice Mathews wrote of her, "She was a very model of a bishop's wife. She had a dignity and a selfhood which stood out by itself and not merely in the shadow of her husband's office. I had the privilege of growing up with some of their children and they were a tribute to the kind of Christian home the Chitambars established. Who among those who knew Mrs. Chitambar could ever forget that she began every letter with the word of Scripture: 'That in all things He (Jesus) might have the preeminence.' That was a word which became flesh in her rich life."

—letter from Eunice Mathews to bishops' wives in India, April 1995; https://en.wikipedia.org/wiki/Jashwant_Rao_Chitambar; http://catalog.gcah.org/publicdata/files/4642/chitambar-bishop-jashwant-rao-and-mrs-chitambar.pdf

Kiok Chang Cho (b. 1950)

In 1975, Kiok married Young Jin Cho (born 1946). He was elected in 2012 out of the Virginia Annual Conference and served the Richmond Episcopal Area (2012-2016), then retired. Kiok and Young Jin have three children and two grandchildren.

Kiok Chang Cho was born into a non-believing family in Seoul, Korea. By God's grace she studied at Christian junior and senior high schools, which were founded by an American Methodist missionary sent by the UMW. She encountered Jesus Christ, was baptized at age 16, and decided to dedicate her life to God. Both she and Young Jin studied at the Methodist Theological Seminary in Seoul, Korea (ThB and ThM), and Wesley Theological Seminary in Washington, DC (MTS). Kiok also studied programs in "Leading Contemplative Prayer Groups and Retreats" and "Spiritual Guidance" at Shalem Institute for Spiritual Formation in Washington, DC. She served as a spiritual director during the 2016 General Conference and has led contemplative prayer workshops for the Bishop's Convocation on Prayer and for churches in the Virginia Annual Conference, as well as district clergy prayer retreats. She is a spiritual director, a member of Wesleyan Contemplative Order, and an ordained deacon in the Virginia Annual Conference. She has served as a minister for adult Christian education and spiritual formation at Korean United Methodist churches in Northern Virginia and for an Anglo church and a Korean United Methodist Church in Richmond, Virginia.

Favorite Scriptures: John 8:31-32; Romans 8:33-39; Proverbs 3:5-6

—*Biographical Directory*, 2012–2016; email communication with Kiok Cho, July 2017

Grace Ying Hom Choy (d. 1977)

In 1940, Grace married Wilbur Wong Yan Choy (b. 1918). He was elected bishop in 1972 out of the California-Nevada Conference and was assigned to the Seattle Episcopal Area. Grace and Wilbur have four children.

—*Biographical Directory*, 2012–2016

Charles E. Logsdon Christopher (b. 1934)

In 1973, Charles married Sharon Ann Brown (b. 1944) and together they took Christopher as their married name. Sharon was elected in 1988 out of the Wisconsin Annual Conference and served the Minnesota Episcopal Area (1988–1996) and the Illinois Great Rivers Episcopal Area (1996–2008), then retired. Charles and Sharon settled in Nashville, Tennessee. They have two children and two grandchildren.

Charles is an ordained member of the Wisconsin Annual Conference in retired status. He grew up in Kentucky and entered the United Methodist ministry in that conference. While serving a charge in the Detroit Conference, he was ordained a deacon in that conference in 1962. Charles attended and graduated from Garrett Theological Seminary in 1963. He was appointed to serve in the East Wisconsin Annual Conference, where he was ordained elder in 1963. Charles loved the pastoral and teaching parts of his ministry best. Early in his retirement he taught adult education classes with emphasis on progressive Christianity. His favorite quote is from Carl Jung: "Bidden or not bidden, God is present."

—*Biographical Directory*, 2004–2008;
email communication with Charles Christopher, August 2017

Ethel Christian Smith Clair (1894–1979)

In 1920, Ethel married Matthew Walker Clair (1890–1968). Matthew, son of Bishop Matthew Wesley Walker, was elected in 1952 out of the Central Jurisdiction after serving churches in Virginia, West Virginia, Florida, Colorado, Indiana, and Illinois; as a chaplain during World War I; and as a professor at Gammon Theological Seminary. He served the St. Louis Episcopal Area (1952–1964), during which time he was sent by the Council of Bishops to "review and appraise" Methodist work in Africa (1954), Singapore (1956), Central and South America (1958), and Europe (1961). Ethel and Matthew had two daughters and six grandchildren.

Ethel was born in West Virginia and raised by a cousin, after her mother and minister father died at a young age. After graduation from Morgan State College, she went on to earn an outstanding reputation as a public school teacher until her marriage. She traveled extensively with her bishop husband and was active in the work of the Women's Division of The United Methodist Church.

—*Encyclopedia of World Methodism, Vol. 1*, 509–510; http://catalog.gcah.org/publicdata/gcah569.htm; *Journal of the Missouri West Annual Conference . . .*, *1969*, 123; *Journal and Yearbook, Northern Illinois Conference . . .*, *1980*, 275

Eva F. Wilson Clair (1880–1975)

In 1926, Eva married Matthew Wesley Clair (1865–1943). Matthew, a son of former slaves, was elected in 1920, one of the first two Black persons to become bishops in The Methodist Episcopal Church. He was sent to oversee mission work in Monrovia, Liberia (1920–1928). He was then assigned to the Covington, Kentucky, Episcopal Area, which covered Black conferences in the Midwest (1928–1936), then retired. Matthew had five sons with his first wife, Fannie Meade Walker Clair, who died in 1925. One of those sons, Matthew W. Clair Jr was elected bishop in 1952.

—https://en.wikipedia.org/wiki/Matthew_Wesley_Clair; http://Wvpublic.Org/Post/June-28-1943-Bishop-Matthew-Wesley-Clair-Senior-Dies#Stream/0;

https://prabook.com/web/matthew_wesley.clair/278345; *Encyclopedia of African American Religions*, Larry G. Murphy, J. Gordon Melton, Gary L. Ward, eds. (New York: Routledge, 2011), 178; https://www.findagrave.com/memorial/184986375/matthew-wesley-clair

Esther Mae Maddox Clark (1922–1991)

In 1945, Esther married Roy Clyde Clark (1920–2014). Roy was elected in 1980 after 36 years of serving local churches in Mississippi and Tennessee. He served the Columbia (South Carolina) Episcopal Area (1980–1988), then retired. Esther and Roy returned to Tennessee. They had two daughters, three grandchildren, and three great-grandchildren.

Esther graduated from Mississippi State College for Women, having served as president of the state's student movement. After graduation, she taught math and chemistry. As the wife of a pastor and bishop, she fulfilled her role with grace, while finding ministries of her own through UMW and Planned Parenthood, where she served as a director. She was known for her efforts to lift women to full personhood and as a supportive and trusted confidant for persons in crisis.

—*Biographical Directory*, 2000–2004; http://www.umc.org/news-and-media/bishop-clark-theologian-relief-leader-dies-at-93; https://www.findagrave.com/cgi-bin/fg.cgi?page=gr&GRid=181082432; *Journal of the South Carolina Conference…, 1991*, 325

Marion Salisbury Hall Clark (1925-2010)

In 1992, Marion married retired Bishop Roy Clyde Clark (1920–2014). Roy and his first wife, Esther, who died in 1991, had two daughters, three grandchildren, and three great-grandchildren.

Marion earned a BS from the University of Kentucky in Lexington. After teaching at the high school in her hometown, Prestonsburg, Kentucky, she moved to Nashville in 1957 to join the staff of the Board of Education of The Methodist Church. Later she was employed as coordinator of voluntary service for Vanderbilt University Hospital and as a personnel director in private business. Marion was an involved Methodist all her life and active in West End United Methodist Church during her years in Nashville. She sang in the choir and taught Sunday school: older youth at first, and then three-year-olds, whom she enjoyed immensely. Marion also served as a member and officer of several groups in the church. She was remarkably generous in her giving to her church, the West End Day School, the Big Sandy Community College, her family, and her friends. She was also known for her strong will and perseverance, which she demonstrated in her struggle with her final illness.

—*Biographical Directory*, 2000–2004; http://www.umc.org/news-and-media/bishop-clark-theologian-relief-leader-dies-at-93; http://www.legacy.com/obituaries/tennessean/obituary.aspx?n=marion-salisbury-clark&pid=141804494

Helen Eloise Graves Clymer (1916–1999)

In 1939, Helen married Wayne K. Clymer (1917–2013). Wayne, who started his ministry in the Atlantic Conference of the Evangelical Church, was elected in 1972 by the North Central Jurisdictional Conference and served the Minnesota Episcopal Area (1972–1980) and the Iowa Episcopal Area (1980–1984), then retired. Helen and Wayne had two children, six grandchildren, and two great-grandchildren.

Helen, born in South Dakota, graduated from Asbury College with a major in English literature. After marrying Wayne, she did graduate work at New York Biblical Seminary while Wayne pastored churches. She also worked as a librarian at Queens County Library. While in Illinois, when Wayne was dean and later president of Evangelical Theological Seminary, she served as homemaker and hostess for a "continuing flow of students, faculty, and visiting guests." In Minnesota, she worked with UMW and UMCOR, as well as volunteering to assist handicapped travelers. She also enjoyed arts and crafts, reading, and art.

—*Biographical Directory*, 2000–2004;
Official Journal and Yearbook Minnesota Annual Conference, 2000, 233–234

Virginia Schoenbohm Clymer (b. 1923)

In 2000, Virginia married retired Bishop Wayne K. Clymer (1917–2013). He and his first wife, Helen, who died in 1999, had two children.

Virginia is from Minneapolis, where she is an active member of the Hennepin Avenue United Methodist Church. A speech therapist by profession, she serves on the Board of Directors at Courage Center, an international treatment and care center for persons with disabilities. Virginia has two children.

—*Biographical Directory*, 2000–2004;
telephone conversation with Virginia Clymer, January 13, 2018

Jane Elizabeth Curry Colaw (1919–2013)

In 1942, Jane married Emerson S. Colaw (1921–2016). Emerson was elected in 1980 after serving churches in the Northern Illinois and West Ohio Annual Conferences. He served the Minnesota Episcopal Area (1980–1988), then retired. Jane and Emerson had four children, nine grandchildren, 12 great-grandchildren, and one great-great-granddaughter.

Jane attended God's Bible School and College in Cincinnati, Ohio, and Asbury College in Wilmore, Kentucky. She married Emerson while he was a student pastor. "Through the years that followed she was unswervingly supportive of her husband in his educational pursuits, as well as his service as a pastor and later as a Methodist bishop. She led over 70 travel tours, including 10 groups to the Holy Land, and five times went to the Passion Play in Oberammergau, Germany. Jane was always there in every way possible, helping the church accomplish its mission" (Service of Celebration bulletin, Hyde Park Community United Methodist Church, April 23, 2013). She worked outside the home only briefly, teaching English and Latin. She was the perfect preacher's wife and a devoted mother who was adored by her children and grandchildren.

—*Biographical Directory*, 2000–2004; http://www.startribune.com/obituary-methodist-bishop-emerson-colaw-was-spellbinding-orator-kind-ministry-leader/399160001/; https://www.gbs.edu/wp-content/uploads/2015/10/1306_gods_revivalist.pdf, 11

Margaret Havens Coors (1891–1983)

In 1917, Margaret married D. Stanley Coors (1889–1960). Stanley was elected bishop in 1952 after serving churches in New York and Michigan. He served the St. Paul Episcopal Area 1952 until his death in 1960. Margaret and Stanley had three children and eight grandchildren.

Margaret was born in Michigan, received college training at Olivet College and the University of Chicago, and worked as a teacher at an orphanage in Chicago. She worked closely with Stanley in his roles as a chaplain, pastor, and bishop, and is described as a pillar of strength for him when he suffered from multiple myeloma. She had a talent for listening and was known as a person of faith and a "confessional saint" until her last days in the convalescent home where she died.

—https://en.wikipedia.org/wiki/D._Stanley_Coors; *Official Journal and Yearbook, 129th session Minnesota Annual Conference, 1983,* 300

Catherine Andrews Copeland (1914–2010)

In 1933, Catherine married Kenneth W. Copeland (1912–1973). He was elected bishop in 1960 out of the Southwest Texas Annual Conference. He served the Nebraska Episcopal Area (1960–1968) and the Houston Episcopal Area from 1968 until his death in 1973. Catherine and Ken had two daughters, five grandchildren, and four great-grandchildren.

Throughout the years, Catherine held many leadership roles in the church: serving on committees, conducting retreats and mission study classes, writing devotional materials, teaching adult church school classes. She was an elected delegate to General and Jurisdictional Conferences in 1980 and 1984. She worked on the administrative staff at Southwest Texas Methodist Hospital in San Antonio for 17 years and also served as a trustee of the Foundation for Evangelism of The United Methodist Church.

Catherine "was known to all as a gentle lady who charmed everyone with her grace and dignity. . . . Her major concern in the life and witness of the church was the Christian witness through world missions. She traveled extensively with her husband including visits to the life and work of the church in Europe, South America,

Southeast Asia, East Asia, the Middle East and the Holy Lands. She spoke in numerous gatherings of church people where the mission of the church around the world was a major concern. She was the recipient of many honors from church organizations, served as president of the Bishops' Wives of the South Central Jurisdiction of the United Methodist Church, and was corresponding secretary of the Council of Bishops' Wives. After her husband's untimely death in 1973, she was part of the Administrative Staff of the Southwest Texas Methodist Hospital of San Antonio and received a Doctor of Humanity from Wiley College in Marshall, Texas, and was for many years an active member of the Foundation for Evangelism of The United Methodist Church" (Council of Bishops Memorial Booklet May 2011).

—*Biographical Directory*, November 1996

Frances Blount Beamon Corson (1900–1997)

In 1922, Frances married Fred Pierce Corson (1896–1985). Fred was elected in 1944 out of the New York East Conference, while serving as president of Dickenson College in Carlisle, Pennsylvania. He served the Philadelphia Episcopal Area (1944–1968), then retired. Frances and Fred had one son, three grandchildren, and five great-grandchildren.

Frances spent some of her early childhood in Charlotte, North Carolina, and her adolescent years in New York City. She never attended college, but like many others of her era, she acquired a good education through self-study and reading. In recognition of contributions she and her husband made toward higher education for African American youth, Claflin University in Orangeburg, South Carolina, conferred upon her an honorary degree of Doctor of Humanities in the 1960s. Frances Corson pursued many interests: Old St. George's Church in Philadelphia, Jefferson Medical College, the Daughters of the American Revolution, the United Christian Colleges of Asia, the Methodist Hospital in Philadelphia, the needs of the people of Puerto Rico (then part of the Philadelphia Episcopal Area), the World Methodist Council, and her own talents as a public speaker. "Frances found it to be very satisfying and 'certainly an education' to be a real helpmate to her husband over the years, whether he was pastor, district superintendent, College President, or bishop."

—*Biographical Directory*, 1996; http://archives.chicagotribune.com/1985/02/19/page/18/article/obituaries; *Wyoming Annual Conference Journal*, June 5–7, 1998, 319; http://static1.squarespace.com/static/5776ca76d2b8573a1eb3d822/t/579276f9f5e231b908ac8d9a/1469216516029/4+Bishop+Fred+Corson+Pierce+.pdf

Marsha Lynn England Coyner (b. 1949)

In 1970, Marsha married Michael J. Coyner (b. 1949). Michael was elected in 1996 out of the North Indiana Annual Conference and served the Dakotas Episcopal

Area (1996–2004) and the Indiana Episcopal Area (2004–2016), then retired. Marsha and Michael have two children and five grandchildren.

Marsha received a BS in Audiology and Speech Sciences from Purdue University and an MA in special education from Ball State University. She has taught in both public and private schools—in classes with middle-school emotionally disabled youth and in a preschool in a local United Methodist church. Marsha's hobbies include music, walking, gardening, quilting, travel, and bike-riding with Mike. She has a special fondness for dogs and the outdoors. She loves being involved in music, gardening, reading, and spending time with grandchildren. She has played in and directed handbell choirs at various churches in Indiana and North Dakota. She has also volunteered many hours of her time with UMCOR; participated in annual conference mission projects; and served in local outreach ministries.

Favorite Scripture: Romans 8:31-39

—*Biographical Directory*, 2004–2008, 2012;
email communication with Marsha Coyner, September 2017

Benja Lee Bell Crutchfield (1916–2015)

In 1941, Benja Lee married Finis Alonzo Crutchfield Jr (1916–1987). Finis was elected in 1972 out of the Oklahoma Annual Conference. He served the New Orleans Episcopal Area (1972–1976) and the Houston Episcopal Area (1976–1984), then retired. Benja Lee and Finis had one son (Bishop Charles Crutchfield) and two grandchildren.

"Bennie" graduated from Southern Methodist University in 1937 with a degree in classical languages. She worked for the Southwest Texas Conference as youth coordinator until her marriage in 1941. She liked to sing, do crossword puzzles, and hike in the Colorado Rockies. Her gift for hospitality was an extension of her grace-filled love of others. She visited many international mission sites and raised donations through numerous programs about the mission work of the church.

—*Biographical Directory*, 1996;
email communication with Karen Crutchfield, 2017

Karen Jenkins Crutchfield (b. 1946)

In 1968, Karen married Charles N. Crutchfield (b. 1943). Charles was elected in 2004 out of the New Mexico Annual Conference and served the Arkansas Episcopal Area (2004–2012), then retired. Karen and Charles have settled in North Carolina. They have two living children, one deceased child, and two grandchildren.

Karen earned degrees from Duke University (music history) and the University of New Mexico (MA in music-bassoon). She was a Woodrow Wilson scholar in 1968. Karen has pursued her musical interests (bassoon, organ, and piano); taught music in public schools; worked as a paralegal; and served as chair of the New Mexico Annual

Conference Board of Pension and Health Benefits for 13 years. She received the Charles Calkins award from the General Board of Pension and Health Benefits and the New Mexico Annual Conference Living Archives award for this work. She enjoys reading, hiking, skiing, and eating Charles' cooking. "I served as a director of the General Board of Pension and Health Benefits 2008–2012, after 19 years of working with the New Mexico Board of Pensions. While reevaluating and refining the current pension plan for United Methodist clergy and their spouses, staff and board members discussed clergy spouses' contributions to ministry and how that should be reflected in pension benefits. I sought to emphasize the indirect contributions spouses make in itinerant ministry, the effect that has on spouses' careers and earning capacity, and the value of supportive spouses to the mission of the church. I enjoyed bringing a spouse's voice to the conversation!"

Favorite Hymn: "When in Our Music God Is Glorified" (*UMH*, 68)

—*Biographical Directory*, 2004–2008;
email communication with Karen Crutchfield, 2016

Maude Estella Hammond Cushman (1878–1971)

In 1902, Maude married Ralph Spaulding Cushman (1879–1960). Ralph was elected in 1932 in The Methodist Episcopal Church, after serving churches in New England and New York State. He served the Denver Episcopal Area (1932–1939), the Minnesota Episcopal Area (1939–1952), then retired. Maude and Ralph had two children, five grandchildren, and three great-grandchildren.

Born in Ellenburg, New York, Maude studied at the Troy Conference Academy in Poultney, Vermont, and the Crane Institute in Malone, New York. She was a life member of the Women's Society of Christian Service and served as president in various parts of the organization.

—https://www.findagrave.com/cgi-bin/fg.cgi?page=gr&GRid=38613177;
Journal of the Rocky Mountain Conference, 1971, 694

Kerike Christiana Dabale

In 1968, Kerike married Done Peter Dabale (1949-2006). In 1992, while serving as a general superintendent of United Methodists in Nigeria, Done became the first elected United Methodist bishop of that African nation, serving the Nigeria Episcopal Area until his death. Kerike and Done Peter have 11 children and 11 grandchildren.

Kerike was born in Northeastern Nigeria and was working as a nurse's aide at Numan District Hospital in Adamawa at the time of their marriage. Kerike contributed to Done's ministry by serving the needy, especially women and children. A devoted housewife, she also took primary responsibility for feeding, teaching, and caring for their large family while her husband concentrated on expanding the church. Kerike now resides in Bawagarki village of Mayo-Lope Ward in Lau Local Government Area of Taraba State, Nigeria. She loves her family and dedicates most of her time to attending church and community meetings. Her hobbies include animal husbandry, educating women's groups, and farming.

Favorite Scripture: Psalm 121:1-2

—*Biographical Directory*, 2004–2008, 2012; http://www.umc.org/news-and-media/first-united-methodist-bishop-in-nigeria-done-peter-dabale-dies-in-us-hospi; email communication with son Wehnam Dabale, January 2018

Virginia Bourne Darlington (1888–1978)

In 1913, Virginia married Urban Valentine Williams Darlington (1870–1954). Urban was elected in 1918 out of the West Virginia Annual Conference of The Methodist Episcopal Church, South. His episcopal areas included North and South Carolina, Illinois, Kentucky, West Virginia, Mississippi, and Europe (Belgium, Poland, and Czechoslovakia). He retired in 1944. Urban had two children with his first wife, Lyda Clarke, who died in 1911. Virginia and Urban had two children also.

Virginia was a music teacher at Marshall College in Huntington, West Virginia.

—https://www.findagrave.com/cgi-bin/fg.cgi?page=gr&GRid=62061444; http://catalog.gcah.org/publicdata/files/4642/darlington-bishop-u-v-w.pdf; https://en.wikipedia.org/wiki/Urban_Valentine_Williams_Darlington

Jennifer Mink Davis (b. 1949)

In 1972, Jennifer married George Lindsey Davis (b. 1948). Lindsey was elected in 1996 out of the Kentucky Annual Conference and served the North Georgia Episcopal Area (1996–2008) and the Louisville Episcopal Area (2008–2016), then retired. Jennifer and Lindsey have settled in Lexington, Kentucky. They have two children and four grandchildren.

Jennifer received her BS from Union College in Kentucky and her MA in guidance and counseling from Eastern Kentucky University. She taught math in Kentucky for 20 years before retiring. Jennifer helped develop a Conference Youth Mission Project, "Hands to Honduras," in North Georgia and Kentucky, hoping to instill a love of missions in young people that would continue throughout their lives. As a result of the North Georgia project, a Christian school, Aldersgate Elementary, was built in Culucco, Honduras, for grades one through six, serving 200 children. United Methodists in Kentucky funded and built a kindergarten building in Carnizuelar. Each summer Jennifer has led week-long youth mission trips to the Agalta Valley.

Favorite Scripture: Joshua 1:9

—*Biographical Directory*, 2004–2008, 2012; http://www.umc.org/bishops/lindsey-davis; email communication with Jennifer Davis, September 2017

Delma A. Millikan Dawson

In 1926, Delma married Dana Dawson (1892–1964). Dana was elected in 1948 after serving churches in Oklahoma, Arkansas, and Louisiana. He served the Kansas-Nebraska Episcopal Area (1948–1952) and the Kansas Episcopal Area (1952–1960), then retired. A world traveler and lecturer, he spent time in Palestine, Egypt, Syria, Russia, Europe, Asia, the Orient, Africa, South America, and the Middle East. Dana had two children with his first wife, Grace Elizabeth, who died in 1924.

—*Encyclopedia of World Methodism, Vol. 1*, 635;
http://prabook.com/web/person-view.html?profileId=679725

Marilina Stella De Jesus Figueiredo DeCarvalho (b. 1941)

In 1966, Marilina married Emilio J. M. DeCarvalho (b. 1933). Emilio was elected in 1972 out of the Angola Annual Conference. He served the Angola Episcopal Area (1972–1988) and, after the division of the area, the West Angola Episcopal Area (1988–2000), then retired. Marilina and Emilio have three children, 13 grandchildren, and one great-grandchild.

Marilina taught in secondary schools and actively participates in The United Methodist Church. She was elected a member of the Africa Church Growth and Development Committee and served as president for seven years. Later she became a member of the General Council on Ministries for four years and served as vice president for four years. In 1995, she was elected president of the Bishops' Spouses' Association, the first African to serve in that role.

—*Biographical Directory*, 2004–2008;
email communication with Marilina DeCarvalho, 2016–2017

Bertha Whitley Decell (1887–1950)

In 1910, Bertha married John Lloyd Decell (1887–1946). John was elected in 1938 out of the Mississippi Annual Conference of The Methodist Episcopal Church, South, and presided over the following annual conferences: Alabama, North Alabama, Georgia and North Georgia, Memphis, Mississippi, and North Mississippi. Bertha and John had two children.

—https://www.findagrave.com/cgi-bin/
fg.cgi?page=gr&GSln=Decell&GSiman=1&GSst=27&GRid=94065315&;
http://www.millsaps.edu/library/archives/resources/library_cain_decell.pdf;
http://prabook.com/web/person-view.html?profileId=280575

Anna Maude Sullivan Dennis (1890–1972)

In 1911, Anna married Fred L. Dennis (1890–1958). Fred was elected in 1941 by the General Conference of the United Brethren Church, after serving churches in Ohio. He served out of Indianapolis (1941–1950) and then Dayton, Ohio, 1950 until his death in 1958. Anna and Fred had six children.

Anna, born in Indiana, "was a great source of strength" to her husband throughout his ministry.

—*Official Journal and Yearbook of the 3rd Session of the West Ohio Annual Conference, 1972,* 285; https://www.findagrave.com/memorial/39254456/Anna-Maude-Dennis; *Encyclopedia of World Methodism, Vol. 1,* 658; *Journal of the Ohio East Conference Evangelical United Brethren Church, 1958,* 90

Prema Devadhar (b. 1953)

In 1976, Prema married Sudarshana Devadhar (b. 1951). Suda was elected out of the North Central New York Conference in 2004. He served the Greater New Jersey Episcopal Area (2004–2012) and was assigned to the Boston Episcopal Area in 2012. Prema and Suda have one adult daughter and three grandchildren.

Prema was born in the city of Mangalore, India. Hailing from a family very actively involved in the church, she, too, became an active participant in the life of her church. After graduating with a BS (majors in Botany and Zoology) from St. Agnes College (affiliated with the University of Mysore), in Mangalore, India, Prema worked for the Vijaya Bank. Deeply supportive of her husband's ministry, Prema migrated with him to the U.S., where she was actively involved in all the churches Suda served as pastor. From 1989 to 2004, Prema worked for the state of New York Correctional Facilities and the State Insurance Fund. Again, to fully support the ministry of her partner in Christ, she resigned from her job when Suda was elected bishop. Since 2004, Prema has accompanied Suda and others on mission pilgrimages, including to Taize. Along with Bishop Devadhar, she regularly visits the churches in their conference. Prema is an ardent supporter of the empowerment of children, youth, and young adults. Currently, with the support of a staff member of the New England Conference, she is collecting used jewelry and selling it as a project to raise money for various youth ministries of the conference. Prema also does volunteer work in the Merrimack Valley Habitat for Humanity Restore in Lawrence, Massachusetts.

She enjoys traveling, gardening, crafts, and volunteering at a local food pantry. Prema makes use of every opportunity to travel to Cincinnati to be with her three precious granddaughters and her daughter and son-in-law.

Favorite Scripture: Psalm 23 / Favorite Hymn: "I Surrender All" (*UMH*, 354)

—*Biographical Directory*, 2012–2016; email communication with Prema Devadhar, July and October 2017

Mae Marie "Mitzi" Eggers Dew (b. 1936)

In 1958, Mitzi married William W. Dew Jr (1935–2010). Bill was elected in 1988 out of the California-Nevada Annual Conference and served the Portland (Oregon) Episcopal Area (1988–1996) and the Phoenix Episcopal Area (1996–2004), then retired. Mitzi and Bill have three children and six grandchildren.

Mitzi attended Union College in Barbourville, Kentucky, to pursue a music degree and met Bill there. Mitzie's favorite positions in church have been in children's work and choral music. Mitzie returned to college for further study in child development and became a certified director of Pre-School and Child Care Centers.

—*Biographical Directory*, 2004–2008, 2012–2016

Annamary Horner DeWitt (1921–2010)

In 1941, Annamary married Jesse Robert DeWitt (1918–2015). Jesse was elected bishop in 1972 out of the Detroit Annual Conference, while serving as associate general secretary of the National Division of the General Board of Global Ministries in New York. He served the Wisconsin Episcopal Area (1972–1980) and the Chicago Episcopal Area (1980–1988), then retired. Annamary and Jesse had two daughters, five grandchildren, and 11 great-grandchildren.

Annamary graduated from a comptometer business school, then later went on to get her BA in sociology from Northern Illinois University and MA in theological studies from Garrett Evangelical Seminary. She has served on the Conference Commission on the Role and Status of Women, the Commission on Family Concerns, and the Commission on Aging. She was a hospital volunteer for 30 years, along with jury watching for the American Civil Liberties Union, working with juveniles, and participating in many church activities. She enjoyed roller-skate dancing, playing golf, making ceramics, doing things with their grandchildren, and doing needlepoint.

"When she knew her death was imminent, she very deliberately defined the terms of her departure. Her last lesson to her family was how to die as you live—loving and caring for those around you and recognizing the importance of each day's blessings."

—*Biographical Directory*, 2000–2004; Council of Bishops Memorial Booklet, May 2011; autobiographical memoir shared by family; email communication with daughters Darla Inman and Donna Wegryn, October–November 2017

Mary Jessie Munroe Dickey (1868–1960)

In 1891, Jesse married James Edward Dickey (1864–1928). James was elected in 1922 out of the North Georgia Annual Conference of The Methodist Episcopal Church, South, after serving churches and as president of Emory College in Oxford, Georgia (1902–1915). As bishop, he served two conferences. Jesse and James had six children.

Jesse graduated from Wesleyan College in Macon, Georgia, and was a charter member of Alpha Delta Pi Sorority.

—https://www.findagrave.com/cgi-bin/fg.cgi?page=gr&GRid=108894006; https://en.wikipedia.org/wiki/James_Edward_Dickey; https://findingaids.library.emory.edu/documents/eua0102dickey/printable/

Ernestine Gray Clark Dixon (1923–2015)

In 1979, Ernestine married Bishop Ernest T. Dixon Jr (1922–1996), who was serving the Kansas Episcopal Area (1972–1980). He served the San Antonio Area (1980–1992), then retired. Ernest had four children, five grandchildren, and two great-grandchildren with his first wife, Lois, who died in 1977.

Ernestine received a BS from Prairie View A&M College, a degree from Columbia University Teachers College in 1950, and a PhD from Texas Woman's University in the field of child development and family living, a subject she taught for 34 years. She also trained high school students to serve as staff members in Day Care Centers for six years and served as a vocational counselor for two years. After moving to San Antonio, she began to teach sewing at the Wesley Community Center. Later she bought and secured sewing machines and supplies and clothing from organizations, churches, and individuals for programs and projects in the Colonias (low-income unincorporated housing-areas), located in the Rio Grande Valley.

—*Biographical Directory*, 1992;
https://riotexas.org/news/2015/7/2/dr-ernestine-gray-clark-dixon

Lois Dixon (1923–1977)

In 1943, Lois married Ernest T. Dixon Jr (1922–1996). He was elected in 1972 while serving as general agency staff member in charge of coordination for the Program Council in Dayton, Ohio. He served the Kansas Episcopal Area (1972–1980) and the San Antonio Area (1980–1992), then retired. Lois and Ernest had four children, five grandchildren, and two great-grandchildren.

—http://www.nytimes.com/1996/07/07/us/ernest-dixon-73-retired-methodist-bishop.html; http://www.lib.utexas.edu/taro/smu/00297/smu-00297.html

Lessie Rush Jackson Dobbs (1883–1951)

In 1906, Lessie married Hoyt McWhorter Dobbs (1878–1954). Hoyt was elected in 1922 out of the North Alabama Annual Conference of The Methodist Episcopal Church, South, and served episcopal areas in Brazil, Alabama, Florida, Louisiana, and Mississippi, then retired in 1944. Lessie and Hoyt had two(?) children, and four grandchildren.

Lessie was born in Louisiana and graduated from Belmont College for young women in Nashville, Tennessee, where she met Hoyt. She pursued graduate training in music and then taught school back at home for two years before their marriage. She was an accomplished musician and "was a pianist of skill and feeling." She taught Sunday school and otherwise supported and participated in Hoyt's ministry. When they were preparing to entertain, they would look up information about their guests' professions and interests, in order to be able to converse intelligently with them.

—https://findagrave.com/cgibin/fg.cgi/%3C/www.linkedin.com/in/johnmacomber/fg.cgi?page=gr&GRid=170620745; http://www.smu.edu/Bridwell/Collections/SpecialCollectionsandArchives/~/media/Site/Bridwell/Archives/BA10409.pdf; https://findagrave.com/cgi-bin/fg.cgi/%3C/www.linkedin.com/in/johnmacomber/fg.cgi?page=gr&GRid=170620894; *Journal of the Louisiana Conference of The Methodist Church, 1952*, 171–173

Elizabeth Greene Law Dodge (d. 1998)

In 1983, Beth married retired Bishop Ralph Edward Dodge. Ralph had four children, all raised in Africa, eight grandchildren, and 18 great-grandchildren with his first wife, Eunice, who died in 1982. Beth was a widow with four grown daughters.

Born in Ohio, she graduated from the former Schauffler College, now a division of Oberlin College, with a BS in religious education. She did graduate study at Scarritt College in Nashville, Tennessee, and earned an MA in 1963. She was commissioned as a deaconess in 1964 and worked as a local church director of Christian education, librarian, and teacher at Vashti School for Girls, a Methodist mission school and home for girls in Georgia. Beth shared Ralph's interests in gardening and in the church.

—https://www.findagrave.com/cgi-bin/fg.cgi?page=gr&GRid=29115838; *Biographical Directory*, 2004–2008; *News from Methodist Board of Missions, January 1964*; https://drive.google.com/drive/folders/0B0ZpPq4CvG95VkNtWUJ4U1lYOG8

Eunice Elvira Davis Dodge (1910–1982)

In 1934, Eunice married Ralph Edward Dodge (1907–2008). After a brief pastorate in North Dakota, the Dodges were recruited as missionaries and sent to the Kennedy School of Missions in Hartford, Connecticut, for orientation, and to Portugal for language study. They served as missionaries in Angola (1936–1950) with the exception of a three-year period when they could not return from furlough because of travel restrictions during World War II. In 1950, Ralph was asked to join the staff of the General Board of Missions as secretary for Africa and Europe, and in 1956 he was elected bishop by the Africa Central Conference and assigned to the Rhodesia (now Zimbabwe) Episcopal Area. After serving there for eight years, he was expelled by the white minority government of Prime Minister Ian Smith. Upon the death of Bishop Sigg in 1965, Bishop Dodge was given interim responsibility for most of the Geneva Area. After his retirement in 1968, the Dodges remained in Africa, and Bishop Dodge served as chaplain of the Mindolo Ecumenical Foundation in Kitwe, Zambia. Returning to the U.S. in 1971, the Dodges settled in Springfield, Missouri. Bishop Dodge was reactivated several times in order to take on special assignments for the Council of Bishops. In 1980, Eunice and Ralph retired to Florida. They had four children, all raised in Africa, eight grandchildren, and 18 great-grandchildren.

Eunice served as a missionary in Angola, Africa, with her husband. When they returned to the United States, she worked as a private secretary in the International Missionary Society and in the Africa Office of the National Council of Churches.

—*Biographical Directory*, 2004–2008; https://www.findagrave.com/cgi-bin/fg.cgi?page=gr&GRid=29115838

Lucrécia Manual Alexandre Domingos (b. 1962)

In 1983, Lucrécia married Gaspar João Domingos (b. 1961). Gaspar was elected in 2000, while serving as the general secretary of the Angolan Council of Christian Churches and was assigned to the Western Angola Episcopal Area. Lucrécia and Gaspar have six children.

Lucrécia, born in the province of Malange, is a physiotherapist. She completed her studies at the Technical Center for Medicine in Luanda and received her BA in clinical analysis and public health from the Methodist University of Angola. She is also an ordained elder in the Western Angola Annual Conference. She grew up in the Maria Madalena UMC, where she sang in the choir and was the youth officer. She also sang in the university choir of Rudge Ramos in Brazil and later was the treasurer of the Women's Society at Emmaus UMC. She is a professor at the Western Angola Women's Training Center, general counsel for the Women's Society, and a member of the conference health board. Her hobbies are agriculture and fish farming.

—*Biographical Directory*, 2004–2008; interview and email communication by translator Donald Reasoner with Bishop Domingos, May 2018

Barbara Langley Dorff (b. 1947)

In 1975, Barbara married James E. Dorff (born 1947). Jim was elected in 2008 out of the North Texas Annual Conference and assigned to the San Antonio Episcopal Area. He resigned in 2016. Barbara and Jim have two grown sons and six grand-children.

Barbara earned a BS in art education (K-12) at Texas Tech University, did graduate work for two years at Southern Methodist University Perkins School of Theology and completed a MEd in early childhood education at Texas A&M University. She worked as an art teacher K–12, junior high youth director, kindergarten teacher, humanities teacher, social studies teacher, assistant director of social studies for Dallas schools, and as a social studies consultant and teacher trainer for a regional Education Service Center. She was chosen Texas Teacher of the Year in 2002 and also as Rising Star by the National Office of English Language Acquisition that same year. Barbara serves on the National Board of Project Transformation, which involves churches and college students in programs to support low-income children and youth, and on the School Boards for Lydia Patterson Institute in El Paso and for Wesley Prep School at Lovers Lane United Methodist Church in Dallas. She volunteers at the Austin Street Shelter in downtown Dallas, where she helped establish a "Sisterhood" program to support homeless women in finding jobs and safe supportive housing, and she serves on the Board of Genesis Women and Children's Shelter for abused women. Barbara also helped start and maintain Little Free Libraries in inner-city Dallas.

She grew up in a strong Methodist family and, in her own words, "Jesus spoke to my heart as a young teenager, and I have been assured of the importance of living a life of kindness, love, service and faith, always encouraging others to join in and believe our God truly knows and loves each of us. Through the joys and the sorrows of my life, my friends and my deep belief in God's comfort and love have lifted me. May that be the same for all his children. He is there, and so willing to do so. Now onward, as there is still much work to be done in His name!"

—*Biographical Directory*, 2010;
email correspondence with Barbara Dorff, November 2017

Gertrude Vaughn Amis Dubose (1872–1948)

In 1899, Gertrude married Horace Mellard Dubose (1858–1941). Horace was elected in 1918 in The Methodist Episcopal Church, South, after serving churches in the Mississippi, Texas, Los Angeles, East Texas, and Georgia annual conferences. He was "stationed" in Berkeley, California. He was a member of the Joint Commission on Unification and "worked hard to bring the two churches together." Gertrude and Horace had six children.

—https://www.lib.ua.edu/Alabama_Authors/?p=1251;
The Christian Advocate, Vol. 93 [May 23, 1918], 643; https://en.wikipedia.org/wiki/Horace_Mellard_DuBose; https://www.findagrave.com/cgi-bin/fg.cgi?page=gr&GSln=Dubose&GSiman=1&GSst=45&GRid=100826295&

Marjorie Louise Clouse Duecker (1924–2012)

In 1948, Marje married R. Sheldon Duecker (1926–2011). Sheldon was elected in 1988 out of the North Indiana Annual Conference and served the Chicago Episcopal Area (1988–1996), then retired. Marje and Sheldon settled in Fort Wayne, Indiana. They had two children, three grandchildren, and a great-granddaughter.

Marje graduated *magna cum laude* from Indiana Wesleyan University. She taught junior high school, directed the only free and interracial kindergarten at Neighborhood House in Kokomo, Indiana (1948–1950), and taught Naturalization classes for German and Japanese war brides following World War II. She was very active in the local church, district, and annual conference UMW, serving as a conference officer and as dean of the School of Christian Mission. She also served as a member of the Board of Directors of the Wesley Foundation at Ball State University and on both the conference and area Commissions on Interreligious Concerns and Ecumenical Affairs. She was a member of H.O.P.E. Ministries of the Northern Illinois Annual Conference (a ministry related to HIV-AIDS) and trained as a tutor for English as a second language through Literacy Volunteers of America. She was a member of the American Association of University Women and P.E.O. She also enjoyed gardening and reading.

"Marje will be remembered as a dedicated Christian who lived her life with enthusiasm. Her quick wit put people at ease and brightened many conversations. She loved her home, was an immaculate housekeeper, loving homemaker and wonderful cook, . . . a devoted wife, mother, grandmother, great-grandmother, aunt, and friend who always looked for opportunities to help others."

—"A Service of Remembrance and Hope," Council of Bishops, November 10, 2013; *Biographical Directory*, 2004–2008; http://www.inumc.org/newsdetail/98933; http://www.legacy.com/obituaries/chicagotribune/obituary.aspx?n=r-sheldon-duecker&pid=154436458

Louise Calhoun Duffey (1921–2010)

In 1944, Louise married Paul Andrews Duffey (1920–2012). Paul was elected in 1980 out of the Alabama-West Florida Annual Conference and served the Louisville Episcopal Area (1980–1988), then retired. Louise and Paul had two children, five grandchildren, and nine great-grandchildren.

Louise graduated from Huntingdon College in Montgomery, Alabama, with a major in home economics and a minor in science. Although Louise began a career as a high school teacher, once she married Paul, she felt her calling to be in tandem with his call to ministry. As Paul served churches in the Tennessee and Alabama-West Florida conferences, Louise served beside him, supporting his ministry in any way she could—teaching children's Sunday school classes, leading in UMW, planning retreats, mentoring young pastors' wives, and later serving as an officer in the bishops' spouses organization, often leading the orientation sessions for spouses of newly elected bishops. An avid reader herself, Louise was an eager volunteer with the Library for the Blind, a tutor for students with special needs, a lifetime member and conference officer in UMW, an active member of the New Era Literary Club, P.E.O. and other civic organizations. Louise was selected to be an honorary senator of the Commonwealth of Kentucky and was named a Kentucky Colonel. In recognition of her accomplishments and loyal support, her alma mater conferred upon her an honorary Doctor of Humane Letters in May 2000.

Louise's friendly and generous nature overflowed into a wide variety of interests: enjoying flowers, birds, trees, snow, and beaches; practicing amateur photography; sewing; reading; traveling; and learning about space (Sputnik, the planets, satellites, and the International Space Station). She frequently called family members outside to view snow angels or to witness the International Space Station pass overhead. She was known to all as a welcoming hostess and excellent cook, and she was regarded as having ability to lead, inspire, and encourage. Louise was a modest and gentle woman, a devout and humble servant of God, and an example of faithful living who viewed life as an opportunity for giving to others. During her lifetime, Louise endeared herself to all whom she met through her considerable creativity, compassionate nature, adventuresome spirit, and ever-present smile.

—*Biographical Directory*, 2004–2008; Council of Bishops Memorial Booklet, May 2011; correspondence and email communication with daughter Melanie Hutto, August 2017

Marion Easterling (b. 1963)

In 1998, Marion married LaTrelle E. Miller (born 1964). Latrelle was elected bishop in 2016 out of the New England Conference and was assigned to the Baltimore-Washington Annual Conference. Marion and LaTrelle have two sons.

Marion was born in Harlem, New York, graduated from Andover Newton Theological School, and currently serves on the President's Advisory Committee. He was serving Parkway UMC in Milton, Massachusetts, when LaTrelle was elected, and he became pastor of Wesley Grove United UMC in Maryland in September 2016. He currently serves on the Board of Ordained Ministry, the Mission Share Relief Committee, and as a candidacy mentor and a certified field supervisor through the Boston University School of Theology Contextual Education Office. Marion is also a member of the Milton Interfaith Clergy Association and the Black Ministerial Alliance of Boston. He enjoys golf, Tibetan Tai Chi, family movie nights, and long walks with Latrelle.

—http://www.wesleygrove.org/about-us/meet-the-pastor/; http://www.umc.org/news-and-media/northeastern-elects-easterling-as-bishop; email communication with Marion Easterling, January 2018

Kenneth P. Ehrman (b. 1951)

In 1976, Ken married Sally Dyck (born 1953). Sally was elected out of the East Ohio Annual Conference in 2004. She served the Minnesota Episcopal Area (2004-2012) and was assigned to the Chicago Episcopal Area in 2012.

Ken graduated from Carleton College in Northfield, Minnesota, and then from Boston University School of Theology with an MDiv. He also earned a DMin in Black Church Ministries from United Theological Seminary. He attended the Ecumenical Institute of the World Council of Churches and the University of Geneva (1978–1979). Ken was ordained in the East Ohio Annual Conference and has served urban and suburban ministries since 1979. He has also provided leadership for the Russia Initiative in East Ohio and urban ministries in the North Central Jurisdiction. He now serves as director of Field Education for Garrett-Evangelical Theological Seminary. Ken is an avid bicycle rider.

—*Biographical Directory*, 2012–2016; email communication with Ken Ehrman, July 2017

Lisa Elphick

In 1926, Lisa married Roberto Valenzuela Elphick (1873–1961). Roberto was elected in 1936 by the Latin America Central Conference of The Methodist Episcopal Church and supervised the work of the churches in Panama, Peru, and Chili (1936–1941). Lisa and Roberto had eight children.

Lisa was active as a deacon, preaching in churches, promoting temperance, and raising funds for a children's home she established.

—*Encyclopedia of World Methodism, Vol. 1*, 770; autobiographical sketch, letter from Lisa to Dr. Ralph Stoody, and death announcement in Roberto's administrative file at the UM Archives and History Center

Eva Rebecca Vines Eutsler (1922–2014)

In 1945, Eva married Kern Eutsler (b. 1919). Kern was elected in 1984 out of the Virginia Annual Conference and served the Holston Episcopal Area (1984–1988), then retired. Eva and Kern have two daughters and four grandchildren.

Eva graduated from Mary Baldwin College and worked as secretary to the headmaster of Staunton Military Academy before marriage. Devoted to her family, she excelled in culinary arts, flower gardening, sewing and needlework. She also loved history, classical music, and art.

—*Biographical Directory*, 2004–2008, 2012; http://www.richmond.com/obituaries/eutsler-eva/article_95d7bb2e-2136-5c4d-a566-f06229094baf.html

Dawn Sparks Fairley (b. 1963)

In 2018, Dawn married Leonard Fairley (b. 1957). Leonard was elected in 2016 out of the North Carolina Annual Conference and assigned to the Louisville Episcopal Area. Leonard has two adult children and three grandchildren from his first wife, Priscilla, who died in 2013. Dawn has two adult children and three grandchildren from her first husband, David Sparks, who died in 2015.

Dawn grew up in the home of Salvation Army officers, ordained ministers. She began working for The Salvation Army's Greater New York Division in New York City immediately following graduation from high school, serving in both their Public Relations and Youth Departments. In 1987, Dawn married David and began a 20-year partnership of ministry with youth and young adults in The United Methodist Church. To this day, she continues to have a great passion for youth and young adult ministries in the Kentucky Conference. Dawn served as administrative assistant in two local United Methodist churches, Middletown UMC and Mosaic UMC. She also served as administrative assistant to the Lexington district superintendent.

While grieving the loss of her first husband, Dawn discovered the extraordinary gift of encouragement through her writing, which has helped Dawn encourage others to find their voice, even in the midst of great loss. In addition to her writing, Dawn has spoken at several local events with other prominent Christian writers, such as Liz Curtis Higgs and Kristy Cambron, including the Be Radiant Women's Conference in 2014 and Shelf Life: A Day with Rachael McRae in 2017.

Dawn met Leonard when he was assigned to the Louisville Episcopal Area following his election in 2016. They believe that only God could have paved the footpath that brought them together. Because of her long history with The United Methodist Church, Dawn brings to her partnership with Leonard a wealth of wisdom and knowledge. She looks forward to the doors God will open as she discovers new possibilities for using her gift for the glory of God's kingdom.

Favorite Scripture: Romans 8:38-39

—email from Kelly McDonald, executive assistant to Bishop Fairley, October 2018

Faye Thomas Fannin (b. 1937)

In 1956, Faye married Robert E. Fannin (b. 1935). Robert was elected in 1992 out of the Florida Annual Conference and served the Birmingham Episcopal Area (1992–2004), then retired. Faye and Robert have three children, nine grandchildren, and 11 great-grandchildren.

Faye completed her freshman year at Florida Southern College, after marrying Bob that spring. Later she earned an AA from Indian River Community College and took classes at Florida Atlantic University. After moving to Miami when Bob became a district superintendent, she enrolled in Florida International University and graduated with honors, earning a BS in secondary English education. She is a member of Pi Kappa Phi. When the children were growing up, she taught preschool for five years, substituted in elementary and high schools, and served as a Girl Scout leader, band parent, football parent, and Sunday school teacher. She also did her share of car-pooling. Later she became involved in Habitat for Humanity and "Paint Your Heart Out Lakeland," as well as participating in DISCIPLE Bible studies and UMW. Her hobbies include cross-stitching, traveling, walking, mountain hiking, cooking, and entertaining, but her primary joy is time spent with their children, grandchildren and great-grandchildren.

—*Biographical Directory*, 2012; email communication with Bishop Fannin, January 2018

Susan R. Farr (b. 1960)

In 1979, Susan married Robert Farr (b. 1959). Robert was elected in 2016 out of the Missouri Annual Conference and assigned to the Missouri Episcopal Area. Susan and Robert have two children and two grandchildren.

Susan earned a BS in education from East Texas State University; an MA in education from Central Methodist University in Fayette, Missouri; and an Educational Specialist Degree in Curriculum and Instruction from Missouri Baptist University in St. Louis. She has now retired after 33 years of teaching and is exploring options for what she will do next. She began her career teaching math and science, then moved to the elementary level. Her last 20 years have been focused on literacy, working with students struggling with reading and writing, and providing professional development to teachers. Susan enjoys gardening, reading and spending time with their grandchildren.

Favorite Hymns: "How Great Thou Art" (*UMH*, 77), "Just as I Am" (*UMH*, 357)

—interview with Susan Farr, May 2017

Luciana da Silva Clementa Fernandes (b. 1940)

In 1961, Luciana married Moises Domingos Fernandes (1938–2017). He was elected in 1988 and served the Eastern Angola Episcopal Area (1988–2000), then retired. Luciana and Moises have eight children and 19 grandchildren.

Luciana taught Sunday school while a young student at Henda School in Malange, Angola. She studied pedagogy at Quessua Mission School, also in Malange, and taught school from 1957 to 1984, while helping Moises with church tasks. She has served God by teaching the gospel; by spreading the Word of God in the community; and organizing and working with women in general, especially UMW, youth, and children. Sometimes she preached on Sundays when Moises was away. When Moises became a bishop, she helped open Women's Training Centers where students learn to sew, cook, and so on. Churches in the United States give much support, donating sewing machines, typewriters, fabrics, knitting needles, and so on. Proceeds from this work go to help the poor, who do not have food and clothing and many of whom live on the streets. In the 1990s, during the time of much war, she was appointed by the conference as coordinator of children living on the streets in Malange, providing food, clothing, education, and lots of love. Luciana has worked to bring evangelism and support to other provinces and to the Republic of Namibia as well. Luciana says, "I thank God first for the privilege of choosing me to serve Him. Without God's love, I am nothing. He empowered me to serve Him humbly with excellence. I thank my late husband who was humbly untiring in the service of God and who always supported me and loved me unconditionally. I also thank my children who are always with me to support me in everything. I extend my gratitude to family members, friends, all the members of the congregations and conference we served, and also the communities. Thank you for the honor of sharing about this humble and wonderful service."

Favorite Scriptures: Psalm 133, Jeremiah 33:3, 1 Corinthians 13:1-13

—https://www.unitedmethodistbishops.org/person-detail/2464066; https://www.umnews.org/en/news/bishop-fernandes-brave-leader-dies; email communication with daughter Isabel de Sousa, January 2018

Emilia V. Rosario Ferrer

In 1934, Emilia married Cornelio M. Ferrer (1908–1988). Cornelio was elected in 1968 out of the Philippine Annual Conference and served the Manila Episcopal Area (1968–1974), then retired. Emilia and Cornelio had four children.

Emilia was described as a real helpmate to her husband, and she continued to work by his side after retirement, doing volunteer work with the fisherfolk and farmers of their country.

—http://catalog.gcah.org/publicdata/gcah741.htm; *Biographical Directory*, 1984

Mamie Lee Ratliff Finger (1918–2006)

Mamie married Homer Ellis Finger Jr in 1942. Ellis (1916–2008) was elected in 1964 from the Mississippi Annual Conference of The Methodist Church. He served the Nashville Area (1964–1976) and the Holston Area (1976–1984). He retired from active service in 1984 and served for 12 years as administrative assistant secretary to the Council of Bishops. Mamie and Ellis had three children and five grandchildren.

Mamie graduated Phi Beta Kappa from Agnes Scott College. She served as president of Ewha Women's University International Foundation and as a member of the Committee for Women's History and Status and of the General Commission on Archives and History. Her hobbies included needlepoint and stitchery.

She followed in the footsteps of her activist mother, Cora Rodman Ratliff, about whom she wrote eloquently in her 1986 work, *The Kaleidoscope Turns Through Nearly a Century of America, 1918–2000.*

When Ellis was president of Millsaps College in Mississippi, an uproar ensued when 28 pastors signed a covenant affirming the official position of The Methodist Church on race, as stated in the 1960 *Discipline*, "Our Lord Jesus Christ teaches that all men are brothers. He permits no discrimination because of race, color, or creed." Mamie visited the wife of one of those pastors and assured her, in spite of criticism from church members, that she and Ellis supported her husband's action (Joseph T. Reiff, *Born of Conviction: White Methodists and Mississippi's Closed Society* [NY: Oxford University Press, 2016], 137).

In 2002, Mamie prepared a devotional booklet *Mysteries and Verities.* Brief quotations address such themes as simplicity, grace and gratitude, power and authority, listening and receptivity, mission and service: "Find and accept the core of your being and know the joy of being your own self."

—*Biographical Directory*, November 1996; Spouses' Scrapbooks, 2000–2004

Welthy Honsinger Fisher (1879–1980)

In 1924, Welthy married Frederick Bohn Fisher (1882–1938). Frederick was elected in 1920, after serving in the North Indiana and New England Annual Conferences and four years as a missionary in India. He served as bishop-in-residence in Calcutta (1920–1930), then resigned and returned to Michigan to serve local churches.

Welthy graduated from Syracuse University and taught at Rosebud College, a one-room school in Haverstraw, New York, then went to China as a missionary teacher in 1906. As headmistress of Baldwin Memorial School in Nanchang, she believed that education could equip girls to become independent Chinese women and modernize their country, often in spite of resistance by their traditional parents. A review of her autobiography noted that she devoted her life to "literacy, feminine education, and the civilizing influence of Christian religion. She did not marry until she was 44, and her husband, a Methodist bishop serving in India, was an admirable man whose activities and credo she shared fully. Long a widow at age 72, she returned to the sub-continent to set up a training school for Indian teachers, from which some 5,000 have already graduated and fill posts administered by the India Literacy Board she helped develop. She and her husband—about whom she has also written a book—were intimates of Gandhi, Nehru, Tagore, and other Indian notables. She has been close to the affairs of Asia for so many years that she can write with the easy familiarity of a native, yet has the keen, observing eye of a journalist. Her affection for the people she has served and her profound enjoyment of life glow warmly from the pages of her story" (https://www.kirkusreviews.com/book-reviews/welthy-honsinger-fisher/to-light-a-candle/).

After her husband's death, she wrote his biography, *Frederick Bohn Fisher: World Citizen*, published by Macmillan in 1944, republished in 2010 and available on Amazon.com. Her autobiography, *To Light a Candle*, was published in 1962 by McGraw-Hill.

In 1952, at the age of 73, Welthy returned to India to work with Frank Laubach, the Christian evangelical missionary and literacy pioneer. She broke with him after deciding that literacy training should be linked with agricultural and industrial development in order to combat poverty. In 1953, she founded Literacy House, offering both literacy and vocational training, which became famous for its effectiveness. Together with other literacy pioneers, she helped start two nonprofit organizations: World Literacy, which became World Education, and World Literacy of Canada. She stayed closely involved with both organizations for many years and traveled throughout the world in her nineties. She made her last trip to India as a guest of the government shortly before her death at the age of 101. In 1966, *Time* magazine featured her work in an article titled "Education Abroad: India's Literacy." In 1980, The Indian government, which based its village literacy programs on her ideas, honored her with the issue of a stamp in her likeness.

—https://en.wikipedia.org/wiki/Frederick_Bohn_Fisher; https://prabook.com/web/frederick_bohn.fisher/280655; *Encyclopedia of World Methodism, Vol. 1*, 846; /;https://www.kirkusreviews.com/book-reviews/welthy-h-fisher/frederick-bohn-fisher/; https://en.wikipedia.org/wiki/Welthy_Honsinger_Fisher; *The Official Journal and Minutes Detroit Annual Conference, 1981*, 1005

Sarah Frances Perry Fitzgerald (1924–2013)

In 1945, Frances married Ernest A. Fitzgerald (1925–2001). Ernest was elected in 1984 out of the Western North Carolina Annual Conference and served the Atlanta Episcopal Area (1984–1992), then retired. Frances and Ernest had two children, three grandchildren, and one great-granddaughter.

Frances graduated from Wingate College and Appalachian State University. She taught home economics for two years, worked as a dietitian at Duke Hospital while Ernest was attending Duke Divinity School, and worked in a public school lunch program. Frances had many interests and hobbies. She served district and local offices in UMW, as president of the Ministers' Wives, on the advisory board of the Health Department in the area of home health care, and as a trustee of Greensboro College. She credited her happiness as a minister's wife to being totally committed to God and the Church. Shortly after Ernest was elected bishop, she was elected president of the Bishops' Spouses' Association. She greatly appreciated the opportunities to travel the world on behalf of United Methodism. Frances loved people, flowers, and handwork and was also an excellent pianist and seamstress.

—*Biographical Directory*, 2000–2004; http://www.journalnow.com/obituaries/fitzgerald-frances-perry/article_731d777e-ef12-54ef-888a-f8d63844711e.html

Elisabeth Flinck [Alsted] (b. 1962)

In 1984, Elisabeth married Christian Alsted (b. 1961). Christian was elected in 2009 out of the Denmark Annual Conference and serves the Nordic and Baltic Episcopal Area of the Northern Europe and Eurasia Central Conference. Elisabeth and Christian live in Copenhagen, Denmark. They have three children and one grandchild.

Elisabeth was born in Naestved, Denmark, and studied at Roenne Gymnasium and Esbjerg Seminarium, majoring in French and earning a BA in teaching and pedagogy. She is a teacher working with innovative school development and a deputy principal at Orestadsskolen, a new school with a virtual esthetic profile. Elisabeth also enjoys crafts (especially sewing), reading, running, and gardening.

—*Biographical Directory*, 2012–2016; https://www.unitedmethodistbishops.org/person-detail/2463475; interview with Elisabeth Flinck, February 2018

Clara Yetta Flint (1878–1958)

Clara married Charles Wesley Flint in 1901. Charles (1878–1964) was elected in 1936 and served the Atlanta Episcopal Area of The Methodist Episcopal Church (1936–1939), the Syracuse Episcopal Area (1939–1944), and the Washington, DC, Episcopal Area (1944–1952), then retired. Clara and Charles had two children, a son who became a Methodist pastor and a daughter who became a college professor.

Clara grew up in a Methodist parsonage in Iowa, her father a presiding elder. In a memoir of her, Bishop Earl Ledden states, "Through pastorates, college and university presidencies, and the manifold ministries of the episcopacy, she was the resourceful partner in the long list of distinguished achievements associated with the name of Flint. . . . She never sought to attract attention to herself. But how she illumined her home and the pathways of all the family." Speaking at his retirement, Bishop Flint said, "I thank God for the wife who for 51 years walked by my side. She has been most understanding and most helpful in all my work. Indeed, I think I was positively stingy when I recently said to the women of our area that 85 percent of all I have done is due to her. I think that was an understatement."

—November 1958 memoir in Spouses' Scrapbooks, 1949–1964;
http://catalog.gcah.org/publicdata/files/4642/flint-charles-wesley-bishop.pdf

Linda Layfield Edwards Foster [Edwards] (b. 1939)

In 1962, Linda married Marion Mortimer Edwards (1939–2011). He was elected in 1996 out of the South Georgia Annual Conference, served the Raleigh Episcopal Area (1996–2004), then retired. The Edwards have three children and four grandchildren.

Linda is a graduate of Emory University (BA) and Vladosta State University (MS). She taught special education, kindergarten, and elementary grades, and also has been a social worker. She served in Christian education for several churches, in addition to volunteering in outreach ministries, congregational evangelism, small-group ministries, scouting, and parent-teacher organizations. More recently she has worked as a licensed realtor specializing in residential sales. Linda married Fred Foster, a retired United Methodist minister from South Georgia, in 2013.

—*Biographical Directory*, 2004–2008;
email communication with Linda Foster, January–February 2017

Restetita Francisco (b. 1955)

In 1982, Restetita married Ciriaco Francisco (b. 1952). Ciriaco was elected in 2012 out of the Philippines Annual Conference and served the Davao Episcopal Area (2012–2016). He was re-elected in 2016 and assigned to the Manila Episcopal Area. Restetita and Ciriaco have three children and three grandchildren.

Restetita earned a Doctor of Education degree and has worked as a counselor and as a teacher. She has been active in UMW.

Favorite Scripture: Psalm 35:27 / Favorite Hymn: "Great Is Thy Faithfulness" (*UMH*, 140)

—https://www.unitedmethodistbishops.org/person-detail/2463476; interview and email conversation with Bishop Francisco, November/December 2017

Wilma Alice Sedoris Frank (1908–2000)

In 1930, Wilma married Eugene Maxwell Frank (1907–2009). Eugene was elected out of the Kansas Annual Conference in 1956, served the Missouri Episcopal Area (1956–1972) and the Arkansas Episcopal Area (1972–1976), then retired. Wilma and Eugene settled in Kansas City. They had four children, seven grandchildren, and 14 great-grandchildren.

Wilma graduated from Pittsburgh State University in Kansas and was employed as a public school teacher and social worker. She was active in the local church, traveled widely with her husband doing church work, organized retreats for clergy spouses in Missouri and Arkansas, and received a 50-year pin for her membership in P.E.O.

—*Biographical Directory*, 2000–2004, 2004–2008; *Journal of the Missouri West Annual Conference, 2000*, §I-11–12; https://www.umnews.org/en/news/bishop-eugene-m-frank-social-activist-dies-at-101

Catherine Fae Luster Lane Franklin (1901–1996)

In 1953, Fae married Bishop Marvin Augustus Franklin (1894–1972), who was serving the Jackson (Mississippi) Episcopal Area. After his retirement in 1963, Fae and Marvin continued to live in Jackson. He had four children with his first wife, Ruth. Fae had one daughter and three grandchildren.

Fae was the widow of a ministerial member of the Mississippi Annual Conference, William Henry Lane, who died in 1950. A native of Mississippi, she attended Hinds Junior College, graduated from Mississippi State College for Women, and taught school. She was active in Galloway Memorial UMC, teaching in the Junior Department of the Sunday school and serving as a UMW officer and as president of the Susannah Wesley Circle. After marrying Marvin, she traveled with him extensively around Mississippi, the United States, and the world, visiting Methodist ministries.

—*Biographical Directory*, 1984; http://prabook.com/web/person-view.html?profileId=1099089#; https://www.findagrave.com/cgi-bin/fg.cgi?page=gr&GRid=19071620; *1996 Journal, Mississippi Conference*, 310

Ruth Tuck Franklin (1893–1952)

In 1915, Ruth married Marvin Augustus Franklin (1894–1972). Marvin was elected in 1948 out of the Alabama-West Florida Annual Conference and served the

Jackson (Mississippi) Episcopal Area (1948–1964), then retired. Ruth and Marvin had four children.

Ruth's memoir in the 1953 North Mississippi Conference Journal states, "Mrs. Franklin impressed those who knew her even slightly with her wonderful Christian virtues. She was a constant source of inspiration to the wives of preachers. Her attitude was that her noble husband's work came first, and she enabled him to give himself wholly to it by reason of that attitude. Even when she was so desperately ill near the end, she "gave no thought to herself" but had a mind to the Kingdom. . . . Likewise, she was inspiring as a mother. She had a wonderful sense of humor which added spice to her homelife and her public contacts."

—*The North Mississippi Conference Journal 1953*, 100; *Biographical Directory*, 1984; http://prabook.com/web/person-view.html?profileId=1099089#; https://www.findagrave.com/cgi-bin/fg.cgi?page=gr&GRid=162832651

Elizabeth Louise Boney Galloway (1910–1998)

In 1932, Elizabeth married Paul Vernon Galloway (1904–1990). Paul was elected in 1960, after serving churches in Arkansas and Oklahoma, and served the San Antonio Episcopal Area (1960-1964), the Arkansas Episcopal Area (1964–1972), then retired. After retirement, he was reactivated to serve the Houston Episcopal Area for three years and the New Orleans Episcopal Area for one. Elizabeth and Paul had two children, a son and a daughter, who died at age six.

Elizabeth attended Galloway Women's College in Searcy, Arkansas, and later received a BA from Randolph-Macon Women's College in Lynchburg, Virginia, with majors in both Latin and English. She did other academic work at the University of Arkansas and taught Latin in two high schools. Later, as the wife of a bishop, she served on the board of the YWCA in San Antonio, Texas. In Arkansas, she was instrumental in getting a state's charter for Lauback Literacy work and was active in support of this cause. She was recognized for leading projects related to the preservation of Arkansas's oldest Methodist church in historic Washington, Arkansas. She served on various boards and pushed for "camperships" for needy and ill youth for Aldersgate Camp at Little Rock. Church-related travels around the world and in the United States were enriching and inspired continuing friendships and unending devotion to the church's mission outreach. In later years, she pursued her interest in reading, writing, needlepoint, cross-stitching, and philanthropy, including Peace Links and hand-gun control efforts.

—*Biographical Directory*, 1984; http://www.nytimes.com/1990/08/07/obituaries/bishop-paul-galloway-dead-of-cancer-at-86.html; https://www.findagrave.com/cgi-bin/fg.cgi?page=gr&GRid=8370366; http://prabook.com/web/person-view.html?profileId=371142; *The Little Rock Annual Conference, 1998 Journal*, 305

Zoraida Freytes Galvan (b. 1960)

In 1986, Zoraida married Elias Gabriel Galvan (b. 1938). Elias, born in Mexico and raised in a Methodist parsonage there, was elected in 1984 out of the Southern California-Arizona Annual Conference and served the Phoenix Episcopal Area (1984–1996) and the Seattle Episcopal Area (1996–2004), then retired. Zoraida and Elias have one son.

Zoraida, a native of Puerto Rico, was raised in a United Methodist parsonage. She earned a degree in health education.

—*Biographical Directory*, 2000–2004; https://www.unitedmethodistbishops.org/person-detail/2463633; interview with Bishop Galvan, November 2017

Edita Bote Gamboa (1927–2015)

In 1986, Edita married José Gamboa Jr (b. 1928). José was elected in 1986 while serving as professor of Christian Education at Union Theological Seminary in Manila, The Philippines. He served the Davao Episcopal Area (1986–1994), then retired. Edita and José have five children.

Edita, known from an early age for her beautiful singing voice, attended Harris Memorial College and served as a deaconess in Nueva Ecija. She met José, then a young pastor, through her ministry with youth and children. After their marriage, she served as deaconess and choir director at the churches her husband pastored. While he was studying at Wesley Theological Seminary in Washington, DC, she studied at the music conservatory of American University there. She also earned a BS in education at Philippine Wesleyan College and taught music and Bible in the elementary school of that college. Later, she served on the faculty of the Elementary School of the Philippine Christian University in Dasmarina, Cavite. In 1975, she received her MA in teaching English from De La Salle University Graduate School Manila and was promoted to principal of Union Elementary School until José was elected bishop. She then joined him in serving the southern Philippines. Edita also grew beautiful and rare orchids but left them behind when they moved to Davao City. She continued to serve with UMW's Society of Christian Service, the preachers' spouses, and the deaconesses there.

—*Biographical Directory*, 2000–2004; https://s3.amazonaws.com/PNWUMC/Annual+Conference/The-Amen-Report.pdf, 5; *Methodism in the Philippines: A Century of Faith and Vision* [Philippines Central Conference, 2003], 249–250; "A Service of Remembrance and Resurrection, November 4, 2018" program book for the Council of Bishops

Nina Fontana Garber (d. 1986 or 1987)

In 1963, Nina married Bishop Paul Neff Garber (1899–1972), who was serving the Richmond Episcopal Area. He served the newly created Raleigh Episcopal Area (1964–1968), then retired. His first wife, Orina, died in 1959.

—http://www.ncpedia.org/biography/garber-paul-neff;
Alaska Missionary Conference Journal for 1986, 95;
Encyclopedia of World Methodism, Vol. 1, 897–898

Orina Winifred Kidd Garber (1903–1959)

In 1927, Orina married Paul Neff Garber (1899–1972). Paul was elected in 1944, while serving as dean of Duke Divinity School. He served the Geneva Episcopal Area (1944–1951) (North Africa, Switzerland, Belgium, Spain, Yugoslavia, Hungary, Austria, Bulgaria, Poland, Czechoslovakia, and the Madeira Islands), the Richmond Episcopal Area (1951–1964), and the newly created Raleigh Episcopal Area (1964–1968), then retired.

Orina, born in Massachusetts, graduated from Pembroke College (Brown's college for women) in 1924. Paul was an instructor at Brown when she was a student there. After their marriage, she and Paul moved to North Carolina, where he began teaching at Duke. She loved her adopted state and co-authored a supplementary textbook called *History of North Carolina*, in addition to teaching school. She and Paul became active in Trinity Methodist Church in Durham. She taught Sunday school, organized and taught the Susannah Wesley class for young women, and served as president of the Woman's Society of Christian Service. A gifted public speaker, she was often invited to speak at meetings of the Women's Society of Christian Service and of the ministers' wives. After Paul's election, she moved with him to Europe, where she accompanied him on visitations to churches struggling to recover from the destruction of World War II, graciously accepting limited accommodations and sharing their resources with pastors and church members. When they returned to the United States, she continued to accompany him and share in his ministry and was known for her personality, friendship, service, and prayer life.

—http://www.ncpedia.org/biography/garber-paul-neff;
Journal of the North Carolina Annual Conference of The Methodist Church 1960, 136–137

Edith Heritage Garrison (1900–1971)

In 1922, Edith married Edwin Ronald Garrison (1897–1995). Edwin was elected in 1960 out of the North Indiana Annual Conference and served the Dakotas Episcopal Area (1960–1968), then retired. Edith and Edwin settled in Kalamazoo, Michigan. They had two daughters, six grandchildren, and four great-grandchildren.

Edith was a graduate of DePauw University and Columbia University and taught school for two years.

—*Biographical Directory*, 1984

Marion Thompson Garrison (1909–2008)

In 1973, Marion married retired Bishop Edwin Ronald Garrison (1897–1995). Edwin had two daughters, six grandchildren, seven great-grandchildren, and one great-great grandchild with his first wife, Edith, who died in 1971.

Marion grew up in a United Brethren church in Indiana and taught Sunday school there, as she did later at a United Methodist church and the Marion County Children's Guardian Home. For a while she worked as a secretary and later operated her own letter shop. For 20 years, she was a member of the Indiana Episcopal Area office staff. Active in church programs, she also enjoyed the children, grandchildren, and great-grandchildren she inherited on her wedding day.

—*Biographical Directory*, 1984; *North Indiana Conference 1995 Journal*, 2407

Lola Mabel Stroud Garth (d. 1947)

In 1922, Lola married Schuyler Edward Garth (1898–1947). Schuyler was elected in 1944 after serving churches in Kansas, Illinois, Florida, and Ohio, and served the Wisconsin Episcopal Area from 1944 until his death. Lola and Schuyler died together in a plane crash near Hankow, China, while on an episcopal visitation there. They had three children.

—*Encyclopedia of World Methodism, Vol. 1*, 904

Minnie E. Gattinoni

Minnie married Juan Ermete Gattinoni (1878–1970). Juan was elected in 1932 after serving churches in Uruguay and Argentina. The first South American to be elected bishop in The Methodist Episcopal Church, he served an episcopal area that included Argentina, Uruguay, and Bolivia (1932–1945), then retired. Minnie and Juan had 10 children.

Minnie was born in England and came to Argentina at the age of five. She attended Methodist and government schools in Buenos Aires and trained to be a teacher at Nicholas Lowe Institute. She helped with educational work in the churches Juan pastored and for years served as president of the Methodist Federation of Women in Argentina. She wrote a book titled *Women Under the Southern Cross* sometime in the 1930s. Juan described her as "a wise counselor, the severe critic of my sermons, and the exemplary mother of my children. She has suffered and rejoiced with me, 'for better, for worse,' always courageous, never complaining, never discouraged by any circumstance."

—http://catalog.gcah.org/publicdata/files/4642/gattinoni-bishop-john-ermette.pdf; https://www.newspapers.com/newspage/21815546/

Lamarr V. Gibson [Lee] (b. 1948)

In 1991, Lamarr married Linda Lee (b. 1949). Linda was elected in 2000 out of the Detroit Annual Conference. She served the Michigan Episcopal Area (2000–

2004) and the Wisconsin Episcopal Area (2004–2012). She then retired, and they settled in Wisconsin. Lamarr and Linda have three children, 12 grandchildren, and three great-grandchildren.

Lamarr graduated from the University of Illinois with a BA in economics and also studied graduate quantitative economics there. Lamarr entered the ordained ministry after an 18-year career in financial and investment services and was ordained an elder in the Detroit Annual Conference, transferring to the Wisconsin Annual Conference in 2005. He holds an MDiv from Garrett Evangelical Theological Seminary in Evanston, IL (1993); MACP and DMin from Ashland Seminary in Ashland, Ohio; and an MADR from Wayne State University in Detroit, Michigan. Lamarr has advanced training in mediation and restorative justice. He has served as an adjunct chaplain at Grace Hospital (1992–1998), a licensed professional counselor at Southfield Michigan Counseling and Development Center (1995–2000), a mediator for the Oakland County Mediation Center, and an adjunct professor for conflict transformation and church growth at Ashland Seminary in Southfield, Michigan. He has held appointments in the Detroit, East Michigan, and Wisconsin Episcopal Areas and is currently a retired elder. Lamarr has served on the Council on Ministries in the Northern Illinois and Michigan Episcopal Areas and on the Board of Congregational Development in the Michigan and Wisconsin Episcopal Areas. He also served as chair of the Northern Illinois Black Methodists for Church Renewal (BMCR) caucus and as president of the Detroit Conference Black Clergy Association.

—*Biographical Directory*, 2012–2016; interview with Bishop Linda Lee, Fall 2017; email communication with Lamarr Gibson, September 2018

Ida Elizabeth Smith Golden

In 1937, Ida married Charles Franklin Golden (1912–1984). Charles, who was born in Mississippi, was elected in 1960 while serving as associate general secretary of the National Division of the Board of Missions. He served the Nashville-Birmingham Episcopal Area of the Central Jurisdiction (1960–1968), the San Francisco Episcopal Area (1968–1972), and the Los Angeles Episcopal Area (1972–1980), then retired.

Ida graduated from Rust College in Mississippi, where she was given special recognition in 1978, and did specialized study at Scarritt College and Fisk University. She taught school and was active in Girl Scout and YWCA work. She served on the Women's Planning Committee of the Interdenominational University of Japan (1960–1968). Widely traveled, she remembered with gratitude the private audience she and Charles had with Pope Paul VI. Her hobbies included knitting and liquid embroidery.

—*Biographical Directory*, 1984

Deborah Phoebe Cox Goodpaster (b. 1950)

In 1971, Deborah married Larry Martin Goodpaster (b. 1948). Larry was elected in 2000 out of the Mississippi Annual Conference and served the Alabama-West Florida Episcopal Area (2000–2008) and the Western North Carolina Episcopal Area (2008–2016), then retired. Deborah and Larry are living in Tucker, Georgia. They have two daughters and five grandchildren.

Deborah attended Wesleyan College in Macon, Georgia; Tallahassee Junior College in Tallahassee, Florida; and the University of Mississippi. She served as a teacher's assistant in the public schools of Oxford, Meridian, and Tupelo, Mississippi. She has also been active in community activities, such as chairing a blood drive; and in many groups and ministries in the life of the congregations where she has been a member, including United Methodist Volunteers in Mission. She enjoys spending time with her family, yard work, tending houseplants, traveling, and needlework.

Favorite Scripture: John 3:16

—*Biographical Directory*, 2012–2016;
email communication with Deborah Goodpaster, September 2017

Thelma Goodrich (1917–2008)

In 1939, Thelma married Robert E. Goodrich Jr (1909–1985). Robert was elected in 1972 out of the Texas Annual Conference and served the Missouri Episcopal Area (1972–1980), then retired. Thelma and Robert had four children, 11 grandchildren, and 15 great-grandchildren.

Thelma attended Shorter College and Southern Methodist University, graduating from the latter in 1938. She was a gifted painter, musician, composer, writer, and lover of the arts. She held several one-woman shows of her oil paintings, designed Christmas cards and book covers for publishers, had religious solos and anthems published, recorded three musical compositions, and three of her television scripts were telecast nationally. She also researched ethnic hymns for a new hymnal.

—*Biographical Directory*, 1992;
http://www.legacy.com/obituaries/dallasmorningnews/obituary.aspx?n=thelma-quillian-goodrich&pid=123070846; Spouses' Scrapbooks, 1977–1979

Martha Ann Ogburn Goodson (1915–2006)

In 1937, Martha married Walter Kenneth Goodson (1912–1991). Kenneth was elected in 1964 out of the North Carolina Annual Conference and served the Birmingham Episcopal Area (1964–1972) and the Richmond Episcopal Area (1972–1980), then retired. Martha and Ken had three children, seven grandchildren, and nine great-grandchildren.

Martha received an AB from the University of North Carolina, with a major in biology. She was active in the local church, teaching Sunday school and participating in the activities of UMW. She enjoyed swimming, watching spectator sports, working in the yard "when I want to," and especially grandmothering.

—*Biographical Directory*, 1984; http://www.legacy.com/obituaries/charlotte/obituary-preview.aspx?n=martha-ann-ogburn-goodson&pid=197124508&referrer=218; Council of Bishops Memorial Booklet, Spring 2007

Elizabeth Thompson Gowdy (1877–1965)

In 1902, Elizabeth married John H. Gowdy (1869–1963). John, a Scottish-American member of the New Hampshire Annual Conference of The Methodist Episcopal Church, was elected in 1930 by the China Central Conference after serving as a missionary teacher there and then president of the Anglo-Chinese College in China. He was assigned to the China Central Conference (1930–1941), then retired. Elizabeth and John settled in Florida.

Elizabeth graduated from Wesleyan University in Connecticut, as did John. She was a member of Phi Sigma sorority and also of Phi Beta Kappa. Elizabeth and John went to China in 1902, where she also taught English at the Anglo-Chinese College (1902-1903), Fukien Christian University (1923–1927), and again at the Anglo-Chinese College (1929–1930). She co-authored a very successful English textbook for Chinese students.

—https://en.wikipedia.org/wiki/John_W._Gowdy; http://divinity-adhoc.library.yale.edu/ChinaCollegesProject/wesleyan/bios/gowdy.html

Juanita Rodriguez Recarey De Balloch Gowland

In 1911, Juanita married Enrique Carlos Balloch Gowland (1885–1979). Enrique was elected in 1941 while serving Methodist churches in Paraguay, Uruguay, and Argentina. He was assigned to the Pacific Episcopal Area, which included Chile, Perú, Panama, and Costa Rica (1941–1952), then retired. Juanita and Enrique then returned to Uruguay, serving as pastors for seven years in different small churches in the interior of that country. They had six daughters.

Juanita was born in Spain and did her studies in Argentina. She became a schoolteacher and a professor in music, song, and choir direction. She wrote and translated or adapted more than 200 hymns. She worked with Enrique in his ministry, especially when he thought the presence of a woman was needed—preaching, visiting, promoting the Women's Society, attending Sunday schools and youth activities, and providing social services (addressing alcohol, drug, and prostitution concerns) with the Mapuches Indians and in other communities. She also worked with him in administering the Pacific Episcopal Area and assisted him with his book, *Mirando a Jesús*. After his death, she lived with one of her daughters in Buenos Aires, Argentina, and wrote an autobiography.

—*Biographical Directory*, 1984

Racelder Grandberry-Trimble (b. 1955)

In 1979, Racelder married Julius Calvin Trimble (b. 1954). Julius was elected in 2008 out of the East Ohio Annual Conference, served the Iowa Episcopal Area (2008–2016), and was assigned to the Indiana Episcopal Area in 2016. Racelder and Julius have three young adult children.

Racelder, born in Chicago, graduated from Methodist Theological Seminary in Ohio with an MA in counseling ministries. She is a professional counselor and family advocate.

Favorite Scriptures: Proverbs 22:6; Luke 12:48b / Favorite Hymn: "He's Got the Whole World in His Hands"

—*Biographical Directory*, 2012–2016;
email communication with Racelder Grandberry-Trimble, January 2018

Doris K. Malin Grant (d. 1975)

In 1921, Doris married Alsie Raymond Grant (1897–1967). Alsie was elected in 1952 after serving churches in Iowa, Minnesota, and California. He served the Portland (Oregon) Area until his death in 1967. Doris and Alsie had one daughter.

Doris, who was born in Iowa, earned a degree in music at Cornell College. Through the years, she sang in church choirs, taught primary grades in Sunday school, volunteered in the offices of the American Association for the United Nations, and did hospital volunteer work as well. Her memoir in the conference journal states that, while she appeared to be quiet and unassuming, she was highly intelligent and a great reader and that she had a passion for world peace and a unique sense of humor.

—*Encyclopedia of World Methodism, Vol. 1*, 1032; *Journal and Yearbook, California-Nevada Annual Conference, 1976*, 293–294;
http://prabook.com/web/person-view.html?profileId=1099111

Nancy Graves (b. 1959)

In 1981, Nancy married David W. Graves (b. 1958). David was elected in 2016 out of the Holston Annual Conference and assigned to the Alabama-West Florida Episcopal Area. Nancy and David have two children and three grandchildren.

Nancy graduated from the University of Tennessee in Chattanooga and worked for three different school systems in Tennessee for the last 19 years. Her hobbies include decorating, cooking, and reading.

—email communication with Nancy Graves, June 2017

Lucy Dickerson Grose (1871–1961)

In 1894, Lucy married George Richmond Grose (1869–1953). George was elected in The Methodist Episcopal Church in 1924, after serving churches in Massachusetts and Maryland and as president of DePauw University in Indiana. He was assigned as a missionary bishop to China and served there until 1929, then retired and returned to the United States, settling in California. Lucy and George had five children.

Lucy, who was born in Ohio, graduated from Ohio Wesleyan University with Phi Beta Kappa honors and was president of the student YMCA organization. While they were in Asia, she devoted much of her time to mission projects. Back in the United States, she served as a trustee of the Methodist Hospital in Arcadia, California, and on the boards of the Pasadena YWCA and Thoburn Terrace Methodist Home for Retired Missionaries.

—https://en.wikipedia.org/wiki/George_Richmond_Grose; Minutes of the North Indiana Annual Conference of The Methodist Church, 1961, 655

Mary Lou Grove (b. 1929)

In 1951, Mary Lou married William Boyd Grove (b. 1929). Bill was elected out of the Western Pennsylvania Annual Conference in 1980, served the West Virginia Episcopal Area (1980–1992) and the Albany Episcopal Area (1992–1996), then retired. Mary Lou and Bill settled back in West Virginia. They have two daughters, five grandchildren, and two great-grandchildren.

Mary Lou shared her talents in the four congregations and two episcopal areas her husband served. A musician, she sang in the chancel choirs of each congregation, directed the children's choir at First Church Pittsburgh, and played cello in instrumental ensembles. She was an active participant and leader in UMW at local church, district, and conference levels. She served as a Girl Scout leader and Sunday school teacher and was active in clergy spouse organizations, both as a pastor's wife and as a bishop's wife. She is also an artist, enjoying painting, sewing, quilting, and knitting.

Favorite Scripture: Psalm 121 / Favorite Hymns: "Fairest Lord Jesus" (*UMH*, 189), "God Whose Love Is Reigning O'er Us" (*UMH*, 100)

—*Biographical Directory*, 2004–2008;
email communication with Bishop Grove, July 2017

Emilia Ramos Guansing

In 1934, Emilia married Benjamin I. Guansing (1908–1968). Benjamin was elected in 1967, after serving as a pastor in the Philippines and as a professor at Union Theological Seminary. He served the Manila Episcopal Area for less than a year before his death. Emilia and Benjamin had three children.

—*Encyclopedia of World Methodism, Vol. 1*, 1047

Mary Lucille Hendrick Gum

In 1919, Lucille married Walter Clarke Gum (1897–1969). Walter was elected out of the Virginia Annual Conference in 1960 and served the Louisville Episcopal Area (1960–1964) and the Richmond Episcopal Area (1964–1968), then retired. Lucille and Walter had one daughter and four grandchildren.

Lucille said she "was very fortunate to have been educated in a very fine private school." She majored in voice. She also noted that she "loved working with my husband in our churches" and traveling with him when he was a district superintendent and then a bishop. She loved to travel and frequently led tours to some "far-off" places.

—*Biographical Directory,* 1992

Basilia Baltazar Gutierrez (b. 1933)

Bessy married Benjamin R. Gutierrez (b. 1931). Benjamin was elected in 1994 by the Philippines Central Conference and served the Davao Episcopal Area (1994-1996). He served on the General Board of Global Ministries (1996-2000). Bessy and Benjamin have five children and six grandchildren.

Bessy earned a degree in Christian education from Harris Memorial College and a BS in elementary education from the University of Pangasinan. She also earned a Masters degree in education from San Carlos College. She served as deaconess-Christian education director for four years at the Mangaldan UMC and worked as a public schoolteacher for 18 years, earning the distinction of master grade schoolteacher.

—*Biographical Directory,* 1996–2000; *Methodism in the Philippines: A Century of Faith and Vision* [Philippines Central Conference, 2003] 250; email from daughter Glenda B. Gutierrez, October 2019

Joyce Hannah Gwinn (b. 1943)

In 1963, Joyce married Alfred W. Gwinn Jr (b. 1943). Al was elected in 2004 out of the Kentucky Annual Conference and served the Raleigh Episcopal Area (2004–2012), then retired. Joyce and Al now live on a 68-acre farm in Winchester, Kentucky. They have two daughters (married to brothers) and four grandchildren.

Joyce received an ADN from Northern Kentucky University and a BS in nursing from the University of Kentucky. She practiced her calling as a registered nurse in several hospitals through the years as she moved about with Al. She specialized in coronary care for 25 years before her retirement in 2004. During their years of ministry together, Joyce taught Sunday school, served on various boards, and loved to work in mission ministries both at home and around the world. She also enjoys journaling and has been actively involved with the Council of Bishops' Spouses' Association. In retirement, Joyce says, "I have become a farmer's wife, expert at weed eating and mowing many acres on the zero turn mower. I operate the tractor and take care of the barn cats. Lots of work, but lots of fun!" Joyce is also active at First UMC Andover Campus in Lexington, where she participates in Bible study and a covenant group. She also serves on the University of Kentucky Wesley Foundation Board of Directors.

Favorite Scriptures: Psalm 100; Romans 8 / Favorite Hymns: "Amazing Grace" (*UMH,* 378), "Jesus, Jesus, Jesus, There's Just Something about That Name!" (*UMH,* 171)

—*Biographical Directory*, 2004–2008, 2012–2016;
email communication with Joyce Gwinn, July 2017

Ruth Marthine Larsen Hagen (d. 1985 or 1986)

In 1926, Ruth married Odd Arthur Hagen (1905–1970). He was elected in 1953 while serving as principal of Methodistkyrkans Nordiska Theologiska Seminarium in Göteborg, Sweden. He was assigned to the Northern European Episcopal Area, with headquarters in Stockholm. Ruth and Odd Arthur had three daughters.

—*Biographical Directory*, 1984;
Odd Hagen biographical lexicon in Norwegian, by Peter Borgen (2009, 13 February) retrieved August 1, 2017, from https://nbl.snl.no/Odd_Hagen

Janet Hagiya (b. 1952)

In 1976, Janet married Grant J. Hagiya (b. 1952). Grant was elected in 2008 out of the California-Pacific Annual Conference and served the Seattle Episcopal Area/ Greater Northwest Episcopal Area (2008–2016), then was assigned to the Los Angeles Episcopal Area. Janet and Grant have three grown children and two grandchildren.

Janet, born in Colorado, graduated from UCLA with a major in psychology and earned her teaching credentials at California State, Long Beach. She has worked as an elementary math resource teacher and is currently a high school librarian.

—*Biographical Directory*, 2012–2016;
email communication with Janet Hagiya, February 2018

Gary Haller (b. 1952)

In 1978, Gary married Laurie Hartzel (b. 1954). Laurie was elected in 2016 out of the West Michigan Annual Conference and assigned to the Iowa Episcopal Area. Gary and Laurie have three children and two grandchildren.

Gary graduated from the University of Michigan and earned an MDiv and Master of Sacred Theology from Yale Divinity School. An ordained elder in the West Michigan Annual Conference, he retired in June 2017 and moved to Iowa, looking forward to being a support to Laurie. Gary and Laurie served as co-senior pastors in two different appointments, one for 13 years and the other for three. Each time, when she moved on to other positions, Gary remained as senior pastor. Gary loves to read, study, hike, and travel.

Favorite Scripture: John 1:1-5 / Favorite Hymn: "Come, O Thou Traveler Unknown" (*UMH*, 386)

—email communication with Gary Haller, May 2017

Williamine Weihrauch Hammaker (d. 1967)

In 1901, Williamine married Wilbur Emery Hammaker (1876–1968). Wilbur was elected bishop in The Methodist Episcopal Church in 1936, after pastoring churches in Ohio. He served the Nanking Episcopal Area in China (1936–1939) and the Denver Episcopal Area (1939–1948), along with other assignments, then retired. Willamine and Wilbur had two sons, four grandchildren, and three great-grandchildren.

Born in Springfield, Ohio, Williamine was one of the early coeds at Wittenberg College, where she was named class poet.

—http://prabook.com/web/person-view.html?profileId=283106;
https://quod.lib.umich.edu/b/bhlead/umich-bhl-851388?view=text;
Official Record and Yearbook of the 29th Annual Session of the North-East Ohio Conference of The Methodist Church, 913

Mariam Flora Crawford Hancock (1924–2012)

In 1946, Mariam married Charles Wilbourne Hancock (1924–2015). Charles was elected in 1988 out of the South Georgia Annual Conference and served the newly created Alabama-West Florida Episcopal Area (1988–1952), then retired. Mariam and Charles settled in Macon, Georgia. They had four children, eight grandchildren, and eight great-grandchildren.

Mariam attended the University of Georgia for two years and received her BS from Purdue University in West Lafayette, Indiana, in June 1945. She worked for Bell South while Charles finished seminary. Mariam was active in all phases of the church's work, especially as a teacher in Sunday school and with the UMW. She was a member of several civic organizations and was active in Girl Scouting. She had a great love of nature; was an enthusiastic birder; and enjoyed hiking, backpacking, camping, and canoeing. She made a thorough study of wildflowers of the Southeast, compiling a large slide collection. She also enjoyed many types of needlework.

—*Biographical Directory*, 2012–2016;
A Service of Remembrance and Hope, Council of Bishops, November 10, 2013

Ruth Odessa Robinson Handy (b. 1925)

In 1948, Ruth married William Talbot Handy Jr (1924–1998). W. T. was elected in 1980 out of the Louisiana Annual Conference and served the Missouri Episcopal Area (1980–1992), then retired. Ruth and W. T. had four children (one deceased) and eight grandchildren.

Ruth graduated from Dillard University in 1949 and then did graduate work at Louisiana State University and Southern University. While W. T. was in seminary, Ruth was employed in Atlanta, Georgia, as an elementary school teacher. This was followed by a fruitful career as a physical education teacher, coordinator for foreign students at Meharry Medical College, and reading and math teacher for special students. She was active in and held offices for the National Ministers' Wives Association, UMW, Church Women United, and the Girl Scouts Council. She received the outstanding Cotillion Award for Woman of the Year and the United Methodist Laity Award for Outstanding Layperson of the Year. Ruth was a charter member of Delta Sigma Theta Sorority and a lifetime member of the NAACP. She traveled extensively with her husband and attended four sessions of the World Methodist Council, meeting in Singapore, Kenya, England, and Portland, Oregon. She also traveled to Italy, Korea, The Philippines, Japan, Switzerland, Finland, Russia, Jordan, Egypt, Alaska, Australia, Austria, Israel, Canada, Hawaii, Puerto Rico, Malaysia, Germany, and Bermuda.

—*Biographical Directory*, 2004–2008; http://archive.wfn.org/1998/04/msg00139.html; http://www.lib.utexas.edu/taro/smu/00295/smu-00295.html; biographical sketch in W. T. Handy's administrative file in the UM Archives and History Center

Jinying Hao [Wang] (d. 1969)

In 1900, Jinying married Chih Ping Wang (1878–1964). Chih Ping was elected in 1930, probably in The Methodist Episcopal Church, after serving as a teacher, professor, and pastor. He was the first Chinese Methodist bishop in China. His work required travel to many places in China, and exhaustion forced him to retire before he reached age 60. Jinying and Chih Ping lived in Beijing and Tianjin during his retirement years.

Jinying was a graduate of Muzhen Girls School.

—https://en.wikipedia.org/wiki/Chih_Ping_Wang

Dorothy Elizabeth Reel Hardin (1904–1992)

In 1927, Dorothy married Paul Hardin Jr (1903–1996). Paul was elected in 1960 out of the Alabama-West Florida Annual Conference and served the new Columbia (South Carolina) Episcopal Area (1960–1972), then retired. Dorothy and Paul settled in the mountains of North Carolina. They had three children.

Dorothy majored in piano in college. Her husband and children were always her primary interests, but she participated in church activities as much as possible. Her hobbies included piano and handwork (knitting, crocheting, and needlepoint). She also compiled scrapbooks for her own and the whole family's enjoyment.

—*Biographical Directory*, 1984; https://en.wikipedia.org/wiki/Paul_Hardin_Jr.

Martha Carson Hardt (b. 1920)

In 1943, Martha married John Wesley Hardt (1921–2017). John was elected in 1980 out of the Texas Annual Conference and served the Oklahoma Episcopal Area (1980–1988), then retired. Martha and John had four children, eight grandchildren, and 12 great-grandchildren.

Martha attended Lon Morris College and Southern Methodist University, receiving her BA in 1942. She has been active in local church activities and enjoys reading and travel. She traveled with her husband to various World Methodist Conferences and on repeated mission trips abroad, with a focus on Zimbabwe and Indonesia. "Martha has always been my confidant, counselor, comforter, encourager, partner and best friend," John Hardt said in an interview with UMW's *response* magazine. In a telephone conversation in September 2018, Martha said she found the Bishops' Spouses' Association to be a wonderful and very helpful organization.

—*Biographical Directory*, 2012;
telephone interview with Martha Hardt, 9/11/2018;
https://www.umnews.org/en/news/bishop-john-wesley-hardt-1921-2017

Rebecca Lamarr Harmon (1896 –1980)

In 1923, Rebecca married Nolan Bailey Harmon (1892–1993). Nolan was elected in 1956 after serving churches of The Methodist Episcopal Church, South, in Maryland and Virginia and then serving as book editor for The Methodist Church. He served the Charlotte Episcopal Area (1956–1964), then retired. Rebecca and Nolan had two sons and eight grandchildren.

Rebecca grew up in a Methodist family, graduated from Randolph-Macon College, and was a member of Phi Beta Kappa. She began her career as a high school teacher and then worked as a French translator for US government agencies and the Red Cross Headquarters in Washington, DC. While Nolan was working as book editor, she worked as training director for Orhbach's department stores and assisted with the opening of the store in Los Angeles. During their years in Western North Carolina, she was recognized for her support of Nolan, her devotion to Christ, and her individuality in her own right. Her strong personal feeling for Susanna Wesley inspired her to undertake eight years of extensive research in England at the various Wesley sites and consultation with renowned Wesley scholars, resulting in a book, *Susanna—Mother of the Wesleys* (Nashville: Abingdon Press, 1968).

—*Biographical Directory*, November 1996; newspaper clipping from the
Lynchburg, VA *The Daily Advance*, stored in Spouses' Scrapbooks, 1965–1968;
The Journal of the Virginia Annual Conference, 1980, 220–221

Amy Patten Walden Harrell (circa 1880–1969)

In 1917, Amy married Costen Jordan Harrell (1885–1972). Coston was elected in 1944, after serving churches of The Methodist Episcopal Church, South, in Tennessee, North Carolina, and in Virginia. He served the Birmingham Episcopal Area (1944–1948), the Charlotte Episcopal Area (1948–1956), then retired. Amy and Costen had one son.

Amy was born and grew up in Ohio, the daughter of a southern Presbyterian minister. She graduated from Agnes Scott Institute in Atlanta. While Coston was a pastor, she taught a young women's Bible study and led an Upper Room small-group Bible study in her home.

—https://en.wikipedia.org/wiki/Costen_Jordan_Harrell; https://beta.worldcat.org/archivegrid/data/173863131; http://www.ncpedia.org/biography/harrell-costen-jordan; Biographical Note in https://www.history.pcusa.org/collections/research-tools/guides-archival-collections/rg-485; newspaper obituary from April 4, 1969, in Coston Jordan Harrell's administrative file at the UM Archives and History Center

Geneva Magnolia Nelson Harris (1909–2010)

In 1931, Geneva married Marquis LaFayette Harris (1907–1966). Lafayette was elected in 1960 and served the Atlanta Area until his death in 1966. Geneva and Lafayette had a son, four grandchildren, and four great-grandchildren.

Geneva, born in Atlanta, Georgia, earned a BA in library science at Clark College there. She later earned an MA at the University of Illinois and was awarded the Doctor of Humane Letters from Philander Smith College in 1977. She worked as an instructor at Samuel Houston College in Texas and served as associate librarian at Philander Smith College, in Arkansas, when her husband was president. When Marquis was elected bishop, they moved to Atlanta, where he died six years later. Although she retired as an educator and librarian, she gave many years of dedicated service through religious, educational, and civic organizations, including the America Association of University Women, the Bethlehem Senior Center, the Salvation Army, YWCA, League of Women Voters, National Council of Negro Women, Alpha Kappa MU National Honor Society, Wesley Woods, Fulton County Agency on Aging, Church Women United, UMW, and AARP. "In a businesslike but deeply caring manner, she served on countless boards of directors for businesses, as well as civic and community organizations."

—*Biographical Directory*, November 1996; Council of Bishops Memorial Booklet, May 2011

Anneliese Fritzsch Härtel

In 1951, Anneliese married Armin E. Härtel (b. 1928). Armin was elected in 1970 by the Central Conference in the German Democratic Republic, the first bishop of the UMC to be elected in a socialist state with full and equal rights in the Council of Bishops. He was re-elected each quadrennium 1976, 1980, and 1984. In 1986, he retired in order to care for Anneliese, who was terminally ill. He continued serving as pastor in then Karl-Marx-Stadt (today Chemnitz). Anneliese and Armin had two children.

—*Biographical Directory*, 1984;
email communication from Urs Schweizer, assistant to Bishop Dr. Patrick Streiff,
Central Conference of Central and Southern Europe, October 2018

Helen Marion Nutter Hartman (1894–1960)

In 1922, Helen married Lewis Oliver Hartman (1876–1955). Lewis entered ministry in the Cincinnati Annual Conference of The Methodist Episcopal Church and served churches and 24 years as editor of *The Zion's Herald* before his election in 1944. He served the Boston Episcopal Area (1944–1948). Helen and Lewis had two children.

Helen, a native of Newton, Massachusetts, graduated from Wellesley College. She taught school before marriage and was a life member of the Boston University Women's Council. She served as president of the Women's Society of Christian Service. Her memoir in the New England Conference Journal, May 1961, states, "She will be remembered by a host of friends who shared experiences in the local churches where she lived and worked, in the councils and administrators of church business, as the mother of fine children. She graced many occasions in company of her husband, who served the church for years as the editor of *Zion's Herald*, and who for four years was the episcopal leader of the Boston Area."

—https://en.wikipedia.org/wiki/L._O._Hartman;
Official Minutes of the New England Conference, May 1961, 537

Dean Harvey (b. 1958)

In 1981, Dean married Cynthia Fierro (b. 1959). Cynthia was elected in 2012 out of the Texas Annual Conference and served the Louisiana Episcopal Area starting in 2012. Dean and Cynthia have one daughter.

— https://www.unitedmethodistbishops.org/person-detail/2463478

Merrill Hassinger (b. 1941)

In 1966, Merrill married Susan Wolfe Hassinger (b. 1942). Susan became a candidate for ministry while a member of Lohr's Evangelical United Brethren Church in Hanover, Pennsylvania; and Merrill became a candidate while a member of Sweitzer's Evangelical United Brethren, Berrysburg, Pennsylvania. Susan was elected in 1996 out of the Eastern Pennsylvania Annual Conference and assigned to the Boston Episcopal Area, where she served (1996–2004), then retired. She served as interim bishop in the Albany Episcopal Area (2006–2010). Merrill and Susan have two daughters and three grandchildren.

Merrill, a graduate of United Theological Seminary, Dayton, Ohio, was ordained elder in 1966 and served local churches in the Eastern Pennsylvania Conference. He also served with the Conference Youth Council, Education Commission, and the Board of Ordained Ministry.

—*Biographical Directory*, 1992–1996; email correspondence with Merrill Hassinger and Susan Hassinger, July–August 2017

Margaret Matilda Gulick Hay (1869–1945)

In 1900, Matilda married Samuel Ross Hay (1865–1944). Samuel was elected in 1922 in The Methodist Episcopal Church, South, after serving churches in Texas. He was appointed bishop in charge of all American Southern Methodist Episcopal Mission work in China (1922–1923), then returned to the United States and presided over episcopal areas that included Texas, Arkansas, Louisiana, New Mexico, Alabama, Florida, and the Pacific coast (1924–1934). He also helped organize The Methodist Church in Mexico. Samuel had two sons by his first wife, Della Binford, who died in 1899. Margaret and Samuel had a daughter.

Margaret was born in Fort Worth, Texas, and when she married Sam, he was the pastor of First Methodist Church in that city. After listing her husband's appointments, her memoir states, "In all these widely scattered fields of service with her husband Mrs. Hay was always the sweet and modest wife and mother. Whether as a hostess or guest, she was the center of attraction and a source of inspiration when and wherever found. She was truly the queen of her parsonage and the inspiration of her preacher-husband. Their home life was beautifully serene—a veritable vestibule of Heaven."

—*Journal of the 7th Annual Session of the Texas Annual Conference of The Methodist Church, 1945*, 132; https://www.findagrave.com/cgi-bin/fg.cgi?page=gr&GRid=76711542; *Encyclopedia of World Methodism, Vol. 1*, 1097; http://prabook.com/web/person-view.html?profileId=281830; https://en.wikipedia.org/wiki/Samuel_Ross_Hay; https://tshaonline.org/handbook/online/articles/fhabf

Deliliah "Dee" Bernard Hayes (b. 1954)

In 2003, Dee married Robert E. Hayes Jr (b. 1947). Bob was elected out of the Texas Annual Conference and served the Oklahoma Area (2004–2012), then retired. Dee and Bob have three grown children.

Dee attended Eastern Michigan University. She worked as an accountant in Texas for over 20 years. In 1995, she was appointed as budget consultant with GTE/Verizon Wireless and held that position until Bob was assigned to the Oklahoma Area in 2004. She loves interior decorating and working with children. She served on the board of Circle of Care, an Oklahoma Conference ministry working with children.

—*Biographical Directory*, 2012–2016; email communication with Dee Hayes, 2017 and 2019

Elizabeth Anne Connaughton Hearn (b. 1931)

In 1952, Anne married James Woodrow Hearn (b. 1931). Woodrow was elected in 1984 out of the Louisiana Annual Conference. He served the Nebraska Episcopal Area (1984–1992) and the Houston Episcopal Area (1992–2004), then retired. After retirement, Anne and Woody settled in Houston. They have four children.

Anne received her undergraduate degree from Louisiana Tech University and has done graduate work at Boston University, McNeese State, and Louisiana State Universities. She has been a member of the World Methodist Council and has taught in conference and regional mission schools throughout the U.S.

—*Biographical Directory*, 2012–2016;
email communication with Anne Hearn, July 2017

Erma Irene Martin Heininger (1901–1983)

In 1925, Erma married Harold Rickel Heininger (1895–1983). Harold was elected in 1954 and assigned to the Northwest Area of the Evangelical United Brethren Church, which included Illinois, Wisconsin, Minnesota, North Dakota, South Dakota, and northwestern Canada. He retired in 1968. Erma and Harold had three children, two of whom died in infancy, and two grandchildren.

Erma attended North Central College in Naperville, Illinois. She was a "faithful companion" and helpmate to her husband throughout his ministry as a seminary professor, college president, and bishop. She traveled extensively with him, including to overseas conferences in Germany, Norway, and Switzerland. She calculated that between 1925 and 1970, they spent 9 years, 7 months, and 26 nights away from home.

—*Official Journal and Yearbook of the 130th Session of the Minnesota Annual Conference, June 11–14, 1984*, 262

Dorothye Carithers Henderson (b. 1938)

In 1959, Dorothye married Cornelius Linton Henderson (1934–2000). Cornelius was elected in 1996 out of the North Georgia Annual Conference and served the Florida Episcopal Area 1996 until his death in 2000. He was the first African American United Methodist resident bishop for the Florida Conference. Dorothye and Cornelius have one child and two grandsons.

Dorothye holds a BA from Spelman College and graduate degrees from Atlanta University and Vanderbilt University. She is a retired science teacher/supervisor, having worked in public schools for 35 years. She served on the Board of Trustees of Gammon Theological Seminary (2002–2015) and on the Board of Trustees for Bethune Cookman University (2005–2015). Since 2000, she has participated in the Clark Atlanta University Guild of Fine Arts and the Chancel Choir at Cascade United Methodist Church in Atlanta.

Favorite Scripture: Ruth 1:16 / Favorite Hymn: "Amazing Grace" (*UMH,* 378)

—*Biographical Directory,* 2012;
https://www.findagrave.com/cgi-bin/fg.cgi?page=gr&GRid=6807388;
email communication with Dorothye Henderson, October 2017

Huldah Jo Chapin Henley (1908–1967)

In 1931, Huldah married James Walton Henley (1901–1990). James was elected in 1960 after serving churches in Tennessee, and served the Florida Episcopal Area (1960–1972), then retired. Huldah and James had two children.

Huldah was born in Arkansas. She was beloved throughout the Florida Annual Conference for her devotion to her husband and sons, honesty, sincerity, compassion, tenderness, joy, and enthusiasm.

—*Encyclopedia of World Methodism, Vol. 1,* 114; *Journal of the 126th Session of the Florida Annual Conference, 1968,* 271

Margaret Hollis Henley (1910–1984)

In 1970, Margaret married Bishop James Walton Henley (1901–1990), who was serving the Florida Episcopal Area and retired in 1972. Margaret had one son with her first husband, who died some years earlier. James had two sons with his first wife, Huldah, who died in 1967. Together they had nine grandchildren and two great-grandchildren.

Margaret and her first husband, L.S. "Sonny" Hollis, were very active in church affairs, and her dedication to educational programs eventually led her to become a member of the staff at the First Methodist Church of Tampa. She was given the role of director of educational programs and went to school for a short time at Scarritt, in Nashville. After his tragic death resulting from an electrical accident, Margaret dedicated herself to church matters and became well known throughout the conference for her work. Through this work, she came into contact with Bishop Henley. Margaret quickly adapted to being a bishop's wife. Her long association with the conference meant that she knew most of the ministers and was well acquainted with Florida Methodism. After his retirement in 1972, she continued her interest in educational work, serving as the faculty director for Educational Opportunities Inc. along with her husband.

—*Encyclopedia of World Methodism, Vol. 1,* 114;
Journal of the 143rd Session of the Florida Annual Conference, 1985, 417–418

Ruth Porter Herrick (d. 1973 or 1974)

Ruth married Paul Murray Herrick (1898–1972). Paul was elected at the General Conference of the Evangelical United Brethren Church in 1956 and was appointed to the Central Area. After the 1968 merger, he was assigned to the Virginia Annual Conference, but resigned in 1972 due to ill health. Ruth and Paul had three children.

Paul is quoted as saying of Ruth, "God gave me a lovely wife who has been a great and helpful companion for more than 50 years."

—*Official Journal and Yearbook West Ohio Annual Conference, June 10–15, 1973,* 243; *The Journal of the Virginia Annual Conference 1973,* 180

Lila Elaine Goodwin Hicks (b. 1926)

In 1946, Elaine married Kenneth William Hicks (b. 1923). Ken was elected in 1976 out of the Nebraska Annual Conference. He served the Arkansas Episcopal Area (1976–1988) and the Kansas Episcopal Area (1988–1992), then retired. Elaine and Ken settled in Little Rock, Arkansas. They have two daughters and two grandchildren.

Elaine graduated from York College, a United Brethren school, in York, Nebraska. She taught school in various communities and worked in doctors' and dentists' offices. She enjoyed the privileges and responsibilities of being a pastor's wife in various communities in Colorado and Nebraska, then as a bishop's wife in Arkansas and Kansas. She enjoyed weaving, and music was very important in her life. She sang in choirs, taught piano, and played the organ in many of her husband's churches. Each community gave her an opportunity to find something interesting to do.

—*Biographical Directory,* 2012–2016

Polly Anne Martin Hodapp (b. 1924)

In 1947, she married Leroy Charles Hodapp (1923–2006). Leroy was elected in 1976 out of the South Indiana Annual Conference and served the Illinois Episcopal Area (1976–1984), the Indiana Episcopal Area (1984–1992), then retired. Polly and Leroy have two daughters and four grandchildren.

Polly earned a BA in education from the University of Evansville. She has always had a special interest in working with children and taught in both secular and church schools. She is also a member of P.E.O., UMW, American Association of University Women, and a local United Methodist church. She enjoys needlepoint and interior design.

—*Biographical Directory,* 2000–2004, 2012–2016

Mary Brown Buckshaw Hodge (1899–1988)

In 1923, Mary married Bachman Gladstone Hodge (1893–1961). Bachman was elected in 1956 out of the North Alabama Annual Conference and served the Birmingham Episcopal Area until his death in 1961. Mary and Bachman had two daughters and five grandchildren.

Mary, a native of Birmingham, Alabama, attended Howard College there and was in nurse training for field service abroad with the American Red Cross when World War I ended. She taught in the Birmingham Public Schools until her marriage to Bachman. She was a faithful and devoted wife, mother, and grandmother and a devout and active church member, having taught church school and participated fully in UMW and in Church and Society organizations and interest groups. She described their life: "We had 38 wonderfully rich, satisfying years, four churches in four conferences, the Nashville District, and the Birmingham Area." She demonstrated her passion for unity among all people by participating in the work of the Fellowship of Reconciliation, American Friends Service, Women's International League for Freedom, the Panel of American Women, U.S.-China Peoples Friendship Association, United Nations Association, the Chattanooga Peace Center, and Church Women United, who named her "Valiant Woman of the Year" in 1984. While she was a strong supporter of her husband's ministry, she was also a forceful person in her own right. She was witty and full of good humor, forthright and unequivocal, but also humble and open. She could make a militant statement in a peaceful manner. In an article entitled "Viewing Life after 50," published in the *Holston United Methodist Reporter*, she commented, "The liberation movement is nothing new. Christ is way out in front leading the movement. He told us to follow him. I believe he is calling us today to build bridges of understanding, compassion and love where walls of ignorance, indifference and hostility have existed."

—*Biographical Directory*, 1984;
Journal of the Holston Annual Conference, June 12–15, 1989, 252

Winifred Maxwell Jackson Holloway (1901–1988)

In 1923, Winifred married Fred Garrigus Holloway (1898–1988). He was elected in 1960, while serving as dean of Drew Theological Seminary. He served the West Virginia Episcopal Area (1960–1968), then retired. Winifred and Fred had two sons.

Winifred graduated from the New Jersey State Teachers' College and taught kindergarten. She was a supportive pastor's wife and helpmate on campus and in the episcopal area, and she delighted in her grandchildren and great-grandchildren.

—*Biographical Directory*, 1984;
https://www.findagrave.com/cgi-bin/fg.cgi?page=gr&GRid=75687401

Felecia Brown Holston (b. 1956)

In 1984, Felecia married Lewis Jonathan Holston (b. 1959). Jonathan was elected in 2012 out of the North Georgia Annual Conference and assigned to the Columbia Episcopal Area. Felecia and Jonathan have two children.

Felecia received a BBA in finance from Georgia State University. She is a board member for Epworth Children's Home and Killingsworth Home. She enjoys volunteering, baking, and walking.

Favorite Scripture: Jeremiah 29:11

—email communication with Felecia Holston, June 2017

Leland Burks Holt (d. 1948)

In 1906, Leland married Ivan Lee Holt (1886–1967). Ivan was elected at the last General Conference of The Methodist Episcopal Church, South, in 1938 and assigned to the North Texas, Central Texas, North Central, and New Mexico Conferences for one year. He was also in charge of all Methodist mission work in Latin America. He served the Dallas Episcopal Area of The Methodist Church (1940–1944) and the Missouri Episcopal Area (1944–1956), then retired. Leland and Ivan had one son.

Leland was born in Missouri and attended Central College in Fayette. After their marriage, she went with Ivan to the University of Chicago, where she earned her MA in New Testament Greek. She was active in patriotic societies and other social clubs, as well as being active in the church.

—http://catalog.gcah.org/publicdata/gcah672.htm; http://shsmo.org/manuscripts/columbia/c2553.pdf; *The Methodist Church, St. Louis Annual Conference, Tenth Session, 1948*, 57; *Encyclopedia of World Methodism, Vol. 1*, 1146–1147

Modena McPherson Rudisell Holt

In 1966, Modena married retired Bishop Ivan Lee Holt (1886–1967). Ivan had one son with his first wife, Leland, who died in 1948. Modena had four children with her first husband, Edmund D. Rudisell Jr, a Methodist minister who died in 1963.

Modena was a graduate of Wesleyan College in Macon, Georgia; a Methodist leader in Georgia; and the widow of a district superintendent there. After Ivan's death, she worked as a Methodist missionary in Hong Kong and married Dr. Karl Quimby, former executive of the Methodist Board of Missions.

—http://shsmo.org/manuscripts/columbia/c2553.pdf; http://catalog.gcah.org/publicdata/files/4642/Done/holt-bishop-ivan-lee.pdf (page 1); *Encyclopedia of World Methodism, Vol. 1*, 1146–1147

Starr Carithers Holt (1893–1958)

In 1950, Starr married Bishop Ivan Lee Holt (1886–1967), who was serving the Missouri Episcopal Area and retired in 1956. Ivan had one son with his first wife, Leland.

Before her marriage, Starr served as a leader in the North Georgia Conference of the Woman's Society of Christian Service and in the Federation of Women's Clubs, as a trustee of the Methodist Children's Home, and in other roles as well. Bishop Arthur J. Moore, in a memoir written after her death, described her as "richly endowed with a noble mind, an energetic temperament and a naturally gracious manner." He noted that "Whether her distinguished bishop husband was at home in his Area; presiding over the Methodist World Council; or traveling as the 'Overseer of the flock of Christ' in the remote parts of the earth, she was at his side with a perceptive helpfulness and an unfaltering contentment. Her faith in God was as firm as her affections were constant. Men and women of many kindreds and tongues will gratefully remember her with lasting affection because of her outgoing personality and her deep loyalty to the Church."

—http://shsmo.org/manuscripts/columbia/c2553.pdf; memoir in Spouses' Scrapbooks, 1940–1964; *Encyclopedia of World Methodism, Vol. 1*, 1146–1147

Isabelle Elliott Holter (1906–2004)

In 1931, Isabelle married Don Wendell Holter (1905–1999). He was elected in 1972 by the South Central Jurisdiction while serving as president of Saint Paul School of Theology. He served the Nebraska Episcopal Area (1972–1976), then retired. Isabelle and Don had three daughters and six grandchildren.

Isabelle earned her AB from Baker University in 1927 and then taught junior high school English in Atchinson, Kansas, for four years. After marriage, she and Don moved to Chicago, where she worked as a case worker in the Unemployment Relief Service, and then to the Philippines as missionaries. While there, Isabelle and Don were interned at Santo Tomas along with their three daughters because they refused to sign a pledge required by the Japanese. Isabelle enjoyed reading, gardening, and furniture refinishing, "but especially the six grandchildren."

—*Biographical Directory*, 1984; http://cnac.org/emilscott/holter01.htm

Elaine M. Smithson Hopkins (b. 1946)

In 1964, Elaine married John Lowry Hopkins (b. 1945). John was elected in 1996 out of the South Indiana Annual Conference, served the Minnesota Episcopal Area (1996–2004) and the Ohio East Episcopal Area (2004–2016), then retired. Elaine and John have three sons and seven grandchildren.

Elaine attended Indiana University and Southern Connecticut State University, graduating *cum laude* with a BS in English. She earned an MA in public relations in 1985 from Ball State University. She worked as director of communications and marketing for the YMCA in Muncie, Indiana; internal education consultant for St. Joseph Medical Center in Fort Wayne; and director of management education for the University of Evansville. In 1993, she founded Hopkins Associates. Elaine has also served as president of several training professional associations, as a member of the board of directors for numerous civic groups, and as facilitator for strategic planning events for business and civic managers and boards. In 2002–2003, Elaine conducted training events for staff members of the General Council on Finance and Administration and the General Board of Church and Society.

Favorite Scripture: Matthew 19:24 / Favorite Hymn: "O God, Our Help in Ages Past" (*UMH*, 117, st. 5)

—*Biographical Directory*, 2004–2008;
email communication with Elaine Hopkins, March 2017

Greta Goo Hoshibata (b. 1951)

In 1974, Greta married Robert T. Hoshibata (b. 1951). Robert was elected in 2004 out of the Pacific Northwest Annual Conference, served the Portland (Oregon) Episcopal Area (2004–2012), and was assigned to the Phoenix Episcopal Area starting in 2012. Greta and Bob have three children.

Greta, who was born in Hawaii, graduated with a BA in English from Connecticut College in New London, Connecticut. She returned to Hawaii and earned her fifth-year credential in secondary education from the University of Hawaii. After her marriage to Bob, Greta taught high school English in California. After raising their children, Greta served as information specialist for a University of Washington study on healthy aging. After 11 years in this job, Greta went on to work for the Office of Educational Assessment at the University of Washington. Greta has served in ministries with children and youth as well as singing in the choir. Her interests include hunger and social justice issues, reading, classical music, professional baseball, golfing, cooking, and baking.

Favorite Hymn: "Here I Am, Lord" (*UMH*, 593)

—*Biographical Directory*, 2012–2016;
email communication with Greta Hoshibata, October 2017

Katherine Higgins Shannon Howard (1905–1994?)

In 1932, Katherine married Paul E. V. Shannon (1898–1957). He was elected in 1957 by the Evangelical United Brethren and assigned to Pittsburgh but died on the day that a reception had been planned to welcome him as bishop. In 1967, Katherine married Bishop John Gordon Howard (1899–1974), a widower who was elected bishop in 1957 to fill the vacancy created by the death of Bishop Shannon. The Howards lived in Pittsburgh until reassigned to the Philadelphia Episcopal Area in 1968, where he served until 1972, then retired. Katherine and John settled in Winchester, Virginia. They had a blended family of four children, seven grandchildren, and 10 great-grandchildren.

Katherine graduated from Bridgewater College, Pennsylvania State University, and Shenandoah College and Conservatory of Music. While a music student at the latter, she played violin in the orchestra, sang in the college choir and glee club, participated in the drama club, and wrote the winning play for commencement presentation. From her college days, she was a member of the Higgins Sisters Quartette, a well-known group that toured evangelistic services, camp meetings, and gatherings of The United Brethren in Christ and other denominations. They recorded for Victor Records and won several state and national awards. She taught school for a number of years and was quite active in the local church and UMW. She taught Sunday school and served as a Girl Scout Board secretary for seven years, and she also enjoyed doing needlepoint, hooking rugs, crocheting, reading, and sewing.

—*Biographical Directory*, 1984;
Journal of the Wyoming Annual Conference, June 5–8, 1997, 362

Mera Gay Hughes (b. 1932)

In 1950, Mera married Harold Hasbrouck Hughes Jr (b. 1930). Harold was elected in 1988 out of the Virginia Annual Conference and served the Florida Episcopal Area (1988–1996), then retired. Mera and Hasbrouck settled in Williamsburg, Virginia. They have four children.

Mera's lifetime career has been that of homemaker for the Hughes family. Her hobbies and interests include furniture refinishing, upholstering, needlepoint, caning, tole painting, ceramics, and vegetable gardening.

—*Biographical Directory*, 2004–2008

Robert Wolff Huie (b. 1946)

In 1970, Bob married Janice Riggle (b. 1946). Janice was elected in 1996 out of the Southwest Texas Annual Conference and served the Arkansas Episcopal Area (1996–2004) and the Houston Episcopal Area (2004–2016), then retired. Robert and Janice have a son, whose younger brother died in an accident at 13, and three grandchildren.

Bob, born and raised in Austin, Texas, graduated from the University of Texas, where he met Janice, and from Perkins School of Theology. While a student there, he served an internship in campus ministry in Buffalo, New York; as a summer intern with the National Council of Churches; and as youth director at Northaven UMC in Dallas. Upon graduation, he was appointed to a small rural church outside Austin, and Janice was appointed as an associate pastor to University UMC, Austin, where Bob had been active while growing up. Both he and Janice were ordained elders in 1974 by the Southwest Texas Annual Conference, and, beginning in 1975, they served as co-pastors of local churches. In 1990, Bob was appointed to the Texas Conference of Churches, where he worked to establish an interfaith network for ministry with persons with HIV/AIDS and began training as a pastoral counselor and psychotherapist. After Janice was elected bishop, Bob served as a licensed marriage and family counselor in Arkansas and Texas, working for the Samaritan Counseling Center in Little Rock and the Krist Samaritan Counseling Center in Houston. Bob retired from the Southwest Texas Annual Conference in 2009 and from counseling in 2010. In retirement, he divides his time between farming and ranching in South Texas, traveling with Janice, and chasing their three lively grandchildren.

—*Biographical Directory*, 2012; email communication with Bob Huie, October 2017

Nancy Mamie Humper

Nancy is married to Joseph Christian Humper (b. 1942). Joseph was elected in 1992 out of the Sierra Leone Annual Conference and served the Sierra Leone Episcopal Area (1992–2008), then retired. Nancy and Joseph have four children.

—*Biographical Directory*, 2000–2004;
https://www.unitedmethodistbishops.org/person-detail/2464023

Mary Ann Hunt (1919–2018)

In 1943, Mary Ann Hunt married Earl Gladstone Hunt Jr (1918–2005). Earl was elected bishop in 1964 out of the Holston Annual Conference. He served the North Carolina Episcopal Area (1964–1976), the Nashville Episcopal Area (1976–1980), and the Florida Area (1980–1988). He retired in 1988 and served as president of the Foundation for Evangelism (1989–1996). Mary Ann and Earl had one son.

Mary Ann earned a BS from East Tennessee State University and taught in elementary schools in Tennessee and in Georgia. She held a variety of positions in Methodist organizations for youth and women and served as director of the first junior camp for the Holston Conference. She directed community drama and local church pageants, as well as participating in Little Theatre and Church Drama Players. Her hobbies include theater, travel, making samplers, and needlepoint.

—*Biographical Directory*, 2000–2004;
email communication with son Stephen Hunt, July 2017

Kay Arcille Hutchinson (b. 1942)

In 1964, Kay married William Wayne Hutchinson (b. 1941). Bill was elected in 2000 out of the New Mexico Annual Conference and served the Louisiana Episcopal Area (2000–2012), then retired. Kay and Bill now live in Louisiana. They have two sons and one grandchild.

Kay was born in Oklahoma and graduated from the University of Oklahoma with a degree in music education. In 1983, she received her MA in vocal performance from New Mexico State University. She has been intensely involved in music education all her life, teaching private voice lessons and directing choral groups and handbell choirs in various churches. In recent years, she has enjoyed working in retail and traveling with Bill.

—*Biographical Directory*, 2012–2016;
email communication with Kay Hutchinson, 2017

Irene Janjay Zeon Innis (b. 1964)

In 1984, Irene married John G. Innis. John was elected in 2000 by the West Africa Central Conference and served the Liberia Episcopal Area (2000–2016), with the addition of Côte d'Ivoire (2003–2005), then retired. Irene and John live in Liberia and Worcester, Massachusetts. They have four children and four granddaughters.

Irene graduated from Worcester State College in Massachusetts in 2001. A devoted Christian, she has served the UMC as UMW president, choir director, choir member, and Sunday school teacher.

—*Biographical Directory*, 2012–2016;
email communication with Irene Innis, January 2018

Inez Rossey Irons (1936–1993)

In 1958, Inez married Neil L. Irons (b. 1936). Neil was elected in 1984 out of the West Virginia Annual Conference and served the New Jersey Episcopal Area (1984–1996) and the Harrisburg Episcopal Area (1996–2004), then retired. Inez and Neil have two children.

Inez was a graduate of Davis and Elkins College and received her MA in social work (specializing in social gerontology) from the University of Tennessee. She taught high school in Coalton, West Virginia, and Dayton, Ohio, and was also employed by Huntington State Hospital (WV). She worked as a community services director in Romney, WV; and she established a Senior Companion Program in Buckhannon, WV, and a Retired Senior Volunteers Program in Champaign, Illinois. She served as the director of an adult day care center in Trenton, New Jersey, and on the Board of Directors of the United Methodist Homes of New Jersey. "Mrs. Irons served well as a teacher, a social worker and a faithful disciple of Christ. Her compassion and love for others will always be remembered."

—*Biographical Directory*, 2000–2004; George Wang, *Southern New Jersey Conference Journal, 1994*, 231–232; email communication with Neil Irons, 2017

Jane Petherbridge Ives (b. 1939)

In 1959, Jane married S. Clifton Ives (b. 1937). Cliff was elected in 1992 out of the Maine Annual Conference and served the West Virginia Episcopal Area (1992–2004), then retired. Cliff and Jane moved back to Portland, Maine. They have three children and seven grandchildren.

Jane has served as an active layperson in the UMC since she was a teenager. She earned a BA in English from the University of Maine and an MA in exceptionality from the University of Southern Maine. She taught in public schools, first as an English teacher and then in Special Education. Jane has been active in UMW, has taught Sunday school and in Schools of Christian Mission, led youth groups, and served as a Volunteer in Mission. In 1974, she and Cliff became certified as a marriage enrichment leader couple through Better Marriages and led many workshops and retreats and worked with many couples and families through the years. Discipleship Resources published two books she wrote about marriage ministries (*Couples Who Care*, 1997 and *Couples Who Cope*, 1999). Upper Room Books published her *Transforming Ventures: A Spiritual Guide for Volunteers in Mission* in 2000, and she served on the General Board of Global Ministries' writing team for *A Mission Journey: A Handbook for Volunteers,* published in 2013. She and Bishop Ives co-authored an update and revision of the *Growing Love in Christian Marriage Pastor's Manual,* published in 2001, revised and updated again in 2013. From 2010 to 2018, Jane worked on contract with the General Board of Discipleship, now Discipleship Ministries, as a consultant for marriage and family ministries, reviewing and promoting resources, writing articles, responding to inquiries, and maintaining a global directory of resource persons and a schedule of upcoming events and training opportunities.

Favorite Scripture: Matthew 11:28 / Favorite Hymn: "Great Is Thy Faithfulness" *UMH,* 140

Rosemarie Jackson [Rivas] (b. 1948)

In 1970, Rosemarie married Rafael Moreno Rivas (b. 1947). Rafael was elected in 2009 by The Methodist Church in Puerto Rico, an Autonomous Affiliated Church whose bishops participate in the United Methodist Council of Bishops. He served as bishop of the Puerto Rico Methodist Church (2010–2016). Rosemarie and Rafael have three daughters and one grandchild.

Rosemarie was born in San Juan, Puerto Rico, and graduated from the University of Puerto Rico, where she majored in social sciences, sociology, and economy. She worked with the Labor Department until their first child was born and resumed her career after all three of their children started school. Rosemarie has also worked closely with her husband in the church, especially with women and seniors. She attended the Council of Bishops with her husband one year and enjoyed meeting other bishops' spouses. Rosemarie also likes to write poetry.

—http://www.metodistauniversitaria.org/ (search for Dr. Rafael Moreno Rivas); conversations with Bishop Hector F. Ortiz Vidal and Alma Y. Varela Deippa, 2017–2018; Facebook Messenger conversation with Rosemarie Jackson, November 2018

Beverly Nadine Ellerbeck Job (b. 1932)

In 1952, Beverly married Rueben Philip Job (1928–2015). Rueben was elected in 1984 out of the Dakotas Annual Conference and served the Iowa Episcopal Area (1984–1992), then retired. Beverly and Rueben have four children and seven grandchildren.

Beverly graduated from Westmar College and has been employed as a junior high school teacher, local church director of Christian Education, and secretary to the state director of Prison Fellowship. She has been very active in spiritual formation events and has led a large number of retreats. She also has been very active in UMW through the years.

Favorite Scripture: Romans 8:28 / Favorite Hymn: "Hymn of Promise" (*UMH,* 707)

—*Biographical Directory,* 2000–2004; email communication with Beverly Job, July 2017

Allen Johnson [Haupert-Johnson] (b. 1961)

In 1997, Allen married Sue Haupert (b. 1962). Sue was elected in 2016 out of the Florida Annual Conference and assigned to the North Georgia Episcopal Area. Allen and Sue have one daughter.

Allen grew up in Gainesville, Florida, near the University of Florida where his father taught in the College of Agriculture. Allen attended the College of Agriculture, intending to become a veterinarian. After graduating, he went to work for the Farm Credit Bank as a loan officer. At the age of 12, he made a public profession of faith and joined the UMC. He was active in the church throughout high school and college, and in his late twenties, he decided to commit his life full-time to the church. In 1990, he entered Candler School of Theology at Emory University in Atlanta. Allen met Sue in 1995, while serving as chaplain at Florida Southern College. In 2003, Allen and Sue requested an appointment as co-pastors and asked for a church that was vital to the annual conference, but currently struggling. After four years and a successful turnaround, they then served another struggling church for five years, with the same good results. Allen continued to serve at Ocala First UMC from 2008–2016, then took personal leave for a year. He now serves at Winters Chapel UMC in Doraville, GA. Allen and Sue also served in Methodist missions in the Dominican Republic and Zambia.

—https://www.flumc.org/suehaupertjohnsonbio;
https://tinyurl.com/y4wmeb9t;
email communication with Allen Johnson, January 2018

Michael C. Johnson (b. 1954)

In 1978, Michael married Peggy Olver (b. 1953). Peggy was elected in 2008 out of the Baltimore-Washington Annual Conference and was assigned to the Philadelphia Episcopal Area. Michael and Peggy have two adult sons.

Michael came from a military family and lived many places during his formative years. He received his BS from Southwest Texas University. An ordained elder, he has served local congregations in the Baltimore-Washington Annual Conference and several interim positions in the Peninsula-Delaware and the Eastern Pennsylvania annual conferences. In 2013, he received a certificate in spiritual direction from Moravian Theological Seminary and now serves in extension ministry as a spiritual director in Pennsylvania.

—*Biographical Directory*, 2012–2016;
email communication with Mike Johnson, July 2017

Sarah Tilsley Johnson (1863–1967)

In 1884, Sarah married Eben Samuel Johnson (1866–1939). Eben, born in England and a direct descendant of one of John Wesley's original helpers, moved to the United States in 1889. He was elected missionary bishop for Africa in 1916 out of the Northwest Iowa Annual Conference of The Methodist Episcopal Church. He served at Old Umtali in Rhodesia and then in Capetown, South Africa. When he retired in 1936, they returned to live near Portland, Oregon. Sarah and Eben had three children.

Sarah, born in England, came to the United States in 1889 with her husband and young son. She served with her husband in various Iowa communities as "wife, mother, mistress of the parsonage, and worker in the church with unfailing devotion and great efficiency," as noted in her memoir in the Journal of the Oregon Annual Conference, 1967. After his election, she served with him in Africa for 20 years, returning to the US with him when he retired. In 1954, when she was 91, she traveled back to South Africa to visit her daughter and many of the places and persons known from their time serving there.

—http://catalog.gcah.org/publicdata/gcah753.htm;
Journal of the Oregon Annual Conference of The Methodist Church, 1967, 124;
Iowa Annual Conference Journal, 1969, 388

Sherrie Boyens Dobbs Johnson (b. 1948)

In 2005, Sherrie married retired Bishop Alfred Johnson (b. 1950). Alfred was elected in 1996 out of the Eastern Pennsylvania Conference, served the New Jersey Area (1996-2004), then retired to serve local churches, teach, and lead training sessions in urban ministry. Sherrie and Al have settled in New Jersey.

Sherrie, now retired, has been a local church pastor, editor of the UMW's *response* magazine, conference council director, and district superintendent. She was on the communication staffs of the General Board of Discipleship, the UM Publishing House, and Clark Atlanta University. She is a contributor to the UM General Board of Discipleship's *21st Century Africana Worship Book,* volumes A, B, and C. She also wrote the Bible studies for the UMW *Program Resource Book* for 2016–2017.

Favorite Scripture: Ephesians 3:20-21 / Favorite Hymn: "How Firm a Foundation" (*UMH,* 529)

—*Biographical Directory,* 1996, 2012–2016;
email communication with Sherrie Johnson, May 15, 2017

Edith Munjoma Jokomo (b. 1957)

In 1983, Edith married Christopher Jokomo (1946–2007). He was elected in 1992 out of the Zimbabwe Annual Conference and was assigned to the Zimbabwe Episcopal Area, where he served until retiring in 2004 because of health issues. Edith and Christopher have two daughters of their own, as well as caring for many other children throughout the country.

Edith earned a diploma in home economics from Gweru Teacher's College, Zimbabwe, and a BSc Education degree from Njala University College in Sierra Leone,

West Africa. She worked as a teacher in several schools before joining the Curriculum Development Unit of the Ministry of Education in Zimbabwe. She has written several high school biology and integrated science textbooks that are used in Zimbabwean schools today. She is also editing Christian education materials for the UMC in the Zimbabwe Episcopal Area. She has worked extensively with many NGOs on several humanitarian issues and served as a director of the General Board of Global Ministries, participating in meetings in New York and visiting programs in Norway, Angola, and Mozambique (April 1992–2000). When Chris retired, the family saw it as an opening to be involved in new opportunities for ministry, hence the formation of the NGO called Gashirai Nyasha Project (*receive the Grace of Christ*). Eventually, miraculously, it gave birth to the Hear Africa Foundation (HAF) where Edith is currently involved in humanitarian activities. She is the executive director of HAF, working with several communities in sustainable agriculture, education, orphan care, empowerment programs and health. The NGO has its head office in Canada where the seven-member Board of Directors is based.

Favorite Scripture: Proverbs 3:5-6 / Favorite Hymn: "My Hope Is Built on Nothing Less" (*UMH*, 368)

—*Biographical Directory*, 2004–2008;
email communication with Edith Jokomo, June 2017

Harriet Elizabeth Brown Jones (1988–1973)

In 1920, Elizabeth married Robert Elijah Jones (1872–1960). Robert was elected in 1920, the first African American elected to the episcopacy of The Methodist Episcopal Church. He served as resident bishop of the New Orleans Episcopal Area, which included seven conferences in Tennessee, Mississippi, Alabama, Louisiana, and Texas, with a total of 1,905 churches. He retired in 1944. Robert had three children with his first wife, Valena McArthur, who died in 1917. Elizabeth and Robert had two children.

Elizabeth, originally from Meadville, Pennsylvania, taught at Sumner High School in St. Louis, Missouri.

—https://en.wikipedia.org/wiki/Robert_Elijah_Jones;
http://amistadresearchcenter.tulane.edu/archon/?p=creators/creator&id=119

Mildred Hawkins Jones (1928–2015)

In 1949, "Tuck" married Lewis Bevel Jones III (1926–2018). "Bev" was elected in 1984 out of the North Georgia Annual Conference and served the Charlotte Episcopal Area (1984–1996), then retired. "Tuck" and "Bev" settled in Atlanta. They had three children and six grandchildren.

"Tuck" attended Wesleyan College in Macon, Georgia, where she was given her nickname because she came from Kentucky. During their pastorates, she was especially active in choir, drama, and UMW. She enjoyed reading, music, art, and needlework.

—*Biographical Directory*, 2000–2004; http://www.legacy.com/obituaries/atlanta/obituary.aspx?pid=175864753; https://www.legacy.com/obituaries/atlanta/obituary.aspx?n=bishop-lewis-bevel-jones&pid=188423375&fhid=5281

Margaret Crawford Jordan (b. 1936)

In 1959, Margaret married Charles Wesley Jordan (b. 1933). Charles was elected in 1992 out of the Northern Illinois Annual Conference and served the Iowa Episcopal Area (1992–2000), then retired. Margaret and Charles settled in California, near their two adult daughters and two grandsons.

Margaret received her BED from National College of Education (now National-Louis University) and her MA in guidance and counseling from Northeastern Illinois University. She taught in public schools in Illinois and served as a school counselor in Chicago and in Iowa. She became a travel consultant in 1985 and continues to book and advise persons about travel. She loves sewing, crafts, digital photography, and machine embroidery. She has designed and made banners, paraments, and displays for her local church, Black Methodists for Church Renewal (BMCR), her sorority, and her service organization. Six of her banner designs were made into a kit that is distributed by Cokesbury. She continues her creativity with stoles, other church paraphernalia, personal greeting cards, and machine embroidery projects. Margaret is an active member of The Links, Inc., and Alpha Kappa Alpha Sorority, Inc., in which she holds life membership. Her favorite song is "If I Can Help Somebody," composed by Alma Androzzo.

—*Biographical Directory*, 2004–2008;
email communication with Margaret Jordan, July 2017

Agnes Karan Singh Joshi

In 1944, Agnes married Ram Dutt Joshi (1916–1976) while he was teaching at the North India Theological College in Bareilly and serving a local church. Ram was elected in 1969 and served the Bombay Episcopal Area until his death in 1976. Agnes and Ram had three sons, a grandson, and a granddaughter.

Agnes worked as a registered nurse in a Methodist hospital until 1954, when Ram was appointed district superintendent and they moved to the northern hills of India. In 1961, they moved back to Bareilly until his election in 1969.

—*Biographical Directory*, 1996

Lurleen Lapuz Juan (b. 1968)

In 1993, Leigh married Rodolfo A. Juan (b. 1961). Rudy was elected in 2008 out of the Philippines Annual Conference and served the Baguio Episcopal Area

(2008–2012). In 2012, he was re-elected and assigned to the Davao Episcopal Area (2012–2016), then to the Manila Episcopal Area in 2016. Leigh and Rudy have two children.

Leigh (Dr. Lurleen Lapuz Juan) is an optometrist. She was born in Manila and graduated with a Doctor of Optometry Degree from Manila Central University in 1990. Leigh is self-employed and has two optometry clinics, one at Mary Johnston Hospital and the other at Malinta, Valenzuela City. She also serves as lead doctor with the MODEL (Medical, Optical, Dental, Evangelism, and Legal) Outreach Program, assisting the office of the bishop. Their mobile bus clinic travels around the whole episcopal area, bringing services to poor people in remote *barangays* (communities). Leigh also enjoys walking, working out at the gym, and a little bit of tennis.

—https://www.unitedmethodistbishops.org/person-detail/2464087; email communication with Bishop Juan, January 2018

Im Hyon Jung

In 1982, Im married Hee-Soo Jung. Hee-Soo was elected out of the Wisconsin Annual Conference in 2004 and served the Chicago Episcopal Area (2004–2012) and the Wisconsin Episcopal Area starting in 2012. Im and Hee-Soo have two grown sons.

Im graduated from Dallas Baptist University and Garrett Evangelical Theological Seminary. She was ordained in the Wisconsin Annual Conference and became an ordained elder and full member in 1996. She has pastored several churches in Wisconsin, is a certified spiritual director, has a passion for leading spiritual formation retreats, and joyfully serves as director, International Relations Asia, Upper Room Ministries/Discipleship Ministries.

Favorite Scriptures: Psalm 8; Isaiah 43; John 15 / Favorite Hymns: "How Great Thou Art" (*UMH*, 77), "Amazing Grace" (*UMH*, 378), "In Christ Alone" (*Baptist Hymnal*, 506)

—*Biographical Directory*, 2012–2016; https://www.unitedmethodistbishops.org/person-detail/2463660; email communication with Im Jung, July 2017

Elizabeth Justo

Elizabeth married Benjamin A. Justo, who was elected out of the Northeast Philippines Annual Conference in 2000. He served the Baguio Episcopal Area (2000–2008), then retired. Elizabeth and Benjamin have two children.

—*Biographical Directory*, 2012

Leigh Kammerer (b. 1948)

In 1970, Leigh married Charlene Payne (b. 1948). Charlene was elected in 1996 out of the Florida Annual Conference and served the Charlotte Episcopal Area (1996–

2004) and the Richmond Episcopal Area (2004–2012), then retired. Leigh and Charlene have settled at Lake Junaluska. They have one son and four grandchildren.

Leigh graduated from Vanderbilt University in Nashville, Tennessee, with a BA in anthropology. He received an MDiv from Garrett Theological Seminary. Leigh worked in the field of alcohol and drug treatment between 1977 and 2012, then retired. He worked in both inpatient and outpatient treatment settings, including with jail inmates, as well as in employee assistance programming and impaired health professional monitoring. In the local church, Leigh has served as an adult Sunday school teacher and DISCIPLE Bible study leader, as well as volunteering in a variety of program work areas.

—*Biographical Directory*, 2010, 2012, 2004–2008;
email communication with Leigh Kammerer, September 2017

Kashala Katembo (b. 1950)

In 1968, Kashala married Kainda Katembo (b. 1944). Kainda was elected out of the Southern Zaire Annual Conference in 1980, then reelected for life in 1984. He served the South Congo Episcopal Area (1980–2017), then retired. Kashala and Kainda have six sons.

Kashala attended a school for students' wives, learning home economics and biblical studies in particular. Kashala was Kainda's "first counselor," encouraging him through very difficult first years in ministry.

—*Biographical Directory*, 2000–2004;
https://www.unitedmethodistbishops.org/person-detail/2464029;
http://www.calpacumc.org/prayer-2/for-bishop-kainda-katembo-south-congo-episcopal-area/; https://www.ngumc.org/newsdetail/bishop-watson-among-retiring-bishops-honored-at-general-conference-4822203

Wife of Z. T. Kaung

Although no name or details were found for the wife of Z. T. Kaung (1884–1958), his obituary mentions a daughter who was a physician in Hong Kong, and a press release notes that six grandchildren attended his memorial service.

Also known as Jiang Changchuan, he was elected bishop of North China in 1941 and served the Peiping Episcopal Area. He was under constant surveillance during the Japanese occupation of North China because of his close ties with the Sung family and Chiang Kai-shek, whom he baptized in 1930. When the Communists came into power, Kaung was among the 19 Protestant leaders who met with Chou En-lai in Beijing in April 1950. He supported the formation of the Three-Self Patriotic Movement, which promoted a strategy of "self-governance, self-support, and self-propagation" in order to remove foreign influences from the Chinese churches and to assure the government that the churches would be patriotic to the newly established People's Republic of China.

—*Encyclopedia of World Methodism, Vol.* 1, 1314; http://methodistmission200.org/jiang-changchuan-z-t-kuang-1884-1958/; newspaper clipping about his death, *New York Times,* August 28, 1958, and "Memorial Service for Bishop Kuang" in his administrative file at the UM Archives and History Center

Alice T. Kearns (1909–2010)

In 1933, Alice married Francis Enmer Kearns (1905–1992). Francis was elected in 1964 by the North Central Jurisdiction and served the Ohio East Episcopal Area (1964–1976), then retired. Alice and Francis had three children, five grandchildren, and six great-grandchildren.

Alice graduated from Ohio Wesleyan University and served as a director of Christian education in Philadelphia. Later she was employed by the National Division of the General Board of Missions to do mission work in the city of Pittsburgh. Alice Kearns was very involved in ministry as an adviser to the Methodist Youth Fellowship and an active member of the Women's Society of Christian Service. As a bishop's spouse, she especially enjoyed traveling to missionary projects in Africa and Asia and organizing retreats for clergy spouses. She also enjoyed flower gardens, travel, and collecting coins and stamps. Francis died 12 years after his retirement; Alice lived for another 22 years in the Copeland Oaks Retirement Community in Sebring, Ohio. "Alice will be remembered as a dedicated Christian who lived life with enthusiasm. She never tired of helping her neighbor and encouraging others to do their best. She was a devoted wife, mother, grandmother, aunt and friend. As her daughter Peggy said, 'Mom is full of love, and it is contagious!'" (Council of Bishops Memorial Booklet, May 2011).

—*Biographical Directory,* 1984

Beverly Keaton (b. 1946)

In 1969, Beverly married Jonathan D. Keaton (b. 1946). Jonathan was elected in 1996 out of the Northern Illinois Annual Conference and served the Ohio East Episcopal Area (1996–2004), the Michigan Episcopal Area (2004–2012), and the Illinois Episcopal Area (2012–2016), then retired. Beverly and Jonathan have three children and two grandchildren.

Beverly worked as an accounts-receivable correspondent for City National Bank of Fort Smith, Arkansas, and Barton and the Aschman Landscaping and Development firm in Evanston, Illinois. She also worked in the circulation department for the *Interpreter* magazine when it was located in Evanston, Illinois. She has participated in many areas of the church and enjoys doing volunteer work in the community. She enjoys reading, biking, walking, calisthenics, choreography, writing, art, taking college courses, and elocution, but most of all being with her family. She has traveled extensively, mainly abroad, and served on various boards.

Favorite Scripture: Isaiah 41:10 / Favorite Hymn: "In the Garden" (*UMH*, 314)

—*Biographical Directory*, 2012; https://www.unitedmethodistbishops.org/person-detail/2464020; email and telephone communication with Beverly and Bishop Keaton, October 2017

Frances Novella Grant Kelly

In 1955, Frances married retired Bishop Edward Wendall Kelly (1880–1964). Edward had one son with his first wife, Oma, who died in 1953.

Frances was the daughter and granddaughter of bishops from the Colored Methodist Episcopal Church.

—*Encyclopedia of World Methodism, Vol. 1*, 1320; wedding announcement in Edward Wendall Kelly's administrative file at the UM Archives and History Center

Oma A. Burnett Kelly (1882–1953)

In 1905(?), Oma married Edward Wendall Kelly (1880–1964). Edward was elected in 1944 out of the Central Jurisdiction and served the St. Louis Episcopal Area (1944–1952), then retired. Oma and Edward had one son.

Oma, born in Texas, attended Prairie View College and taught in Texas for several years.

—*Encyclopedia of World Methodism, Vol. 1*, 1320; wedding and funeral announcements in Edward Wendall Kelly's administrative file at the UM Archives and History Center

Lucy Gordhall Campbell Kern

In 1907, Lucy married Paul Bentley Kern (1882–1953). Paul was elected in 1930 out of the Tennessee Annual Conference of The Methodist Episcopal Church, South, after serving as a pastor, a missionary in Asia, and a charter member of the faculty at Southern Methodist University. As bishop, he served in China (1930–1934), the North and South Carolina Episcopal Areas (1934–1938), and the Nashville Episcopal Area (1938–1952), then retired. He was active in the 1939 unification. Lucy and Paul had three children.

—http://catalog.gcah.org/publicdata/gcah755.htm; http://socialarchive.iath.virginia.edu/ark:/99166/w6fj3511; http://www.ncpedia.org/biography/kern-paul-bentley

Victoria Nogay Khegay (b. 1973)

In 2000, Victoria married Eduard Khegay (b. 1970). Eduard was elected in 2012 out of the Central Russia Annual Conference and serves the Eurasia Episcopal Area. Victoria and Eduard have two daughters and live in Moscow.

Victoria was born in Tselinograd, Kazakhstan, former Soviet Union (presently Astana, the capital of Kazakhstan) in 1973. She graduated from Oil and Gas State University in Moscow, Russia. She worked as a sales manager and marketing director. In the church, she has been active with church newspapers and leading small groups. Her interests include fashion and design, traveling and reading.

—*Biographical Directory*, 2012–2016;
email communication with Bishop Khegay, January 2018

Bradley Kiesey (b. 1945)

In 1975, Brad married Deborah Kiesey (b. 1951). Deb was elected in 2004 out of the Iowa Annual Conference and served the Dakotas Episcopal Area (2004–2012) and the Michigan Episcopal Area (2012–2016), then retired. Brad and Deb have settled back in Iowa. They have two sons and one grandchild.

Brad obtained a BA in journalism in 1968 and a Juris Doctorate in 1971. Since then he has been in the private practice of law in his hometown of Washington, Iowa. Occasionally, he has taught commercial law and criminal justice courses at Iowa Wesleyan College in Mt. Pleasant, Iowa, and has lectured at numerous gatherings of new clergy on income tax issues unique to pastors. He has frequently served as a member of the Iowa Annual Conference and serves on a number of boards of directors of charitable and business organizations. He has directed choirs in several churches and enjoys his weekly participation with Old Capitol Barbershop Chorus in Iowa City, Iowa. In his spare time, Brad also enjoys restoring and showing antique automobiles.

—*Biographical Directory*, 2004–2008; interview with Brad Kiesey, May 2016

Wha-Sei P. Kim (b. 1937)

In 1935, Wha-Sei married Hae Jong Kim (b. 1935). Hae Jong was elected in 1992 out of the Northern New Jersey Annual Conference. He served the New York West Episcopal Area (1992–2000) and the Pittsburgh Episcopal Area (2000–2005). Wha-Sei and Hae-Jong, who have returned to New Jersey, have three children and four grandchildren.

Wha-Sei is also a seminary graduate, having attended the same schools as her husband: The Methodist Theological Seminary in Seoul (South Korea), METHESCO, and Drew. She is musically gifted and has played the organ in churches since she was 12 years old.

—*Biographical Directory*, 2000–2004; http://www.deseretnews.com/
article/605153388/First-Korean-American-bishop-resigns-his-post.html;
email and telephone communication with Hae Jong Kim, February 2018

Emma C. Arnold King (1893–1976)

In 1944, Emma married Willis Jefferson King (1886–1976). Willis was elected in 1944 in the Central Jurisdiction of The Methodist Church after serving churches in

Texas and Massachusetts and as a college professor and president. He served in Liberia, Africa (1944–1946) and the New Orleans Episcopal Area (1956–1960), then retired. He had three daughters by his first wife, Parmela J. Kelly King, who died in 1943.

Emma was born in Atlanta, Georgia, and attended Clark College and Cheyney Teachers College in Clark, Pennsylvania, where she specialized in elementary education. After graduation, she worked as a youth secretary for the YWCA in Washington, DC, and in Maryland, remaining committed to and volunteering in that organization throughout the rest of her life. She taught in Atlanta public schools. Immediately after their marriage, Emma and Willis traveled to Liberia, where they did missionary work for 12 years. She was especially interested in helping women both at home and abroad and is quoted in the 1997 Louisiana conference journal as saying, "You know I am married to the ministry."

—https://en.wikipedia.org/wiki/Willis_J._King; https://www.findagrave.com/memorial/89637192; https://www.tshaonline.org/handbook/online/articles/fki56; *Journal of the 7th Session of the Louisiana Annual Conference, May 31–June 3, 1977*, 174; https://findagrave.com/cgi-bin/fg.cgi/pages.suddenlink.net/http//fg.cgi?page=gr&GRid=73840671

Louise Marie Watts King

In 1903, Louise married Lorenzo Houston King (1878–1946). Lorenzo, son of former slaves, was elected in 1940 at the first Jurisdictional Conference of the Central Jurisdiction, having served in The Methodist Episcopal Church as a pastor, teacher, and editor. He served the Atlantic Coast Episcopal Area 1940 until 1946, when he died. Louise and Lorenzo had three sons.

—https://en.wikipedia.org/wiki/Lorenzo_Houston_King; Thomas Yenser, ed., *Who's Who in Colored America Corporation: A Biographical Dictionary of Notable Living Persons of African Descent in America, 1941-1944* (New York: Thomas Yenser); *Encyclopedia of World Methodism, Vol. 1*, 1337

Margaret Rosetta Hayden King (b. 1944)

"Rose" married James R. King, who was elected in 2000 after serving churches in Alabama, California, and Tennessee. James served the Louisville (Kentucky/Redbird Mission) Episcopal Area (2000–2008) and the South Georgia Episcopal Area (2008–2016), then retired. Rose and James have three children.

Rose was born in Alabama and graduated from Bennett College in North Carolina with a BA in psychology. She also did graduate work in psychology at Howard University. She taught school and worked as a hairdresser. When her husband was bishop in South Georgia, she especially enjoyed the opportunity to host the Council of Bishops at least four times, giving her the privilege of working closely with bishops' spouses from all over the world.

—*Biographical Directory*, 2012–2016; https://www.ledger-enquirer.com/news/local/article29009152.html; interview with Rose King, May 2018

Annegret Klaiber (b. 1938)

In 1965, Annegret married Walter Klaiber. Walter (b. 1940) was elected in 1989 out of the South Germany Annual Conference. He served the West Germany Episcopal Area (1989–2005), then retired. The Klaibers moved back to Tübingen in South Germany. Annegret and Walter have three sons and seven grandchildren.

Annegret served in the Sunday school and choir of the local EUB Church in Tübingen from her childhood days. She studied medicine, earned an MD, and worked as a doctor in different hospitals and as an associate of general practitioners. After her sons were born, she taught hygienics for childcare workers and gave lectures in the church and in public institutions on medical and psychological subjects. During Walter's active years as a bishop, she served as a medical counselor and later as head of the Evangelical Church in Frankfort's consulting center for alcohol addicts. She also served as chair of the Committee against Addiction in the South Germany Central Conference.

—*Biographical Directory*, 2012–2016;
email communication with Bishop Klaiber, 2017

Edith Laney Strawn Knox (1928–2008)

In 1951, Edith married James Lloyd Knox (1929–2014). While serving in the Florida Annual Conference, Lloyd and Edith were assigned as missionaries to Cuba (1958–1960) and Argentina (1961–1964). Lloyd was elected in 1984 and served the Birmingham Episcopal Area (1984–1992) and the Atlanta Episcopal Area (1992–1996), then retired. Edith and Lloyd had two children.

Edith attended Tulane University and graduated from Mather School of Nursing, Southern Baptist Hospital, New Orleans, Louisiana. As a registered nurse, she did surgical and obstetrical nursing in Louisiana, Georgia, and Florida. While in Cuba, she ran a clinic in Santiago de las Vegas. She was the supervisor of the Student Outpatient Clinic of the University of Miami and of the S.W. Florida Blood Bank at Tampa General Hospital.

—*Biographical Directory*, 2000–2004

Julia Nolen Knox (b. 1947)

In 2009, Julia married retired Bishop James Lloyd Knox (1929–2014). Lloyd had two children with his first wife, Edith, who died in 2008, and Julia has a son by her first husband, Thirwell Nolen Jr, who died in 2004.

Julia graduated from the University of Alabama with a degree in education. She was a homemaker and, she said in a telephone interview, "Church was my hobby." She was also a philanthropist, actively involved in civic activities, and served on the Committee of One Hundred at Candler Theological Seminary. She knew Lloyd and his family since 1984, having served on the Committee on Episcopacy in Alabama.

—*Biographical Directory*, 2000–2004;
telephone interview with Julia Knox, January 2018

Raphael K. Koikoi [Moore-Koikoi] (b. 1966)

In 2013, Raphael married Cynthia Moore (b. 1966). Cynthia was elected in 2016 out of the Baltimore-Washington Annual Conference and assigned to the Pittsburgh Episcopal Area.

Raphael, who is a Liberian and a Licensed Local Pastor, married Cynthia in the chapel at Africa University in Zimbabwe when they were participating in the Baltimore-Washington Conference joint pastors' school there. Raphael was serving Sharp Street UMC in Baltimore when Cynthia was elected and continued to do so until February 2017, when he began to serve in an extension ministry appointment as the Upper Allegheny Valley Director of Ministry and Community Development in the Western Pennsylvania Annual Conference. He retains his membership in the Baltimore-Washington Annual Conference and is under the supervision of the bishop there. Raphael, in collaboration with a church pastor and laity, is designing and implementing community-based creative outreach programs to meet physical and spiritual needs, working with government and non-governmental agencies on developing food security for the community, planning and implementing community asset-based educational opportunities, and planning and conducting community worship services designed to be inclusive of the growing diversity of the community. Raphael describes his work as building relationships by connecting and reconnecting congregations and communities, discovering needs in response to which the outreach programs emerge. Raphael believes the church must be involved in and with the community in which it exists, as "faith without works is dead" (James 2:26).

—https://www.unitedmethodistbishops.org/person-detail/2462486;
https://www.umnews.org/en/news/new-bishop-recalls-questions-about-segregated-church; https://www.wpaumc.org/newsdetail/koikoi-to-build-ministry-in-allegheny-valley-7382542;
email communication with Raphael Koikoi, September 2019

Gloria Doe Kulah (b. 1963)

In 2016, Gloria married retired Bishop Arthur Flumo Kulah (b. 1936). Arthur has seven children and 27 adopted homeless and parentless children with his first wife, Violet, who died in 2012. Gloria has one son.

Gloria holds a BPA in public administration from the University of Liberia and an advanced certificate in data processing from AT&T's computer school. She worked as a research assistant with the Ministry of Foreign Affairs, Republic of Liberia. Presently, she works with the civil service agency Biometric Center in Liberia as an assistant director for data management. Gloria is the financial secretary and treasurer for the women's organization of E.J. Goodridge UMC in Monrovia, Liberia. She is interested in church ministries with women and children.

Favorite Scripture: Psalm 37:4 / Favorite Hymn: "A Charge to Keep I Have" (*UMH*, 413)

—interview and email communication with Gloria Kulah, 2017

Violet Mamusu Sackie Kulah (1939–2012)

In 1956, Violet married Arthur Flumo Kulah (b. 1936). Arthur was elected in 1980 out of the Liberia Annual Conference, and in 1984 he was elected for life. He served the Liberia Episcopal Area (1980–2000), then retired. He was called out of retirement to serve the Nigeria Episcopal Area from about 2007 to 2012 (*Interpreter* [January/February 2013], 25) Violet and Arthur have seven children, and at the end of the civil war in 1997, they adopted 27 more homeless and parentless children.

Violet was born in Kakata, Liberia; when she was 10 years old, she was sent to Gbarnga to attend the newly opened Methodist School, where she met Arthur. After completing high school, Violet attended the Mendolo Ecumenical Center where she studied home arts. When Arthur came to the United States to study, Violet came, too, as a missionary to the Baltimore Annual Conference. She also took specialized courses in home arts. Upon returning home, Violet became director of the Home Economics Department of the Gbarnga School of Theology and also taught first grade at the W.V.S. Tubman United Methodist School.

—*Biographical Directory*, 2004–2008; conversation with Arthur Kulah, 2018

Harriett Lang Boutelle Lacy (d. 1966)

In 1918, Harriett married George Carleton Lacy (1888–1951). George, an American missionary and son of American missionaries in China, was elected bishop of the China Central Conference in 1941, the last Methodist bishop in Mainland China. He was assigned to Foochow, and in 1950, when all foreign missionaries were forced to withdraw from China, he was the only Westerner in that area denied an exit permit. He was detained under house arrest and died shortly thereafter. Harriett and George had a son and a daughter.

Harriet graduated from Mount Holyoke College and went to Canton, China, as a YWCA secretary. She and George married in Chelsea, Massachusetts, and returned to China, where their children were born. She served as a missionary teacher in Canton, Kiukiang and Shanghai. During World War II, while George was supervising the church behind enemy lines, she worked with the American Bible Society in New York. She returned to China in 1947, but from 1949 on she was forced to remain in the United States while her husband remained in Communist China until his death.

—https://www.findagrave.com/cgi-bin/fg.cgi?page=gr&GRid=122093443; https://www.revolvy.com/main/index.php?s=George%20Carleton%20Lacy; Harriet's death notice in George's administrative file at UM Archives and History Center; https://kihm4.wordpress.com/2013/09/07/at-silver-bay/

Sushila Sentu Lance

In 1944(?), Sushila married Joseph R. Lance (1925–2003). Joseph, born in India, was elected in 1969 by the Southeast Asia Conference after serving as pastor and as executive secretary of the Council of Christian Concerns for The Methodist Church in India. He served the Lucknow Episcopal Area.

Sushila was a graduate student nurse.

—*Encyclopedia of World Methodism, Vol. 2*, 1379

Martha Ellen Pegram Lawson (1930–2015)

In 1950, Martha married David Jerald Lawson (1930–2007). David was elected out of the Indiana Annual Conference in 1984 and served the Wisconsin Episcopal Area (1984–1992) and the Illinois Episcopal Area (1992–1996), then retired. Martha and David had two children and three grandchildren.

Martha studied at the University of Evansville. Martha's employment included: a position in Sears Credit Department, bank teller in several banks, legal secretary, public school system treasurer, and secretary/conference coordinator for Indiana State Association of Elementary School Principals. She served in a variety of church leadership positions, such as conference UMW officer and church school team teaching trainer, and she was a member of P.E.O. Martha also served as an election judge, a retreat leader, and a speaker on the life of Susanna Wesley. She and David were certified Marriage Enrichment trainers.

—*Biographical Directory*, 2000–2004; http://archives.gcah.org/bitstream/handle/10516/4145/article0.aspx.htm?sequence=2; http://prabook.com/web/person-view.html?profileId=1709458

Henrietta Gibson Ledden (1890–1981)

In 1964, Henrietta married retired Bishop Walter Earl Ledden (1888–1984). Walter had three children with his first wife, Lida, who died in 1957.

Henrietta graduated from Vassar College and was the first woman to serve on her local church board, as well as the first president of both the Troy Annual

Conference Women's Society and the Conference Board of Missions. She served on the staff of the Women's Division (1943–1955). She also served as president of Ewha Women's University Cooperation Board and assistant treasurer for the Japan International University Foundation. In 1971, she was awarded an honorary doctorate by Ewha Women's University in Seoul, Korea, and was honored by the government of the Republic of Korea for her service to education in that country. After marrying Walter, she played an important role in the life of the Wesley Theological Seminary in Washington, DC, where Walter served on the faculty.

—*Encyclopedia of World Methodism, Vol. 2,* 1404–1405; *Northern New York Annual Conference 1958 Journal and Yearbook,* 633–634; *Yearbook and Minutes of the 146th Session Southern New Jersey Annual Conference, 1982,* 248

Mary (Lida) Iszard Ledden (1889–1957)

In 1913, Lida married Walter Earl Ledden (1888–1984). Walter was elected in 1944 out of the Southern New Jersey Annual Conference and served the Syracuse Episcopal Area (1944–1960), then retired. Mary and Walter had three children, one of whom died in 1949, and six grandchildren.

Lida grew up in Glassboro, New Jersey, as did Walter. She graduated from Trenton State Teachers College with a degree in English. She taught for a few years before marrying Walter, after which she served with him in each appointment and later as "First Lady" of the Syracuse Area. She was recognized for her quiet confidence, appreciation of the gifts of others, deep faith, and sense of humor.

—https://www.findagrave.com/cgi-bin/fg.cgi?page=gr&GRid=104488370; https://www.findagrave.com/cgi-bin/fg.cgi?page=gr&GRid=104488493; *Encyclopedia of World Methodism, Vol. 2,* 1404-1405; *Northern New York Annual Conference 1958 Journal and Yearbook,* 633–634

Dorothy Stricklin Lee (1932–2017)

In 1951, Dot married Clay Foster Lee Jr (b. 1930). Clay was elected in 1988 out of the Mississippi Annual Conference and served the Holston Area (1988–1996), then retired. Dot and Clay settled in Jackson, Mississippi. They have five children and eight grandchildren.

Dot attended Millsaps College in Jackson, Mississippi, and graduated from Jones County Junior College in Ellisville, Mississippi in 1951. She taught kindergarten and for 16 years worked as secretary of a State Farm Insurance Agency in Jackson, Mississippi. As a hobby, she especially enjoyed needlework, and her grandchildren were her primary interest. She was an excellent cook, known for the more than 30 pecan pies she baked and gave away between Thanksgiving and Christmas. She was also known for her green thumb and the marvelous landscaping she did at the new episcopal residence in the Holston conference.

—*Biographical Directory*, 2012–2016;
email communication with Bishop Clay Lee, September 2017; Hasbrouck Hughes Jr, speaking at the Council of Bishops Memorial Service, November 5, 2017

Edna Dorman Lee

In 1909, Edna married Edwin Ferdinand Lee (1884–1948). Edwin was elected a missionary bishop in 1928 at the General Conference of The Methodist Episcopal Church, after serving local churches in Iowa and Manila and missionary assignments in Batavia, Java, Malaya, and Singapore. He served the Manila Episcopal Area, which included Malaysia and the Philippines.

—https://en.wikipedia.org/wiki/Edwin_Ferdinand_Lee

Janet Elaine Dowell Leeland (b. 1949)

In 1968, Janet married Paul Lee Leeland (b. 1948). Paul was elected in 2008 out of the North Carolina Annual Conference and served the Alabama-West Florida Episcopal Area (2008–2016), then was assigned to the Charlotte Episcopal Area. Janet and Paul have three children and six grandchildren.

Janet was born in Washington, DC, and graduated from North Carolina State University with a BA and from East Carolina University with an MSW. She served as director of the Council on Aging while doing graduate work and later as director of Kitty Askins Hospice Center in Goldsboro, North Carolina. When they moved to Raleigh, she became director of development with Community Home Care and Hospice, opening 25 offices and two hospice houses across North and South Carolina. She is now retired. While living in Alabama, she served on the Board for the Stegall Foundation, as well as tutoring children in kindergarten and second grade. Since moving to the Charlotte area, she has been serving on a "Congregations for Children" team, which works to meet needs of children in the community and addresses hunger among children in Haiti. Other interests include sewing, music, and crafts.

—*Biographical Directory*, 2012–2016;
email communication with Janet Leeland, December 2017

Jeanette Gertrude Fuller Leete (1868–1952)

In 1891, Jeanette married Frederick Deland Leete (1866–1958). Frederick was elected in 1912 out of the Detroit Annual Conference of The Methodist Episcopal Church (after transferring from the Central New York Annual Conference in 1903). He served the Atlanta Episcopal Area (1912–1920), the Indianapolis Episcopal Area (1920–1928), and the Omaha Episcopal Area (1928–1936), then retired. Jeanette and Frederick had three children.

Before her marriage, Jeanette was an instructor. She was descended from Edward Fuller of the Mayflower through the line of Chief Justice Fuller.

—https://www.findagrave.com/cgi-bin/fg.cgi?page=gr&GRid=80170284; https://www.findagrave.com/cgi-bin/fg.cgi?page=gr&GRid=79948494; https://www.familysearch.org/photos/artifacts/17077059; http://www.lib.utexas.edu/taro/smu/00155/smu-00155.html

Mary Luella Day Leonard (1874–1956)

In 1901, Mary married Adna Wright Leonard (1874–1943). Adna was elected in 1916 out of the Cincinnati Annual Conference of The Methodist Episcopal Church. He served the San Francisco Episcopal Area (1916–1924), the Buffalo Episcopal Area (1924–1932), the Pittsburgh Episcopal Area (1932–1940), and the Washington, DC, Episcopal Area (1940–1943). In 1943, President Franklin D. Roosevelt asked him to tour the American forces in Europe and Africa as a representative of the Commission on Chaplains of the Federal Council of Churches. It was on this mission that Bishop Leonard was killed in an airplane crash over Iceland. He was buried there. Mary and Adna had two children and five grandchildren.

Mary, born in New Jersey, studied art at the Cooper Institute of New York and later taught art at Centenary Collegiate Institute in New Jersey. After their marriage, she and Adna lived in Rome, Italy, where he served an American church for two years. They returned to the United States and served churches in Ohio and Seattle, Washington, before his election. She was active in the church and in the Women's Society of Christian Service.

—http://catalog.gcah.org/publicdata/gcah2396.htm

Janet Mae Dean Lewis (b. 1931)

In 1951, Janet married William B. Lewis (b. 1931). Bill was elected in 1988 out of the Southern Illinois Annual Conference and served the Dakotas Episcopal Area (1988–1996), then retired. Janet and Bill settled in Illinois and Door County, Wisconsin. They have three children, seven grandchildren, and three great-grandchildren.

Janet received her BA and MA in elementary education from Southern Illinois University and taught for 15 years. She has been active in UMW, camping activities, and musical programs wherever they have lived. She also enjoys quilting, sewing, crafts, and being a grandmother.

—*Biographical Directory*, 2012–2016; https://www.unitedmethodistbishops.org/person-detail/2464113

Mina Wood Locke (1859–1944)

In 1882, Mina married Charles Edward Locke (1858–1940). Charles was elected in 1920 after serving churches in the East Ohio Conference; Pittsburgh; Portland, Oregon; San Francisco; Buffalo, New York; Brooklyn, New York; and Los Angeles.

He served as bishop in the Philippine Islands (1920–1924) and in St. Paul, Minnesota (1924–1932), then retired. According to the Encyclopedia of World Methodism, they had "a son and a number of daughters."

Mina, born in Pittsburgh, met Charles at Allegheny College. She was an accomplished musician, having graduated from the Pittsburgh Conservatory before attending college. During one of Charles' early pastorates, a wealthy man gave him a large sum of money to spend on a "needy cause." Charles turned the money over to Mina, who used it to start the Bethesda Home, forerunner of the Florence Crittenden Homes for unwed mothers. Later she assisted a Latin American Mission in distributing coffee sacks of clothing, which were the forerunners of the Goodwill bags. The income from sales of the clothing helped start a medical clinic. Mina was also the first president of the Columbia River Branch of the Women's Foreign Missionary Society and vice president of the Pacific Branch. She also served as president of the Women's Conference in the Philippines when they lived there.

—*Encyclopedia of World Methodism, Vol. 2,* 1442; *Journal of the Southern California-Arizona Annual Conference, The Methodist Church, 1944,* 250–251; https://www.findagrave.com/cgi-bin/fg.cgi?page=gr&GRid=81041934

Mildred Shay Loder (1916–1999)

Mildred married Dwight Ellsworth Loder in 1939. Dwight (1914–2002) was elected in 1964 after serving churches in Pennsylvania and Minnesota and as head of Garrett Theological Seminary in Illinois. He served the Michigan Episcopal Area (1964–1976) and the West Ohio Episcopal Area (1976–1984), then retired. They had three children, six grandchildren, and three great-grandchildren.

Mildred attended the Lawrence Memorial Hospital School of Nursing in Medford, Massachusetts, and worked there as an RN and assistant to the head surgical nurse. She was an active member of the Women's Society of Christian Service, served as president of the local PTA in Ohio and of her P.E.O chapter, in addition to other community and church-related activities. A friend described her in the *2000 West Ohio Conference Journal*: "Mildred Loder was a beautiful, serene, genuine, joyful lady. She was quietly and deeply committed to Christ and the faith, expressed best in profound love for family and friends. Her personal faith, her commitment to and love for the Church, and her love for the people of Michigan and West Ohio endeared her to all. Without intending it, she was a role model for not only the ministers' wives but also for everyone who knew her. The world is a better place because of Mildred. Each life touched by her has been blessed."

—*West Ohio Conference Journal–2000,* 145, 394

Carolyn Adele McKeithen Looney (1930–2009)

Carolyn married Richard Carl Looney in 1957 (b. 1934). Richard was elected out of the Holston Conference in 1988 and served the South Georgia Episcopal Area (1988–2000), then retired. Carolyn and Richard have three children and four grandchildren.

Carolyn graduated from Asbury College with a diploma in piano and from Candler School of Theology with a degree in Christian education.

"Carolyn was an exceptional musician and an excellent teacher. She taught music in public schools and gave private piano lessons. . . . She showered her love and concern on family, parishioners, friends and acquaintances. She was a woman of rare beauty and grace, exhibiting an unmistakable radiance even in trying circumstances. While facing a multitude of physical challenges, she demonstrated a quiet strength and independence that inspired everyone" (Council of Bishops Memorial Booklet, 2009). Her husband shared this story, "After a severe stroke in which she lost her speech, her young therapist began singing to her one day. Carolyn chimed in clearly with every word. This was the beginning of her recovery. Her amazing spirit was demonstrated on our first day at home from the hospital. I was confused by the instructions about her medications, and she was trying to tell me what they meant. I wasn't sure about her understanding at that point. With great difficulty, she spoke her first sentence, 'I–have–had–a–stroke.–I–am–not–stupid.' With quiet persistence, she made a remarkable recovery."

—*Biographical Directory*, 2000–2004;
email communication with Bishop Looney, 8/19/2016

Margaret Farrington Ratcliffe Lord (1902–1997)

In 1931, Margaret married John Wesley Lord (1902–1989). John was elected in 1948 out of the Newark Annual Conference. He served the Boston Episcopal Area (1948–1960) and the Washington Episcopal Area (1960–1972), then retired to Lakeland, Florida, and Wolfeboro, New Hampshire. Margaret and John had one daughter and two grandchildren.

Margaret attended the New York School of Fine and Applied Arts and later, with her husband, did graduate work at Rutgers University in the field of human emotions. She was a member of P.E.O. and Zeta Tau Alpha Sorority. Her many activities included membership in the National Committee of 100 United Church Women and in the Corporation of the New England Deaconess Hospital. She was also a member of the Women's Planning Committee of Japan International Christian University Foundation. While living in Washington, DC, she served as a volunteer tutor in remedial reading, working with inner city children, and had a number of articles concerning that work published in church periodicals. The Baltimore Conference of the Women's Society of Christian Service established the Margaret Lord Scholarship. She traveled around the world twice. Her lifelong concern for missions in Africa was inspired by an extended tour of Methodist Missions there in 1955.

—*Biographical Directory*, 1984

Virginia L. Ross Love (1896–1974)

In 1923, Virginia married Edgar Amos Love (1891–1974). Edgar was elected in 1952 out of the Washington Annual Conference of the Central Jurisdiction and served the Baltimore Episcopal Area of the Central Jurisdiction of The Methodist Church (1952–1964), then retired. Virginia and Edgar had one son and two grandsons.

Virginia, named for the state in which she was born, completed the Teachers Normal Course at Morgan College Annex in Lynchburg and taught public school in her hometown, Staunton, for several years before her marriage. She later enrolled in Miner Teacher's College in Washington, DC, while Edgar was serving in that area, and earned a BA in education. After teaching for a year in Maryland, she enrolled in Howard University School of Religion and earned an MA in religious education. Later she worked in the Religious Education Department of St. Mark's Methodist Church in New York City and taught in a neighborhood school in Jamaica, New York. After Edgar's election to the episcopacy, she traveled and lectured with him during visits to mission stations in Malaysia, Hong Kong, the Philippines, Japan, India, Burma, Africa, England, France, Belgium, Switzerland, West Germany, Italy, Lebanon, and the Holy Land. She was a member of Delta Sigma Theta Sorority, the Order of Eastern Star, and many other organizations in the Baltimore area.

—https://en.wikipedia.org/wiki/Edgar_Amos_Love; *Eastern Pennsylvania Conference, Journal Vol. 2 Conference Proceedings, 1975*, 781

Bonnie Faye Pressley Lovern (1908–1982)

In 1935, Faye married James Chess Lovern (1909–1987). James was elected in 1976 out of the Oklahoma Annual Conference and served the San Antonio Episcopal Area (1976–1980), then retired. Faye and James had two children.

Faye graduated as valedictorian of her high school class in Smyrna, Georgia, attended Monroe A&M College for a while, then worked in Detroit. While James was serving Laurel Heights Church in San Antonio, Texas, she enrolled in Incarnate Word College, where she majored in dialectics and graduated with honors. Her main interests, outside her family and her church, were sewing, interior decorating, and gourmet cooking. She also did volunteer work with senior citizens. As a preacher's wife and as a bishop's wife, as Bishop Eugene Slater noted in her Texas Conference Journal 1983 memoir:

"Faye's gifts and graces were graciously given and gratefully received. Although in pain often, she lived through the last three and one-half years of her life without complaint. She continued to be active in the ministry she had always shared with her husband. . . . Faye Lovern was an altogether lovely and loving person, gentle and genuine, unassuming and unselfish. She never clamored for place or position. She never demanded recognition. She was an authentic human being."

—Central Texas Conference Journal, 1983, 177); *Biographical Directory*, 1984; https://www.findagrave.com/memorial/106666067/bonnie-faye-lovern

Edith Eglantine Egloff Lowe (1876–1955)

In 1913, Edith married Titus Lowe (1877–1959). Titus was elected in The Methodist Episcopal Church in 1924 after serving churches in Pennsylvania, India, Iowa, and Nebraska. He was assigned to the Singapore Episcopal Area (1924–1928), Portland (Oregon) Episcopal Area (1928–1939), and the Indianapolis Episcopal Area (1939–1948), then retired. Titus had two daughters and a son, who died in infancy, with his first wife Anna Bessie Creed Lowe (1880–1911). Edith and Titus had one daughter.

—http://prabook.com/web/person-view.html?profileId=279050; https://en.wikipedia.org/wiki/Titus_Lowe

Ellen Louise Stoy Lowe (1890–1977)

In 1957, Ellen married retired Bishop Titus Lowe (1877–1959). Titus had three children, one of whom died in infancy, with his first wife, Anna Bessie Creed Lowe (1880–1911) and a daughter with his second wife, Edith Eglantine Egloff Lowe (1876–1955).

As a young adult in Indiana, Ellen taught teenagers in public schools and was active in the programs of the UMC in New Albany. When she married Titus, his health was failing, and she cared for him at home for more than a year and a half. She served as a "Pink Lady" volunteer at Methodist Hospital in Indianapolis until shortly before her final illness.

—*North Indiana Annual Conference Journal, 1977,* 246–247; https://en.wikipedia.org/wiki/Titus_Lowe

Jolynn Lowry (b. 1949)

In 1976, Jolynn married John Michael Lowry (b. 1950). Mike was elected in 2008 out of the Southwest Texas Annual Conference and assigned to the Fort Worth Episcopal Area. Jolynn and Mike have two children and four grandchildren.

Jolynn graduated from Oklahoma Baptist University with a BSN in nursing and from Texas Woman's University with an MSN in psychiatric nursing and education.

She has practiced clinically in the psychiatric-mental health field and served as a director of inservice education, an infection control practitioner, and a risk management director in psychiatric facilities. Jolynn has taught psychiatric-mental health nursing, fundamentals of nursing, and health promotion/disease prevention in university settings (Texas Woman's University, Del Mar College, Texas A&M Corpus Christi, The University of Texas at Austin, University of Health Sciences in San Antonio, and University of the Incarnate Word). She has also worked as Central Texas conference secretary at United Community Centers, Inc. and as a conference Partners in Ministry trainer. She serves as a Faith Community Nurse and currently has a ministry with older adults at the United Community Poly Center. Jolynn also likes to travel, read, do crafts, and watch movies. She co-authored articles in several professional publications: "Hispanic and female college students: Evidence for increased risk for cardiac disease" in *Journal of Hispanic Higher Education* 4, no. 1 (January 2005); "Cardiac health: Relationships among hostility, spirituality and health risk" in *Journal of Nursing Care Quality* 20, no.1 (2005); "Cardiovascular risk among older Hispanic women" in *American Association of Occupational Health Nurses Journal* 54, no. 3 (2006).

Favorite Scripture: 2 Corinthians 4:16-18 / Favorite Hymn: "I'll Praise My Maker While I've Breath" (*UMH*, 60)

—*Biographical Directory*, 2012–2016;
email communication with Jolynn Lowry, August 2017 and August 2018

Elizabeth Frances Hall Lundy

In 1944, Elizabeth married Robert Fielden Lundy (1920–2003). Robert was elected in 1964, after serving churches in Tennessee and as a missionary to Malaysia and Singapore. He served the Singapore Episcopal Area one term (1964–1968). Believing in the importance of indigenous leadership, he proposed legislation that ensured he would not be re-elected. They returned to the United States, where he served with the General Board of Missions and then as General Secretary of the Southeastern Jurisdiction, returning to the Holston Annual Conference to serve a local church until his retirement in 1990. Elizabeth and Robert had three children and five grandchildren.

Elizabeth, according to Robert's memoir in the Holston Conference Journal, was a "gifted and dedicated layperson" and "a highly significant and creative part of the Lundy leadership team."

—*The Journal of the Holston Annual Conference, 2003*, 308–309;
https://www.findagrave.com/memorial/7126582; http://prabook.com/web/person-view.html?profileId=582072; *Encyclopedia of World Methodism, Vol.* 2, 1470

Julienne Dembo Lunge (b. 1962)

In 1979, Julienne married Daniel Onashuyaka Lunge (b. 1958). Daniel was elected in 2017 out of the Central Congo Annual Conference, while serving as dean of the faculty of theology of Wembo-Nyama University and pastor of a local French-speaking church in the Democratic Republic of Congo. He was assigned to the Central Congo Episcopal Area. Julienne and Daniel have seven children.

Julienne lost both parents when she was 10 years old. She is president of the women's group in Wembo-Nyama and also directs the choir. She enjoys preparing food for large groups when there is a party at the local church. She also enjoys sewing and designing dresses.

Favorite Scripture: John 3:16

—interview with Julienne Lunge by Heidi Streiff at Council of Bishops meeting, fall 2016; https://www.umnews.org/en/news/lunge-elected-bishop-in-congo

Eleanor Lyght (b. 1942)

In 1971, Eleanor married Ernest S. Lyght (b. 1943). Ernest was elected in 1996 out of the Northern New Jersey Annual Conference. He served the New York Episcopal Area (1996–2004) and the West Virginia Episcopal Area (2004–2011), then retired and moved back to New Jersey. Eleanor and Ernest have two sons and four grandchildren.

Eleanor earned a BA from Montclair State University and worked in the Paterson, New Jersey, public school system as a vocal music teacher (K–12). She was able to continue in her work there for the first eight years after Ernest's election and retired when he was assigned to West Virginia in 2004. She has also been an active volunteer in local churches, specializing in hand bell choirs. When they moved to West Virginia, she served as a substitute organist at several different local churches. Since their return to New Jersey, she continues to substitute for organists and has volunteered as a tutor for students transitioning from the Cadets to the full-fledged Philadelphia Boys Choir. Eleanor comments, "It was hard for me to move away from my job and family in 2004. Our first grandchild was just 16 months old at the time. When we arrived in West Virginia, we were received with such gracious hospitality, and the welcoming service was phenomenal, with outstanding music. Seven years later, when Ernest retired early because of illness, we left West Virginia with mixed feelings. Although we were glad to return to home and family, which includes three more grandchildren born since we moved away, we love the people of West Virginia and are so grateful for the experiences we had there."

—*Biographical Directory*, 2000–2004;
interviews with Eleanor Lyght, 4/10/17 and 8/28/17

Nocia Madonela Machado (b. 1948)

In 1975, Nocia Madonela married Joao Somane Machado (b. 1946). He was elected in 1988 out of Mozambique and served the Mozambique Episcopal Area until 2008, then retired. Nocia and Joao have four children and six grandchildren.

Nocia has given her life to help women and youth through literacy and adult education programs. Through the Public Health and Community Development Project of the South Mozambique Annual Conference, she has helped train women and young adults to promote public health in their congregations and on the district level. The persons trained through this project teach those in their congregations and communities more healthy ways to live and how to prevent common illness. Caring for persons infected and affected by HIV/AIDS is a primary concern. The project maintains two health centers in each of the two districts.

—*Biographical Directory*, 2004–2008; interview with Bishop Machado, May 2017

Harriet Ammie Keeler Magee (1880–1943)

In 1902, Harriet married Junius Ralph Magee (1880–1970). Junius was elected in 1932 in The Methodist Episcopal Church, after serving churches in Iowa, Massachusetts, and Washington State. He served the St. Paul Episcopal Area (1932–1939), the Des Moines Episcopal Area of The Methodist Church (1939–1944), and the Chicago Episcopal Area (1944-1952). Harriet and Junius had two children and two grandchildren.

Born in Iowa, Harriet graduated from the State Teachers College at Cedar Falls in 1900 and taught music there until their marriage. She was active in church work and especially in mission support, corresponding with about 96 missionaries at home and abroad. While they were in Minnesota, she was elected president of the Minnesota Women's Foreign Missionary Society, which group published *Beads of Silver*, a souvenir volume of her poetry. She also had poems published in *The Christian Advocate* from time to time and sometimes served as a poetry reviewer for that magazine.

—https://en.wikipedia.org/wiki/Junius_Ralph_Magee; https://prabook.com/web/junius_ralph.magee/1102421; https://www.revolvy.com/topic/Junius%20Ralph%20Magee&uid=1575; *Official Records of the 89th Session of the Upper Iowa Annual Conference of The Methodist Church, 1944*, 165; *Journal of the Pacific Northwest Annual Conference of The Methodist Church, 1944*, 88

Derrick Malone (b. 1970)

In 1993, Derrick married Tracy Smith (b. 1968). Tracy was elected in 2016 out of the Northern Illinois Annual Conference and assigned to the Ohio East Episcopal Area. Derrick and Tracy have two daughters.

Derrick was born in Illinois and earned a BS from North Central College, where he met Tracy. He has owned his own business as a State Farm Insurance agent in Chicago since 1998. In his free time, he enjoys playing basketball, golf, fishing, and cooking.

— https://www.umnews.org/en/news/tracy-smith-malone-elected-bishop-in-north-central; email communication with Derrick Malone, February 2018

Mildred Helen Fryer Martin (1920–2003)

In 1920, Mildred married Paul Elliott Martin (1897–1975). Paul was elected in 1944 out of the North Texas Conference of The Methodist Church and was assigned to the Arkansas-Louisiana Episcopal Area (1944–1960), then to the Houston Episcopal Area (1960–1968), then retired.

Mildred was active in many church-related and community organizations, including Southern Methodist University and Perkins School of Theology. She was awarded an honorary Doctor of Law degree by Hendrix College in Conway, Arkansas, and was a strong supporter of Methodist missions, traveling with her husband to Africa, China, and India. After her husband's death, she spent much time organizing and cataloging his sermons, articles, and other historical information now stored in the Bridwell Library at SMU and in the Paul E. Martin Narthex and Heritage Area in First UMC of Wichita Falls, Texas.

—*2004 Lousiana Annual Conference Journal*, p. 263; Howell Clinton, *Prominent Personalities in American Methodism* (Birmingham, AL: Lowry Press, 1945); Leete, Frederick, *Methodist Bishops* (Nashville: MPH, 1948); Texas Conference Journal for 2004, K–24

Sally Katherine Beene Martin

In 1918, Sally married William Clyde Martin (1893–1984). William was elected in 1938 out of The Methodist Episcopal Church, South, and assigned to the Pacific Coast Episcopal Area. When The Methodist Church was formed the next year, he was assigned to the Kansas-Nebraska Episcopal Area, then to the Dallas-Fort Worth Episcopal Area (1948–1964), then retired. Sally and William settled in Little Rock, Arkansas. They had three children, nine grandchildren, and seven great-grandchildren.

Sally greatly loved music, reading, and travel. She was genuinely supportive of William and his ministry, but because she suffered from ill health and depression, she often stayed home while he traveled. She loved her grandchildren generously and enjoyed indulging their wants and giving them treats.

—James E. Kirby, *Brother Will: A Biography of William C. Martin* (Nashville: Abingdon Press, 2000), 421–422; *Biographical Directory*, 1984; https://www.ancestry.com/boards/topics.obits/108654/mb.ashx?pnt=1

Raquel Mora Martinez (b. 1940)

In 1961, Raquel married Joel Neftali Martinez (b. 1940). Joel was elected out of the former Rio Grande Annual Conference in 1992. He served the Nebraska Episcopal Area (1992–2000) and the San Antonio Episcopal Area (2000–2008), then retired. Raquel and Joel have three children and three step-grandchildren.

Raquel was born in Mexico, the daughter of a Methodist pastor. Her parents instilled in her a love for the church, a love for music, and a desire to serve. In 1952, Raquel's family came to the U.S., and she attended Lydia Patterson Institute in El Paso, Texas, where she met Joel. Raquel has a degree in music education from the University of Texas at El Paso and an MA in sacred music from Perkins School of Theology, SMU Dallas. She also holds an honorary Doctor of Music degree from Nebraska Wesleyan University, Lincoln, Nebraska. During Joel's first pastoral assignment in 1965, Raquel served as a kindergarten director and part-time pianist, in addition to her work with UMW. She continued working as pianist and choir director in some of the other churches where they served. From 1975 to 1981, when Joel took a staff position with the General Board of Global Ministries, Raquel worked as administrative assistant in the former Women's Division (now UMW) and as a director (1984–1992). During those years, she was often called to serve as pianist and/or song leader, besides her other duties. She has continued to function as pianist and/or song leader for various jurisdictional and conference gatherings of UMW, occasionally giving workshops on worship and music (Perkins School of Theology, the Lutheran School of Theology in Chicago, and the Consultation on Town and Country Mission). She has served as visiting professor at Perkins School of Theology, the Evangelical Seminary in San Juan, Puerto Rico, and at the Methodist Seminary in Mexico City. Since Joel was elected a bishop in 1992, she has been asked to play the piano for worship at Council of Bishops' meetings on numerous occasions. She received the Perkins School of Theology Distinguished Alumni Award in 1997. In 2010, Perkins presented her with the Soli Deo Gloria Award for excellence in church music. She was the editor of the Spanish UM Hymnal, *Mil Voces Para Celebrar*, presented to General Conference in 1996, and in 2003 she and Joel co-edited a partly bilingual Book of Worship Resources titled *Fiesta Cristiana*, published by Abingdon.

Some of her work (translations, arrangements, original text and music) has been included in the following denominational hymnals: *Glory to God* (Westminster John Knox Press); *Lift Up Your Hearts* (Faith Alive Christian Resources); *Psalms for All Seasons* (Faith Alive Christian Resources); *Las Voces del Camino* (Unitarian Universalist Association of Congregations); *The United Methodist Hymnal* (The United Methodist Publishing House); *El Himnario Presbiteriano* (Geneva Press); *Libro de*

Liturgia y Cántico (ELCA, Augsburg); *Mil Voces Para Celebrar* (Abingdon); *Chalice Hymnal* (Chalice Press, St. Louis, MO); *Oramos Cantando / We Pray in Song* (GIA Publications); *The Faith We Sing* (Abingdon); *Worship & Song* (Abingdon). She has also composed other music related to special days and special events, including theme songs for UMW and MARCHA, the Hispanic caucus.

Favorite Scripture: 1 Corinthians 10:31 / Favorite Hymn: "When in Our Music God Is Glorified" (*UMH*, 68)

—*Biographical Directory*, 2004–2008;
email communication with Raquel Martinez, June 2017

Eunice Treffry Jones Mathews (1914–2016)

In 1940, Eunice married James Kenneth Mathews (1913–2010). Jim was elected bishop in 1960, while working as associate general secretary of Global Mission for the UMC. He served the Boston Episcopal Area (1960–1972) and the Baltimore-Washington Episcopal Area (1972–1980), then retired. They settled in Bethesda, Maryland, and in retirement, he served several interim assignments: Zimbabwe Episcopal Area (1985–1986), the Albany Episcopal Area (1990–1992), and the New York Episcopal Area (1995–1996). Jim and Eunice had three children, six grandchildren, and three great-grandchildren.

Eunice was born in Sitapur, India, the daughter of missionary and evangelist E. Stanley Jones and missionary and educator Mabel Lossing Jones. She attended Oberlin College Music Conservatory, graduated from American University in Washington, DC, and trained at Baylor Secretarial School in Dubuque, Iowa. She then served as her father's secretary and assistant for three years, until her marriage. She met Jim, a young American missionary in India, when he came to hear her father speak. While Jim was serving in the US Army during World War II, Eunice became a typist at the Office of Strategic Services, the forerunner to the CIA. After the war, they moved to New York, and then New Jersey, where Eunice focused on raising their three children. As a bishop's wife, she traveled extensively with her husband and worked on his autobiography, while at the same time making her own mark, researching and writing about drug abuse, clergy spouses, and the role of women. She was twice elected vice president of the UM Commission on Archives and History. In the spouses' organization she was gracious and kind to all, while also providing significant leadership. And always she advocated for missions, especially in India.

—*Biographical Directory*, November 1996; interview with Eunice Mathews, 2009

Barbara Walker Matthews (b. 1941)

In 1974, Barbara married Marcus Matthews (b. 1946). Marcus was elected out of the Baltimore-Washington Annual Conference in 2004. He served the Philadelphia Episcopal Area (2004–2008), the Upper New York Episcopal Area (2008–2012), and the Washington, DC, Episcopal Area (2012–2016), then retired. They have two grown children and five grandchildren.

Barbara is a graduate of both St. Paul's College and the University of Virginia with an MA in reading. During her career, Barbara taught elementary school in Virginia and was a reading specialist in the public schools in Washington, DC, and in Maryland. She retired as an educator in June 2005. Barbara's hobbies include reading, gardening, and arts and crafts.

—*Biographical Directory*, 2004–2008;
email communication with Barbara Matthews, April 2018

Jessica Mavula

Jessica married Kefas K. Mavula (1967–2008). He was elected out of the Nigeria Annual Conference in 2007 during a special session of the West African Central Conference and assigned to the Nigeria Episcopal Area. Kefas died less than a year later. Jessica and Kefas have six sons.

—http://tnumcgmeth.blogspot.com/2008/01/nigerian-united-methodist-bishop-mavula.html

Phyllis Elizabeth Henry May (b. 1935)

In 1963, Phyllis married Felton Edwin May (1935–2017). Felton was elected in 1984 out of the Peninsula Annual Conference and assigned to the Harrisburg Episcopal Area (1984–1996) and the Washington Episcopal Area (1996–2004). In 1990, he served as bishop-on-special-assignment to organize and coordinate the United Methodist Bishops' Initiative on Drug and Alcohol Abuse and Violence in Washington, DC. Upon retirement in 2004, he served as dean of the Harry R. Kendall Science and Health Mission Center at Philander Smith College, Little Rock, Arkansas. Phyllis and Felton have two children and 10 grandchildren.

Phyllis attended Bennett College, graduating with a BA in 1957. She continued her studies at Boston University School of Theology, where she received an MRE in 1959. She taught philosophy and religion at Bennett College and served as director of youth for the West Wisconsin Conference. A teacher and director of Christian education, Phyllis May has taught and counseled in schools and Head Start programs and authored curriculum materials. She was instrumental in founding the *Phyllis Elizabeth May Child Development Center* at Congress Heights UMC in Washington, DC. She has also served as a Volunteer in Mission in Africa, working with children in refugee camps.

Favorite Scripture: Psalm 139 / Favorite Hymn: "Great Is Thy Faithfulness" (*UMH*, 140)

—*Biographical Directory*, 2012–2016;
email communication with daughter Daphne Brown, July 2016

Lynn Barkley McAlilly

Lynn married William T. McAlilly. He was elected in 2012 out of the Mississippi Annual Conference and was assigned to the Nashville Episcopal Area. Lynn and William have two children and four grandchildren.

Lynn graduated from Mississippi State University with a BS in business and worked in banking and retail sales. After enjoying her time as a stay-at-home mom, Lynn pursued alternate route certification in the field of education and later earned a Master of Education in reading and literacy. She taught lower elementary in several public schools and in a Choctaw Tribal School in Mississippi. Since her husband's election to the episcopacy, Lynn's passion for children and literacy has involved her in ministries such as Project Transformation and Trinity Community Ministry. She is encouraging churches in the Memphis and Tennessee Annual Conferences to engage in their communities by forming Church-School Partnerships. Lynn also served on the board of Miriam's Promise, an adoption agency of the Tennessee Annual Conference. Lynn enjoys traveling, reading, working in the yard, and spending time with family.

Favorite Scripture: Proverbs 3:5-6

—*Biographical Directory*, 2012–2016;
email communication with Lynn McAlilly, May 2016

Margaret Fowler McCleskey (b. 1942)

In 1963, Margaret married James Lawrence McCleskey (b. 1940). James was elected in 1996 out of the Western North Carolina Annual Conference and served the Columbia Episcopal Area (1996–2004) and the Charlotte Episcopal Area (2004–2008), then retired. Margaret and James have settled in Lake Junaluska. They have three children and four grandchildren.

Margaret holds a BA in education and an MA in community education, with a certificate in resource development. From 1983 to 1991, she was the first director of development for The United Methodist Agency for the Retarded in Western North Carolina (UMAR WNC, Inc.), an agency related to the Western North Carolina Conference providing residential and other services for persons with developmental disabilities. She led in the establishment of this ministry, which now has over 25 church-related group homes. In 2012, a UMAR apartment complex in Huntersville, North Carolina, was named for her in recognition of her pioneering work in this ministry, and in 2013, she was recognized with the UMAR Legacy Award. She is also a former trustee of Gammon Theological Seminary, and she is active in several community service and church organizations. She enjoys riding her spotted saddle horse, Ranger, and walking their dogs, Barkley and Cricket, with Lawrence.

—*Biographical Directory*, 2012;
email communication with Margaret McCleskey, September 2017

Eva Thomas McConnell (1871–1968)

In 1887, Eva married Francis McConnell (1871–1953). Francis was elected in 1912 out of the New York Annual Conference of The Methodist Episcopal Church. He served the Denver Episcopal Area (1912–1920), the Pittsburgh Episcopal Area (1920–1928), and the New York Episcopal Area (1928–1944), then retired.

Eva served as vice president of The Women's Foreign Missionary Society of The Methodist Episcopal Church and traveled widely with her husband. She was elected the first president of the Bishops' Wives Fellowship, formed in 1940, and served for the quadrennium.

—Francis J. McConnell Family Collection, Drew University Methodist Collection, Madison, NJ; Spouses' Scrapbooks, 1949–1964; http://www.depauw.edu/news-media/latest-news/details/27386/

Mary Carolyn Bamberg McConnell (1931–1986)

In 1952, Mary married Calvin McConnell (b. 1928). Cal was elected in 1980 out of the Rocky Mountain Annual Conference. He served the Portland Episcopal Area (1980–1988) and the Seattle Episcopal Area (1988–1996). Mary and Cal had two sons and three grandchildren.

Mary earned an AB in psychology at Stanford University, an MEd at Harvard, and a PhD in philosophy at the University of Colorado. She worked as a social studies teacher at the secondary level and as a writer and curriculum developer for Biological Sciences Studies. Mary also worked as education director for the Oregon Museum of Science and Industry. She was active in the adult education program of local churches and was a popular leader for workshops and seminars on faith development.

—*Biographical Directory*, November 1984, 2004–2008

Velma Duell McConnell (b. 1924)

In 1988, Velma married Bishop Calvin McConnell (b. 1928), who was serving the Portland (Oregon) Episcopal Area and was assigned to the Seattle Episcopal Area (1988–1996). He retired in 1996, and they moved to back to Portland, Oregon. Cal has two sons and three grandchildren with his first wife, Mary, who died in 1986. Velma has four sons and five grandchildren with her first husband, Paul Duell, who died in 1983.

Velma grew up in a devout Methodist family in western Kansas. She earned a BS in home economics and sociology from Fort Hays Kansas State University, where she was active in the Wesley Foundation, YWCA, and Kappa Phi. Velma has worked as a secretary in a YMCA Marriage Clinic, a coordinator of classroom volunteers, a remedial reading tutor in elementary schools, a mentor for ADD students, and coordinator and home-stay host. Her lifelong commitment led her to a volunteer staff position in Lay Pastoral Care in her local church. After her marriage to Cal and move to the Pacific-Northwest Area, she sought out a Reconciling congregation and placed her membership there at Wallingford UMC. She volunteered with the Multi-faith AIDS Project of Seattle and continues to speak out for full inclusion, openness, and acceptance.

—*Biographical Directory*, 2004–2008; personal notes by Velma McConnell, May 2016

Milah Dodd Gibson McDavid (1916–2011)

In 1942, Milah married Joel Duncan McDavid (1916–2003). Joel was elected in 1972 out of the Alabama-West Florida Annual Conference and served the Florida Episcopal Area (1972–1980) and the Atlanta Episcopal Area (1980–1984), then retired. Milah and Joel had three children, six grandchildren, and five great-grandchildren.

Milah worked as a secretary at Candler School of Theology while Joel was in seminary. She later worked in the registrar's office at a high school in Mobile, Alabama, and gave over 1,500 hours of volunteer service at a local hospital. She devoted the early years of her marriage to working as a homemaker and wife, spending many hours attending sporting events and using her sewing and culinary skills. Later in life, she made doll clothes for her grandchildren's dolls and also left special treats on their pillows each night when they came to visit. Her recipe for strawberry shortcake was used in a local Montgomery, Alabama, restaurant, and she served as hostess for many meetings and church functions. She always fixed snacks and lunch when the Cabinet met in the office, which was in their home, and if they did not break in time for lunch, she would open the door and ring a dinner bell to announce that lunch was ready. She was a popular Sunday school teacher and was active in UMW and other church activities.

As a bishop's wife, she accompanied Joel on mission trips to India and South Africa, after which she made many presentations to groups around the conference. She was presented a trophy by the Florida Annual Conference for being "The Bishop's Chauffeur," which was especially meaningful to her because she learned to drive at the age of 45. According to her son Ben, while she drove, Joel wrote letters or worked on his sermon or presentation for wherever they were going. Her number one commitment was to support her husband and his ministry.

—*Biographical Directory*, 2000–2004; Council of Bishops Memorial Booklet, November 2011; correspondence with son Ben McDavid, July 2017

Joan Craig McKee (b. 1950)

In 1975, Joan married Michael McKee (b. 1952). He was elected in 2012 out of the Central Texas Annual Conference and assigned to the Dallas Episcopal Area. Joan and Michael have two adult children and two grandchildren.

Joan was born in Texas and earned her BA from Austin College. She worked as an educator in public schools and for 18 years taught pre-school at the Museum of Science and History in Ft. Worth ("the greatest job I ever had," she said in an email). She has taught Sunday school, led Bible studies, and worked on Lord's Acres (a ministry that started by asking farmers to donate the earnings from one acre of farmland) and mission-related efforts. Joan has also worked as a docent at the Amon Carter Museum of American Art, served on education boards and committees, and volunteered with Habitat for Humanity and with Mission Central in the Mid-Cities. Presently she serves as chair of the board for Project Transformation North Texas and on the National Advisory Board for Project Transformation. She loves to travel, read, attend book reviews, work in the yard, take nature walks, and spend time with family and friends.

—*Biographical Directory*, 2012–2016;
email communication with Joan McKee, January 2018

Eleanor M. Smith Mead (1874–1955)

In 1896, Eleanor married Charles Larew Mead (1868–1941). Charles was elected in The Methodist Episcopal Church in 1920 after serving churches in New Jersey, Maryland, New York, and Colorado. He served the Denver Episcopal Area (1920–1932) and the Kansas City Episcopal Area (1932–1939). Eleanor and Charles had five children and seven grandchildren.

—https://www.findagrave.com/memorial/84381520/Eleanor-Maren-Mead; http://prabook.com/web/person-view.html?profileId=279379; *Official Record, 3rd Annual Session, The Kansas Conference, The Methodist Church, 1941*, 330

Hannah Campbell Meadors (1935–2003)

In 1954, Hannah married Marshall LeRoy (Jack) Meadors Jr (b. 1933). Jack was elected in 1992 out of the South Carolina Annual Conference and served the Mississippi Episcopal Area (1992–2000). When he retired in 2000, Hannah and Jack moved back to South Carolina. They have four children, 10 grandchildren, and four great-grandchildren.

Hannah was an educator and early childhood consultant, working with schools, churches, universities and community groups in the areas of public policy, interagency collaboration, curriculum, parenting, and guidance. She served as director of Early Childhood Development in the Education Division of South Carolina under Governor Richard W. Riley and a coordinator of Early Childhood in the Greenville County School District Office. Governor Riley conferred on her the state's highest award, "The Order of the Palmetto." While living in Mississippi, she worked through the State Departments of Education and Human Services and chaired the committee mandated to develop a state plan for the education of young children. She participated in the development of a study document, "Education: The Gift of Hope," sponsored by the UM Board of Higher Education and Ministry and served on the task force for the Bishops' Initiative on Children and Poverty. She traveled to Russia, Estonia, Angola, Mozambique, and Mexico and visited refugee camps in Palestine, Macedonia, and Kosovo. In 1999, she recruited a team of UM bishops' spouses to visit Kosovo with UMCOR staff to deliver school kits to children there.

She also served as president of the Board of Trustees of the International Foundation of Ewha Womans University in Seoul, Korea. Chang Hynun Sin Geer, representing that foundation, included these words in her eulogy for Hannah, "Hannah deeply touched many who met her and worked with her . . . a guiding light for many of us. She demonstrated integrity, individuality, and leadership. Her deep faith in the Lord and sense of humanity inspired me profoundly. . . . One of her deepest concerns was to improve the lives of neglected people . . . [including] . . . Korean women who were no strangers to adversity, torment, injustice, pain and suffering. Her dream was to help those in need by improving the quality of life through education. Hannah was a woman warrior with a tenacious will. . . . She wanted the Foundation to be inclusive and united. In spite of her illness, she traveled tirelessly to work towards implementing her vision."

—*Biographical Directory*, 2000–2004; notes shared by Bishop Meadors and email communication with him, February 2017

Socorro Mella-Granadosin (b. 1926)

In 1952, Socorro married Paul Locke A. Granadosin (1925–2001). Paul was elected in 1968 out of the Philippine Central Conference and served the Baguio Episcopal Area (1968–1974), the Manila Episcopal Area (1974–1980), and both the Manila and Baguio Episcopal Areas (1980–1992), then retired. In 1996, he was reactivated to serve the Davao Episcopal Area (1997–2000). Socorro and Paul have six sons.

Socorro graduated from Union Theological Seminary in Manila, with majors in religious education and sacred music. Socorro was president of the National Clergy Spouses Association of the UMC in the Philippines for seven years, has been very active in assisting seminary students, and also participated in community projects in the episcopal areas where they were assigned. She is an active member of the Hope UMC in Imus, Cavite; has served on various church council committees; and at the age of 92 still serves as choir director. She is an accomplished soloist. She is very active in community work, especially in children's development projects. "The Granadosin Brothers" were privileged to sing at the 1992 and 2000 General Conferences.

Favorite Scripture: Psalm 121:1-2 / Favorite Hymns: "Great Is Thy faithfulness" (*UMH*, 140), "His Eye Is on the Sparrow" (*TFWS*, 2146)

—*Biographical Directory*, 2000–2004; email communication with son Genesis Granadosin, June 2017

Hanna Eckhard Melle (d. 1958)

In 1907, Hanna married F. H. Otto Melle (1875–1947). Otto was elected in the German Methodist Episcopal Church in 1936, after serving as a missionary in Budapest, Hungary (1907–1911) and in Vienna, Austria (1911–1920) and as president of Frankfurt Theological Seminary. He served as resident bishop of the Germany Central Conference in Berlin (1936–1946). In spite of the fierce warfare during those years, he refused to go west for safety, because he "did not want to leave the Berlin Methodists alone in the day of darkness." Hanna and Otto had three children.

Hanna and their daughter Edith stayed with him in Berlin. Bishop Wunderlich remembered Hanna for her faithfulness and loving kindness through the years.

—September 8, 1958 letter in Spouses' Scrapbooks, 1949–1964; https://hu.wikipedia.org/wiki/Melle_Ottó; *Encyclopedia of World Methodism, Vol. 2*, 1545

Jack Dale Middleton (b. 1939)

In 1961, Jack married Jane Stewart Allen (b. 1940). Jane was elected in 2004 out of the New York Annual Conference. She served the Harrisburg Episcopal Area (2004–2012), retired in 2012, and then served the New York Episcopal Area (2014–2016). In retirement, Jack and Jane settled in Connecticut. They have two children, four grandchildren, and one great-grandchild.

Jack has worked in community organization and development for the Archdiocese of Hartford Office of Urban Affairs, Junior Achievement, Economics America, the University of Oklahoma, and the University of Hartford. His avocation is the history of automobiles, automobile racing and automobile memorabilia. He and Jane have served on several Volunteer in Mission teams in Bolivia and have traveled widely.

—*Biographical Directory*, 2004–2008;
email communication with Jack Middleton, July 2017

Miriam Kathleen Horst Middleton (1908–2000)

In 1931, Miriam married William Vernon Middleton (1902–1965). William was elected in 1960 out of the Eastern Pennsylvania Annual Conference and served the Pittsburgh Episcopal Area 1960 until his death in 1965. Miriam and William had two children.

Miriam graduated from Dickinson College. While her husband served local churches, she shared in his ministry, but when he became general executive secretary of the Division of National Missions, she managed the home and cared for their two children. During those years, she enjoyed entertaining dinner guests from all over the world when they came to Philadelphia on National Missions business. During their time in the Pittsburgh Episcopal Area, they hosted the 1964 General Conference. After his sudden death *en route* to the Council of Bishops meeting in the fall of

1965, Miriam moved back to Chambersburg to be near her elderly parents. She spent seven "very happy years" teaching in the Tuscarora Public School system in eastern Pennsylvania and earned an MA in education at Shippensburg State Teacher's College. Over the years, she pursued interests in ancient history, biblical archeology, and parapsychology. In retirement, she participated in volunteer projects.

—*Biographical Directory*, November 1992; *Western Pennsylvania Conference Journal* for 2000, 369–370; *Philadelphia Conference Journal* for 1966, 1001

Mary Francis Noblitt Milhouse (1911–2008)

In 1932, Mary Francis married Paul William Milhouse (1910–2005). Paul was elected bishop in 1960 out of the Illinois Annual Conference of the Evangelical United Brethren church. He served the Southwestern Area of the EUB (1960–1968) and the Oklahoma Episcopal Area of the UMC (1968–1980), then retired. Mary Frances and Paul had three children, seven grandchildren, and 19 great-grandchildren.

"Frances was very active in the life of the church wherever her husband's position took them. . . . Frances was well-known for her hostess skills, and she always seemed to be entertaining someone, from foreign students studying at Oklahoma City University to the spouses of her husband's district superintendents" (Council of Bishops Memorial Booklet, November 2009). She enjoyed flowers, reading, travel, listening to classical music, and letter-writing, especially to the ill and shut-ins. Frances often traveled overseas with her husband. After retirement, they both spent time with foreign students at Oklahoma City University, frequently inviting them into their home.

—*Biographical Directory*, November 1996; http://www.barkesweaverglick.com/obituaries/Mary-Milhouse-42463/#!/Obituary

Margaret Ross Miller (1870–1955)

In 1894, Margaret married George Amos Miller (1868–1961). George was elected in The Methodist Episcopal Church in 1924 after serving local churches in California and missionary assignments in Manila and Costa Rica. As bishop, he served one quadrennium each from headquarters in Mexico City, Buenos Aires, and Santiago. He retired in 1934. Margaret and George had two daughters.

Margaret attended Stanford University in California, as did George, and served with him in local church ministry and missionary assignments. She served as president of the Pacific branch of the former Women's Foreign Missionary Society and also of the Women's Society of Christian Service. She began her efforts to organize women's groups in the mission fields while living in Chile. These groups were later organized into the Federation of Women's Societies, for which she wrote several study books. She also wrote and published *Women Under the Southern Cross* for the 16 denominations in the U.S. that combined their missionary study courses.

—http://catalog.gcah.org/publicdata/gcah527.htm

Mary Ann Minnick (1928–2013)

In 1946, Mary Ann married Carlton Printess Minnick Jr (b. 1927). C.P. was elected in 1980 out of the Virginia Annual Conference and served the Jackson Episcopal Area (1980–1984) and the Raleigh Episcopal Area (1984–1996), then retired. Mary Ann and C.P. have four children, nine grandchildren, and two great-grandchildren.

After graduating as valedictorian of her high school class, Mary Ann attended Farmville State Teachers College (now Longwood University) in Virginia, with a straight A academic record. C.P recalls clearly how disappointed and distressed her family was when he persuaded her to marry him (she was 18 and he was 19) after she had completed only one year of her college education and he had completed only two. She never earned her own college degree, but she gave devoted support to C.P. while he completed seven more years of college and graduate school education. She was truly a self-educated person, a voracious reader of books on every subject and every period of history. She once made the comment that she felt like she had had an education in law after typing her daughter Ann's law school papers and a theological education from typing C.P.'s seminary papers.

She was a proud and affectionate grandmother and a lover of most sports, but her favorite was college basketball (her favorite team, of course, the Duke Blue Devils). She also enjoyed sewing, cooking, playing bridge, ballroom dancing, and traveling. She visited many parts of the world on episcopal visits, UMCOR travels, and personal journeys. She was a person of deep and abiding faith, and she loved the UMC. She often expressed her hope that the church would continue to expand its outreach ministries and become truly inclusive.

For three years before her death, Mary Ann suffered severe symptoms of Parkinson's disease, but demonstrated undying faith and patience. When her doctor shared with her that the end of her life was near, she asked for hospice to come and care for her during her remaining days. Two years before the end of her earthly life she had planned her memorial service, selecting the scripture passages, the hymns and the solos she wanted in the service. Two nights before her death, four of her grandchildren stood beside her bed and sang for her all of the music that she had selected for her service of resurrection. At the end, as throughout her life, she bore witness to this truth: "Even though I walk through the valley of the shadow of death, I fear no evil; for thou art with me" Psalm 23:4a (RSV).

—*Biographical Directory*, 2004–2008;
https://www.dignitymemorial.com/obituaries/raleigh-nc/mary-minnick-5523902;
"A Service of Remembrance and Hope," Council of Bishops, November 10, 2013;
email communications with son Jay Minnick, August 2017

Gerlinde Johanna Mueller Minor (b. 1938)

In 1964, Gerlinde married Rüdiger Rainer Minor 1939–2017). Rüdiger was elected in 1986 out of the Middle German Annual Conference, while serving as director of the United Methodist Theological Seminary, Bad Klosterlausnitz. He was assigned to the Dresden Episcopal Area in 1986 and, as episcopal coordinator, to the Commonwealth of Independent States (Russia and its neighbor countries) in 1991, with the task of reorganizing Methodist work after Communism. He was elected bishop of the Eurasia Episcopal Area in 1993 and served the newly emerging church until his retirement in 2005. Gerlinde and Rüdiger settled in Dresden, Germany. They have three children, nine grandchildren, and one great-grandchild.

Gerlinde, born in Germany, grew up in difficult times during World War II. Bombardments destroyed churches and schools, and often they had nothing to eat and could not get clothing. She attended school under the socialist system of the German Democratic Republic. As a Christian, it was not easy to get higher education. A fourth generation Methodist, grandchild of Methodist preachers, she found faith at an early age. She worked as a medical assistant and was active in Methodist youth work, both in her home church and on the ecumenical level. She served as a delegate to European Youth Conferences, taught Sunday school, sang in youth quartettes and choirs, and acted in church plays. As a volunteer, she pursued her interests in politics, ecumenism, languages, and social issues in several different countries. She was Rüdiger's only caregiver while he struggled with ALS. Now she is grateful for the beautiful landscape in which she lives and works and for the support of their family and church community. "Thanks be to God!"

Favorite Hymn Lyrics: "Christ, from Whom All Blessings Flow" (UMH, 550, st. 6)

—*Biographical Directory*, 2012–2016; email communication with Gerlinde Minor, January 2018; email communication with Urs Schweizer, assistant to Bishop Dr. Patrick Streiff, October 2018

Clara Aull Mitchell (1855–1944)

In 1888, Clara married Charles Bayard Mitchell (1857–1942). After serving large Methodist Episcopal churches in eight different annual conferences from New Jersey to Minnesota, Charles was elected in 1916 and served the St. Paul Episcopal Area (1916–1924), then was sent to the Philippines, where he served until his retirement in 1928.

—https://ar.billiongraves.com/grave/Clara-Aull-Mitchell/11941019; https://en.wikipedia.org/wiki/Charles_Bayard_Mitchell

Wife of Eric Algernon Mitchell

In 1946, a woman, whose first name we were unable to find, married Eric Algernon Mitchell (1917–1997). Eric, born in India, was elected in 1969, while serving as pastor in the Bengal Annual Conference, by the Central Conference of The Methodist Church in Southeast Asia. He was assigned to the Hyderabad Episcopal Area. Mrs. Mitchell and Eric had one son.

—*Encyclopedia of World Methodism, Vol. 2*, 1649

Jewell Lena Wells Moncure (b. 1947)

In 1967, Jewell married Rhymes H. Moncure Jr (1945–2006). Rhymes was elected in 2000 out of the Missouri East Annual Conference and served the Dallas Episcopal Area until his death in 2006. Jewell and Rhymes have two children and four grandchildren.

Jewell graduated from the University of Missouri, St. Louis, Missouri, with an MA in counseling. She has worked as a guidance counselor in Missouri, Kansas, Nebraska, and Texas school districts. Jewell is a member of Ousley UMC in Stonecrest, Georgia, a dedicated Stephen Minister Leader, and an active member of UMW. She volunteers in the DeKalb County schools and library. Recent travels include trips to South Korea, China, Ghana, Zimbabwe, Brazil, Dubai, Australia, and New Zealand.

Favorite Scripture: Psalm 46:1 / Favorite Hymn: "Give Me a Clean Heart" (*TFWS*, 2133)

—*Biographical Directory*, 2004–2008;
email communication with Jewell Moncure, August 2017

Carolyn Belle Osburn Mondol (1901–1987)

In 1929, Carolyn married Shot Kumar Mondol (1896–1985). In 1940, he became the second citizen of India to be elected bishop in The Methodist Church there. He served the newly created Hyderabad Episcopal Area (1940–1956) and the Delhi Episcopal Area (1956–1965), then retired. He also served the Manila Episcopal Area as an interim in 1966. Carolyn and Shot retired in Dayton, Ohio. They had three sons.

Carolyn was born in the U.S., but spent part of her childhood in India, where her father, a building engineer and missionary, was working for The Methodist Church. Carolyn attended the University of Southern California and then was commissioned to be a missionary in India, where she met Shot. She was president of the All-India Woman's Society of Christian Service for 12 years and also traveled with her husband.

—*Biographical Directory*, 1984;
https://www.geni.com/people/Carolyn-Carrie-Mondol/6000000024805992550

Martha Storey Morgan (b. 1938)

In 1958, Martha married Robert Crawley Morgan (1933–2014). Bob was elected in 1984 out of the North Alabama Annual Conference and served the Mississippi

Episcopal Area (1984–1992) and the Louisville Episcopal Area (1992–2000), then retired. Martha and Bob returned to Birmingham, Alabama. They have four children and nine grandchildren.

Martha studied piano at Mississippi State College for Women and at Franklin Academy in Columbus, Mississippi, and gave a graduate piano recital at the academy. She majored in religion at Birmingham-Southern College and received an honorary Doctor of Humanities degree from UM-related Rust College in Mississippi. Her main involvement in the churches and episcopal areas where Bob served was with music and worship. Martha especially enjoyed entertaining in their home. During the 10 years Bob taught at Birmingham-Southern College, Martha prepared a meal for his students twice each semester because having people in their home allowed them all to get to know one another.

—*Biographical Directory*, 2004–2008;
email communication with Martha Morgan, August 2017

Bessie Harris Moore (1892–1956)

In 1901, Bessie married John Monroe Moore (1867–1948). John was elected in The Methodist Episcopal Church, South, in 1918, while serving as secretary of the Department of Home Missions of the M.E.C.S. He was assigned to supervise work in Brazil (1918–1922), then Oklahoma and eastern Texas (1922–1926), western Texas and New Mexico (1926–1930), Georgia and Florida (1930–1934), and Missouri and Arkansas (1934–1938). John is noted for his work toward union (see J. A. Earl, "Bishop John M. Moore: Premier Prophet of Methodist Union," *The Christian Education Bulletin* [February 1953], 6). He retired in 1938.

Bessie was born in Texas and educated at the Coronal Institute of San Marcos and the Waco Female College. She was organist at Travis Park Church in San Antonio, Texas, when she met and married John. They served First Church in Dallas for four years, during which she endeared herself to the community. They moved to Nashville when John was elected managing editor of the *Christian Advocate*, then to St. Louis, Missouri, when he was appointed pastor of St. John's Church. There she became "queen of the parsonage" again. In 1910, the General Conference elected John mission secretary, which took them back to Nashville again, where she stayed after his election and assignment to foreign service in 1918 until his assignment to Dallas in 1922. She made her home in Dallas the rest of her life and was active in church and community, including the Women's Society of Christian Service and many social groups, such as the Dallas Women's Club, Daughters of the American Revolution, and others.

—http://prabook.com/web/person-view.html?profileId=279658;
Yearbook and Minutes of the Southwest Texas Annual Conference, The Methodist Church, 1942, 92–93; http://explorekyhistory.ky.gov/items/show/279

Carolyn Lee Moore (1904–1985)

In 1926, Carolyn married Noah Watson Moore Jr (1902–1994). Noah was elected in 1960 out of the Delaware Annual Conference of the Central Jurisdiction and served the Gulf Coast Episcopal Area (1960–1968) and the Nebraska Episcopal Area (1968–1972), then retired. Carolyn and Noah had one child, a daughter, two grandchildren, and one great grandchild.

Carolyn attended the Princess Anne Academy (now University of Maryland Eastern Shore), a Methodist school serving African American youth. She met Noah there. She took courses at Temple University for Home Service Work with the American Red Cross and worked with families who had soldiers overseas during World War II. In Nebraska, she worked with the Salvation Army, ringing bells on street corners soliciting donations to help the poor. She was also active in the church, participating in the ministries of the Women's Society, the Guild, and Ministers' Wives, and working with youth. She was a life member of the National Council of Negro Women, Inc. She had a beautiful soprano voice and enjoyed playing the piano and singing both at home and in churches.

—*Biographical Directory*, 1992;
Southern New Jersey Annual Conference Journal 1986, 286–287

Martha J. McDonald Moore (1884–1964)

In 1906, "Mattie" married Arthur James Moore (1888–1974). Arthur was elected in 1930 in The Methodist Episcopal Church, South, after serving churches in Georgia, Texas, and Alabama, and also as a roving evangelist. As bishop, he supervised the Pacific Coast Area (1930-1934); missionary activity in China, Japan, Czechoslovakia, Belgium, Belgian Congo, Poland, and Korea (1934–1940); the Atlanta Episcopal Area of The Methodist Church comprising Georgia and Florida (1941–1948); and Georgia (1948–1960). Mattie and Arthur had five children.

Mattie received an honorary Doctor of Laws degree from La Grange College. She traveled internationally, speaking in churches and mission outposts. She authored a number of articles in national publications.

—https://en.wikipedia.org/wiki/Arthur_James_Moore; http://socialarchive.iath.virginia.edu/ark:/99166/w62j7r0q; handwritten death notice in Arthur James Moore's administrative file at the UM Archives and History Center

Mary Virginia Head Morris (1934–2005)

In 1969, Mary married William Wesley Morris (1937–2015). William was elected in 1992 out of the Tennessee Annual Conference and served the Alabama-West Florida Episcopal Area (1992–2000) and the Nashville Episcopal Area (2000–2004), then retired. Mary and William had four children.

Mary graduated from Bennett College in Greensboro, North Carolina, and received an MA from New York University as a reading specialist. She worked as a reading coordinator teacher in elementary, junior high, high schools, and in college. She also served as principal of Haynes Elementary School. Her church activities included serving as children's coordinator, serving as a district officer of the UMW, and teaching in several Schools of Mission. Her favorite activities included reading, attending Sunday school, and teaching the Bible course in Schools of Mission.

—*Biographical Directory*, 1996; *Alabama-West Florida Conference Journal* for 2005, 481; http://www.gcumm.org/news/in-memoriam-bishop-william-w-morris/; https://obits.tennessean.com/obituaries/tennessean/obituary.aspx?pid=177321936

Princilla Smart Evans Morris (b. 1950)

In October of 2006, Princilla married retired Bishop William Wesley Morris (1937–2016). Bill had four children with his first wife, Mary, who died in 2005.

Professionally, Princilla has worked in higher education continuously for 41 years. She started as an instructor of pharmacology at Meharry Medical College. She participated in studies of abnormal growth (keloid research) and partnered with her first husband, Dr. Stanley L. Evans, in anti-cancer drug synthesis and discovery. They were married for 27 and one-half years until his sudden death in 1999. Princilla moved across the street and began teaching chemistry at Fisk University. There, she taught graduate and undergraduate students, served as the first female chair of the Department of Chemistry, became director of Graduate Studies, and held the title dean of General Education and Graduate Studies just prior to her appointment as executive vice president and provost. Presently, she serves as the first executive director of the Center for Teaching and Learning and is the Commission on Colleges of the Southern Association of Colleges and Schools liaison for Fisk.

At her church home, Clark Memorial UMC in Nashville, Princilla is an instructor for the New Members Orientation Class, teaches Sunday school, brings Children's Church messages monthly, and serves as the co-chair of the Room in the Inn Ministry. In the summer, she works with crafts in Vacation Bible School. Additionally, she is a member of the board for the Fisk University Wesley Foundation. Princilla has also provided "food for thought" in the Saints and Sinners Sunday School Class at First UMC in Gallatin. Her passion is teaching, and she gives God all glory and honor for the gifts He freely gave her.

In her spare time, Princilla enjoys being creative. She cooks (and is known for her homemade rolls), sews, makes wall hangings in mixed media, and claims to have earned a PhD in home decorating by paying close attention while watching HGTV.

Favorite Scripture: Psalm 121:1-2

—*Biographical Directory*, 1996; https://obits.tennessean.com/obituaries/tennessean/obituary.aspx?pid=177321936;
email communication with Princilla Morris, March 2018

Karen Goodman Mueller (b. 1952)

In 2016, Karen married Bishop Gary E. Mueller (b. 1953). Gary was elected bishop in 2012 out of the North Texas Annual Conference and assigned to the Arkansas Episcopal Area starting in 2016. Karen and Gary share four children and two grandchildren.

Karen earned her BA in business administration from Stephen F. Austin State University in Nacogdoches, Texas. She worked in various business offices before settling into education. Karen is a retired teacher with a special interest in the area of gifted and talented education. Since retirement, Karen has specialized in grandparenting, with side interests of quilting, gardening and reading.

Favorite Scripture: Psalm 139 / Favorite Hymn: "Here I Am, Lord" (*UMH*, 593)

—*Biographical Directory*, 2012;
email communication with Karen Mueller, July 2017

Magdalene Stauffacher Mueller (1892–1975)

In 1919, Magdalene married Reuben Herbert Mueller (1897–1982). Reuben was elected in 1954 in the Evangelical United Brethren Church after serving in Minneapolis and Indiana. He served an episcopal area that included Canada, Germany, Indiana, Michigan, and Switzerland, then retired in 1972. Magdalene and Reuben had one daughter and one grandchild.

Magdalene was born in Wisconsin, received a degree from North Central College, and taught in public schools. Active in the church, she corresponded extensively with missionaries and prepared manuals, guides, and teaching aids for Christian education teachers. She also provided secretarial service in the General Church Office in Cleveland. She was active in Eastern Star, the American Association of University Women, UMW and its antecedents, the Women's Christian Temperance Union, and the Women's Department Club of Indianapolis. In 1971, Indiana Central University conferred upon her an honorary degree, Doctor of Humane Letters. She was also known as a gracious hostess and a helpful traveling companion to her husband.

—https://www.findagrave.com/memorial/50650044;
Minutes of the North Indiana Annual Conference, 1983, 1967–1968;
Journal of the South Indiana Conference, 1976, 242–243

Etta Mae McClurg Mutti (b. 1938)

In 1959, Etta Mae married Albert Frederick Mutti III (b. 1938). Fritz was elected in 1992 out of the Missouri West Conference and served the Kansas Episcopal Area

(1992–2004), then retired and returned to Missouri. Etta Mae and Fritz have three sons: Tim, Fred, and Marty.

Etta Mae attended Northwest Missouri State University and has enjoyed a career as a church secretary. For a period of time, she operated her own transcribing business. She has been a Christian Education Laboratory leader and frequently leads small-group experiences in the church. She has published a book of recipes and is noted for her sensitivity as a listener. She is a strong advocate for the oppressed and a courageous worker for justice. When two of their sons, Tim and Fred, died of AIDS, her faith and courage were exemplary. Etta Mae and Fritz are the authors of a book, *Dancing in a Wheelchair* (Nashville: Abingdon, 2001), about that experience.

Etta Mae served as a "very part-time" coordinator of the UM Global AIDS Fund (UMGAF) in its first quadrennium, while her husband was chair. The UMGAF was established by vote of the 2004 General Conference, and its mandate was renewed for eight more years by the General Conference in 2016. The responsibilities of the UMGAF include educating the church about HIV and AIDS, advocating for persons living with HIV, and developing various programmatic efforts to help the church address HIV and AIDS as an integral dimension of global health. During the first 12 years, UMGAF raised approximately $3.5 million. Legislation urges annual conferences to keep and use 25 percent of funds raised in their conference, and the remaining 75 percent is administered through UMCOR (#982345). Etta Mae and Fritz have served as ambassadors for this project, traveling the world to share their story, lead workshops, and advocate for AIDS ministries, educating people about how to prevent the spread of the disease and encouraging support for those affected by it.

Favorite Scripture: Isaiah 40:27-31 / Favorite Hymn: "Be Thou My Vision" (*UMH*, 451)

—*Biographical Directory*, 2004–2008;
email communication with Etta Mae Mutti, May 2017

Maggie Muzorewa (1932–2009)

In 1951, Maggie married Abel Tendekayi Muzorewa (1925–2010). Abel was elected in 1968, the first African bishop of the UMC in Central Africa and served the Zimbabwe Episcopal Area (1968–1992), then retired. He also served briefly as the first Black prime minister of Zimbabwe-Rhodesia (1979–1980). Maggie and Abel had five children, 10 grandchildren, and one great-grandson.

Maggie was raised by a missionary couple at Old Mutare Methodist Mission in Zimbabwe. She served as matron of a girls' boarding school there before following her husband to the U.S., where he was a student. When they returned to Zimbabwe, she provided strong leadership for the UMW through revival meetings, retreats, music, preaching, and self-help projects for women. Her memoir in the Council of

Bishops Memorial Booklet for November 2009 includes this statement: "The Zimbabwe [Episcopal] Area best remembers her prayerfulness, unassuming nature, exceptional generosity, hospitality and an industrious passion for gardening and caring for poultry. She was also courageous, fearlessly speaking out when Abel and later two sons were unjustly detained. In exile, during Zimbabwe's liberation armed struggle, Maggie volunteered at Maputo Hospital (Mozambique), where the wounded were brought from the war front. She then went to Nashville, Tennessee, for safety and in 1979 she returned to Zimbabwe to assume the role of First Lady of the nation of Zimbabwe." Among her interests were improving social consciousness, music, preaching, raising poultry, sewing and church activities in general.

—*Biographical Directory*, 2000–2004, 2008–2012;
Council of Bishops Memorial Booklet, November 2009;
https://www.britannica.com/biography/Abel-Tendekayi-Muzorewa

Angelina Baron del Rosario Nacpil (1929–2017)

In 1956, Angelina married Emerito Pimental Nacpil (b. 1932). Emerito was elected in 1980 out of the Philippines Annual Conference, while serving as executive director of the Association of Theological Schools in Southeast Asia and dean of the Southeast Asia Graduate School of Theology. He served the Manila Episcopal Area (1980–2000), then retired. Angelina and Emerito have three children.

Angelina studied at Harris Memorial College, the same school for deaconesses where her mother had studied. After graduation and consecration as a deaconess, she was assigned to a local church in Tarlac province in Central Luzon, where she met Emerito, who was working as janitor there to pay for his studies to become a pastor. After their marriage, she worked as a babysitter and as a reader for the blind and elderly. Later she took up library science and became a cataloguer and then librarian at Union Theological Seminary. She also raised pigs and smoked mango trees in order to help provide for the education of their three children. Throughout Emerito's years of service, Angelina supported and encouraged him. At her memorial service, Daniel Arichea said of her, "A God-fearing woman, she always believed that God had a purpose for putting her and her family in a position of leadership in the church. In fact, service to the Lord with commitment became her life's goal. She was very much involved in women's activities, giving inspirational messages, and if needed, representing her husband. At Christmas time, she and the other bishops' spouses would raise money to help support and give gifts to church workers and their families. But her support was not limited to church workers. As her daughter Cynthia put it during the necrological service, her mother repeatedly told them to never refuse anyone who came to them for help, and she repeatedly demonstrated this to them."

—*Biographical Directory*, 2012; memorial by Daniel Arichea, Council of Bishops Memorial Service, November 2017

Melvena M. Morris Nagbe (1935–2018)

In 1958, Melvena married Stephen Trowen-Weati Nagbe Sr (1933–1973). They came to Atlanta, Georgia, for three years of study and returned to serve a pastorate in Liberia in 1961. Stephen was elected in 1965 and served the Liberia Episcopal Area until his death in 1973. Melvena and Stephen had three children and three grandchildren.

Melvena, born in Liberia, graduated from Cuttington College there with a degree in Christian education. She worked with the UMW in Liberia and taught in local schools. She served as conference officer for UMW there and also in Florida, where she lived later. While living in Daytona Beach, Florida, she worked at Bethune-Cookman College as a foreign student advisor and counselor. She later moved to Smyrna, Georgia, where she stayed active in a local UM church. Her interests included reading and being with people.

—*Biographical Directory*, 1984, 1996; telephone conversation and email communication with daughter Melvena Nagbe, July 2018

Frances M. Mahaffie Nall (1902–1999)

In 1929, Frances married Torney Otto Nall Jr (1900–1989). Otto was elected bishop in 1960 out of the North Central Jurisdiction and served the Minnesota Episcopal Area (1960–1968). He continued in active service in order to administer the Hong Kong-Taiwan Episcopal Area, preparing the conferences in those regions for autonomy. After retirement, Frances and Otto wrote five books. They had two daughters and three granddaughters.

Frances earned an AB from DePauw University, an AM from the University of Illinois, and a LittD from Iowa Wesleyan College. She taught weekday religious education (1929–1941), was professor of European history at Kendall College (1941–1952), and edited the Methodist Bulletin Service for Abingdon Press (1943–1961). She also wrote church school lessons for junior high youth and 10 books published by Friendship Press and Abingdon Press. She held offices in UMW, from local to national levels, and was vice president of the Women's Division (1956–1960). She was secretary of the World Federation of Methodist Women (1961–1966) and a member of the Word Family Life Committee. She served as a trustee of Pfeiffer College and on the boards of several honorary and scholastic societies. She was also active in her local church, serving on many different committees.

Among the books written or co-authored by Frances Nall: *One Church for One World; A Course for Intermediate or Junior High School Groups in Vacation Church*

Schools (with Olive L. Johnson, 1951); *This Globe—a Neighborhood: An Elective Unit for Intermediates, for Use in Church Schools, Christian Adventure Weeks, and Special Groups* (with Henry M. Bullock, 1953); *The Church in Today's World* (with Olive L. Johnson, 1959); *The Church Through the Centuries* (1949); *One World—One Family* (1946); and *When Are We Patriotic?* (two units in weekday religious education for Christian citizenship series for grades seven and eight, 1940).

—*Biographical Directory*, 1984; https://www.geni.com/people/Frances-Nall-Dr/327221517710006972; https://www.worldcat.org/search?q=au%3ANall%2C+Frances+M.&qt=hot_author; https://www.journals.uchicago.edu/doi/abs/10.1086/482648?mobileUi=0&

Sabine Ngeza Ndoricimpa (1943–2011)

In 1972, Sabine married John Alfred Ndoricimpa (1946–2005). John was elected in 1980 out of the Evangelical Episcopal Church in Burundi and led the negotiations that brought his church into the Africa Central Conference of the UMC in 1984. Sabine and John were forced to move to Kenya in March 1994, after the 1993 assassination of the first democratically elected president in Burundi, President Melchoir Ndadaye. Since John had served as his spiritual advisor, he was warned that his life might be in danger. During his time in Kenya, the bishop continued to work with the church in Burundi and expanded mission into Kenya, Rwanda, Tanzania, Uganda, and Sudan. Those areas are now part of the East Africa Conference. John and Sabine returned to Burundi in 2000, by which time the conflict between Hutu and Tutsi tribes had claimed some 200,000 lives, and he served there until his death. Sabine and John have two children.

Sabine graduated from Lyceé Notre Dame of Bujumbura, a Roman Catholic Mission school, with a diploma in accounting. She went to work with the Commercial Bank of Burundi and later worked as the manager of Gitega Branch. She was active in and generously supportive of the church and from 1984 through 2010 served as president of the UMW's organization in the Burundi Annual Conference, which later became the East Africa Annual Conference. She suffered from diabetes for over 30 years and for 11 of those years survived on dialysis, but never missed Sunday worship, even when in pain. She is described as "a brave and courageous woman of God" (Council of Bishops Memorial Booklet, November 2013).

—*Biographical Directory*, 2000–2004; http://archive.wfn.org/2005/08/msg00006.html

Emily Louise Lewis Newell (1892–1978)

In 1919, Emily married Frederick Buckley Newell (1890–1979). Frederick was elected in 1952 out of the New York East Annual Conference of The Methodist Church and served the New York Episcopal Area (1952–1960), then retired. He served as interim bishop for the Pittsburgh Episcopal Area (1965–1968). Emily and Frederick had two children, eight grandchildren, and five great-grandchildren.

Emily was born in New Jersey but grew up in Hartford, Connecticut, where she met Frederick, a student at Wesleyan University. After their marriage, she assisted him with his work for the New York City Society, a missionary project of The Methodist Church, and served in her local church and beyond. She served on the Board of Managers for The Methodist Home in the Riverdale section of New York City—and as its secretary for 15 years. She represented the Women's Missionary Society on the Board of Trustees for the Methodist Hospital of Santo Domingo and was also conference president of the New York East Women's Society of Christian Service. After Frederick's election, she traveled extensively with him throughout their area and abroad. As noted in the 1978 Western Pennsylvania Conference Journal, "She became a confidant to ministers' wives wherever she went, providing support, encouragement and counsel to parsonage families."

—https://www.findagrave.com/memorial/79289554; https://en.wikipedia.org/wiki/Frederick_Buckley_Newell; *Journal of the 181st Session of the New York Annual Conference, 1980*, 256–257; *Official Journal and Yearbook Western Pennsylvania Annual Conference, 1978*, 414–415

Thelma Heard Newman (1923–2017)

Thelma married Ernest Wilbur Newman (1928–2008). Ernest was elected in 1984 out of the Florida Annual Conference and served the Nashville Episcopal Area (1984–1992), then retired. He was the first Black bishop elected by the Southeastern Jurisdictional Conference since the formation of the UMC in 1968. Thelma and Ernest had two children, five grandchildren, and seven great-grandchildren.

Thelma graduated from Clark College and did graduate work at Atlanta University and Florida State University. She taught school in Atlanta, Georgia, and in Ocala, Jacksonville, Melbourne and Ft. Lauderdale, Florida. She devoted much time to civic and community activities, including registering voters and working at the polls during elections, and was deeply involved in UMW.

—*Biographical Directory*, 2000–2004; http://www.legacy.com/obituaries/atlanta/obituary.aspx?page=lifestory&pid=185299630; https://tinyurl.com/y64eb2xk; https://www.umnews.org/en/news/2017-remembering-notable-church-members; email communication with daughter Kathy McCoy, October 2017

Blandine Mujinga Ngoy [Muyombo] (b. 1975)

In 2002, Blandine married Mande Muyombo (b. 1972). Mande was elected in 2017 out of the North Katanga, Tanganyika, and Tanzania Annual Conferences. The first graduate of Africa University to be elected bishop, he had been serving as executive director for Global Mission. He was assigned to the North Katanga Episcopal Area in the Democratic Republic of Congo. Blandine and Mande have four children.

Blandine has a BA in education. Currently she is at home with her children, since they are young. She looks forward to working with pastors' spouses in general and especially with those who are widows and widowers. She wants to empower them to use their skills to be financially independent and to be able to send their children to school. Many pastors' spouses who are widows or widowers rely mostly on the church for financial support, which she would like to change by helping them earn their own income. She also has a passion for working with orphans.

Favorite Scripture: Psalm 139:23-24

—https://www.umnews.org/en/news/muyombo-elected-bishop-in-congo; email communication with Blandine Ngoy, May and June 2017

Greater Taremeredzwa Munesi Nhiwatiwa (b. 1950)

In 1979, Greater married Eben K. Nhiwatiwa (b. 1949). Eben was elected in 2004 out of the Zimbabwe Episcopal Area, to which he was assigned. Greater and Eben have one child.

Greater completed her diploma in nursing from Bonda School of Nursing, Zimbabwe, and graduated with a BS in occupational health and safety (OHS), with a minor in biology, from Illinois State University, Normal, Illinois. She later graduated with a diploma in OHS specializing in safety in forestry from the National Institute for Working Life in Sweden. She worked for a long time as a factories inspector in the government of Zimbabwe. After taking early retirement from the government, she worked with the Family AIDS Caring Trust (FACT), monitoring and evaluating orphans and vulnerable children of AIDS victims in Zimbabwe. Currently Greater's main activities as a bishop's spouse include working with and leading the UMC women in the episcopal area.

Favorite Scripture: Jeremiah 29:11 / Favorite Hymn: "Amazing Grace" (*UMH*, 378)

—*Biographical Directory*, 2004–2008; email communication with Greater Nhiwatiwa, 5/21/2017

Ruth Richardson Nichols (1920–2006)

In 1944, Ruth married Roy Calvin Nichols (1918–2002). Roy was elected in 1968 and served the Pittsburgh Episcopal Area (1968–1980) and the New York Episcopal Area (1980–1984), then retired. Ruth and Roy had three children, seven grandchildren, and three great-grandchildren.

Ruth, born in Spokane, Washington, attended the Eastern Washington College of Education. After graduating from the California College of Podiatric Medicine, she practiced as a podiatrist for 20 years in San Francisco and Berkeley. Ruth always showed her concern for youth, as a Sunday school superintendent, counselor for various youth groups, teacher of confirmation classes, Campfire Girls' leader, and president of Parent Teacher Associations. She was also active in other community and church programs: teaching in Schools of Mission, serving on YWCA Boards, organizing programs for local American Association of University Women groups, and giving of herself in many ways. She was a world traveler. Her hobbies included hiking and backpacking, especially in the Sierras; collecting wooden elephants from various parts of the world; coordinating table settings; and dressmaking. She served as a docent in the Natural Science Gallery of the Oakland City Museum, on the Alameda County Grand Jury for two consecutive one-year terms, and as chairperson of the Scholarship Committee of Delta Sigma Theta Sorority.

—*Biographical Directory*, 2000–2004; Council of Bishops Memorial Booklet Spring 2007; http://archive.wfn.org/2002/10/msg00135.html

Evelyn Riley Nicholson (1873–1967)

In 1917, Evelyn married Bishop Thomas Nicholson (1862–1944). Thomas was elected in 1916 and served the Chicago Episcopal Area (1916–1924) and the Detroit Episcopal Area (1924–1932), then retired. Thomas had two children with his first wife, Jane Boothroyd, who died in 1915.

Evelyn was a missionary leader and peace advocate. She graduated Phi Beta Kappa from DePauw University in Indiana. After graduate studies, she taught at Crandon International Institute in Rome and spent a year at the American School for Classical Studies, where she also edited *Roman World.* She was a teacher and head of the Latin Department at Cornell College in Iowa (1906–1917). She was co-founder and president of the Woman's Foreign Missionary Society of The Methodist Episcopal Church. She was a member of other international organizations as well, such as the International Missionary Council and the World Alliance for International Friendship through the Churches. In 1924, Abingdon Press published a book by Evelyn, titled *The Way to a Warless World.*

—https://www.amazon.com/warless-world-Evelyn-Riley-Nicholson/dp/B0008BZD8U; https://billiongraves.com/grave/Evelyn-Riley-Nicholson/16331471; *Encyclopedia of World Methodism, Vol.* 2 1754–1755; Charles Yrigoyen Jr and Susan E. Warrick, *Historical Dictionary of Methodism* [Scarecrow Press, 2013], 271; 1967 Rock River Conference Journal, 293

Nshimba Ntambo Nkula [Ntanda] (b. 1950)

In 1967, Nshimba married Ntambo Nkulu Ntanda (b. 1947). Ntambo was elected in 1996 out of the North Sheba Annual Conference and served the North Katanga Episcopal Area of the Democratic Republic of Congo (1996–2016), then retired. Nshimba and Ntambo have eight children.

Nshimba was born in Lubumbashi and attended college. She provides training for pastors' wives, counsels with church members, and works with groups of UMW. She maintains a hospitable home for visitors, who have included many government officials, ministers, bishops, and missionaries. She also created a foundation for orphans, serving 300 children.

—*Biographical Directory*, 2012–2016; https://www.westohioumc.org/conference/news/bishop-ntambo-nkulu-retirement; interview with Bishop Ntanda, February 2018 and November 2019

Mackie L. Harper Norris

In 1961, Mackie married Alfred L. Norris Sr. Alfred was elected in 1992 out of the Louisiana Annual Conference while serving as president/dean of Gammon Theological Seminary in Atlanta, Georgia. He served the Northwest Texas/New Mexico Episcopal Area (1992–2000) and the Houston Episcopal Area (2000–2004), then retired. In retirement, he served an interim assignment as bishop of the Dallas Episcopal Area (2006–2008). Mackie and Alfred live in Georgia. They have two children and four grandchildren.

Mackie graduated from Dillard University in New Orleans, Louisiana, with a BS in nursing. Mackie shares in her spouse's ministry and she is also engaged in her own calling as a nurse, serving as practitioner, educator, consultant, and health promoter. She received MSN and PhD degrees from Emory University, where she spent several years as a faculty member and was the first African American to hold a faculty appointment in the Nell Hodgson Woodruff School of Nursing at Emory University. She continues to use her education as a professional nurse to assist in raising the level of wellness for individuals, families, communities, and other aggregates. She has a particular passion for clergy spouses and families and is frequently called upon to lead seminars, retreats, workshops, and other gatherings that focus on health and wholeness.

Mackie also served as a consultant with the General Board of Global Ministries division on Health and Relief in the mid 1990s, developing information and guidelines for Congregational Health Ministries. Later she served as an evaluation consultant with the Council of Bishop's Initiative on Children and Poverty. In 2002, she served as a consultant for the Commission on the Role and Status of Women (COSROW), updating information on UM Clergy Spouses as COSROW prepared for the 2004 General Conference. She also served as a consultant with the General Board of Pensions and Health Benefits (2008–2010), as a part of the Church Systems Task Force. Mackie H. Norris wrote all 28 devotionals for the month of February for the 2010 and 2011 editions of *African American History Month Daily Devotions* (Nashville: Abingdon Press, 2009, 2010).

—*Biographical Directory*, 2004–2008;
interview with Mackie Norris, 2016, and email communication, 2017

Florence Engle Northcott (1891–1970)

In 1917, Florence married Harry Clifford Northcott (1890–1976). Clifford was elected in 1948 out of the Rock River Annual Conference and served the Wisconsin Episcopal Area of The Methodist Church (1948–1960), then retired. Florence and Clifford had one daughter and two grandchildren.

Florence was born in Abilene, Kansas, lived next door to the Eisenhower family, and was a schoolmate and lifelong friend of President Eisenhower. She attended Western College for Women in Oxford, Ohio, for two years and then transferred to the University of Kansas in Lawrence, where she graduated with a BS. She taught high school English in Kansas for two years prior to her marriage, which took place while Clifford was in Army training, having enlisted during World War I. Florence and Clifford met at a church summer camp at Lake Geneva, where they were both in leadership positions. Florence was active in the church, including the Women's Society of Christian Service, and traveled extensively with her husband, to England in 1935 and after his election, to Africa, Southeast Asia, and South America.

—http://prabook.com/web/person-view.html?profileId=1099249;
Encyclopedia of World Methodism, Vol. 2, 1779;
Yearbook and Journal Wisconsin Annual Conference, 1970, 384

Mary Louise Nunn (b. 1958)

In 1978, Mary married James Gregg Nunn (b. 1956). James was elected in 2016 out of the Northwest Texas Annual Conference and assigned to the Oklahoma Episcopal Area. Mary and James have two children and one grandchild.

Mary earned a BA in music from McMurry University and an MA in Christian education from Asbury Theological Seminary. She works full-time teaching piano at a private school and at her music studio. She also enjoys working out in the gym and swimming.

Favorite Scripture: Proverbs 3:5-6 / Favorite Hymn: "Joyful, Joyful, We Adore Thee" (*UMH*, 89)

—email communication with Mary Nunn, July 2017

Marilyn Brown Oden (b. 1937)

In 1957, Marilyn married William B. Oden (1935–2018). Bill was elected out of the Oklahoma Annual Conference in 1988. He served the Louisiana Episcopal Area (1988–1996) and the Dallas Episcopal Area (1996–2004), then retired, serving as ecumenical officer for the Council of Bishops until 2008. Marilyn and Bill settled in Santa Fe, New Mexico. They have four children and four grandchildren.

Marilyn holds MAs in counseling and creative writing and received the Distinguished Achievement Award from Dillard University in New Orleans. She worked as a teacher, school counselor, director of volunteers for an urban school system, and district liaison for a U.S. congressman.

Marilyn is the award-winning author of three novels: *Crested Butte: A Novel* (2000), *The Dead Saint* (2010), and *The Santa Fe Secret* (2018). She has also published nine nonfiction books: *The Minister's Wife: Person or Position* (1966), *Beyond Feminism: The Woman of Faith in Action* (1971), *The Courage to Care* (1979), *Wilderness Wanderings: A Lenten Pilgrimage* (1988), *Through the East Window: Prayers and Promises for Dealing with Loss* (1988), *Land of Sickles and Crosses: The United Methodist Initiative in the Commonwealth of Independent States* (1992), *Manger and Mystery: An Advent Adventure* (1999), *Abundance: Joyful Living in Christ* (2002), and *Hospitality of the Heart* (2002). Marilyn has also written 25 seasonal devotions and articles on varied topics: gratitude, homelessness, the empty nest, jury duty, leadership, Russian Methodism, and clergy spouses. Some of her writings are translated into Russian and Indonesian. Marilyn taught spiritual formation at Perkins School of Theology (2004–2008), leads workshops on Christian hospitality for local congregations and annual conferences, and has been the McCormick Lecturer (Lovers Lane UMC, Dallas), the Fenn Lecturer (Central UMC, Albuquerque), and the Holland Lecturer (Crown Heights UMC, Oklahoma City). She has served on several boards, including St. Paul School of Theology, and on the faculty for training new district superintendents and council directors.

Marilyn's life has been enriched through experiences on six continents with diverse people—refugees and royalty, women in prison and prime ministers, Gypsies and presidents. Working with Russians in a transitional long-term project, visiting refugee centers in the war zones of Bosnia-Herzegovina during the NATO bombing, and participating with Israelis and Palestinians in an ecumenical fact-finding peace delegation reshaped her worldview. She enjoys good times with family and friends, walking to the Santa Fe Plaza, and cross-country skiing in the moonlight.

—*Biographical Directory*, 2012–2016;
email communication with Marilyn Oden, May 2017

Nancy Kelley Oliphint (1927–2009)

In 1952, Nancy married Benjamin Ray Oliphint (1924–2007). Ben was elected in 1980 out of the North Texas Conference and served the Kansas Episcopal Area (1980–1984) and the Houston Episcopal Area (1984–1992). He retired in 1992, and they settled in Houston. Nancy and Ben had four children.

Nancy graduated from Louisiana State University with a BA in 1948. She then worked as traffic director for radio station KALB in her hometown, Alexandria,

Louisiana. When Ben concluded his year as associate pastor at First UMC there, they married and moved to Monroe, Louisiana, to start a new church. Nancy was active in UMW and enjoyed working with children, serving as hostess, and attending concerts and sports events. Her obituary states, "Nancy's kitchen was legendary. Countless persons have been served scrumptious meals and affirmed by her gracious hospitality. Hundreds have been comforted in time of need by her loaves of hot homemade bread. Multitudes have ecstatically discovered a 'foretaste of glory divine' in her magnificent desserts. When her family gathered around her table, it was as close to heaven on earth as possible. Nancy set a eucharistic table of graciousness and welcome; her Christ-like compassion and genuine concern for others will warm and inspire us always."

Her daughter, Mary Brooke Casad, shared, "Her favorite hymn was 'Leaning on the Everlasting Arms.' I remember her singing it and saying that this was the hymn that came to mind when she faced times of uncertainly and crisis. I remember our family singing it, gathered around my father's deathbed. When my father was elected bishop, a friend said to me, 'Everyone is saying that sure, Ben will be a good bishop, but won't Nancy make a great bishop's wife!' In both roles, as a pastor's wife and as a bishop's wife, she was able to be who she authentically was: a person of faith in Christ, who showed great compassion and care for others. To this day, I hear from people about the way she cared for them, or even just that she remembered their names, which she had an amazing ability to do."

—*Biographical Directory*, 2000–2004; https://www.legacy.com/obituaries/houstonchronicle/obituary.aspx?n=nancy-brooke-kelley-oliphint&pid=124419546; email communication with Mary Brooke Casad, 4/12/2017

Toril Olsen (b. 1946)

In 1967, Toril married Øystein Olsen (b. 1944). Øystein was elected in 2001 out of the Norway Annual Conference and served the Nordic and Baltic Episcopal Area (2001–2009), then retired. Toril and Øystein live in Norway. They have three children and seven grandchildren.

Toril has worked as a special education teacher for 43 years, first in elementary school, later in high school, and finally in a psychiatric clinic for youth. In the church, she has taught Sunday school, led mission groups and church choir, served as a member of church boards, and participated in Bible study groups. She has also served as co-chair of the Norway Annual Conference Women's Division. Toril enjoys gardening, cooking, baking, and knitting.

—*Biographical Directory*, 2012–2016; https://www.unitedmethodistbishops.org/person-detail/2464069; email communication with Bishop Olsen, November 2017

Ekoko L. Onema

In 1952, Ekoko married Fama Onema (b. 1936). Fama was elected in 1972 out of the Democratic Republic of Congo and served the all Congo Episcopal Area (1972–1976) and the Central Congo Episcopal Area 1976 until his retirement in 2005. Ekoko and Fama have nine children.

Ekoko was a student and had special class training for pastoral studies at the seminary which is part of the Methodist Patrice Emery Lumumba University in the Democratic Republic of Congo, graduating in 1994. She has served as a local pastor and has traveled many times within Africa and to Asia, Europe, and America. She was president of the Federation of Protestant Women in the Congo and was elected president of UMW several times. She was director of Social Affairs of the UMC since 1972 and a volunteer director of Young, Single Mothers at Kananga in the UM Social Center and in Kinshasa. She was a delegate to the General Conference six times and to the Africa Central Conference seven times.

—*Biographical Directory*, 2000–2004;
interview with Bishop Onema, November 2018

Janet Edith Pass Ott (1942–2015)

In 1963, Jan married Donald A. Ott (b. 1939). Don was elected out of the Wisconsin Annual Conference in 1992 and served the Michigan Episcopal Area (1992–2000), then retired. Don and Jan settled in Wisconsin. They have two children and seven grandchildren.

Janet graduated from Carroll College, held a teaching certificate, and was employed in education. She also worked in a counseling center, trust department office, and as an assistant to curators at the Milwaukee Zoological Park. As a volunteer, she served at a home for battered women, taught English as a second language, and presented recycling education in classrooms. She was also involved in congregational evangelism, missions, and small group ministries. Jan was known for her smile and genuine care for others, birthday greetings and notes, and love of reading.

—*Biographical Directory*, 2000–2004; Council of Bishops Memorial Booklet, November 2015; email communication with Don Ott, 2017

Charlene Ann Feldner Ough (b. 1947)

In 1976, Char married Bruce R. Ough (b. 1958). Bruce was elected in 2000 out of the Iowa Annual Conference and served the West Ohio Episcopal Area (2000–2012) and the Minnesota-Dakotas Episcopal Area starting in 2012. He also provides episcopal oversight of the UMC's mission in Vietnam, Laos and Thailand. Char and Bruce have three sons and four grandchildren.

Charlene received an Associate degree in secretarial science from the North Dakota School of Forestry and Liberal Arts and later received a BA in child development/family relations from North Dakota State University. Later she took graduate courses in social work at the University of Iowa. Char's first husband, Don Henning, drowned in a canoing accident when she was 26, leaving her with two young sons. Two years later Bruce came into their life, bringing joy and healing. Char has worked as director of social services in a Methodist hospital, counseling supervisor for recovering alcoholics at a detox center and halfway house, hospitality coordinator at a retreat center, minister of Christian education, and director of two preschools and a before/after school program. Char has served locally as a youth counselor, acolyte training coordinator, DISCIPLE Bible study leader, and member of various committees. She attended the two-year Upper Room Academy for Spiritual Formation. She has also been active in prison ministries, including the Kairos Outside program, and leads numerous retreats and workshops for women. She collects nativity sets and also enjoys travel, reading, movies, theater, concerts and sports events, especially the Big Ten.

—*Biographical Directory*, 2012–2016; email communication with Char Ough, 2017

Lavelle Owen (1933–2015)

In 1952, Lavelle married Raymond Harold Owen (1932–2010). Ray was elected in 1992 out of the Oklahoma Annual Conference and served the San Antonio Episcopal Area (1992–2000). Upon retirement, Ray and Lavelle settled in the Oklahoma City area to be closer to family. Lavelle and Ray had three children: Dana, the eldest, who died in 1973; Darryl and Dyton, both of whom are pastors; and four grandchildren.

Lavelle was a trained physician's assistant, secretary, salesperson, and cashier. For 10 years she gave herself tirelessly to volunteer work at the Jane Phillips Hospital and Medical Center in Bartlesville, Oklahoma. Throughout her life, she was unwavering in her support of Ray and his ministry, as well as providing a rock-solid foundation for her family. She was a certified Stephen Minister, and "quiet care-taker" of persons with special needs. Lavelle was a loving, gracious and generous mother, grandmother, and delightful friend. She was widely traveled and enjoyed walking, reading and creative handcrafts.

—*Biographical Directory*, 2012–2016; *Council of Bishops Memorial Booklet 2011*; http://www.scjumc.org/wp-content/uploads/2017/03/2016-SCJ-Journal.pdf; email communication with son Dr. Dyton L. Owen, August 2017

Ruth Fisher Oxnam (d. 1975)

In 1914, Ruth married Garfield Bromley Oxnam (1891–1963). G. Bromley was elected in 1936 out of the Southern California Annual Conference and served the

Omaha Episcopal Area (1936–1939), the Boston Episcopal Area (1939–1944), the New York Episcopal Area (1944-1952), and the Washington Episcopal Area (1952–1960), then retired. Ruth and G. Bromley had three children, eight grandchildren, and six great-grandchildren.

Ruth, a native of Nebraska, traveled the world with her husband.

—https://en.wikipedia.org/wiki/Garfield_Bromley_Oxnam; http://catalog.gcah.org/publicdata/gcah2412.htm;
Minutes of the 191st Annual Session of the Baltimore Annual Conference, 1975, 342;
Encyclopedia of World Methodism, Vol. 1, 1840–1841

Lee Padgett [Wallace-Padgett] (b. 1955)

In 1981, Lee married Debra Kaye Wallace (b. 1958). Debra was elected in 2012 out of the Kentucky Annual Conference and serves the Birmingham Episcopal Area. Lee and Debra have two young adult children.

Lee graduated from Ouachita Baptist University with a BS in physics and served as youth director/assistant to the minister at his hometown church in the Little Rock Annual Conference for seven years. He then went to Scarritt College and Graduate School, where he earned an MA in Christian education and met Debra. He was consecrated as a diaconal minister in 1983 in Kentucky at the same worship service as was Debra. He was ordained deacon in 1997. He served as director of program ministries at Trinity Hill UMC in Lexington for seven years and then was assigned to Aldersgate Camp and Retreat Center, where he served as executive director for 24 years. Lee retired as executive director at Sumatanga Camp and Conference Center in North Alabama in 2018. His hobbies include woodworking, fixing and restoring old radios and other antique machines and appliances. He used to restore, repair, and build pipe organs for churches that needed such assistance. Lee also loves backpacking and camping and has ventured 14 times around the Maroon Bells near Aspen, Colorado, leading backpacking trips for adults over four mountain passes at altitudes up to 12,700 feet elevation. Lee's teaching parable is Matthew 13:1-9, the sower and the seeds, about which he says, "I have always felt that my calling was to sow seeds for Christ, then allow God to see the harvest through."

—*Biographical Directory*, 2012–2016;
email communication with Lee Padgett, 2017, and interview, 2018

Wife of Federico Jose Pagura

Although no name or details were found for the wife of Federico Jose Pagura (1923–2016), he is described as married and the father of three children in the *Encyclopedia of World Methodism*. Federico was elected bishop in 1969 after serving as a pastor, district superintendent, and professor and chaplain at Union Theological

Seminary in Buenos Aires, Argentina. He was elected at the last session of the Latin America Central Conference, the annual conferences of which would become autonomous during that quadrennium. Federico served Panama and Costa Rica (1969–1973), then returned to seminary teaching in Argentina, where he was active in speaking up for human rights and ecumenism. He participated in the vigils of the Mothers of the Plaza de Mayo to protest the abduction of thousands of children. He was elected bishop of The Evangelical Methodist Church of Argentina and served (1977–1989).

—*Encyclopedia of World Methodism, Vol.* 21847;
https://en.wikipedia.org/wiki/Federico_Jos%C3%A9_Pagura

Cynthia Palmer

In 1976, Cynthia married Gregory Vaughn Palmer (b. 1954). Gregory was elected bishop in 2000 out of the East Ohio Annual Conference and served the Iowa Episcopal Area (2000–2008), the Illinois Great Rivers Episcopal Area (2008–2012), and the West Ohio Episcopal Area starting in 2012. Cynthia and Greg have two children.

Cynthia graduated with honors in religion from Duke University. She is a senior sales director with Mary Kay Cosmetics. She has served as a director of Christian education and as staff of several community action agencies focused on Welfare to Work projects. A biographical sketch on the West Ohio conference website notes that "She is an outstanding student and teacher of the scriptures and has a strong interest in women's leadership development."

—*Biographical Directory*, 2012–2016;
https://www.westohioumc.org/conference/bishops-biography

Florence Ruth Wales Palmer (1903–1993)

In 1927, Florence married Everett Walter Palmer (1906–1971). Everett was elected in 1960 while serving a church in Glendale, California, and served the Seattle Episcopal Area (1960–1968) and the Portland (Oregon) Episcopal Area 1968 until his death in 1971. Florence and Everett had three daughters.

After working her way through normal schools in South Dakota, Florence taught in a one-room country school for three years and an elementary school for another year. When her husband, who was working in a gold mine, decided to become a minister, she was his helpmate as he completed his studies at Dakota Wesleyan University and Drew University, while serving student pastorates. Florence and Everett studied together at Oxford University and then moved to Glendale, California, where he served until his election nine years later. Florence is quoted in the Biographical Directory for November, 1992, as saying, "I did all I could to help with his work, the most important in the world: the work of a minister." She taught church school, participated in Methodist and ecumenical women's activities, and focused especially on missionary education and spiritual life development. During her husband's years as a bishop, she traveled with him to Europe, India, Africa, and the Middle East. They took a special interest in foreign students.

—*Biographical Directory*, November 1992; https://findagrave.com/cgi-bin/fg.cgi/http%22/%3C/fg.cgi?page=gr&GRid=85924528

Elizabeth (Lisa) Hyeja Park (b. 1950)

In 1974, Lisa married Jeremiah Jungchan Park (b. 1952). Jeremiah was elected out of the Greater New Jersey Annual Conference, served the New York Episcopal Area (2004–2012) and was assigned to the Harrisburg Episcopal Area starting in 2012. They are the parents of two children and three grandchildren.

Lisa was born in Seoul, Korea and graduated from Ewha Women's University with a BA, with a major in English literature. She served on the staff of the World Vision of Korea in Seoul. In 1976, Lisa and Jeremiah emigrated to the U.S. Lisa earned a degree in data processing in the U.S. and worked as an IT manager at Bristol Myers Products and Proctor and Gamble. She enjoys reading, movies, swimming, hiking, and travel.

Favorite Scripture: 1 Thessalonians 5:16-18 / Favorite Hymn: "O Spirit of the Living God" (*UMH*, 539)

—*Biographical Directory*, 2004–2008;
email communication with Lisa Park, July 2017

Phyllis Jeanne Shaeffer Armstrong Paul [Armstrong] (1925–2018)

In 1942, Phyllis married Arthur James Armstrong (1924–2018). Jim was elected in 1968 after serving churches in Florida and Indiana. He served the Dakotas Episcopal Area (1968–1980) and the Indiana Episcopal Area (1980–1983), then resigned. Phyllis and Jim divorced in the mid-80s. They had five children.

Phyllis was born in Kansas. She enjoyed interior design and led retreats for clergy wives, encouraging them to speak up for themselves and to be themselves in their dress, makeup, and activities. She is fondly remembered for her interest in the clergy wives and encouragement to be all they could be. She married Henry Paul (1915-2004) in November, 1988. Her daughter, Rebecca Putens, writes, "At 93, she was still sassy, lovely and vibrant, and had chosen the memories she would dwell on and those she would dismiss. I want her to be remembered for the love and joy she showered on those who might have expected it the least. Long before it was accepted, my mother was a friend to those not accepted fully in society. Her five children all acknowledge that our mother was a remarkable person who made something of herself and of her life. She loved us. We loved her. We continue to feel heartbreak with her absence, but can also feel her presence, and even at times her guidance, as we continue to walk the path of life."

—https://en.wikipedia.org/wiki/Arthur_James_Armstrong, *Biographical Directory*, November 1981; *Encyclopedia of World Methodism, Vol. 1*, 142–143; http://um-insight.net/in-the-church/remembering-a-former-bishop-social-activistt/; email communication with Don Messer, Boyd Blumer, and daughter Rebecca Putens, 2018–2019

Carol L. Paup (b. 1945)

In 1965, Carol married Edward W. Paup (1945–2012). Ed was elected in 1996 out of the Rocky Mountain Conference and served the Portland (Oregon) Episcopal Area (2000–2004), the Seattle Episcopal Area (2004–2008), then resigned from the episcopacy to become the general secretary of the United Methodist Board of Global Ministries. He resigned from that position in 2009 because of health issues. Carol and Ed have three daughters and five grandchildren.

Carol studied at the University of New Mexico and has worked in medical clinics through the years. She is a master gardener and enjoys flowers and landscaping. She also enjoys swimming at least half a mile three times each week.

—*Biographical Directory*, 2000–2004; https://www.umnews.org/en/news/paup-former-bishop-executive-dies-at-66; telephone and email communication with Carol Paup, July 2017

Elizabeth Lytch Peele (1882–1965)

In 1911, Elizabeth married William Walter Peele (1881–1959). William was elected in 1938 out of the Western North Carolina Annual Conference of The Methodist Episcopal Church, South, and served "at large" (1938–1940) and the Richmond Episcopal Area (1940–1952), then retired.

Born in North Carolina, Elizabeth graduated from Littleton College, a Methodist college for women, and taught in public schools for several years. After marrying William, she was active in the Sunday schools where he served and in the Women's Society of Christian Service, once serving as president of the Raleigh District. At least two churches in North Carolina have a "Betsy Peele class" named in her honor. She took a personal interest in persons in their churches and later, when he became a bishop, in the clergy spouses and children in their area. During his retirement celebration, William remarked that he could not have "rendered his service without the daily inspiration and assistance of his good wife."

—https://en.wikipedia.org/wiki/William_Walter_Peele; http://www.ncpedia.org/biography/peele-william-walter; *Journal of the North Carolina Annual Conference Raleigh Area of The Methodist Church (Southeastern Jurisdiction) 1960*, 168–169

Lois May Sheppard Pendergrass (1905–2004)

In 1929, Lois married Edward Julian Pendergrass Jr (1900–1995). Edward was elected in 1964 out of the Florida Annual Conference and served the Jackson Episcopal Area (1964–1972), then retired. Lois and Edward returned to Florida. They had three children, five grandchildren, and eight great-grandchildren.

Lois attended North Carolina College for Women, Greensboro, and business college in Columbus, Ohio. She met Edward at a church where he was teaching a Sunday school class; two weeks later they married and moved to Fort White, Florida, for his first church assignment. She assisted her husband with his ministry throughout Florida. Avid travelers, they visited Europe, the Holy Lands, Africa, and Canada.

—*Biographical Directory*, 1992;
https://www.findagrave.com/memorial/66302152/lois-may-pendergrass;
https://www.findagrave.com/cgi-bin/fg.cgi?page=gr&GRid=66302116

Angelina Joaquim Garrine Penicela (1919?–1998)

In 1957, Angelina married Almeida Penicela (1929–2003). Almeida was elected in 1976 out of the Mozambique Annual Conference and served the Mozambique Episcopal Area (1976–1988), then retired. Angelina and Almeida had four children.

—*Biographical Directory*, 2000–2004;
http://archive.wfn.org/2003/05/msg00171.html

Janene Deloris Pennel (b. 1940)

In 1962, Janene married Joe Edward Pennel Jr (b. 1939). Joe was elected in 1996 out of the Tennessee Annual Conference. He served the Richmond Episcopal Area (1996–2004), then retired. Janene and Joe have two daughters.

Janene graduated from Lambuth College and earned an MA from the University of Memphis. She taught at the University School of Nashville for 18 years, where her classroom included children of all races, nations, and cultures of the world. She enjoys reading, travel, counted cross-stitch, and cooking. Janene received an honorary Doctorate in Humanities from Shenandoah University.

Favorite Scripture: Micah 6:8

—*Biographical Directory*, 2004–2008;
email communication with Janene Pennel, 2017

Navamani Peter

Navamani married Mamidi Elia Peter (1922–2014). Mamidi was elected in 1972 by the Southern Asia (India) Central Conference after serving as a teacher and administrator and assigned to the Southern Asia area until his retirement in 1989. Navamani and Mamidi had four children.

Navamani was a former teacher at the UM Stanley Girls' High School in Hyderabad and served as president of the Women's Society of Christian Service in Hyderabad and Jabalpur.

—news release from UM Communication, December 1972, in the election file for M. Elia Peter at the UM Archives and History Center; http://firstfridayletter.worldmethodistcouncil.org/2014/06/bishop-m-elia-peter-1922-2014/

Ruth Estella Clinger Phillips (1892–1969)

Ruth married Glenn Randall Phillips (1894–1970). Glenn was elected in 1948 after serving churches in California and served the Denver Episcopal Area (1948–1964), then retired. Ruth and Glenn had one son.

Ruth was born in Ohio and graduated from Ohio Wesleyan University, where she studied music, the first woman in her family to graduate from college. She worked as a music teacher while waiting for her husband to return from World War I. In an obituary written by their son, she is described as a seeker of perfection—for herself, her family, the church, and the world: "Traveling in Africa, India, Europe, Japan, The Philippines, Malaysia, Hong Kong and Israel, she had a firm belief that people could live together in love if they would only work at it."

—*Journal of the Yellowstone Conference, 1969*, 102–103;
Encyclopedia of World Methodism, Vol. 2 1902–1903

Ruth Robinson Pickett (1895–1983)

In 1916, Ruth married Jarrell Waskom Pickett (1890–1981). Waskom, born in Texas, was appointed to lead an English-speaking congregation in Lucknow, India, for the Methodist Board of Foreign Mission. He became a member of the North India Conference of The Methodist Church and was elected bishop in 1935 by the Central Conference of Southern Asia. He served the Bombay Area (1935–1945) and the Delhi Area (1945–1956), then retired from the mission field and taught missions at Boston University School of Theology for three years. Ruth and Jarrell spent their last years at a retirement village in Columbus, Ohio. They had four children, all born in India.

Ruth, the daughter of John Wesley Robinson (a missionary to India who was elected bishop in 1912), was born in Lucknow and met Jarrell there, but insisted on obtaining a college degree before their marriage. She graduated from Northwestern University in Chicago, Illinois, in 1916 and married Jarrell soon after. They returned to India and began serving together as missionaries.

—https://en.wikipedia.org/wiki/J._Waskom_Pickett;
https://www.asbury.edu/offices/library/archives/biographies/j-waskom-pickett;
http://www.bu.edu/missiology/missionary-biography/n-o-p-q/pickett-j-waskom/

Kate Sayle Pope (d. 1985)

In 1930, Kate married William Kenneth Pope (1901–1989). William was elected in 1960 after serving churches in Texas. He served the Arkansas Episcopal Area (1960–1964) and the Dallas-Fort Worth Episcopal Area (1964–1972), then retired. Kate and William had two children.

Kate grew up in Breckenridge, Texas, and met William when he came to serve the church she attended. He "persuaded her to change her role from that of parishioner to pastor's wife." She graduated from Samuel Houston State University and later took classes in political science at Southwestern University. Her memoir notes that she understood "the Christian life as having to do with justice, mercy, compassion and respect for persons," and we assume she supported her husband in his speaking out against the Ku Klux Klan and the Vietnam War.

—*Encyclopedia of World Methodism, Vol. 2* 1934; http://prabook.com/web/person-view.html?profileId=370457; https://en.wikipedia.org/wiki/William_Kenneth_Pope; *Journal of the 120th Session of the North Texas Annual Conference, 1986*, 275–276; *Official Journal 1990 Central Texas Annual Conference*, 308

Alice Wuerfel Pryor (1905–1984)

In 1925, Alice married Thomas Marion Pryor (1904–1979). Thomas was elected in 1964, after serving churches in the Detroit and Michigan Annual Conferences, and served the Chicago Episcopal Area (1964–1972). Alice and Thomas had four children, 11 grandchildren, and three great-grandchildren.

Alice studied at the University of Michigan, as did Thomas, and later earned an MA. She did volunteer work with drug addicts and later, after her first bout with cancer, with cancer patients. She and Thomas traveled widely, including China, Borneo, and Tanzania, where she walked the slopes of Kilimanjaro.

—http://prabook.com/web/person-view.html?profileId=1096490; *Encyclopedia of World Methodism, Vol. 2* 1959; *Official Journal and Minutes Detroit Annual Conference, 1985*, 1010

Ida Bernice West Purcell (1887–1967)

In 1920, Ida married Clare Purcell (1884–1964). Clare was elected in 1938 out of the North Alabama Annual Conference of The Methodist Episcopal Church, South, and served the Charlotte Episcopal Area (1938–1948) and the Birmingham Episcopal Area (1948–1956), then retired. Ida and Clare had three children.

—https://en.wikipedia.org/wiki/Clare_Purcell; https://findingaids.library.emory.edu/documents/P-MSS319/printable/

Laurinda Vidal Quipungo (b. 1956)

In 1975, Laurinda married José Quipungo (b. 1950). José was elected in 2000 out of the East Angola Annual Conference and assigned to the East Angola Episcopal

Area. In 2004, he was reelected for life. Laurinda and José have five children and 10 grandchildren.

Laurinda, a physician, graduated from the School of Medicine of the University Agostinhho Neto in Luanda, Angola in 1999. Before her husband's election, she worked as a pediatrician in the largest hospital in Luanda. Since moving to Malange, she has opened a clinic for children and adults, an orphanage, and a Women's Training Center for domestic sciences and literacy. She visits churches with her husband, offering spiritual support and health care resources. She has also served as director of the Provincial Health government agency and director of the Provincial Hospital for women and children in Malange. A deaconess, she is active in her local church.

—*Biographical Directory*, 2012–2016;
email communication with Bishop Quipungo, May 2017, and interview, Fall 2017;
Mission Support Network minutes, November 5, 2003

Richlain K. Quire (b. 1967)

In 1989, Richlain married Samuel J. Quire (b. 1959). Samuel was elected in 2016 out of the Liberia Annual Conference and assigned to the Liberia Episcopal Area. Richlain and Samuel have five children and one granddaughter.

Richlain has her MA in education supervision. She lectures on curriculum development and instructional methods at the College of Education/United Methodist University in Monrovia, Liberia. She also works with the Rural Pastor's Spouse Skills Training Programs. Teaching is her passion.

Favorite Scripture: Matthew 19:26 / Favorite Hymn: "How Great Thou Art" (*UMH*, 77)

—email communication, June 2017, and interview with Richlain Quire, May 2018

Blaine B. Rader

In 1962, Blaine married Sharon Zimmerman (b. 1939). Sharon was elected in 1992 out of the West Michigan Annual Conference and served the Wisconsin Episcopal Area (1992–2004), then retired. Blaine and Sharon settled in Evanston, Illinois. They have two children and four grandchildren.

Blaine was born in Monroe, Michigan, and raised in the Evangelical United Brethren Church. He graduated from The University of Michigan, Wayne State University, United Theological Seminary, Drew University, and the University of Notre Dame. He was ordained in 1964 in the Michigan Area; served on the faculty of Adrian College; taught at Evangelical Theological, Western Theological, and Garrett Evangelical Theological Seminaries; and directed Samaritan Counseling Centers in Michigan and Wisconsin. He also served congregations in Wisconsin and Northern Illinois. He was secretary/treasurer of the American Association of Pastoral Counselors and is licensed as a psychologist/pastoral counselor in Michigan, Wisconsin, and Illinois. Blaine has also trained more than 150 pastoral counselors, developed three pastoral counseling centers, and served as a consultant to congregations in conflict. He enjoys practicing his violin, mandolin, bass, and guitar.

—*Biographical Directory*, 2000–2004, 2012–2016;
interview with Bishop Rader, November 2017

Lucille Marguerite Arnold Raines (1897–1980)

In 1920, Lucille married Richard Campbell Raines (1898–1981). Richard was elected in 1948 after serving churches in Massachusetts, Rhode Island, and Minnesota. He served the Indianapolis Episcopal Area (1948–1968), then retired. Lucille and Richard moved to Lakeland, Florida, and spent summers in Glen Arbor, Michigan. They had four children and at least three grandchildren.

Lucile was born in Iowa to a farming family and began her schooling in a one-room schoolhouse. She earned a BA from Cornell College in Iowa, where she and Richard fell in love. They went to Boston University together and then lived in England, France, and Germany while Dick pursued his studies at Oxford. Later she traveled the world with her husband and came back to Indiana to interpret that world (Africa, in particular); they traveled throughout Indiana, visiting churches large and small, offering encouragement and affirmation. She was granted an honorary Doctorate by DePauw University, and the Lucille Raines Residence, a UMW project in Indiana for persons recovering from addictions, was named in her honor, recognizing her efforts on behalf of women. Lucille and Dick were known for the closeness of their relationship and their loving outreach to others.

—https://www.findagrave.com/cgi-bin/fg.cgi?page=gr&GRid=67677138;
http://www.tributes.com/obituary/show/Richard-R.-Campbell-94772317;
Minutes of the North Indiana Conference, 1981, 733–734

Mary Lou Reece [Jones] (b. 1955)

In 1979, Mary Lou married Scott J. Jones (b. 1954). Scott was elected out of the North Texas Conference in 2004. He served the Kansas Episcopal Area (2004–2012) and the Great Plains Episcopal Area (2012–2016), then was assigned to the Houston Episcopal Area. Mary Lou and Scott have three children and five grandchildren.

Mary Lou graduated from the University of Kansas with a BA and from Southern Methodist University with an MBA. She is president of Reece Construction Company and the first woman to serve on the Board of Directors for the Associated General Contractors of Texas. She also serves on the Board for the Kansas Contractors Association. Mary Lou participates in extensive volunteer work, mostly in the church, construction industry, and civic organizations in Kansas. She teaches Sunday school and Bible studies for adults, children, and youth and also sponsors youth events and trips. She serves on the Board for the Dallas Emmaus Community and is a lay director. She also served as president of Kansas Native Sons and Daughters. She enjoys traveling with Scott and supporting his ministry; offering hospitality, which she considers her spiritual gift; and especially being Nanny to her grandchildren.

—*Biographical Directory*, 2012–2016;
email communication with Mary Lou Reece, January 2018

Mary Esther Kirkendall Reed (b. 1894)

In 1917, Mary Esther married Marshall Russell Reed (1891–1973). He was elected in 1948 out of the Detroit Annual Conference and served the Detroit Episcopal Area (1948–1964), then retired. Mary Esther and Marshall had three daughters, 12 grandchildren, and five great-grandchildren.

Mary Esther attended Grinnell College and graduated from Northwestern University with a BA and a teacher's certificate. She spent the 31 years before his election as a pastor's wife in various churches in Michigan and as homemaker for her husband and three daughters.

—*Biographical Directory*, 1984;
https://en.wikipedia.org/wiki/Marshall_Russell_Reed

Anna Elizabeth Isenberg Richardson (1869–1956)

In 1897, Anna married Ernest Gladstone Richardson (1874–1947). Ernest was elected in The Methodist Episcopal Church in 1920, after serving churches in Connecticut and New York City. He served the Atlanta Episcopal Area (1920–1928) and the Philadelphia Episcopal Area (1928–1954), including the Puerto Rico Conference (1933–1944). Anna and Ernest had three children, four granddaughters, and five great-grandchildren.

Anna, born in Pennsylvania, graduated from Dickinson College with Ernest in 1896. Before their 10th anniversary, she was stricken with tuberculosis, crippled, and diagnosed as beyond hope of recovery. She recovered so fully, however, that in spite of an artificial leg, she was able to keep house and travel with Ernest with limited use of a wheelchair. She was active in the local church and especially interested in the Women's Society of Christian Service and the Ministers' Wives Association. She was interested in people and especially in children and families.

—Official Journal and Yearbook of the Philadelphia Annual Conference of The Methodist Church, 1956, 231–233; https://www.ancestry.ca/genealogy/records/anna-elizabeth-isenberg_167655642; http://prabook.com/web/person-view.html?profileId=278718; *Encyclopedia of World* Methodism, *Vol.* 2, 2014–2015

Robin Ridenour [Oliveto] (b. 1957)

In 2014, Robin married Karen P. Oliveto (b. 1958). Karen was elected in 2016 out of the California-Nevada Annual Conference and assigned to the Mountain Sky Episcopal Area.

Robin worked as a pediatric registered nurse for 10 years, then earned her MS in Nurse Anesthesia at the Mayo Clinic and worked as a certified registered nurse anesthetist for 18 years, then retired after Karen was elected bishop. Robin and Karen met at a UM junior high camp in 1991, where Karen served as program director and Robin as camp nurse. They have been together since 1999 and married after the Supreme Court upheld Marriage Equality in 2013. Robin is a deaconess in the UMC and is now starting in Denver a Project Transformation Nonprofit chapter, which has three purposes: a summer program for child literacy, vocational exploration for college students, and church revitalization.

Favorite Scripture: Micah 6:8

—email communication with Robin Ridenour, November 2017

Iris Janet Rivera [Mendez] (d. 2014)

Janet married Juan A. Vera Mendez. Juan was elected in 1998 by The Methodist Church in Puerto Rico, an Autonomous Affiliated Church whose bishops participate in the UM Council of Bishops by special agreement. Janet and Juan have three children.

Janet was an engineer. According to the dedication published on the website of The Methodist Church of Puerto Rico: "Janet was a woman of great human value, she carried with her a whole life and dedication to the service of her family, her Church and loved ones. A woman of solidarity, of untiring faith, in solidarity with social causes, and of testimony as a sign of her immeasurable love for the risen Christ. Iris Janet actively participated in common causes against cancer and developed a ministry for children in the community of Santana in Arecibo, which is sponsored by The Methodist Church of Bethel, where she attended."

— https://www.umnews.org/en/news/la-iglesia-metodista-de-puerto-rico-celebra-la-vida-de-iris-janet-rivera-ca

Helen Cady Rockey (1898–1988)

In 1922, Helen married Clement Daniel Rockey (1889–1975). Clement, born in India, a son of a Methodist missionary and a Methodist missionary himself, was elected in 1941 and served the North India Annual Conference (1941–1965), then retired to Eugene, Oregon. Helen and Clement had three children and 10 grandchildren.

Helen was born in China, the daughter of American missionaries serving there. She earned an MA in psychology from Northwestern University in 1922. She is author of stories and books, including *The Promise,* a collection of stories adapted from the Southern Asia Methodist Centenary Celebrations pageant in 1956. Helen and Clement were active in the church in Eugene and invited several thousand children and other people into their home to tell them about India and Pakistan and to show artifacts and pictures. In her memoir in the 1988 Oregon-Idaho Annual Conference Journal, Helen was described as an "advisor and counselor" to Clement during his years of active service. One of their sons, Dr. Harold Rockey, described her as a "mainstay and comfort" to his father later in life.

—*Journal 20th Session of the Oregon-Idaho Annual Conference, 1988,* 145; https://en.wikipedia.org/wiki/Clement_Daniel_Rockey; http://archiveswest.orbiscascade.org/ark:/80444/xv96432

LuReese Ann Watson Robertson (1918–1999)

In 1941, LuReese married Frank Lewis Robertson (1917–1992). Frank was elected in 1972 out of the South Georgia Annual Conference and served the Louisville Episcopal Area (1972–1980) and the Birmingham Episcopal Area (1980–1984), then retired. LuReese and Frank had two children and five grandchildren.

LuReese was born in Alberta, Canada, after her parents moved there from Tennessee to help with wartime production of wheat for the Allied cause. After the war ended, the family moved to Macon, Georgia, where she met and fell in love with Frank. After their wedding, she followed him to Connecticut while he finished his studies at Yale. She audited some of his classes, skipping the final exams. After his graduation in 1942, they moved back to Georgia, where Frank was appointed to the Baker Village Church. At first, LuReese was shy and uncertain of her role as wife and helpmate to a minister, but she quickly learned to embrace various tasks through which she could support Frank. She also took care of the children and the home to free him for church work. After his election as bishop, LuReese became the "First Lady of Kentucky Methodism" in spite of the rheumatoid arthritis that made traveling with and assisting Frank difficult.

—*Biographical Directory,* 1984; http://www.opentohope.com/fathers-of-faith/; The Journal of the South Georgia Annual Conference, 2000, 518–520

Elizabeth Fisher Robinson (1863–1945)

In 1891, Elizabeth married John Wesley Robinson (1866–1947). John, a missionary to India from the Des Moines Annual Conference of The Methodist Episcopal Church, was elected a missionary bishop for Southern Asia in 1912 and bishop in 1920. He retired in 1936 but was reappointed to episcopal work in 1939 serving the Lucknow Area of The Methodist Church. He resigned in 1942. Elizabeth and John settled in Delhi, India. They had three children.

—http://prabook.com/web/person-view.html?profileId=279423; http://catalog.gcah.org/publicdata/gcah2090.htm

Silvia Rückert (b. 1959)

In 1983, Silvia married Harald H. Rückert (b. 1958). Harald was elected in 2017 out of the Germany South Annual Conference and assigned to the Germany Episcopal Area. Silvia and Harald have three children and one grandchild.

Silvia works as a cytology technical assistant. She is also active in church choir, migrant ministry, and church work for and with elderly people. She enjoys reading, listening to music, and singing in the choir.

Favorite Scripture: Psalm 36:6-11 / Favorite Hymn: "*Meine Hoffnung und Meine Freude*" (*UM Hymnbook Germany*, 2002, #361)

—email communication with Silvia Rückert, May 26–June 10, 2017

Mary Jean Russell (b. 1926)

In 1947, Mary Jean married John William Russell (b. 1926). John was elected in 1980 out of the Oklahoma Annual Conference and served the Dallas-Fort Worth Episcopal Area (1980–1988) and the newly created Fort Worth Episcopal Area (1988–1992), then retired. Mary Jean and John have two daughters and a son (deceased).

Mary Jean attended Oklahoma College for Women and graduated from the University of Oklahoma with a BS in music education. Mary Jean taught elementary music one year and has been the director of children's choirs in local churches, substitute organist in some of these churches, and choir director in one. She has always sung in the choirs of churches she attended. In addition to all aspects of music, Mary Jean likes to sew, crochet, and do needlepoint.

—*Biographical Directory*, 2012–2016

Juana Puch Sabanes (d. 1979/80)

In 1923, Juana married Julio Manuel Sabanes (1897–1963). Julio was elected in 1952 and again in 1956 out of the Latin American Central Conference, after serving churches in Uruguay, Montevideo, and Argentina. He served the Santiago Episcopal Area, including Chili, Peru, Panama, and Costa Rica (1952–1960), then retired due to ill health.

Juana was the daughter of an Argentinian Methodist minister.

—http://catalog.gcah.org:8080/exist/memoirs/memoirs.xql?query=Juana+Sabanes; *Encyclopedia of World* Methodism, *Vol.* 2, 2065

Maye Saenz (b. 1962)

In 1981, Maye married Ruben Saenz Jr (b. 1961). Ruben was elected in 2016 out of the Rio Texas Annual Conference and assigned to the Great Plains Episcopal Area. Maye and Ruben have four children and six grandchildren.

Maye has been involved with moving into a new episcopal residence and making it a welcoming and warm home. She loves decorating; praying; visiting with her children and grandchildren, family and friends; visiting churches with Ruben; meeting new people; cooking and cleaning; exercising; and keeping in touch with friends and family through text messages.

Favorite Scripture: 1 Peter 5:7

—interview with Maye Saenz, November 2017

Billie Jo Sanders (1927–2012)

In 1997, Billie Jo married retired Bishop Carl Julian Sanders (1912–2007). Widowed in 1995, Carl had two daughters and three granddaughters from his first marriage. Widowed in 1979, Billie Jo had two daughters and three grandchildren from her first marriage. Billie Jo and Carl made their home in Birmingham, Alabama.

Billie Jo was born and raised in Alabama. In 1948, she married Thomas B. Perry, who died in 1979. She served as administrative secretary in the bishop's office in Birmingham (1972–1993), under four different bishops. She enjoyed attending several General Conferences and Southeastern Jurisdictional Conferences during that time. After retiring in 1993, she volunteered at Carraway Methodist Medical Center and continued to enjoy her long-standing bridge club.

—*Biographical Directory*, 2000–2004; http://archives.gcah.org:8080/bitstream/handle/10516/4062/article45.aspx.htm?sequence=2&isAllowed=y; http://obits.dignitymemorial.com/dignity-memorial/obituary.aspx?n=Billie+Jo-Sanders&lc=4397&pid=159400145&mid=5216241; http://obits.al.com/obituaries/birmingham/obituary.aspx?page=lifestory&pid=159419379

Eleanor Lupo Sanders (1916–1995)

In 1935, Eleanor married Carl Julian Sanders (1912–2007). Carl was elected in 1972 out of the Virginia Annual Conference and served the Birmingham Episcopal Area (1972–1980, then retired. Eleanor and Carl had two daughters and three granddaughters.

Eleanor graduated from Winthrop College in Rock Hill, South Carolina, and loved to travel. According to a memoir about her posted on the Virgina Annual Conference website, "Eleanor and Carl met back in 1934 when, as a theology student, he came to talk with her father about an appointment. There was an instantaneous attraction between them and they were married on September 28, 1935. She became a very loving and supportive wife and the mother of two daughters. . . . In every appointment Eleanor shared the ministry of her husband. She loved the United Methodist Church and the fellowship of the ministry. It was as if she had heard God's call to serve as positively as her husband and lived her life fully to respond to the joy of that call. Throughout her life with Carl, from the beginning years on the Eastern Shore of Virginia to the years in the episcopal residence in Alabama, she expressed her love for Christ and his church in many ways but primarily through the giving of herself in a very personal ministry of love and supportive caring."

—https://www.vaumc.org/page.aspx?pid=3710; *Biographical Directory*, 2000–2004

Heidi Niederhauser Schäfer (1929–1987)

In 1951, Heidi married Franz Werner Schäfer (1921–2016). Franz was elected in 1966 out of the Switzerland Annual Conference and served the Geneva Episcopal Area, which included 10 diverse countries (1966–1989). Heidi and Franz had five children.

Heidi was born in Switzerland and attended school in Basel, Birsfelden, and Montreux. She could not accompany her husband on his many travels but focused on bringing up their children. She always preferred concrete, practical action over intellectual activities and had an eye and ear for those people who are not often seen or heard. She advocated for those who were not in the public eye, but who faithfully served in families, communities, and the church. She often reminded her husband, "Don't forget the pastors' wives. Don't forget the children. Don't forget the widows."

—*Encyclopedia of World Methodism, Vol. 2* 2104; http://worldmethodistcouncil.org/bishop-franz-w-schafer-1921-2016-building-bridges-between-worlds/; *Biographical Directory*, November 1981; obituary in *Kirche + Welt*, the magazine of the UMC in Switzerland, Vol. 49 [December 6, 1987], summarized by Urs Schweizer, assistant to Bishop Dr. Patrick Streiff, Central Conference of Central and Southern Europe, October 2018

Esther W. Schnase (b. 1958)

In 1980, Esther married Robert C. Schnase (b. 1957). Robert was elected out of the Southwest Texas Annual Conference in 2004. He served the Missouri Episcopal Area (2004-2016) and was assigned to the Rio Texas Episcopal Area in 2016. Esther and Robert have two grown sons.

Esther graduated from the University of Texas at Austin in the Plan II Honors program with a focus on education. She has served as a high school English teacher in Harlingen and McAllen, Texas. Esther enjoys reading, travelling, knitting, and singing.

—*Biographical Directory*, 2012–2016

Beverly Anne Schol (b. 1956)

In 1978, Beverly married John R. Schol (b. 1956). John was elected out of the Eastern Pennsylvania Annual Conference in 2004 and served the Washington Episcopal Area (2004–2012). He was assigned to the Greater New Jersey Episcopal Area in 2012. Beverly and John have three grown children and three grandchildren.

Beverly is an educator and administrative leader. She is from Philadelphia, Pennsylvania, where she was active in the St. James UMC. She earned her BS at Arcadia University in early childhood and elementary education and taught both pre-school and elementary age children in Philadelphia. She also served as the director of a childcare center (1999–2004), leading it to financial health, completely renovating the facilities, increasing enrollment, and strengthening the curriculum.

After Superstorm Sandy, Beverly was an organizing staff member of A Future with Hope, which was started by the UMC of Greater New Jersey. Over the last five years, the organization rebuilt and built new more than 250 homes, using more than 12,000 volunteers from 46 states and three countries. It has raised more than $17 million for this effort. Beverly was the regional manager for the Southern Region, which was the most devastated area. A Future with Hope worked with community residents, nonprofit organizations, churches and local, state and federal agencies to assess damage and repair homes, particularly for the elderly, disabled, and low-income persons whose insurance and other agency support did not cover all of their needs.

Beverly also enjoys gardening, reading, traveling, and spending time with her children and grandbabies.

—*Biographical Directory*, 2012–2016;
email communication with Beverly Schol, 2018

Ina Edmondson Schowengerdt (b. 1926)

In 1951, Ina married Louis Wesley Schowengerdt (1926–1988). He was elected in 1980 out of the Missouri West Annual Conference and served the Northwest Texas-New Mexico Episcopal Area (1980–1992), then retired. Ina and Louis have two sons and four grandchildren.

Ina attended Oklahoma College for Women, receiving the O'Neal Award for "leadership, scholarship and service" and a BA in English. She studied bassoon with Stephen Maxym of the Metropolitan Opera and played professionally, full-time and freelance, with the Kansas City Philharmonic and St. Louis Symphonies. She also has had short stories published in several magazines.

—*Biographical Directory*, 1984, 1996, 2004–2008

Bess Kyle Beckner Selecman (1874–1943)

In 1899, Bess married Charles Claude Selecman (1874–1958). Charles was elected in 1938 in The Methodist Episcopal Church, South, after serving churches in Missouri, Los Angeles, and Dallas, Texas, and as president of Southern Methodist University. He served the Oklahoma Episcopal Area (1938–1944) and the Dallas Episcopal Area (1944–1948), then retired. Bess and Charles had two children and three grandchildren.

—https://www.findagrave.com/cgi-bin/fg.cgi?page=gr&GRid=71996209; https://en.wikipedia.org/wiki/Charles_Claude_Selecman; http://www.lib.utexas.edu/taro/smu/00041/00041-P.html; https://www.revolvy.com/main/index.php?s=Charles%20Claude%20Selecman

Mable Edna White Mason Selecman (1883–1968)

In 1945, "Jackie" married Bishop Charles Claude Selecman (1874–1958), who served the Dallas Episcopal Area (1944–1948), then retired. Charles had two children and three grandchildren with his first wife, Bess, who died in 1943.

Jackie was born in Missouri and educated at the Central College for Women in Lexington, Missouri. She lived in Kansas City and worked in the Methodist Settlement Home until her family moved to Los Angeles, California, in 1913. There she worked as an assistant to a businessman and was active in Trinity Methodist Church, volunteering as church secretary for a time. She was married in 1939 and widowed two years later. After her marriage to Charles, whom she knew when he was pastor at Trinity, she lived in Dallas and maintained a close relationship with Southern Methodist University. She enjoyed relating to the annual conferences during Charles' last three years as bishop there, as well as traveling with him to mission fields and on other official journeys. Her friends recalled her artistic sensitivity and exquisite taste in clothes, furniture, and everything surrounding her.

—https://en.wikipedia.org/wiki/Charles_Claude_Selecman; https://www.findagrave.com/memorial/71996569/mabel-e.-selecman; http://www.lib.utexas.edu/taro/smu/00041/00041-P.html; https://www.revolvy.com/main/index.php?s=Charles%20Claude%20Selecman; *1969 Journal of the 2nd Annual Session North Texas Conference,* 152

Maribel Bonilla Serrano [Bonilla]

Maribel married Victor L. Bonilla, who in 1993 became bishop of The Methodist Church of Puerto Rico, newly autonomous and formerly part of the Philadelphia Episcopal Area of The United Methodist Church. Under the special provisions drafted in 1992 or later, Puerto Rican bishops participate in the United Methodist Council of Bishops.

http://www.gcah.org/history/united-methodist-church-timeline; https://www.umnews.org/en/news/united-methodists-continue-relationship-with-puerto-rican-methodists; conversations with Bishop Hector F. Ortiz Vidal and his wife Alma, 2017–2018

Virginia Maude Late Shamblin (b. 1916)

In 1937, Virginia married J. Kenneth Shamblin (1917–1983). Ken was elected in 1976 after serving churches in Texas and Arkansas. He served the Louisiana Episcopal

Area from 1976 until his death in 1983. Virginia and Ken had two children and two grandchildren.

Virginia attended the University of Arkansas. She liked to do needlepoint.

—*Biographical Directory,* 1996; http://www.la-umc.org/obituary/1547382; https://www.upi.com/Archives/1983/10/04/Funeral-services-were-scheduled-Wednesday-for-J-Kenneth-Shamblin/5291434088000/

Evelyn Mary Michael Shaw (b. 1912)

In 1934, Evelyn married Alfred Jacob Shaw (1906–1981). Alfred, formerly pastor of Central Methodist Church in Lucknow, India, and district superintendent, was elected in 1965 while serving as educational secretary of The Methodist Church in Southern Asia. He served the Bombay Episcopal Area (1965–1969) and the Delhi Episcopal Area (1969–1972), then retired. Evelyn and Alfred settled in Bareilly, where their home was a center of continuing Christian concern and fellowship. They had three children.

Evelyn was very active in conference women's work during her husband's episcopacy. She was president of the All-India Women's Society of Christian Service (1969–1972).

—*Biographical Directory,* 1984

Lottye Blanche Simon Shaw

In 1911, Lottye married Alexander Preston Shaw (1879–1966). Alexander, the son of former slaves, was elected in The Methodist Episcopal Church in 1936, after serving churches in Maryland, Virginia, Arkansas, and Los Angeles. He served the New Orleans Episcopal Area (1936–1940), the Baltimore Episcopal Area of the Central Jurisdiction, including 1,300 African American Methodist churches in Delaware, East Tennessee, North Carolina, and Washington, DC (1940–1952), then retired. Lottye and Alexander had six children, six grandchildren, and one great-grandchild.

Born in Atlanta, Georgia, Lottye studied at Spelman College there. Her memoir in the 1975 *Baltimore Annual Conference Journal* notes that "She served humanity well in all her years, loving Christ, standing with her husband, making her family a haven of peace and serving the church."

—*Minutes of the 191st Annual Session of the Baltimore Annual Conference, 1975,* 344; https://en.wikipedia.org/wiki/Alexander_Preston_Shaw;

Robert Glenn Sherer Jr (1940–2017)

In 1968, Robert married Amelia Ann Brookshire (b. 1942). Ann was elected in 1992 out of the Texas Annual Conference and served the Missouri Episcopal Area (1992–2004) and the Nebraska Episcopal Area (2004–2012), then retired. Robert and Ann divorced in 1995. They have two children and two grandsons.

Robert earned his PhD from the University of North Carolina in 1969. He taught at Stetson University, Wiley College, and Alcon College. He was a university archivist at Tulane University (1991–2006).

—*Biographical Directory*, 2004–2008;
email communication with Bishop Sherer-Simpson, 2017

Louise Clay Baird Short (1906–2016)

In 1926, Louise married Roy Hunter Short (1902–1994). Roy was elected in 1948 out of the Louisville Conference (formerly part of The Methodist Episcopal Church, South). He served the Jacksonville Episcopal Area (1948–1952), the Nashville Episcopal Area (1952–1964), and the Louisville Area (1964–1972), then retired, providing episcopal supervision to the Philippines Central Conference (1972–1974). Louise and Roy had three sons, seven grandchildren, and 21 great-grandchildren.

Louise attended the University of Louisville and graduated from Louisville Normal School. She taught in the Louisville Public Schools and also held a position in her family's business, Baird Dairy. Louise traveled with Roy, but also found time to be active in church and civic organizations, often in the role of teacher and lecturer. Her interests included antiques, political history and social studies, and her grandchildren and great-grandchildren.

—*Biographical Directory*, 2012–2016;
email communication with son Riley Short, June 2017

Justina Lorenz Showers (1885–1984)

In 1911, Justina married John Balmer Showers (1879–1962). John, born in Canada, came to the U.S. in 1900 and was ordained in the Church of the United Brethren in Christ in 1902. He was elected bishop in 1945 out of the Evangelical United Brethren Church while serving as professor of New Testament literature and interpretation at Bonebrake Theological Seminary (now United Theological Seminary) in Dayton, Ohio. He served the Eastern (Harrisburg) Episcopal Area (1945–1950) and the North Central (Indianapolis) Episcopal Area (1950–1955), then retired. Justina and John settled in Dayton.

Justina was known for her warm hospitality. While John was connected to the seminary, their home was always open to students. Later they offered hospitality to missionaries on furlough and remodeled their home to provide accommodations for missionaries temporarily in Dayton. Justina said, "Rich memories tell me Life has been good! First there was the heritage of Christians serving the Church: bishops, conference superintendents, local pastors, editors; then parents who created a Christian home with high ideals of service: a father who used his ministerial training and his musical talent to serve churches of all sizes in their worship, and a mother who passed on to me her concerned interest in missions; and finally my own home where my husband, as professor, gave me the joys of contact with young men and women preparing for ministry, as editor, made me think in broader terms, as publishing agent, shared his burdens with me in the terrible years when he saved the publishing house from bankruptcy, and finally the responsibilities of shepherding churches. Meantime I was working with the women in the cause of world-wide missions, in the local church, in a conference, in the nation. What a fellowship . . . ! And now my hobby, Mission Manor, where missionary families come for furlough renewal and keep my world vision keen and my admiration for witnessing Christians all around the world challenging. Yes, Life has been good: which is just another way of saying God has blessed me far, far beyond my deserving. I am grateful, GRATEFUL." Justina turned over Mission Manor to a retired missionary couple before moving to the Otterbein Home near Lebanon, Ohio. She co-authored a book, *Missions at Home and Abroad,* which was reprinted in 2017 by Forgotten Books.

—*Journal of the 102nd Annual Session of the Michigan Conference of the Evangelical United Brethren, 1963*, 134–136; *Biographical Directory*, 1984; *Western Pennsylvania Conference Journal* for 1984, 413; https://www.amazon.com/Missions-Home-Abroad-Classic-Reprint/dp/0259338443/ref=sr_1_1?s=books&ie=UTF8&qid=1505331684&sr=1-1

Louise Lutshumba Shungu

In 1936, Louise married John Wesley Shungu (1917–2007). John was elected in 1964 out of the Central Congo Annual Conference and served the Congo Episcopal Area (1964–1972). They had 13 children.

—*Encyclopedia of World Methodism, Vol. 2*, 2152; http://archives.gcah.org/bitstream/handle/10516/4179/article34.aspx.htm?sequence=2

Alice Mumenthaler Sigg (1904–1953)

In 1929, Alice married Ferdinand Sigg (1902–1965). Ferdinand was elected in 1954 in the Central and Southern Europe Central Conference and served the Geneva Episcopal Area (1954–1965), when he died.

Alice was born in Basel, Switzerland, where she also attended school. Later, she served in the office of Bishop Nuelsen and, although she struggled with severe health issues throughout her life, she committed much of her time and energy to the Women's Mission and Youth Ministry, where she led camps for girls. Her faith and love was a response to Jeremiah 31:3 and had a lasting impact on the lives of many. She was described as Bishop Sigg's "equal in devotion and as a leader."

—*Encyclopedia of World Methodism, Vol. 2*, 2154; https://en.wikipedia.org/wiki/Ferdinand_Sigg; obituary in 1954 minutes of the Annual Conference of The Methodist Church in Switzerland, summarized by Urs Schweizer, assistant to Bishop Dr. Patrick Streiff, October 2018

Wayne Eldon Simpson [Sherer-Simpson] (b. 1935)

In 2009, Wayne married Bishop Ann Brookshire Sherer (b. 1942), who was serving the Nebraska Episcopal Area (2004–2012), then retired. Wayne and Ann live in Lincoln, Nebraska. Wayne has three children from his first marriage and three grandchildren; Ann has two children and two grandchildren from hers.

While in high school, Wayne was enrolled in the Civil Air Patrol and was awarded an International Cadet Exchange to Canada. He was received, along with 100 or so other CAP cadets, by President Dwight Eisenhower in 1953. Wayne graduated from the University of Nebraska with a BS in mechanical engineering. He graduated from Naval Officer Candidate School in Newport, Rhode Island, and served as a transport officer at Norfolk Naval Air Station, then as an aeronautical engineering officer with the Progressive Aircraft Rework division. Upon release from active duty in 1963, he was employed by Goodyear Tire and Rubber as an industrial engineer and manager of plant planning and safety, including radiation safety. Wayne has written a book about the life of his mother, who was born in Sweden. He enjoys reading history and working Kakuro and other types of puzzles, but his favorite hobby is skiing, which he has enjoyed for 51 years as of May 2017 and about which he is writing a book.

—*Biographical Directory*, 2004–2008, 2012–2016;
email communication with Wayne Simpson, 2017

Shirley Skeete (b. 1934)

In 1952, Shirley married F. Herbert Skeete (b. 1930). Herb was elected out of the New York Annual Conference in 1980. He served the Philadelphia Episcopal Area (1980–1988) and the Boston Episcopal Area (1988–1996), then retired. He was reactivated to serve the Zimbabwe Episcopal Area in 2002 for one year. Shirley and Herb have two sons and three grandchildren.

Shirley earned a BA from Queens College and an MS and a Professional Degree in education, supervision and administration from City College, New York. She was employed by Columbia University, the American Management Association, and she served 19 and one-half years as a public school teacher in New York City, retiring in 1997. Shirley has served in many community and religious organizations, including local churches. She also enjoys singing, crewel, ceramics, and travel, and—most of all—time with family.

—*Biographical Directory*, 2004–2008

Eva B. Richardson Slater

In 1931, Eva B. married Oliver Eugene Slater (1906–1997). Gene was elected in 1960 out of the West Texas Annual Conference and served the Kansas Episcopal

Area (1960–1964) and the San Antonio Episcopal Area (1964–1976), then retired. Eva B. and Gene had two children.

Eva B. earned a BA from Southern Methodist University. She taught high school and church school, as well as participating in UMW at various levels. She was a member of the SMU Women's Club and was one of the founders of the University Women's Oral History Project. She liked to read, sew, and travel.

—*Biographical Directory*, November 1996

Bess Owens Smith (1901–1992)

In 1920, Bess married William Angie Smith (1894–1974). William was elected in 1944 out of The Methodist Episcopal Church, South. (His older brother, Angie Frank Smith, had been elected in 1930.) William had served churches in Texas; Louisiana; Tennessee; Washington, DC; and Alabama. He served the Oklahoma-New Mexico Episcopal Area (1944–1968), then retired. Bess and William had three sons, eight grandchildren, and 10 great grandchildren.

Bess was born in Texas and received an honorary doctorate from Oklahoma City University, where a hall on campus was named for her. A scholarship was named in her honor as well.

—http://catalog.gcah.org/publicdata/gcah5071.htm; http://catalog.gcah.org/DigitalArchives/memoirs/SmithBessOwens.pdf; https://www.findagrave.com/memorial/47220111/angie-frank-smith

Bess Patience Crutchfield Smith (1891–1964)

In 1914, Bess married Angie Frank Smith (1889–1962). Angie was elected in 1930 out of the North Texas Conference of The Methodist Episcopal Church, South, and was assigned to serve annual conferences in Missouri and Oklahoma, including the Oklahoma Indian Missionary Conference. From 1934 to 1960, he served the Houston Episcopal Area, which included five different annual conferences at different times. Before the 1939 merger, he served on the joint commissions that produced a new hymnal and the plan of union and directed the churchwide Aldersgate Commemoration (1937–1938). He was the first president of the Council of Bishops of The Methodist Church. Bess and Angie had four children.

—https://tshaonline.org/handbook/online/articles/fsm14

Ida L. Martin Smith (1876–1954)

In 1899, Ida married Harry Lester Smith (1876–1951). Harry was elected in 1920, after serving Methodist Episcopal churches in New York State. He served in Bangalore, India, supervising missions there (1920–1924); the Helena Episcopal Area (1924–1928); the Chattanooga Episcopal Area (1928–1932); the Cincinnati

Episcopal Area (1932–1944); and the Ohio Episcopal Area starting in 1944. Ida and Harry had one son.

Ida was an active youth worker in one of the churches Harry pastored, and she became his partner in the churches he pastored and during his episcopal service. When their son died at the age of 35, "she was never quite the same again" and suffered from ill health. She responded to a preacher's sermon about loneliness by commenting about how lonely it is when the church places people on a pedestal and leaves them there, instead of loving them.

—*Official Journal and Yearbook of the 17th Annual Session of the Ohio Annual Conference of The Methodist Church, 1955*, 1312; https://en.wikipedia.org/wiki/Harry_Lester_Smith; http://prabook.com/web/person-view.html?profileId=1102595; *Official Record and Yearbook, the 17th session of the Northeast Ohio Conference, The Methodist Church, 1955*, 965

Mildred Brown Smith (1902–1995)

In 1924, Mildred married John Owen Smith (1902–1978). John was elected in 1960 after serving parishes in South Carolina and served the Atlanta Episcopal Area (1960–1972), then retired. Through the turbulent 60s, when the Central Jurisdiction was abolished in 1964, he gave strong leadership to merging former Central Jurisdiction churches with the two conferences in his area. Mildred and John had two daughters, seven grandchildren, and nine great-grandchildren.

Mildred was born in South Carolina, studied the classics at Converse College, and taught high school English for a short time after her graduation. After their marriage, she and John went to Yale for his senior year and then to Montana to do mission work for a few months until he was given an appointment in South Carolina. During their 34 and one-half years in local churches, she served as a Sunday school teacher, leader of circles and mission studies, president of the Women's Society of Christian Service and Church Women United, and district director of Children's Work. They bought a home at Lake Junaluska in North Carolina, and she sometimes taught summer leadership and laboratory classes for the Southeastern Jurisdiction there. During his years as an active bishop, she served a term as a trustee for Clark College, inspired the establishment of ministers' wives organizations in both the North Georgia and South Georgia Annual Conferences, and became known as the "ring-leader" for fun and fellowship at retreats. In 1972, during the General Conference session in Atlanta, she hosted Methodist bishops' wives from around the world at a luncheon at the Governor's mansion. Governor Jimmy Carter arranged for his mother, Miss Lillian, to help welcome the wives to Atlanta. Mildred and John traveled widely, and she was inspired by a mission trip to Africa to help raise funds for scholarships for training women to become "better mothers, nurses, and teachers." She was also an associate at Emory School of Nursing and helped raise money for scholarships there. In retirement, she was active in garden clubs and a sewing group, as well as continuing to attend annual conference meetings.

—http://pitts.emory.edu/archives/text/mss242.html;
The Journal of the North Georgia Conference, 1996, 362–362;
Journal of the North Georgia Conference, 1980, 212–213

Joy B. Solomon (1936–2009)

In 1957, Joy married Dan Eugene Solomon (b. 1936). Dan was elected in 1988 out of the Southwest Texas Annual Conference and served the Oklahoma Episcopal Area (1988–1996) and the Louisiana Episcopal Area (1996–2000), then retired. Joy and Dan divorced in 2002. They have three children.

Joy graduated from McMurry College in Abilene, Texas, with a major in elementary education. She taught elementary children, served as president of the PTA for three schools, worked in Volunteers for Vision (screening elementary school children), and provided leadership in the Texas War on Drugs. She was very active in all phases of church work. She enjoyed music and directed a bishops' spouses' choir during some Council meetings. She also enjoyed traveling.

—*Biographical Directory*, 1996; interview with family, November 2017

Marcia Ann Stamm Solomon (b. 1945)

In 2004, Marcia married Dan Eugene Solomon (b. 1936). Dan was elected bishop out of the Southwest Texas Annual Conference and served the Oklahoma Area (1988–1996) and the Louisiana Area (1996–2000), then retired. Dan and Marcia have five children and nine grandchildren.

Marcia owned and operated an accounting business, MAS Business Service, for 32 years and is now semi-retired. She enjoys reading, travel, gardening and exercise. She has also enjoyed scuba diving and cross-country running.

Favorite Scripture: Psalms 51:10-12

—*Biographical Directory*, 2012–2016;
email communication with Marcia Solomon, July 2017

Beatrice Dibben Sommer (d. 1983/1984)

Beatrice married Johann Wilhelm Ernst Sommer (1881–1952). Ernst was elected in 1946 by the Germany Central Conference and assigned to the Frankfort-on-Main Episcopal Area. Beatrice and Johann had four children.

—https://en.wikipedia.org/wiki/Johann_Wilhelm_Ernst_Sommer;
Encyclopedia of World Methodism, Vol. 2, 2196–2197; http://catalog.gcah.org:8080/exist/memoirs/memoirs.xql?query=beatrice+sommer

Klara Auguste Beatrice Schuchardt Sommer (b. 1909)

In 1938, Beatrice married Carl Ernst Sommer (1911–1981), the son of Bishop J. W. Ernst Sommer. Carl was elected bishop in 1968 out of the Southwest Germany

Annual Conference and served the Frankfurt Episcopal Area (1968–1977), then retired. Beatrice and Carl had two children.

Beatrice, born in Germany, was active in the church and served as treasurer for the Women's Division in West Germany. She enjoyed gardening, music, and horses.

—*Encyclopedia of World Methodism, Vol. 1*, 2196;
Biographical Directory, November 1981

Dania Aben Soriano (b. 1951)

In 1978, Dania married Leo A. Soriano (b. 1950). Leo was elected out of the Philippines Mindano Annual Conference in 2000 and again in 2004 and 2008. He served the Davao Episcopal Area (2001–2012), then retired. Dania and Leo settled in Davao City. They have four children and six grandchildren.

Dania earned a BA in social work at Wesleyan University, Philippines, and entered Union Theological Seminary in 1977, where she met Leo. She is a commissioned diaconal minister. She served as a national officer of the Women's Society of Christian Service and also of the National Clergy Spouses' Association. She and Leo went to Jamkhed, India, for a short-term training in Community Based Primary Health Care (CBPHC), a General Board of Global Ministries project with a preventative approach to health care and disease. This ministry trains volunteer health workers and organizes them to teach and implement preventative health measures, including use of herbal and traditional medicine, classes for mothers, and seminars for out-of-school youth. Dania served as a consultant for this program until Leo's election in 2000.

Favorite Scripture: Romans 8:28 / Favorite Hymn: "So Send I You" (*Baptist Hymnal*, 2008, 362)

—*Biographical Directory*, 2012–2016; https://www.unitedmethodistbishops.org/person-detail/2464045; email communication with Dania Soriano, September 2017

Syble Mink Spain (b. 1926)

In 1948, Syble married Robert Hitchcock Spain (b. 1925). Robert was elected in 1988 out of the Tennessee Annual Conference and served the Louisville Episcopal Area (1988–1992), then retired. Syble and Bob settled back in Brentwood, Tennessee. They have two children, five grandchildren, and three great-grandchildren.

Syble attended Martin Methodist College and Middle Tennessee State University to become a teacher in Tennessee public schools. After providing financial support for her husband's continuing education, Syble turned her attention to the home and the church. Now in retirement, she devotes much time to being a good grandmother and working in the garden in Brentwood.

—*Biographical Directory*, 2012–2016;
email communication with Bishop Spain, 2017

Thomas Lucas Spaniolo [Carcaño] (b. 1949)

In 1988, Thomas married Minerva Garza Carcaño (b. 1954). Minerva was elected out of the Oregon-Idaho Annual Conference in 2004. She served the Phoenix Episcopal Area (2004–2012), the Los Angeles Episcopal Area (2012–2016), and was assigned to the San Francisco Episcopal Area in 2016. Thomas and Minerva have one daughter.

Thomas was born in Michigan and graduated from Michigan State University and Hamline University School of Law in St. Paul, Minnesota. Thomas is a lawyer specializing in immigration and criminal law, work he approaches from a deep commitment to social justice. He reads voraciously, arising early every morning to read the *New York Times*. He also loves to cook, particularly the dishes of his Italian cultural roots. He grounds his life and hope in the words of Mark 8:36 and Matthew 25:31-46.

—*Biographical Directory*, 2012–2016;
email communication with Bishop Carcaño, February 2018

Blanche May Frank Sparks (1906–1989)

In 1931, Blanche married W. Maynard Sparks (1906–1999). After serving EUB churches, Maynard was elected in 1958 during the General Conference session in Harrisburg. He served the Western Area (EUB) until 1968, then was assigned, through the UMC, to the Seattle Episcopal Area (1968–1972). From 1970 to 1973, he also had episcopal oversight of the Sierra Leone Annual conference, West Africa. Blanche and Maynard had three sons, four grandchildren, and two great-granddaughters.

Blanche was born in Pennsylvania and worked as a secretary for Lebanon Steel Foundry, Metropolitan Edison Electric Company, and later for the Jantzen and Pretzfeld Silk Mill. She also worked as assistant to the librarian in the Annville, Pennsylvania public library. After moving to the west coast, she provided secretarial services in the Evangelical United Brethren episcopal office. Blanche showed great passion for and interest in music and was active in church choirs throughout her adult life. She was awarded a life membership in the Women's Society of World Service while still living in Pennsylvania and later a special membership in UMW at Faith Church in Sacramento, California. In retirement, she co-chaired a Committee on Visitation to shut-ins for two years. Her memoir in the 2000 *California-Nevada Conference Journal* states, "Blanche was a treasured part of the team throughout the 41 years and 10 months of Maynard's pre-retirement ministry." In retirement, they lived in Sacramento, and "Blanche continued to be a blessing to Maynard" until her death.

—*2000 California-Nevada Conference Journal*, 226;
Journal and Yearbook the California-Nevada Annual Conference, 1990, 282

Diane Sprague (b. 1939)

In 1959, Diane married C. Joseph Sprague (b. 1939). Joe was elected in 1996 out of the Ohio West Annual Conference and served the Chicago Episcopal Area

(1996–2004), then retired. Diane and Joe settled in Columbus, Ohio. They have four children, 10 grandchildren, and three great-grandchildren.

Diane was born in Ohio and graduated from Miami Jacobs and North Central Colleges there. For over 55 years, Diane was a devoted supporter of Joe's ministry as pastor and bishop, while distinguishing herself as a Head Start teacher and recreational therapist in nursing homes and the former Central Ohio Psychiatric Hospital in Columbus. Her students, co-workers, and patients highly regarded Diane in large measure because of her empathetic heart. She possesses the rare capacity of valuing all people, equally. Diane enjoys cooking delicacies to share with family and neighbors, a practice acquired from her mother. She enjoys watching OSU women's basketball, giving birthday parties (even for her adored dogs), working out with a trainer, and singing in church choirs. Most of all, the abiding joy of Diane's life is their treasured family. A former athlete herself, she remains an avid fan of her family's athletic involvements. Diane is proud of her children and grandchildren's athletic, academic, professional, and community accomplishments. She is overjoyed by their values and grateful for all they do for others and for the strong family tradition they represent.

—*Biographical Directory*, 2004–2008, 2010, 2012;
email communication with Bishop Sprague, January 2018

Helen Emily Springer (1868–1946)

In 1905, Helen married John McKendree Springer (1878–1956). John was elected missionary bishop for Africa in 1936 at the General Conference of The Methodist Episcopal Church, after 35 years of missionary service in Africa. He continued to travel throughout the African continent, retiring in 1944 and returning to the U.S. in 1950.

Helen became a missionary at the age of 21, and shortly thereafter married missionary William Rasmussen and served with him in the Congo (Zaire) until his death from a fever in 1895. After spending time in the U.S. to recover from the fever herself, she returned to Africa in 1901, this time to Rhodesia, as the first missionary there of the Methodist Episcopal Woman's Foreign Missionary Society. Living in the villages to study Shona, she translated the Scriptures and hymns, publishing *A Handbook of Chikaranga* in 1905 and laying the foundation for education of Methodist girls there. After she married John Springer, they served together at mission stations and throughout the African countryside, walking between remote villages, sometimes riding in a hammock carried by natives. They walked across Northern Rhodesia (Zambia) and founded Methodist missions in the Congo (Zaire). They led worship, provided health care, taught individuals and classes, learned native languages and translated materials, wrote articles, and shared the love of Christ with all they met, introducing Protestant work among the Lunda and in Katanga Province. Helen worked with the women, conducted ministerial training, and continued translating the Scriptures. On furlough in 1919, she was a powerful speaker, recruiting for the Student Volunteer Movement. After John's election, Helen still traveled with him, happily encouraging and learning from all she met and enjoying the conferences and visits.

—http://www.bu.edu/missiology/missionary-biography/r-s/springer-helen-emily-chapman-rasmussen-1868-1946/; John McKendree Springer, *I Love the Trail: A Sketch of the Life of Helen Emily Springer* (Nashville: The Parthenon Press, 1952); http://catalog.gcah.org/publicdata/gcah660.htm; http://www.bu.edu/missiology/missionary-biography/r-s/springer-helen-emily-chapman-rasmussen-1868-1946/

Helen Newton Everett Springer

Helen married retired Bishop John McKendree Springer (1878–1956) sometime after the death of his first wife in 1946. John had been serving as missionary bishop for Africa, retired in 1944, and returned to the U.S. in 1950.

Helen Newton Everett Springer was a graduate of Mount Holyoke College and Massachusetts General Hospital, where she earned a BA and a nursing degree. She arrived in Africa in 1921 and served as a missionary/nurse for 21 years, working in Kapanga, Kanene, and Elisabethville in the Congo, as well as in Mount Silinda in Southern Rhodesia.

—http://catalog.gcah.org/publicdata/gcah660.htm

Clinton Stanovsky (b. 1956)

In 1977, Clint married Elaine J. Woodworth (b. 1953). Elaine was elected in 2008 out of the Pacific Northwest Annual Conference and served the Denver Episcopal Area (2008–2016), which became the Mountain Sky Episcopal Area in 2012, and the Greater Northwest Episcopal Area starting in 2016. Clint and Elaine have three sons.

Clint has an undergraduate degree in mechanical engineering from the University of Washington, an MA in public policy from Massachusetts Institute of Technology, and a second MA in public administration earned recently from the University of Colorado Denver School of Public Affairs. He has been a consultant in environmental management since 1981and a regulatory analyst for the Washington State Department of Ecology since 2015. He is a trained community mediator practicing through a local dispute resolution center. Clint is particularly interested in the problems and policies of local communities involved in cleaning up contaminated sites.

—*Biographical Directory*, 2010;
email communication with Clint Stanovsky, February 2018

Lisa Henzler Sticher (b. 1930)

In 1958, Lisa married Hermann Ludwig Sticher (1927-2014). Hermann was elected in 1977 by the Central Conference in the Federal Republic of Germany and

West Berlin. He served an episcopal area that included the Federal Republic of Germany and West Berlin (1977–1989), then retired. Lisa and Hermann have three sons, five grandchildren, and one great-grandson.

Favorite Scripture: Hebrews 13:8

—*Biographical Directory*, 2000–2004;
email communication with son Thomas Sticher, August 2017,
and Urs Schweizer, assistant to Bishop Dr. Patrick Streiff, October 2018

Josephine Mitchell Stith (b. 1935)

In 1960, Jo married Forrest C. Stith (b. 1934). Forrest was elected out of the Baltimore-Washington Annual Conference in 1984 and served the New York West Episcopal Area (1984–1992) and the New York Area (1992–1996), then retired. In retirement, he and Jo served the UMC of East Africa (1996–2000), then returned to Upper Marlboro, Maryland. Josephine and Forrest have a daughter.

Jo earned a BA with a major in English literature at Howard University and an MS as a reading specialist at Morgan State University. In 2000, she ended a 35-year teaching career, having taught in Washington, DC; Maryland; New York; and in East and West Africa. In retirement, she has been enjoying art (needle art, pen and ink drawing) and learning to play the flute. Jo writes poetry, is a letter writer, and sends cards to celebrate special occasions. She goes to Bible study and sings in her church choir. For six years, she has traveled to New York City to attend a week-end seminar at the Church Center, where women and men study issues relevant to poor mothers and their children globally. She works with UMW and has facilitated a weekend retreat to study Women of the Bible. Jo is a cheerleader for pre-natal and new mother wellness. She sends books (stories, poems, and music) to help new mothers create healthy climates to foster happiness and well-being. She also champions literacy and has continued to work tirelessly on behalf of young people in the church and community. In 2000, she traveled to Central and South America to observe Community Based Primary Health Care, wrote a moving account of that experience, and spoke on behalf of poor mothers and children of the developing world at a Council of Bishops' meeting and elsewhere. Jo journals daily and has belonged to the Bishops' Spouses journaling group and to its Mission Support Network.

—*Biographical Directory*, 2004–2008; notes provided by Jo Stith, November 2017

Jean Stevens Stockton (1930–2017)

In 1953, Jean married Thomas Barber Stockton (b. 1930). Tom was elected in 1988 out of the Western North Carolina Annual Conference and served the Richmond Episcopal Area (1988–1996), then retired. Jean and Tom settled back in North Carolina. They have three children and nine grandchildren.

Jean received her BS from the University of North Carolina at Greensboro in 1952 and an MA in education in 1953. She taught in the physical education departments at Duke University, Mars Hill College, and Queens College, specializing in interpretive dance. An obituary published in the *Charlotte Observer* November 12, 2017, described her thus: "Jean was a multi-talented person. As a pioneer in liturgical dance, she inspired worship services and taught others. She was a great student of the Bible and was widely loved as a teacher of the Scriptures, especially by her High Point Bible Group. She studied counseling and was a confidante and supportive friend to many. With boundless creativity, she painted, sculpted, and knitted. Among the many hobbies at which she was competitive were golf, tennis, bridge, croquet, pool, and board games. Her disciplined devotional life was deeply meaningful for her and influential in the lives of others. Above all else, and in everything, she was God's servant, and strived with every fiber of her being to give her utmost for God's highest."

—*Biographical Directory*, 2004–2008; https://www.legacy.com/obituaries/charlotte/obituary.aspx?n=jean-weaver-stockton-stevens&pid=187215284&fhid=17624

Vera Loudon Stockwell (1897–1969)

In 1922, Vera married Bowman Foster Stockwell (1899–1961). Bowman, who was born in Oklahoma and sent by the Board of Missions of The Methodist Episcopal Church to teach at Union Seminary in Argentina, was elected in 1960 by the Latin America Central Conference of The Methodist Church. He served the Pacific Episcopal Area of that Central Conference until his death, 13 months later. Vera and Bowman had two children, one of whom died in infancy. The other, Eugene, became a missionary and served as the director of the Commission on World Mission and Evangelism for the World Council of Churches.

Vera was born in Ohio, graduated in 1919 from Ohio Wesleyan, where she played in the Student Volunteer Band and served on the YWCA Cabinet. She also studied for an MA at Boston University Graduate School, completing a thesis titled "St. Paul's Christ–Mysticism" in 1926.

—https://en.wikipedia.org/wiki/Bowman_Foster_Stockwell; https://www.findagrave.com/memorial/147799911/bowman-foster-stockwell; https://open.bu.edu/handle/2144/5635; *Encyclopedia of World Methodism, Vol. 2*, 2257–2258; email communication with grandson Robert Stockwell, December 2017

Ada Rose Yow Stokes (1920–2008)

In 1942, Rose married Marion Mack B. Stokes (1911–2012). Mack was elected in 1972 out of the North Georgia Annual Conference and served the Jackson Episcopal Area (1972–1980), then retired. Rose and Mack settled at Lake Junaluska, North Carolina. They had two children, seven grandchildren, and one great-grandchild.

Rose attended Peace Junior College in Raleigh, North Carolina; graduated with an AB from East Carolina Teachers College; and studied at the Presbyterian General Assembly's Training School for Lay Workers in Richmond, Virginia. Rose not only taught in the Atlanta public schools, but also assisted her seminary professor husband with research and writing, hosted hundreds of theological students in their home, and actively participated in the UMW as a study leader.

Her memoir in the November 2009 Council of Bishop Memorial Booklet states, "Passionate about education for all children, she was the sole white teacher to show up for the first day of class at her elementary school after the Atlanta schools desegregated in 1961. Assigned to a school in a poor area, Rose was one of the first elementary teachers in the nation to bring black studies into the classroom by exploring the lives of great African Americans. In 1972, when Mack was elected Bishop and assigned to Mississippi, the couple moved to Jackson, where, working against strong resistance, Rose was a tireless advocate for merger of the African American and White Methodist conferences." Her husband said of her, "She was a woman of great poise, faith, and creativity, and an unfailing support to me."

—*Biographical Directory*, 2000–2004;
Council of Bishops Memorial Booklet, November 2009

Clara Morgan Straughn (1882–1965)

In 1904, Clara married James Henry Straughn (1877–1974). James, after serving churches in the mid-Atlantic region and as president of West Lafayette College and of the General Conference of The Methodist Protestant Church, was elected bishop in 1939 in preparation for the coming union. He was assigned to the Pittsburgh Episcopal Area of The Methodist Church (1940–1948), then retired. Clara and James had a daughter and a granddaughter.

Born in Maryland, Clara graduated from Western Maryland College in 1902, *summa cum laude*. She taught in Allegheny County public schools for two years before her marriage. Later, when James was president of the West Lafayette College, she taught French and Latin. In her memoir in the 1966 *Baltimore Annual Conference Journal*, Bishop John Wesley Lord describes her as "A wide reader of the best in books, a woman of intelligence and charm, richly talented, and coming from a home of affluence, her very presence in any company produced the most delightful impression."

—*Minutes of the 182nd Annual Session of the Baltimore Annual Conference of The Methodist Church, 1966*, 408;
https://www.findagrave.com/cgi-bin/fg.cgi?page=gr&GRid=75320694;
http://prabook.com/web/person-view.html?profileId=284121

Heidi Albrecht Streiff (b. 1952)

In 1979, Heidi married Patrick Phillip Streiff (b. 1955). Patrick was elected in 2005 out of the Switzerland-France-North Africa Annual Conference and was assigned to the Central and Southern Europe Episcopal Area, with Methodist presence in 16 countries. Heidi and Patrick have four children and four grandchildren.

Heidi was born and grew up in the region of Zurich in a small farmer's village, later moving to a small town nearby. She became a kindergarten teacher and was active in youth work in the local UM church and in the regional unit. She got to know Patrick when he served her local church before going to seminary for theological studies. When their children were born, she stopped teaching and stayed home with them until they were grown up. Then she began work in a home for elderly people. She loves working with persons near the end of life and discovered she is especially gifted to work with them. When she was 62, her first grandchild was born and she gave up work to spend time with her grandchildren and to be available for her parents, who were in their 90s. She loves to be out in nature, especially when it is warm and sunny, and enjoys hiking and reading. She and Patrick often go for long hikes when on vacation.

Favorite Scripture: 1 Corinthians 15:10

—*Biographical Directory*, 2004–2008;
email communication with Heidi Streiff, May 2017

Mary Ella Stuart (1909–2001)

In 1933, Mary Ella married Robert Marvin Stuart (1910–2003). Marvin was elected in 1964 out of the California-Nevada Annual Conference and served the Denver Episcopal Area (1964–1972) and the San Francisco Episcopal Area (1972–1980), then retired. Mary Ella and Marvin settled in Palo Alto, California. They had three children, two of whom died in infancy.

Mary Ella attended Taylor University in Indiana, where she met Marvin. Before their marriage, she taught high school English and history in Illinois for two years. After their marriage, she used her educational skills to develop a year-long curriculum for seventh grade confirmation classes, which she taught for 20 years. Very active in the local church, Mary Ella sang in choirs, taught, counseled youth, led retreats, and participated in other activities of a team-ministry with Marvin, which she loved. She also enjoyed homemaking, cooking, gardening, music, drama, writing, and oil painting. In 1977, Abingdon Press published her book *To Bend Without Breaking*, in which she speaks honestly about her experiences with depression and shares what she learned while trying to recover. She traveled widely to speak and lead workshops, and her book is still used as a resource for stress management.

—*Biographical Directory*, 2000–2004; http://catalog.gcah.org:8080/exist/memoirs/memoirs.xql?query=Mary+Ella+Stuart; *To Bend Without Breaking: Stress and How to Deal with It* (Nashville: Abingdon Press, 1977)

Dorothy Sinclair Day Subhan

In 1926, Dorothy Day married John Abdus Subhan (1899–1977). John, born into a Muslim family, had recently become a Methodist and was teaching in the Department of Islamic Studies at Bareilly Theological Seminary. In 1930, he was ordained, and in 1945 he was elected out of the North India Annual Conference. He served the Bombay Episcopal Area (1945–1956) and the Hyderabad Episcopal Area (1956–1964), then retired and moved to the U.S., where he taught theology at Boston University until they returned to Hyderabad. They had three children.

—*Biographical Directory*, 1996;
https://library.syr.edu/digital/guides/s/subhan_ja.htm

Rajabai Ruth Peters Sundaram (b. 1902)

In 1930, Rajabai married Gabriel Sundaram (1900–1984), a teacher at Hyderabad Boy's School and a widower. Gabriel was elected in 1956 by the Southern Asia Central Conference. He served the Hyderabad Episcopal Area (1957–1964), then retired. Gabriel had two children by his first wife, and Rajabai and Gabriel had one child together.

Rajabai earned both a BA and an MA in science. At one time she was a reader in chemistry and head of the Department of Science at Osmania University, where she started the Women's College with just five girls. When she retired 25 years later, there were 500 students with a staff to teach physics, organic and inorganic chemistry, botany, and zoology. She was president of the Women's Conference of the Hyderabad Annual Conference for four years and of the Lucknow Conference for eight years, and she represented the Women's Society of Christian Service at the World Methodist Council held in London (circa 1966).

—*Biographical Directory*, 1984; http://worldmethodistcouncil.org/about/

Delphine Yvonne Ramsey Swanson (b. 1954)

In 1986, Delphine married James E. Swanson Sr (b. 1950). James was elected in 2004 out of the South Georgia Annual Conference. He served the Holston Episcopal Area (2004–2012) and then was assigned to the Mississippi Episcopal Area in 2012. Delphine and James have six children and 10 grandchildren.

Delphine graduated from Morris Brown College in Atlanta, Georgia, with a BS in elementary education. She received an MA, specialist degree, and certification in leadership from Troy State University in Phoenix City, Alabama. Additionally, she attended Georgia Southern University in Statesboro, Georgia, and Savannah State College in Savannah, Georgia. She taught school in Columbus and Savannah, Georgia. Delphine enjoys traveling with her husband. Her interest and hobbies include reading, sewing, shopping, decorating, swimming, cooking, and entertaining.

Favorite Scripture: Psalm 27:1 / Favorite Hymn: "Hymn of Promise" (*UMH*, 707)
—*Biographical Directory*, 2004–2008;
email communication with Delphine Swanson, 2017

Jeff Swenson (b. 1943)

In 1968, Jeff married Mary Ann McDonald (b. 1947). Mary Ann was elected in 1992 out of the Pacific-Northwest Annual Conference and served the Denver Episcopal Area (1992–2000) and the Los Angeles Episcopal Area (2000–2012), then retired. Jeff and Mary Ann settled in Pasadena, California.

Jeff Swenson graduated from the University of Puget Sound in Tacoma, Washington, with a degree in fine arts. He served in the Navy in Vietnam. On their 25th wedding anniversary, the Swensons received a tandem bicycle. They have become avid riders, completing a California coast tour in 1994, an Oregon coast tour in 1995, a Washington State tour in 1996, and riding to and from annual conference sessions and to Sunday services. In the summer of 1998, they rode across the U.S. from the Pacific Ocean to the Atlantic Ocean, covering 4,059 miles in 58 days. In the spring of 1999, they joined a group touring Bryce Canyon and Zion National Park in Utah.

—*Biographical Directory*, 2004–2008; https://www.unitedmethodistbishops.org/person-detail/2464055; interview with Bishop Swenson, February 2018

Ethelou Douglas Talbert (1932–1999)

In 1961, Ethelou married Melvin George Talbert (b. 1934). Mel was elected in 1980 out of the Southern California/Arizona Annual Conference (while serving as general secretary for the General Board of Discipleship in Nashville) and was assigned to the Seattle Episcopal Area (1980–1988) and the San Francisco Episcopal Area (1988–2000), then retired. Ethelou and Mel adopted a daughter, who gave them three grandchildren.

Ethelou majored in voice at Dillard University and later attended Scarritt and Vanderbilt, majoring in behavioral science. She also studied in the Graduate School of Social Work, Tennessee State, receiving many honors along the way. She taught music education, served as director of admissions and recruitment at the School of Theology at Claremont, and worked as administrative assistant to the director of a home for the aging in New Orleans. She was an officer of Church Women United and a member of the YWCA Board of Directors, the Greater Seattle Chapter of the United Nations Association, and the board for the Atlantic Street Center in Seattle. She also worked part-time at the Learning Resource Center at Merritt College, Oakland, still finding time for writing, needlecraft, backgammon, camping, voter registration, and providing wedding consultation, as well as being a most gracious hostess.

—*Biographical Directory*, 1996–2000, 2012–2016;
email communication with Bishop Talbert, 2017

Marilyn Ruth Williams Magee Talbert (b. 1940)

In 2000, Marilyn married Bishop Melvin G. Talbert (b. 1934), who retired from the San Francisco Episcopal Area that same year. Marilyn and Mel settled in Brentwood, Tennessee. Mel has one daughter and three grandchildren with his first wife, Ethelou, who died in 1999. Marilyn has two children and four grandchildren.

Marilyn grew up in Illinois and earned degrees from Illinois State University in elementary education and special education. She was a Danforth Foundation Scholar and received honors from the John F. Kennedy Center on Mental Retardation at Vanderbilt University. She was widowed at age 30 with two children. Marilyn earned graduate degrees from Loyola University of Chicago, and has been a case worker, teacher, counselor, administrator, and corporate executive. She was the first lay executive director of Chicago Black Methodists for Church Renewal (BMCR). She has served in various staff positions at the General Board of Discipleship. Marilyn has traveled extensively in Africa and staffed two episcopal travel groups. She is an author, speaker, workshop and seminar leader, and a trustee at Garrett-Evangelical Seminary, where she chaired the Academic Affairs Committee for six years.

Marilyn has published several resources for our church. Most recently, in *The Past Matters: A Chronology of African Americans in The United Methodist Church* (2003), she carefully and clearly chronicled significant events and persons in the history of African Americans in our church. Marilyn also coauthored a book with Evelyn Burry, *Making a Difference You Can See: How to Plan for Ministry* (1987) and contributed to *Church and Family Together, A Congregational Manual for Black Family Ministry* (1996).

Favorite Scripture: Proverbs 3:5-6 / Favorite Hymn: "Amazing Grace" (*UMH*, 378)

—*Biographical Directory*, 2012;
email correspondence with Marilyn Talbert, 2016–2017

Annie Belle Thaxton Taylor (1903–1995)

Annie Belle married Prince Albert Taylor Jr in 1929. Prince (1907–2001) was elected in 1956 by the Central Jurisdictional Conference, having served churches in North Carolina and New York City and as assistant to the president at Bennett College, professor at Gammon Theological Seminary, and editor of *The Central Christian Advocate*. He was assigned to the Monrovia (Liberia) Episcopal Area (1956–1964) and the New Jersey Episcopal Area (1964–1976), then retired. Annie Belle and Prince had one daughter.

Annie Belle graduated from Columbia University and worked as a teacher. She is closely identified with her husband's ministry and also pursued her own interests in church and community work. She and Prince were the first episcopal couple to reside permanently in New Jersey, and he was the first Black bishop to be appointed to lead an essentially white area.

Neil Irons recalls how Belle would chuckle while telling about their experience as the first Black family to live in a certain section of Princeton. When unwanted salesmen or solicitors came to their door, she would simply say that the "missus" was not at home and close the door. Neil also noted that Belle was such an excellent seamstress that she would make replicas of clothing she saw in store windows for her daughter. Although she was reduced to a wheelchair by a stroke in later life, she never lost her sense of humor. Inez Irons was a close friend and would take Belle to meetings of bishops' wives in her wheelchair so that she could enjoy the fellowship.

—Robert B. Steelman, *What God Has Wrought: A History of the Southern New Jersey Conference . . ., 1836–1986* [Pennington, NJ: The UMC Southern New Jersey Annual Conference Commission on Archives and History, 1986], 245; email communication with Bishop Irons, 2011; *Biographical Directory*, November 1992, November 1996

James "Rusty" Russell Taylor (b. 1950)

In 1973, Rusty married Mary Virginia (Dindy) Kilgore (b. 1950). Dindy was elected out of the Holston Annual Conference in 2004. She served the Columbia Episcopal Area (2004-2012) and was assigned to the Holston Episcopal Area in 2012. Rusty and Dindy have two grown children and three grandchildren.

Rusty is a graduate of Tennessee Wesleyan College and Candler School of Theology at Emory University. He began his ministry at the Rising Fawn Circuit in Dade County, Georgia, and has served a variety of churches over the years. He served as director of congregational development for the South Carolina Annual Conference and now serves as director of congregational development in the Holston Conference. He enjoys hunting, playing guitar, singing, and horseback riding.

Favorite Scripture: John 14:27 / Favorite Hymn: "In the Sweet By and By" (https://hymnary.org/text/theres_a_land_that_is_fairer_than_day_an)

—*Biographical Directory*, 2008–2012; email communication with Rusty Taylor, 2017

Ruth Naomi Wilson Thomas (1921–2017)

In 1945, Ruth married James S. Thomas (1919–2010). Jim was elected in 1964 out of the Central Jurisdiction, while serving as the associate general secretary of the General Board of Education in charge of the Black Methodist Colleges. He served the Iowa Area (1964–1976) and the East Ohio Area (1976–1988), then retired. He taught at Southern Methodist, Clark Atlanta, and Emory Universities in retirement. Ruth and Jim had four daughters, four grandchildren, and two great-grandchildren.

Ruth earned a diploma from Barber-Scotia Junior College and finished her college work at North Carolina College for Negroes. Later she did graduate work at Cornell University. She worked as a dietitian and public school teacher. In addition to church activities, she participated in programs of the YWCA, AAUW, PTA, National

Council of Christians and Jews, Girl Scouts, and other organizations. She thoroughly enjoyed travel in the U.S. and abroad. Her hobbies included reading, cooking, sewing, swimming, gardening, and playing Scrabble. She also enjoyed attending lectures and musical and drama performances.

—*Biographical Directory*, 2004–2008;
email communication with daughter Patricia Thomas, spring 2017

Susan Thomas [Irons] (b. 1947)

In 2002, Susan Thomas married Bishop Neil L. Irons (b. 1936), who was serving the Harrisburg Episcopal Area (1996–2004), then retired. Susan and Neil live in Mechanicsburg, Pennsylvania. Neil, whose first wife, Inez, died in 1993, has two children. Susan has two children and four grandchildren.

Susan graduated from Grove City College and did post-graduate work at Penn State University and Shippensburg University. She has been actively working as a residential realtor since September 1989. Her interests include singing in the church choir, gardening, distance walking, and being with her grandchildren.

Favorite Hymn: "You Satisfy the Hungry Heart" (*UMH*, 629)

—*Biographical Directory*, 2000–2004, 2004–2008;
email communication with Susan Thomas, spring 2016

Kathleen Ann Thomas-Sano (1946–2016)

In 1975, Kathy married Roy Isao Sano (b. 1931). Roy was elected in 1984 out of the California-Nevada Annual Conference. He served the Denver Episcopal Area (1984–1992) and the Los Angeles Episcopal Area (1992–2000), then retired. Roy has three children and two grandchildren from a previous marriage.

Kathy served on the staff of the National Division of the General Board of Global Ministries (1967–1975) in Philadelphia and then in New York City. She was a third-generation Korean on her mother's side, with her father a descendant of Irish, Welsh, German, French, English, Scottish, and Canadian Acadian ancestors. This richly diverse ancestry energized what became her passion for inclusiveness in church and community.

Kathy, as she is generally known, served as associate director of the Council on Ministries of the California-Nevada Conference (1976–1984) and as a UM representative on the Governing Board of the National Council of Churches (1976–1985). Kathy was a delegate to the 1980 Western Jurisdictional Conference and then became a part-time consultant to the Western Jurisdiction Inter-Ethnic Coordinating Committee and an advisor to United Methodist Pacific Islanders who created their National Plan in 2012. Earlier, Kathy edited three quadrennial interethnic proposals (1976–1984) for United Methodism's Missional Priorities on "Developing and

Strengthening the Racial Ethnic Minority Churches." Kathy also served as associate general secretary at the General Commission on Religion and Race (2000–2009). Kathy joined others in promoting interreligious healing through the Commission on Christian Unity and Interreligious Concerns. She also served as director of PACTS, the Pacific and Asian American Center for Theologies and Strategies at Pacific School of Religion, and later as the executive director of NFAAUM, the National Federation of Asian American United Methodists. As Rev. Michael Yoshii, a pastor and community organizer based in California, said, Kathy, "was always reaching out to diverse communities—and always mentoring us in ways the connection could support emerging ministries for congregations and caucus ministries."

—*Biographical Directory*, 2004–2008;
email communication with Bishop Sano, 2016–2017

Ruth Lena Underwood Tippett (1893–1980)

In 1922, Ruth married Donald Harvey Tippett (1896–1982). Donald was elected in 1948 after serving churches in Colorado. He served the San Francisco Episcopal Area (1944–1968), then retired. Ruth and Donald had two sons and six grandchildren.

Ruth, born in Nebraska, earned an AB from the University of Nebraska and an MA from the University of Wisconsin. She taught physics in Council Bluffs, Iowa, where she and her students built a wireless, which earned them a front-page story in the local paper. She traveled with her husband around the world, visiting every continent except Australia. In her memoir in the 1981 *California-Nevada Conference Journal*, Donald is quoted as saying, "She was part of everything I did."

—https://www.wikitree.com/wiki/Tippett-14;
Encyclopedia of World Methodism, Vol. 1, 295;
Official Journal and Yearbook, The California-Nevada Annual Conference, 1981, 295

Eugenio Tomas [Nhanala] (b. 1948)

In 1976, Eugenio married Joaquina Filipe Nhanala (b. 1956). Joaquina was elected in 2008 out of the Mozambique Annual Conference and assigned to the Mozambique Episcopal Area. She was re-elected for life in 2012. Eugenio and Joaquina have four children.

Eugenio, at a very young age, went to live with the family of a UM evangelist, where he cared for the flock, mainly goats. Through the witness of the evangelist, Eugenio became the first generation of Christians in his family. The evangelist sent Eugenio to Cambine, a UMC mission, where he attended school. He went from there into the military and then looked for work in the capital city, where he rejoined the UMC. After working with various companies and then the Ministry of Agriculture in the Department of Entomology, he attended Gbarnga School of Theology in Liberia,

Trinity College in Ghana, St. Paul's College and Nairobi Evangelical Graduate School of Theology in Kenya, from which he graduated with a MDiv. Ordained as a UM elder, Eugenio served in various positions in the church and retired in 2011. His hobbies include music and watching soccer. He proclaims, "My life journey has been strengthened by seeing God's hand in my everyday life and witnessing this love to others."

—https://www.umnews.org/en/news/united-methodists-in-africa-elect-first-female-bishop; email communication with Bishop Nhanala, March 2018

Alegria Hembrador Toquero (1939–2010)

In 1970, Alegria married Solito K. Toquero (b. 1942). Solito, a member of the Bulacan Philippines Annual Conference, was elected in 2001 at a special session of the Philippine Central Conference and again in 2004. He served the Manila Episcopal Area (2001–2008), then retired. Alegria and Sol have two children and one grandchild.

Alegria, born in the Philippines, earned her BA in elementary education from the National Teachers College and specialized in home economics at the Philippine Normal College. She worked as an elementary school teacher for over 20 years. She loved to cook, read, and take care of her granddaughter.

According to the Memorial Booklet of 2011, "Alegria was a good partner of Sol in the ministry for 40 fruitful years in various congregations in the Provinces of the Philippines. Alegria and Sol also served as Filipino missionaries in Hong Kong for four years, from 1997–2001. She served as Matron in the Methodist Shelter, taking care of five to 20 domestic helpers, mostly Filipino and Indonesian women, terminated from work. ....She joined her husband in returning to the Philippines when he was elected bishop on July 17, 2001. She traveled with him much of the time and visited many local churches within the Manila Episcopal Area where he was assigned until his retirement. As a bishop's spouse, she supported and joined the ministry of the UMW nationwide; she inspired the ministers' spouses to organize, have their own meetings, and report during annual conference sessions. She helped in the senior citizens' ministry of Kapatiran Kaunlaran Foundation by regularly attending their Bible study and fellowship every Friday in Manila. A year after her husband's retirement from the episcopacy, she suffered a stroke that paralyzed her for a year until she succumbed on July 13, 2010. She was a very jovial person even in her sickness, befitting her name, 'Alegria,' meaning 'joy.'"

—*Biographical Directory*, 2004–2008; Council of Bishops Memorial Booklet May 2011; email communication with Bishop Toquero, September 2017

Joyce Orpilla Torio (b. 1974)

In 2006, Joyce married Pedro M. Torio Jr (b.1965). Pete was elected in 2012 out of the Northwest Philippines Annual Conference and assigned to the Baguio Episcopal Area (2012–2016) and again in 2016. Joyce and Pete have four children.

Joyce is a systems analyst, writer, and composer, whose latest work won first place in the National Clergy Spouses Association Hymn-writing and Logo-making Contest in 2012. She is the former president of the Northwest Philippines Annual Conference United Methodist Young Adult Association (NWPAC UMYAF). She is also an active advocate for HIV/AIDS awareness and prevention.

—*Biographical Directory*, 2012–2016;
email communication with Joyce Torio, 2017 and 2018

Marjorie Ida Tuell (b. 1926)

In 1946, Marji married Jack Marvin Tuell (1923–2014). Jack was elected in 1972 out of the Pacific Northwest Annual Conference and served the Portland (Oregon) Episcopal Area (1972–1980) and the Los Angeles Episcopal Area (1980–1992), then retired. They moved to Washington State. Marji and Jack have three children and five grandchildren.

Marji attended Willamette University and the Children's Hospital School of Nursing in Denver. She received a BA in church music from the University of Puget Sound in 1961 and did graduate work there and at Portland State University. Marji has held district and conference offices in UMW. In addition to more than 20 years of experience as a choir director, she has also taught in public schools, volunteered as a music teacher for mentally disabled youth, and frequently served as a song leader and lecturer on hymnology. Marji chaired the Women's Committee of the Campaign for the Archives and History Center (1982–1983), raising over $700,000 (which was not acknowledged when the Center was dedicated). Marji has published several articles related to church music and compiled *Tell the Blessed Tidings*, a collection of hymn texts by women. Marji also served on the Hymnal Revision Committee (1984–1988), chairing the Text Sub-committee and working into 1989 proofreading and developing the topical index for the *UM Hymnal*.

—*Biographical Directory*, 2000–2004;
email communication with Marji Tuell, June 2017

Katherine Crum Irwin Tullis (b. 1925)

In 1997, Kit married retired Bishop Edward Lewis Tullis (1917–2005), who was living at Lake Junaluska. Ed had two children, four grandchildren, and three great-grandchildren with his first wife, Mary Jane, who died in 1996. Kit has two sons and a daughter (deceased) from her first marriage to Frank M. Irwin, an engineer who died in 1996.

Kit was born in Columbia, South Carolina, but lived most of her life in Durham, North Carolina. Kit was active in church and community affairs, as well as working in real estate and owning an antiques business. She and Ed were actively involved in ministries at Lake Junaluska Assembly and Long's Chapel UMC.

—*Biographical Directory*, 2000–2004;
https://www.wellsfuneralhome.com/obituary/Bishop-Tullis

Mary Jane Tullis (1917–1996)

In 1937, Mary Jane married Edward Lewis Tullis (1917–2005). Ed was elected in 1972 out of the Kentucky Annual Conference and served the Columbia (South Carolina)Episcopal Area (1972–1980) and the Nashville Episcopal Area (1980–1984), then retired. Mary Jane and Ed had two children, four grandchildren, and three great-grandchildren.

Mary Jane, born in Kentucky, studied at Kentucky Wesleyan College, where she met Ed, and later at the University of Edinburgh, Scotland. She was socially active and never let her marriage to a bishop overshadow her own projects and passions. She served as a leader of Methodist Women at the local, district, and conference levels throughout her adult years. In Kentucky, she organized schools for children with cerebral palsy and other special needs. In South Carolina, Mary Jane organized an annual retreat for clergy spouses and helped establish the Killingsworth Home for Women, a residence for women coming out of crisis situations. She traveled extensively around the world with Ed and led retreats for clergy spouses, missionaries, and military chaplains. Mary Jane also enjoyed needlepoint, gardening, and golf.

—*Biographical Directory*, 1992, 2000–2004;
https://en.wikipedia.org/wiki/Edward_Lewis_Tullis; *Journal of the Kentucky Annual Conference, 1996*, 110; *1996 South Carolina Conference Journal*, 326

Manafundu Diandja Marie-Claire Unda (b. 1964)

In 2017, Marie-Claire married Gabriel Yemba Unda (b. 1951). Gabriel was elected in 2012 and again in 2017 and serves the East Congo Episcopal Area. Gabriel has eight surviving children with his first wife, Omba Olela Charlotte, who died in 2007. Marie-Claire has six children from a previous marriage.

Marie-Claire is an MD assigned to a hospital in Kinshasa and also teaches in several medical schools in Kinshasa, Mbuji-Mayi, and Wembo-Nyama. She works with a non-governmental organization (National Multi-Sector Program against HIV/AIDS) specializing in the care of HIV/AIDS orphans, aging persons, and single mothers. She also works with a food and agriculture organization providing care and distributing supplies for farmers and fishermen of the Sankura province. In the church, she is in charge of the Maternal and Child Health Department and directs a children's choir. She is seeking funding for a training project for pastors' wives. A May 17, 2018 UMNS article by Judith Osongo Yanga of the Congo describes a new endeavor at Kindu Methodist University, where wives of theology students have the opportunity to learn trades to help support and care for their families. Courses offered include culinary science, sewing, hygiene, literacy, religion, and languages. The article quotes Marie-Claire, who is studying Swahili, affirming the program and expressing the hope to extend it throughout the episcopal area.

—https://tinyurl.com/y5jxcsyo; https://www.umnews.org/en/news/unda-elected-bishop-of-the-united-methodist-church; email communication and interview with Bishop Unda, January-February 2018

Billye Kathryn Whisnand Underwood (1924–1996 / 1997)

In 1946, Billye married Walter L. Underwood (1925–1987). Walter was elected in 1984 after serving churches in the North Texas, Memphis, Central Texas, and Texas Annual Conferences and served the Louisiana Episcopal Area until his death in 1987. Billye and Walter had three sons and three grandchildren.

On the day after her memorial service, Billye's son, Don Underwood, wrote, "When my mother was told three months ago that she had only a matter of weeks to live, she responded with the same calm strength and equanimity that she had demonstrated all her life. She kindly thanked the doctor for all his care, and for his candor. She went to the funeral home and picked out her own casket so 'the boys won't spend too much' and then got back to the business of living. She went shopping, she cooked for her family, she entertained friends and attended church until she was too weak. We had a grand time of living during these past three months. . . . Her calm and strong faith constantly reassured us that, though Death can take much from you, it cannot take from you that which is most important. And in that discovery, you begin to taste the exhilaration of life lived on the edge, the sweetness of life lived for the moment, the joy of a life that comes from God as a pure gift."

—*Texas Annual Conference, 1997,* K–19; *Biographical Directory,* 1984; http://www.la-umc.org/obituary/1547277; *Official Journal of the 1987 Central Texas Annual Conference,* 243

Manuela Lorenzana Lardizabal Valencia (1905–1984)

In 1930, Manuela married José Labarrete Valencia (1898–1994). José was elected in 1948 out of the Philippines Central Conference and served there until his retirement in 1968. Manuela and José had two children.

Manuela trained to be a teacher and worked as one briefly but gave that up when she married José in order to serve full-time through the church. As the wife of a pastor, district superintendent, and bishop, she worked by his side, as well as pursuing unique ministries of her own: preaching and teaching, organizing, and promoting tithing and stewardship.

—*Biographical Directory,* 1992; José Labarrete Valencia, *After thy will: Story of the life of Manuela Lardizabal-Valencia (handmaiden of God)* (Board of Women's Work, United Methodist Church in the Philippines, 1987)

Alma Y. Varela Dieppa [Vidal] (b. 1946)

In 1987, Alma married Hector F. Ortiz Vidal (b. 1951). Hector was elected in 2016 out of The Methodist Church of Puerto Rico and serves the Puerto Rico Episcopal Area. Alma and Hector have three children and three granddaughters.

Alma has both a BA and MS in psychology. She is a local, district, and conference speaker on issues related to mental health and a member of the Puerto Rico Association of Psychologists. She served as a member of the General Board of Discipleship (1987–1992) and of the Board of Directors for the Evangelical Seminary of Puerto Rico, among other institutions. Alma likes to play chess, tennis, and Ping-Pong, and she also enjoys working as a volunteer with elderly persons.

Favorite Scripture: Psalm 121 / Favorite Hymn: "Amazing Grace" (*UMH*, 378)

—email communication with Alma Varela Dieppa, July 2017; interviews with Alma and Bishop Hector Ortiz Vidal, November 2017, November 2018

Kaija-Riikka Växby (b. 1946)

In 1968, Kaija-Riikka married Hans Växby (b. 1944). Hans was elected in 1989 out of the Finland Swedish Provisional Annual Conference and served the Baltic and Nordic Episcopal Area (1989–2001), then returned to serving local churches in his annual conference, according to the rules of the Northern Europe and Eurasia Central Conference. In 2005, he was elected bishop again and served the Eurasia Episcopal Area (2005–2012), then retired. Kaija-Riikka and Hans live in Helsinki, Finland, and have two sons and four grandchildren.

Kaija-Riikka is a UM pastor and has served churches in the Finland Swedish Provisional Annual Conference.

—*Biographical Directory*, 2000–2014, 2012–2016; https://www.unitedmethodistbishops.org/person-detail/2464424; email communication with Bishop Växby, July 2017

Eleanor Hemstead Dodge Voigt (d. 1955)

Eleanor married Edwin Edgar Voigt (1892–1977). Edwin was elected in 1952 after serving as a teacher, pastor, and college president in Illinois, Iowa, and elsewhere. He served the Dakota Episcopal Area (1952–1960) and the Illinois Episcopal Area (1960–1964), then retired. Eleanor and Edwin had two children.

Eleanor was born in California, graduated from Mills College, and did graduate work in religious education at Yale. She taught school in California before her marriage. For a number of years, she was an approved teacher in the Sunday School Teacher Training program of the former Methodist Episcopal Church. Eleanor was a delegate to the North Central Jurisdictional Conference in 1952, when her husband was elected bishop. She had served as president of the Iowa-Des Moines Conference Women's Society of Christian Service, was a delegate to the Women's Assembly in

1950 and to the Constituting Conference of the National Council of Churches of Christ in America in 1950, and served on the General Board of Education of The Methodist Church (1948–1952). She was also a member of P.E.O., the American Association of University Women, and other civic groups.

—https://library.syr.edu/digital/guides/v/voigt_ee.htm;
Yearbook of the South Dakota Conference of The Methodist Church, 1955, 121;
Official Minutes of the 70th Session of the North Dakota Conference The Methodist Church, 1955, 124; *Encyclopedia of World Methodism, Vol. 2,* 2436

Myrtle L. Mudge Wade (1889–1969)

In 1913, Myrtle married Raymond J. Wade (1875–1970). Raymond was elected in 1928 out of the North Indiana Annual Conference of The Methodist Episcopal Church and assigned to the Stockholm Episcopal Area in Europe (1928–1939), the Detroit Episcopal Area (1940–1948), then retired. Raymond had three children with his first wife, Ella L. Yarian, who died in 1909, and several great-grandchildren.

Myrtle was president of the World Federation of Methodist Women while Raymond was in Sweden. Her travel notes and observations are included with her husband's papers in the UM Archives and History Center in Madison, New Jersey.

—http://catalog.gcah.org/publicdata/gcah582.htm;
Minutes of the West Michigan Annual Conference,1969, 217–218;
The Official Journal and Minutes of the Detroit Annual Conference, 1970, 952

Kasongo Maria Ngolo Wakadilo (b. 1942)

In 1959, Kasongo Maria Ngolo married Ngoy Kimba Maurice Wakadilo (1937–1994). Ngoy was elected bishop in 1976 out of the Central Africa Annual Conference and served the Shaba (now called Katanga) Episcopal Area (1976–1980) and the North-Shaba (now called North-Katanga) Episcopal Area from 1980 until his death in 1994. Kasonga Maria and Ngoy have 10 children.

Maria was very supportive of her husband's ministry, visiting, praying for, and supporting the needy. Her education at a sewing and culinary school prepared her to do what she enjoys most, helping others to be independent. She started sewing classes around 1983, teaching pastors' spouses and disabled, needy people to learn how to make a variety of clothing items, dresses, rompers and so on. Unfortunately, the April 24, 1990, killings and pillage and multiple other pillages in the Democratic Republic of Congo destroyed the training school. She also spent a lot of time listening to and counseling pastors' spouses, often teaching them how to take care of their homes.

Favorite Scripture: Psalm 23 / Favorite Hymn: "*Sepelela tata udi mulu wampee*..." (trans. from Kiluba: "I am happy my heavenly father gave me...")

—*Biographical Directory*, 1992;
email communication with son Steve Wakadilo, July 2017

Flora Janet Irish Waldorf (1876–1963)

In 1902, Flora married Ernest Lynn Waldorf (1876–1943). Ernest was elected in 1920 after serving churches in the Central New York and Genesee Conferences of The Methodist Episcopal Church. He served the Kansas City Episcopal Area, which included Kansas, Oklahoma, Texas, and Louisiana (1920–1924) plus Arkansas and Missouri (1924–1932) and the Chicago Episcopal Area (which included Methodist Episcopal Churches in Illinois and bilingual conferences of Swedish and Norwegian-Danish work between the Atlantic Ocean and Rocky Mountains) starting in 1932. Flora and Ernest had five children, nine grandchildren, and five great-grandchildren.

Born in Philadelphia, Flora grew up on a farm in New York. Her memoir in the 1964 Rock River Conference Journal describes her thus: "Flora Waldorf was a warm and friendly person with a genuine interest in people. Her gracious spirit made of every parsonage and Episcopal Residence in which she lived, a center of activity and hospitality. She traveled extensively with her husband, going to Europe and to South America with him when he held conferences there. She attended almost every conference her husband held and followed the work of the church with keen interest. She had a rare capacity for friendship, and kept in touch with her friends through the years, being a constant writer of letters."

—*Journal and Yearbook, the Official Proceedings of the 125th Annual Session of Rock River Annual Conference of The Methodist Church, 1964*, 251–252;
https://en.wikipedia.org/wiki/Ernest_Lynn_Waldorf;
https://www.findagrave.com/cgi-bin/fg.cgi?page=gr&GRid=43837301;
https://prabook.com/web/ernest_lynn.waldorf/281333

Mildred Henry Walton (1904–1999)

In 1930, Mildred married Aubrey Grey Walton (1901–1978). Aubrey was elected in 1960 after serving churches in Arkansas and served the Louisiana Episcopal Area (1960–1972), then retired. Mildred and Aubrey had two children, six grandchildren, and four great-grandchildren.

Mildred was born in Alabama, attended the University of Arkansas, and taught school for several years. She is remembered as an inspirational writer and for her skill at reciting poetry. Her stories—such as one about the outhouse at one of their parsonages or the time all the families in a church brought Jell-O salad to a potluck dinner—are considered classics "in the memory of Louisiana Methodism."

—*Journal of the 30th Session of the Louisiana Annual Conference, 2000,* 259–260;
http://www.la-umc.org/obituary/1547485;
http://www.lib.utexas.edu/taro/smu/00186/smu-00186.html;
Journal–The Little Rock Annual Conference, 1978, 286–287

Betty Wandabula (b. 1979)

In 2005, Betty married Daniel A. Wandabula (b. 1965). Daniel was elected in 2006 at a special session of the East Africa Annual Conference held at Africa University, Mutare, Zimbabwe, and was assigned to the East Africa Episcopal Area. Betty and Daniel have six children.

Betty earned a BA in divinity and has worked for 10 years with DEJOLISA (u) LTD, a poultry company she started. She ministers with orphans and vulnerable children through a Hope for Africa children's ministry which she started in 2007, bringing hope to children and families who have lost it all. Betty shared, "My involvement with these children and especially when I see smiles on their faces, really makes me very happy. My hobbies are making friends, listening to Gospel music, and swimming."

Favorite Scripture: John 3:16 / Favorite Hymn: "To God Be the Glory" (*UMH*, 98)

—*Biographical Directory*, 2004–2008;
email communication with Betty Wandabula, July 2017

Arleen Burdick Ward (1909–2000)

In 1933, Arleen married William Ralph Ward Jr (1908–1988). After serving churches in New England and Pennsylvania, Ralph was elected by the Northeastern Jurisdiction in 1960. He served the Syracuse Episcopal Area (1960–1972) and the New York Episcopal Area (1972–1980), then retired. Arleen and Ralph had three sons and six grandchildren.

Arleen earned both undergraduate and graduate degrees in Christian education at Boston University. "Throughout her life she espoused the social gospel and ecumenical approach to religion and was a ceaseless worker for social justice and reform. She participated especially in youth and adult educational activities and in the UMW. She served on many commissions and committees and, even into her eighties, she frequently attended General and Jurisdictional conferences. She had a wide circle of friends to whom she was loyal and devoted. She was always willing to help anyone and everyone who needed her. Notable for her lack of pretension and unaffected air, Arlene made friends easily and her home was always open and welcome to all. She was a colorful and amusing storyteller. Having visited every corner of the globe, she was often called upon to give lectures on her world travels. She blessed her family with her love, her humor and wit, and her wisdom, and imparted to them her abiding interest in history and world affairs and her concern for other people. Possessed of an indomitable courage and blessed with an extraordinary mind and memory, she lived life to its fullest" (*The Northern New Jersey Annual Conference Journal, 2000,* UMC, 152–153). Neil Irons recalls Arleen responding, when asked about her home life with Ralph after his election, "We don't have much of a home life, but we have a great car life."

—email communication with Bishop Irons, 2011; https://www.nytimes.com/1988/07/01/obituaries/w-ralph-ward-jr-methodist-bishop-79.html; http://catalog.gcah.org/publicdata/gcah748.htm

Katherine Boeye Ward (1900–2005)

In 1948, Katherine married Bishop Ralph Ansel Ward (1882–1958), who served in China. Ralph had two daughters with his first wife, Mildred, who died in 1947.

Katherine was a former missionary to China. In 1977, Luther Seminary published Katherine's "Midwest China Oral Interviews" in its China Oral Histories series (http://digitalcommons.luthersem.edu/china_histories/74). After Ralph's death, Katherine wrote "Our 10-plus years together were a priceless jewel—perfect in love, palship, and work."

—January 1959 letter in Ralph's administrative file at the UM Archives and History Center; https://billiongraves.com/grave/Katherine-Boeye-Ward/19255318

Michael E. Ward (b. 1953)

In 1977, Michael married Hope Morgan (b. 1951). Hope was elected out of the North Carolina Annual Conference in 2004, served the Mississippi Episcopal Area (2004–2012), and was assigned to the Raleigh Episcopal Area starting in 2012. Hope and Mike have two children and two grandchildren.

Mike has a BS in education and an MA and PhD in educational administration. He served as a high school teacher and coach, high school principal, and local superintendent. For the eight years prior to Hope's election as bishop, he served as North Carolina's elected State Superintendent of Public Instruction. He also served as president of the National Council of Chief State School Officers and is now a professor of education leadership and a consultant to state and local education leaders. In the aftermath of Hurricane Katrina, Mike worked with recovery teams and also participated in research projects related to the effects of the storm by the University of Southern Mississippi, which named Mike as one of the "Heroes of Katrina." Mike enjoys running, sailing, and being a granddad. He is an active and adventurous missioner and has traveled to Afghanistan and Haiti to assist in food distribution.

Published works by Mike Ward include: *Delegation and Empowerment: Leading With and Through Others* (with B. MacPhael-Wilcox, 1999); "Schools and students in disaster recovery," in E. Blakely, E. Birch, R. Anglin, & H. Hayashi, eds., *Managing Urban Disaster Recovery* (2012); "The long haul," in *American School Board Journal*, 197, no. 9 (2010); and three articles in *The Journal of Education for Students Placed at Risk*, 13.2–3 (2008): "Hurricane Katrina: A longitudinal study of the achievement and behavior of displaced students" (with K. Shelley, K. Kaase, and J. Pane); "Hurricane Katrina's impact on students and staff members in the schools of Mississippi" (with K. Shelley); "Katrina and the schools of Mississippi: An examination of emergency and disaster preparedness" (with D. Lee, G. Parker, , R. Styron, and K. Shelley).

Favorite Scripture: Amos 5:24

—*Biographical Directory*, 2012–2016;
email communication with Mike Ward, July 2017

Mildred May Worley Ward (1883–1947)

In 1905, Mildred married Ralph Ansel Ward (1882–1958). Ralph was elected bishop in 1937 after serving churches in Massachusetts and then serving as a missionary to China. As bishop, he served in Chengtu, China (1937–1941) and then at Soochow University, Shanghai, China. Mildred and Ralph had two daughters.

Mildred, known to some as "Lady Ward," served with Ralph for many years, both in and for China. Mildred endured what must have been three particularly difficult years when Ralph was imprisoned by the Japanese (1942–1945) and was not allowed to write to her.

—letter from Arthur Bruce Moss in Ralph's administrative file at the UM Archives and History Center; https://www.findagrave.com/cgi-bin/fg.cgi?page=gr&GRid=79593085; http://prabook.com/web/person-view.html?profileId=280618; *Encyclopedia of World Methodism, Vol. 2*, 2450–2451

Annie Owings Sansbury Warman (1916–2006)

In 1939, Annie O. married John Boyle Warman (1915–1993). John was elected in 1972 out of the Pittsburgh (later Western Pennsylvania) Annual Conference and served the Harrisburg Episcopal Area (1972–1984), then retired. Annie and John had three children, 10 grandchildren, and three great-grandchildren.

Annie graduated from Western Maryland College with a major in English. She then attended Strayer's Business College in Washington, DC. During John's tour as a US Navy Chaplain during World War II, Annie worked at the Navy Hydrographic Office in Suitland, Maryland. Annie O. enjoyed being the homemaker and hostess in parsonages and the episcopal residence, as well as traveling in the Harrisburg Area and abroad with John. She loved music, especially by the big bands; baseball; and old poetry. She survived two cancers.

—*Biographical Directory*, 1992; http://www.tributes.com/show/77587548; *The Wyoming Annual Conference 1994 Journal and Yearbook*, 327–328; *Council of Bishops Memorial Booklet*, Spring 2007; *Central Pennsylvania Conference Journal for 1994*, 488

Ada May Visick Warner (1903–1985)

In 1937, Ada married United Brethren Bishop Ira David Warner (1886–1964), a widower. Ira had been elected bishop in 1929 and served the Pacific Coast area. When they returned from a honeymoon in Great Britain, they established their home and opened a new mission in Pomona, California. When Sierra Leone was added to his responsibilities in 1946, they spent many months in Africa laying the foundation for forming an annual conference. He retired in 1958. Ira had two children with his first wife, Edna May Landis, who died in 1934. There were four grandchildren, two of whom Ada raised after the death of her stepdaughter.

Ada, born in California, was a public school teacher and "a much-loved and much-sought-after public speaker and leader of retreats." At one time she was president of California State Christian Endeavor, and she was active in the Church of the Brethren until her marriage to Ira. She served as pastor for the new mission they established in Pomona, California, for eight and a half years. After that church was firmly established, they moved to LaPuent, California, where they established another new mission and building program in the Hillgrove area. She traveled with her husband to Sierra Leone, visited most of the United Brethren mission stations in the Orient, and served as a mission interpreter.

—*Biographical Directory*, 1984; *Encyclopedia of World Methodism, Vol. 2*, 2455; *Journal of the 104th Annual Session of the Michigan Conference of the Evangelical United Brethren Church, 1965*, 136–137; *Journal of the California-Pacific Annual Conference, 1985*, 176

Anna Harmon Warner (b. 1938)

In 1963, Anna married Bennie de Quency Warner (b. 1935). Bennie was elected in 1973 out of the Liberia Annual Conference, while serving as principal at the College of West Africa and also pastoring a church. He was assigned to the Liberia Episcopal Area, and in 1977, he was also elected vice president of Liberia. In 1980, while he and Anna were attending the Council of Bishops' meeting and General Conference in Indiana, he learned that the military had taken over the government of Liberia. Shortly thereafter he was removed from ecclesiastical power as well. Anna and Bennie remained in the United States, where he taught at Oklahoma City University and served as a pastor in Syracuse, New York, and in Arkansas, then retired in 2004. Anna and Bennie have four children, one deceased.

Anna was born in Liberia, attended the College of West Africa, a UM high school in Monrovia, and did undergraduate work at the University of Liberia, after which she worked at the Lamco International School in Liberia. After their marriage, both she and Bennie taught at the Gbarnga Methodist Mission in Bong County until 1968, when they both matriculated at Boston University. She earned an ME while he earned a ThM. When they returned to Liberia, Anna taught in Monrovia at a Methodist school, now called J. J. Roberts Elementary Junior High School. After 1980, when they could not return to Liberia, she became certified to teach and taught in Texas, New York, Arkansas, and Oklahoma, retiring in 2006 after 37 years of teaching. In retirement, Bishop Warner and Anna, along with family and friends, have been raising funds for a village school in Liberia. The Kaymah H. Warner New Hope Academy (grades pre-K–9), named in memory of Bishop and Anna's daughter, who died in 2014, was dedicated in February 2016.

—https://en.wikipedia.org/wiki/Bennie_Dee_Warner; https://prabook.com/web/bishop_bennie_d.warner/243421; http://www.liberiapastandpresent.org/RitualKillingsSecondHalf20thF.htm; http://grandbassacountyassociation.org/docs/Bishop%20Bennie%20Warner%20img037.pdf; letter from Bishop Warner, October 2018

Kathryn Elizabeth Fischer Washburn (1914–1990)

In 1937, Kathryn married Paul Arthur Washburn (1911–1989). After serving Evangelical United Brethren churches in Illinois, Paul, who was instrumental in the unification of the Evangelical United Brethren and Methodist Churches, was elected bishop in 1968 and was the first to be consecrated in the UMC. He served the Minnesota Episcopal Area (1968–1972) and the Chicago Episcopal Area (1972–1980), then retired. Kathryn and Paul had four children and six grandchildren.

Kathryn graduated from the Evanston Hospital School of Nursing and did advanced studies at the Illinois School of Psychiatric Nursing and Northwestern University. She worked as a staff nurse at Copley Hospital in Aurora, Illinois. While a pastor's wife and a bishop's wife, she spent a great deal of time doing volunteer work and enjoyed visiting. She also enjoyed music, reading, and taking care of house plants. Her memoir in the 1991 Minnesota Conference Journal states, "Kathryn loved the church, and she had a deep and informed faith. She and Paul would read and pray together, and he was known to have said, 'and she's a good theologian.' Over the years she sang in church choirs, taught Sunday School classes, and worked in a church resale shop. Kathryn cherished her family. . . . She was devoted to her husband, and with a quiet strength she cared for him during several years of declining health toward the end of his life. She liked entertaining family and friends, and she enjoyed playing the piano and solving crossword puzzles."

—*Biographical Directory*, 1984; *Official Journal and Yearbook Minnesota Annual Conference, 1991*, 356

Frances Edith Hancock Watkins (1891–1967)

In 1914, Edith married William Turner Watkins (1895–1961). William was elected in 1938 out of the North Georgia Annual Conference of The Methodist Episcopal Church, South, at the last general conference of that denomination. He served the Columbia Episcopal Area of the newly formed Methodist Church (1940–1944) and the Louisville Episcopal Area (1944–1956). Edith and William had five children, 12 grandchildren, and three great-grandchildren.

Born in Kentucky, Edith, according to her memoir, never planned for or desired to live among the leaders of the church, but "served in her role of episcopal hostess with the grace and willingness to service which only the truly dedicated are able to manage."

—*The Louisville Conference Journal 1968 Session*, 201–202;
https://en.wikipedia.org/wiki/William_Turner_Watkins;
Encyclopedia of World Methodism, Vol. 2, 2468–2469

Margaret Lee Watson (b. 1950)

In 1973, Margaret married Benjamin Michael Watson (b. 1949). Mike was elected in 2000 out of the Alabama-West Florida Annual Conference and served the South Georgia Episcopal Area (2000–2008) and the North Georgia Episcopal Area (2008–2016), then retired. Margaret and Mike have two children and six grandchildren.

Margaret earned a BA in history and English and an MA in counseling and guidance, both from the University of Alabama. She worked as a high school teacher for three years and a high school guidance counselor for 13 years. She also organized a UMW unit, taught Sunday school and Vacation Bible School, and served as a youth counselor. She was president and retreat chair of the Alabama-West Florida Conference Spouses, president of two district spouse groups, president of an ecumenical association, and a member of the executive committee for the Southeastern Jurisdiction's larger church consultation. Equally involved in community and professional organizations, Margaret served as a Girl Scout and Boy Scout leader, a member of Delta Kappa Gamma educators' honorary society, president of a Girls' Club board of directors, president of the Alabama Counseling Association chapter and two divisions, and a member of the American Association of Spiritual, Ethical, and Religious Values in Counseling Board of Directors. She was recognized in 1991 as a Distinguished Alumna of The University of Alabama and in 1996 as the state of Alabama's Secondary School Counselor of the Year. Margaret served as the president of the National Alumni Association of The University of Alabama in 1996 and national vice president of alumnae for Kappa Delta Sorority (2007–2011). Since 2003, she has worked part time for Educational Opportunities serving as staff aboard cruise ships all over the world.

Favorite Scripture: Matthew 5:16

—*Biographical Directory*, 2012–2016;
email communication with Margaret Watson, August 2017

Minnie Euphemie Keyser Watts (1891–1985)

In 1913, Minnie married Henry Bascom Watts (1890–1959). Henry was elected in 1952, after serving churches in Oklahoma, Texas, and Arkansas. He served the Nebraska Episcopal Area 1952 until his death. Minnie and Henry had two children and five granddaughters.

—*Biographical Directory*, 1984; https://www.findagrave.com/memorial/99596767/minnie-watts; *Official Record of the Seventh Annual Session of the Oklahoma Conference of The Methodist Church, 1960*, 190

Linda Sells Weaver (b. 1946)

In 2006, Linda married Bishop Peter D. Weaver (b. 1945). Pete was elected bishop in 1996 and served the Philadelphia Episcopal Area (1996–2004) and the Boston Episcopal Area (2004–2012), then retired. Linda and Pete have settled in Williamsburg, Virginia. Together they have eight daughters and 13 grandchildren.

Linda, who grew up in Pittsburgh, Pennsylvania, attended Mount Union College in Alliance, Ohio, and graduated from the University of Pittsburgh. She earned an MA in psychology and early childhood education from Penn State. She taught kindergarten and first grade until she and her first husband adopted a daughter from the Children's Home of Pittsburgh. They adopted another daughter two years later, then gave birth to a daughter two years after that. Linda began a small daycare in her home until the girls were old enough for school and preschool, then taught in that preschool until they moved to Williamsburg, Virginia, where they adopted two more daughters, biological sisters ages five and two and a half. They continued work they had begun in Pittsburgh, serving the elderly with home health care and Meals on Wheels, and built five Assisted Living homes in southeastern Virginia. Later they began a School for Holistic Health and Well-Being, offering massage therapy as well as other services. While taking course work in massage and holistic health, Linda also taught four-year-olds in a local preschool, cutting back to half time as her massage practice grew. After her divorce, Linda continued to work and, in time, reconnected with Pete, a long-time friend. Since their marriage, she has continued to teach adults and volunteer with little children in schools. As a bishop's wife, she has enjoyed many wonderful opportunities and worldwide travels. Although Pete has continued to be active, first as executive secretary for the Council of Bishops and then as bishop-in-residence at

Drew University in New Jersey, they are now enjoying more time with grandchildren and traveling for pleasure. Linda, who loves animals and has had many pets through the years, enjoys their dog Angel, reading, photography, and needlework.

Favorite Scripture: Matthew 19:16b

—*Biographical Directory*, 2004–2008;
email communication with Linda Weaver, September 2017

Joy Diane Brockway Webb (b. 1966)

In 1989, Jodi married Mark J. Webb (b. 1964). He was elected in 2012 out of the Central Pennsylvania (now Susquehanna) Annual Conference and assigned to the Upper New York Episcopal Area. Jodi and Mark have two sons.

Jodi graduated from Bloomsburg University. She worked for The United Methodist Home for Children in Mechanicsburg, Pennsylvania, beginning as the director of public relations and later serving as the program administrator for residential services. She served as director of youth ministries at Aldersgate UMC, Mechanicsburg, Pennsylvania, and as director of youth and young adult ministries at Zion UMC, York, Pennsylvania.

—*Biographical Directory*, 2012–2016;
email communication with Jodi Webb, January 2018

Marie Schnake White Webb (b. 1921)

In 1991, Marie married retired Bishop Lance Webb (1909–1995). Lance had three daughters with his first wife, Mary Elizabeth, who died in 1990. Between them, Marie and Lance have seven children, 15 grandchildren, and one great grandchild.

Marie received her BA from Bradley University in Peoria, Illinois, and her MA from Illinois State. She taught church school and served as a lay speaker and leader. She was director of older adult ministries at First UMC in Enid, Oklahoma, before her marriage to Lance. In 1999, her book *The Power of the Dream: Looking Forward in the Later Years of Life* was published by Dimensions of Living, and in 2006, Discipleship Resources published her *Building a Ministry for Homebound and Nursing Home Residents*. Marie's first husband, Dr. James K. White, who died in 1990, was the first district superintendent appointed by Bishop Webb when he came to the Illinois Episcopal Area. Marie recalls, "When Lance introduced me to the Council at Epworth-by-the-Sea at the family night dinner in 1992, he said 'I want you to meet Marie White, wife of the first district superintendent I ever appointed.' Quick as a wink, Bishop DeCarvalho remarked, 'Now, that's what I call looking ahead.' Everyone laughed. I suggested to Lance that maybe he should introduce me as the widow, rather than the wife of his district superintendent. I want to thank the Association for making us second wives feel so welcome."

—letter from Marie, 11/19/2008; *Biographical Directory*, November 1992; http://catalog.gcah.org/DigitalArchives/memoirs/WebbLance-cen-tx-1996.pdf

Mary Elizabeth Hunt Webb (1908–1990)

In 1933, Elizabeth married Lance Webb (1909–1995). Lance was elected in 1964 by the North Central Jurisdictional Conference and assigned to the Illinois Episcopal Area (1964–1976) and to the Iowa Episcopal Area (1976–1980), then retired. Elizabeth and Lance had three daughters.

Elizabeth received a BA from McMurray College (which was founded by her father), studied at the University of Chicago Divinity School, and received an MA from Southern Methodist University in 1934. Her interest in drama led to directing church plays and participating in little theaters. She taught church school, participated in UMW and Church Women United, sang in church choirs, and was president of the Women's Club when they lived in Columbus. She also liked to paint in oils and acrylics.

Her daughter Mary wrote of her, "The 16 years she served with him as bishop's wife were completely devoted to the ministry she assumed to support Lance. With an endearing sense of humor and loving compassion, Elizabeth loved being his partner in ministry, especially within his episcopal travels around the world for the Church. Her dramatic flair contributed to her being a memorable and beloved part of their team."

—*Biographical Directory*, November 1992;
email from daughter, Mary Webb Edlund, 1/9/2018

Adelaide Frances McGee Welch (1866–1958)

In 1890, Adelaide married Herbert Welch (1862–1969). Herbert was elected in 1916 from the West Ohio Annual Conference of The Methodist Episcopal Church, served in Korea and Japan (1916–1928), the Pittsburgh Episcopal Area (1928–1932), and in the Shanghai Episcopal Area (1932–1936), then retired. Adelaide and Herbert had two daughters, one grandson, three great-grandsons, and two great-great-grandchildren.

Bishop James Baker wrote a memoir of Mrs. Welch, dated November, 1958, quoting another source, "her married life was spent in able fulfillment of the duties, successively, of pastor's wife (15 years), college president's wife (11 years), wife of an 'effective' bishop (22 years) and for 20 years partner of a retired bishop whose activities and honors as an octogenarian and nonagenarian are world-known." Bishop Baker continued, "Bishop and Mrs. Welch have been incomparable comrades and fellow servants of the Eternal for 68 years. Sometimes the life of a wife is swallowed up in that of her husband and her sharp individuality is lost. Not so in the case of Mrs. Welch." He quotes one of Bishop Welch's many tributes to his wife: "From the first day I met her 75 years ago, she has held a decisive place in my life as sweetheart, wife, comrade, counsellor and joy—a refreshing breeze blowing through the shut in areas of life" and concludes with a declaration that her faith "was the dynamic force of her life, the source of her awe, tenderness, dignity, and noble humanity."

—November 1958 memoir in Spouses' Scrapbooks, 1949–1964; http://catalog.gcah.org/publicdata/gcah5099.htm; https://findagrave.com/cgi-bin/fg.cgi?page=gr&GRid=109773806

Tobias Wenner (b. 1959)

In 1983, Tobias married Rosemarie Beisel (b. 1955). Rosemarie was elected in February 2005, out of the Germany South Annual Conference and served the Germany Episcopal Area (2005–2017). Rosemary was the first woman elected to the UM episcopacy outside of the U.S.

Tobias is a computer scientist and currently serves as a volunteer on a team developing software applications for the use of the conferences in Germany. His passion is chess.

—*Biographical Directory*, 2004–2008; interview with Bishop Wenner, November 2017, and email communication, July 2018

Catherine Stewart Werner (1895–1978)

In 1924, Catherine married Hazen Graff Werner (1895–1988). Hazen was elected in 1948 after serving churches in the Detroit Annual Conference and as a professor at Drew University for three years. He served the Ohio Episcopal Area (1948–1964) and was based in Manhattan (1964–1968) as bishop of Hong Kong and Taiwan. He retired in 1968. Catherine and Hazen had two children.

—*Biographical Directory*, 1996; https://new.findagrave.com/memorial/150489684/catherine-s.-werner; *Encyclopedia of World Methodism, Vol.* 22489; https://en.wikipedia.org/wiki/Hazen_Graff_Werner

Helen E. Jenkins Werner

In 1983, Helen married retired Bishop Hazen G. Werner (1895–1988). Hazen had two children with his first wife, Catherine, who died in 1978.

—*Biographical Directory*, 1996; *Encyclopedia of World Methodism, Vol. 2*, 2489; https://en.wikipedia.org/wiki/Hazen_Graff_Werner

Betty Rowe Wertz (1919–1999)

In 1938, Betty married D. Frederick Wertz (1916–2013). Fred was elected in 1968 out of the Central Pennsylvania Annual Conference. He served the West Virginia Episcopal Area (1968–1980) and the Baltimore-Washington Episcopal Area

(1980–1984), then retired. They settled in Carlisle, Pennsylvania. Betty and Fred had four children, 10 grandchildren, and 15 great-grandchildren.

Betty was born in Pennsylvania and studied at Juniata College there for two years, then married Fred and moved with him to Boston, where he was attending seminary. In addition to raising their four children, Betty was an accomplished singer and pianist. Later she began to write poetry and became a sought-after speaker at women's retreats. She also loved knitting, crocheting, and enjoying nature.

—*Biographical Directory*, 2004–2008;
email communication with daughter Donna Ream, September 2017

Luisa Teresa Bissio Wesley (d. prior to 1975)

In 1945, Luisa married Bishop Arthur Frederick Wesley (1885–1975). Arthur was elected in 1944, after serving churches in the Detroit and Michigan Annual Conferences and as a missionary to Argentina, by the Latin American General Conference. He served the Atlantic Area (1944–1949) and then served a church in Santiago, Chile, for eight years, retiring in 1955. Luisa and Arthur had three children. He also had four children with his first wife, Grace Margaret, who died in February 1944, before his election in November. Together Luisa and Arthur had eight grandchildren and eight great-grandchildren.

—*The Official Journal and Minutes Detroit Annual Conference, 1976*, 371;
Encyclopedia of World Methodism, Vol. 2, 2490

Lucile Elizabeth Maris Wheatley (1917–2017)

In 1939, Lucille married Melvin E. Wheatley Jr (1915–2009). Mel was elected in 1972 out of the California-Pacific Annual Conference and served the Denver Episcopal Area (1972–1984), then retired. Lucille and Mel returned to California. They had three sons (one deceased), three grandchildren, and one great-grandson.

Lucile was born in Oregon and attended American University in Washington, DC, graduating *cum laude* in 1938 with an AB. Lucile has held offices in civic and interfaith organizations, and she and Mel were active in mental health programs in California. Lucile had a keen interest in many political, justice, and peace issues and was a member of League of Women Voters. She served on the Conference Commissions on Religion and Race and Status and Role of Women in the Denver Area. She was chair of Portraits of American Women, an outreach project of the Community Relations Conference of Southern California, which involved panels of women representing five different racial/ethnic groups speaking to groups of women in Southern California, attempting to challenge prejudice and bigotry. After Mel's retirement, they concentrated their efforts on gay rights, working actively as members of an international organization of Parents and Friends of Lesbians and Gays (PFLAG) and as supporters of Affirmation and Reconciling Congregations within the UMC. Lucile enjoyed music, drama, books, travel, and their grandchildren.

—*Los Angeles Times* [June 24, 1969] §4, 1; *Biographical Directory*, 2004–2008; http://www.latimes.com/local/obituaries/la-me-melvin-wheatley15-2009mar15-story.html; email communication with son Jim Wheatley, 2017

Melba Jarvis Whitaker (b. 1950)

In 1971, Melba married Timothy W. Whitaker (b. 1948). Timothy, a member of the Virginia Annual Conference, was elected at a special session of the Southeastern Jurisdictional Conference in 2001 and served the Florida Episcopal Area (2001–2012), then retired. Melba and Timothy live in Virginia. They have two children and one grandchild.

Melba, a native of Mississippi, studied special education and anthropology at Longwood College in Farmville, Virginia, and the University of Virginia in Charlottesville. She worked as a special education teacher specializing in the emotionally handicapped at the elementary level. Melba loves to travel and has visited many parts of Latin America, New Zealand, and Angola. She shares her journeys with others through writing and giving speeches. She has worked with laity and clergy to develop Shade and Fresh Water, a ministry for clergy and their families. Melba is an avid reader and a quilter.

—*Biographical Directory*, 2012–2016; email communication with Melba Whitaker, October 2016

Gwendolyn Ruth Horton White (1924–2017)

In 1946, Gwen married C. Dale White (b. 1925). Dale was elected in 1976 out of the New England Annual Conference. He served the New Jersey Episcopal Area (1976–1984) and the New York Episcopal Area (1984–1992), then retired to Newport, Rhode Island. Gwen and Dale have six children, seven grandchildren, 10 great-grandchildren, and three great-great-grandchildren.

Gwen attended Wayne State Teachers College in Nebraska, Buena Vista College in Iowa, Colorado State College of Education, and Morningside College in Iowa. A musician at heart, in addition to singing beautifully, she played piano, organ, violin, snare drum, and timpani. During World War II, she played drums in an all-female dance band. She taught music in Nemaha, Iowa, Dale's hometown, where they met; and also served as an organist-choir director in local churches. Gwen led retreats, taught in conference and regional Schools of Christian Mission, and wrote for UM publications. She led workshops on the spirituality of the family, journaling, intergenerational education and ministries, women's issues, and child advocacy. She also shared leadership with her husband in marriage enrichment events and seminars on spirituality for social witness and action for clergy and laity. She also traveled with him to Africa, China, the Philippines, Korea, India, Bangladesh, Pakistan, and the Middle East, studying world hunger and peace and justice issues. Gwen created a training program for retreat leaders and served for more than two years as director of Spiritual Life for Scarritt-Bennett Center in Nashville, TN.

—*Biographical Directory*, 2004–2008; http://concordfuneral.tributes.com/obituary/show/Gwendolyn-Horton-White-104619789; email communication with daughter Rebecca Blair, 2017–2018

Jennie May "Kim" Tolson White (b. 1939)

In 1961, Kim married Woodie W. White (b. 1935). Woodie was elected in 1984 out of the Detroit Annual Conference and served the Central Illinois Episcopal Area (1984–1992) and the Indiana Episcopal Area (1992–2004), then retired to Kennesaw, Georgia. Kim and Woodie have five children and eight grandchildren.

Kim, a native of Worcester, Massachusetts, attended Clark University there and holds degrees from Howard Community College and Towson University. She has done graduate studies at the University of Maryland and Butler University. Kim is an elementary school teacher and was honored as the Teacher of the Year by the Springfield, Illinois, School District in 1992. She is recognized for her work in the areas of special needs children and English as a second language. An artist, Kim has painted, sculpted, and directed liturgical dance. Kim is active in numerous church and civic organizations.

—*Biographical Directory*, 2012–2016; interview with Kim White, 2016, and email communication, 2018

Valerie Vaughn Whitfield (b. 1947)

In 1993, Valerie married David Max Whitfield (b. 1944). Max was elected in 2000 out of the North Arkansas Annual Conference and served the Northwest Texas-New Mexico Episcopal Area (2000–2012), then retired and settled in Richardson, Texas. Valerie's first husband died in 1988, and Max's first wife died in 1991. Their combined family includes five children and 12 grandchildren. They lost a granddaughter, Mercy, to Trisomy 13.

Valerie attended Memphis State University (now University of Memphis) where she worked on her BFA in graphic design. She worked as a local church secretary, an administrative assistant to two district superintendents, and an administrative assistant to the director of the Conference Council on Ministries, in addition to being a wife and mother. She worked with children and young adults in the ALLSTAR program, was president of a Parent Teacher Association, and led numerous local church activities. She loves photography, sewing, travel, and drawing.

Favorite Scriptures: Micah 6:8b; Romans 8:38-39

—*Biographical Directory*, 2000–2004; email communication with Valerie Whitfield, November 2017

Eunice LeBourveau Ensley Wicke (1911–2002)

In 1935, Eunice married Francis Gerald Ensley (1907–1976). Gerald was elected in 1952 after serving as a professor at Boston University School of Theology and as a pastor in Columbus, Ohio. He served the Iowa Episcopal Area (1952–1964) and the newly created West Ohio Episcopal Area (1964–1976), then retired. Gerald died shortly after retirement, and, in 1979, Eunice married retired Bishop Lloyd Christ Wicke (1901–1996). Eunice and Gerald had four children and 11 grandchildren. Lloyd had two daughters, seven grandchildren, and 11 great-grandchildren with his first wife, Gertrude, who died in 1978.

Eunice graduated from Boston University with an AB. She taught in Norwich (Connecticut) Free Academy for two years, then became her husband's helpmate as he finished his doctoral studies, became a professor, and then a pastor and bishop.

—*Biographical Directory*, 1992; http://www.nytimes.com/1976/09/22/archives/bishop-f-gerald-ensley-dies-leader-of-ohio-methodist-area.html; https://www.findagrave.com/cgi-bin/fg.cgi?page=gr&GRid=49670046

Gertrude Jane Allen Wicke (1901–1978)

In 1924, Gertrude married Lloyd Christ Wicke (1901–1996). Lloyd was elected in 1948 out of the Pittsburgh Annual Conference. He served the Pittsburgh Episcopal Area (1948–1960) and the New York Episcopal Area (1960–1972), then retired. Gertrude and Lloyd had two daughters, seven grandchildren, and 11 great-grandchildren.

Gertrude attended the Library School at Syracuse University. After Lloyd's election to the episcopacy, she was, according to her memoir in the 1978 *Northern New Jersey Conference Journal,* "his constant companion and helper, making friends from conference to conference, both at home and around the world. . . . Those who knew her for 40 years or more extol her as a wonderful friend, a remarkable maker of friends wherever she went. One observed that she was always naturally and serenely herself, free from all affectation and pretentiousness, as magnanimous as she was perceptive in her appraisal of others, gifted with the grace of an understanding heart."

—*Biographical Directory*, 1992;
The Northern New Jersey Annual Conference Journal and Yearbook, 1978, 216

Julia Kitchens Wilke (1932–2016)

In 1953, Julia married Richard B. Wilke (b. 1930). Dick was elected in 1984 after serving churches in Kansas for 30 years. He served the Arkansas Episcopal Area (1984–1996), then retired to Winfield, Kansas. They have four children and nine grandchildren.

Julia and Dick met at Southern Methodist University, where she earned a BS in education. She taught school in Connecticut while Dick earned an MDiv at Yale. After they returned to Dick's native Kansas to begin his ministry, Julia was his partner in service to the church while raising their children. Over the years, Julia taught every age in Sunday school and became a recognized authority on Christian education and Bible study. As a couple, Julia and Dick also led marriage enrichment retreats, and Julia lectured and taught on the subject of marriage and family as well. In 1986, Julia and Dick co-wrote the first of their four-part DISCIPLE Bible study series, a UM Publishing House curriculum that has been studied by millions worldwide. Over the years, the couple traveled the globe to extend the reach of *DISCIPLE* and guide its translation into several languages.

Julia served on several church-related boards and received numerous awards for her volunteer work and fundraising activity. In 1986, she was given the President's Award for her service to Camp Aldersgate, a UM camp in Arkansas serving children and youth with special needs. She was president of the International Foundation Board of Ewha University in Seoul, South Korea, for eight years and served as a board member for 20 years. Julia's hobbies included oil painting, gardening, scrapbooking, and photography, but she derived her greatest joy from her four children and nine grandchildren. "Julia placed her faith and her family at the center of her life," a tribute in the May 2016 Council of Bishops Memorial Booklet affirmed, "and she drew an ever-widening circle to her with her vibrant spirit, her playful sense of humor, and her boundless ability to love."

—*Biographical Directory*, 2010; Council of Bishops Memorial Booklet, May 2016; email communication with daughter Sarah Wilke, July 2017

Patricia Parker Willimon (b. 1945)

In 1969, Patsy married William Henry Willimon (b. 1946). Will was elected out of the South Carolina Annual Conference and served the Birmingham Episcopal Area (2004–2012), then retired. Patsy and Will have two children and four grandchildren.

Patsy earned a BA from Winthrop University and an MA from Southern Connecticut University. She was manager of the Cokesbury Bookstore at Duke Divinity School for 10 years and worked for a number of years as an early childhood educator. Patsy and Will have co-authored books on distinguished southern leaders as well as the International Lesson Annual. Patsy has led DISCIPLE and CHRISTIAN BELIEVER groups for students and faculty at Duke University as well as a student mission trip to Haiti. She has served on the boards of a number of organizations that minister to children and to the hungry. Her hobbies are reading, knitting and travel.

Favorite Scripture: Psalm 16:5-6

—*Biographical Directory*, 2004–2008; https://www.unitedmethodistbishops.org/person-detail/2464115; email communication with Patsy Willimon, August 2017

Eileen W. Wills (b. 1945)

In 1965, Eileen married Richard "Dick" J. Wills Jr (b. 1942). Dick was elected out of the Florida Annual Conference in 2004 and served the Nashville Episcopal Area (2004–2011), then retired. Eileen and Dick have four grown children and 14 grandchildren.

Eileen, born in Florida, went to Florida Southern College and graduated from Georgia State University. She taught in Florida public schools and earned both an MA and an EdD from Florida Atlantic University. Eileen is most excited about having started an International Baccalaureate Elementary Program, which is academically challenging and focuses on student attitudes and thinking skills, in Fort Lauderdale, Florida. She served as principal of Andrew Jackson Elementary School in Old Hickory, Tennessee, and of Julia Green Elementary School in Nashville, Tennessee.

—*Biographical Directory*, 2012–2016;
telephone interview with Eileen Wills, February 2018

Zoe Strickland Wilson (b. 1935)

In 1959, Zoe married Joe A. Wilson (b. 1937). Joe was elected in 1992 out of the Texas Annual Conference and served the Fort Worth Episcopal Area (1992–2000), then retired. Zoe and Joe live in Georgetown, Texas. They have two children and five grandchildren.

Zoe earned a BS from Southwestern University in Georgetown, Texas. As a teacher, she specialized in early childhood education. She has been an active partner in ministry, concentrating her efforts on raising the family and on various activities in the local church. Her particular interests have been in caring ministries at the local church level—intercessory prayer, visitation, grief support—and conference-wide support of the UMW. Her hobbies include music (she is a pianist) and teaching young children through tutoring in the public schools.

—*Biographical Directory*, 2008–2012;
email communication with Zoe Wilson, June 2017

Walter Woods [Shamana]

In 2002, Walter married Bishop Beverly J. Shamana (b. 1939). Beverly was elected in 2000 out of the California-Pacific Annual Conference and served the San Francisco Episcopal Area (2000–2008), then retired. Walter and Beverly live in Los Angeles, California. Walter has two adult children.

Walter spent his early childhood and teen years in Barbados, returning to Brooklyn at age 16 to finish his secondary schooling. He spent two years in the Army and many years as a police officer in the New York Police Department. In 1966, he moved to Los Angeles, California, where he earned a BS from California State University at Los Angeles and a lifetime teaching credential. He was employed by Union Bank in system software engineering and as a senior systems analyst at the Metropolitan Transit Authority in Los Angeles, retiring in 2003. He continues to work as a consultant on call for the MTA. Walter enjoys writing, poetry, cooking, building and repairing computers, and high-end vintage sports cars.

Favorite Scripture: Psalm 23 / Favorite Hymn: "Jesus, Keep Me Near the Cross" (*UMH*, 301)

—*Biographical Directory*, 2004–2008;
email communication with Bishop Shamana, November 2017

Maria Straube Wunderlich (1910–1980)

In 1930, Maria married Friedrich Wunderlich (1896–1990). Friedrich was elected in 1953 while serving as president of the Methodist seminary in Frankfurt-am-Main. He served the Eastern and Western Germany Episcopal Area (1953–1968), then retired. He was recalled to active service to supervise the Stockholm Episcopal Area briefly in 1970. Maria and Friedrich had four children.

After raising her children during the horrors of World War II, Maria devoted herself to work in the church, and especially to women's work. Maria served as secretary of the Methodist West German Conference (1950–1968) and then, with the union of 1968, became chair of women's service in the Federal Republic of Germany and Berlin (West). She was vice president of Continental Europe in the World Federation of Methodist Women (1971–1977). She championed the independence of women and advocated for them to take responsibility in church and society; and she worked ardently for peace, raising concerns about the role of multinational corporations. According to her daughter, she based her life upon the New Testament.

—*Biographical Directory*, 1984;
http://www.emk-frauen.de/pdfs/Lebensbild_M-Wunderlich.pdf

Millicent Yambasu (b. 1958)

In 1986, Millicent married John Kpahun Yambasu (b. 1956). John was elected in 2008 out of the Sierra Leone Annual Conference and serves the Sierra Leone Episcopal Area. Millicent and John have five children and one grandson.

Millicent was born in Southern Sierra Leone and has a Bachelor's degree in Educational Administration. She has taught high school for 38 years. Millicent works with the pastors' wives in their area and also volunteers with the UMC Prison Ministry. She loves singing gospel songs and cooking.

—https://www.unitedmethodistbishops.org/person-detail/2463383;
email communication with Millicent Yambasu, February 24, 2019

Lois Josephine Yeakel (1927–2014)

In 1948, Lois married Joseph Hughes Yeakel (b. 1928). Joe, who was a member of the Central Pennsylvania Annual Conference of the former Evangelical United Brethren Church, was elected bishop in 1972 while serving as general secretary of the Board of Evangelism of the UMC. He served the New York West Episcopal Area (1972–1984) and the Washington Episcopal Area (1984–1996), then retired. Lois and Joe have five children, nine living grandchildren and one deceased, and four great-grandchildren.

Lois earned a teaching certificate and MA in elementary education from Syracuse University, with a specialization in early childhood education. She served as a teacher in a Parent Cooperative Nursery School. She had a special interest in the concerns of marriage and family, in people's interaction with the environment, and in early childhood education, as well as a great appreciation of music, art, and growing plants.

—*Biographical Directory*, 2000–2004, 2012–2016;
conversation with Bishop Yeakel, November 2017

Henriette K'Untu Yemba (b. 1952)

In 1969, Henriette married David K. Yemba (b. 1943). David was elected in 2005 out of the West Congo Annual Conference and re-elected in 2008. He served the Central Congo Episcopal Area (2005–2016) and as an interim in retirement (2016–2017). Henriette and David have five children and five grandchildren.

Henriette was born in the Democratic Republic of the Congo (DRC) and attended UM schools in Minga and Lodja-Diengenga Missions there. She participated in several workshops and meetings initiated by the General Board of Global Ministries in the Congo as well as in other African countries. Henriette served as a member of the African Church Growth and Development Committee of the GBGM. She also served as director of the women's school of Protestant Interdenominational Seminary in Kinshasa for many years. Henriette likes teaching and working with women and youth. She loves singing, and for that reason she has joined local church choirs where she has lived in Kinshasa and in Mutare, Zimbabwe.

Favorite Scripture: Psalm 116:12 / Favorite Hymn: "I Will Sing of My Redeemer" (https://hymnary.org/text/i_will_sing_of_my_redeemer)

—*Biographical Directory*, 2012–2016; https://www.unitedmethodistbishops.org/person-detail/2463624; interview, November 2017 and February 2019;
email communication with Henriette Yemba, January 2018

Asmau Yohanna

Asmau married John Wesley Yohanna (b. 1963). John was elected in 2012 out of the Mungo Dosso area of Nigeria and assigned to serve the Nigeria Episcopal Area. Asmau and John have six children and two grandchildren.

Asmau was born in Munga Dosso, has a diploma in theology from Banyam Theological Seminary Bambur, and is an ordained deacon. Recently she graduated from Taraba State University with a BSc in Public Administration. She has worked in churches, but currently teaches in grammar schools and focuses on home and family.

—https://um-insight.net/in-the-church/john-wesley-yohanna-elected-bishop-of-nigeria-area/; interview with Asmau Yohanna, February 25, 2019

Agnes Elphick Dunstan Zottele (b. 1907)

In 1929, Agnes married Pedro Roberto Zottele (1903–1988). He was elected in 1962 while serving in Chile and was assigned to lead an episcopal area that included Chile, Peru, Panama, and Costa Rica. Pedro retired in 1969 when The Methodist Church of Chile was organized as an autonomous entity, a project that he oversaw. Agnes and Pedro had one son and four grandchildren.

Agnes played the organ for services at which her father preached, then took courses at Boston University School of Religious Education with her husband and worked with him leading Chilean Methodism in Christian education. When he became a bishop, Agnes joined in the visitation work. After retirement, Agnes and Pedro served, without salary, a small Methodist congregation in the outskirts of Santiago. They ran a kindergarten with 100 children, giving them breakfast, lunch, and mid-afternoon snacks each weekday.

—*Biographical Directory,* November 1992;
Encyclopedia of World Methodism, Vol. 2, 2631–2632

Thelma E. Zunguze (1915–2006)

In 1941, Thelma married Escrivao Anglaze Zunguze (1914–1980) and influenced him to become a Christian. Escrivao taught school in Cambine, Mozambique, while serving as lay pastor of a local church. After a three-year missionary appointment in South Africa, he went on to Portugal and the U.S. for continuing education. He was elected bishop in 1964, the first indigenous pastor to be elected in Mozambique. He served the Mozambique Episcopal Area (1964–1976), then retired. He was reactivated while his successor recovered from an automobile accident. Thelma and Escrivao returned to their beloved Cambine. They had a number of children, five of whom were still living in 1996, and two grandchildren.

Thelma graduated from Hartzell's Girls School in Chicuque, Mozambique, where she was an outstanding student, and then became a teacher in that school. She and Escrivao maintained a Christian home, standing side by side in the work of the church for almost 40 years. Thelma kept the family together in Mozambique while Escrivao was serving as a missionary and continuing his studies abroad.

—*Biographical Directory,* 1996;
email communication with Mozambique Episcopal Office, January 2020;
https://methodistmission200.org/zunguze-escrivao-anglaze-1914-1980/

NAME INDEX

CPSIA information can be obtained
at www.ICGtesting.com
Printed in the USA
LVHW080726090221
678758LV00006B/30

9 781501 893551